# HISTORY OF LIBRARIES
# IN THE
# WESTERN WORLD

*Third Edition,
completely revised*

*by*

## Elmer D. Johnson

*and*

## Michael H. Harris

The Scarecrow Press, Inc.

Metuchen, N.J.     1976

Library of Congress Cataloging in Publication Data

Johnson, Elmer D
   History of libraries in the Western World.

   Includes bibliographies and index.
   1. Libraries—History. I. Harris, Michael H.,
joint author. II. Title.
Z721.J63 1976     021'.009   76-25422
ISBN 0-8108-0949-4

# PREFACE

The present work is an attempt to trace the history of libraries in the western world; to indicate the way in which libraries developed and how they influenced and were influenced by their coeval cultures. The book is intended for the student of library science, for the thousands of practicing librarians throughout the world, for students of cultural history, and finally, for the general reader interested in the development of western civilization. Due to the scope of the subject many interesting facts had to be omitted from the text, and in order to aid the interested reader in filling in the details, additional readings have been included at the end of each chapter.

The reception of the first two editions of this work has been gratifying. This third edition, up-dated and revised in the light of recent scholarship, is presented with the hope that it will continue to serve a useful purpose. It seemed particularly appropriate to revise the work at this time, since 1976 marks the centennial of the founding of the American Library Association, and 1977 marks the one hundredth anniversary of the founding of the Library Association (Great Britain). These two events have stimulated a substantial reexamination of the history of libraries in England and America, a fact that is reflected in the extensive reorganization and revision of the latter half of this book.

Thanks and heartfelt appreciation are due many people for the encouragement and assistance that made this book possible: to the students who have listened to us patiently and on occasion have contributed insights which have influenced our thinking; to the librarians, particularly those at Cornell University, Indiana University, The Library of Congress, the University of North Carolina, The University of Kentucky, and The University of Virginia, who have aided in the location of needed materials; and finally, to our friends and colleagues, both historians and librarians, who have encouraged and enlightened us greatly. Without them, and the

iii

constant support of our wives, this book could never have been written.

Elmer D. Johnson

Michael H. Harris

# CONTENTS

PART I

LIBRARIES IN THE ANCIENT WORLD

Chapter 1


THE ORIGIN OF LIBRARIES


The origin of libraries, like the origins of speech and of writing, is not known. Unlike speech and writing, however, the beginning of libraries came after the end of the prehistoric era, since the preservation of written records is considered to have begun the historic age. Conceivably, it should be possible to decide just when and where the first library existed, but all we know is that at certain times and in certain locations early libraries existed. Before that, there were undoubtedly collections of graphic materials approaching the form of libraries, but specific details are more difficult to pin down. One of the purposes for the development of writing was to preserve human communication--to extend its duration beyond the sound of the human voice and beyond the memory of mortal man, and it is probable that written communications were kept almost from the beginning of writing. Early written forms were often considered sacred, which was another reason for their careful preservation. If these early records were kept in an orderly manner, suitable for future use when needed, then they had all the earmarks of a proto-library or archive.

In order to discuss the history of libraries, it is necessary to have a working definition for the term library. What is a library? What distinguishes it from a collection of graphic materials or from an archive? For the purposes of this work it is assumed that a library is a collection of graphic materials arranged for relatively easy use, cared for by an individual or individuals familiar with that arrangement, and available for use by at least a limited number of persons. This definition includes early religious and governmental archives. The distinction between a library and an archive is relatively modern, and for historical purposes the two can be considered together, although where they diverge distinctively, only the library proper will be considered.

3

Before we discuss the kinds of libraries to be found
in the ancient world, it would seem appropriate to pause for
a moment to consider the societal conditions which contribute
to the rise of libraries.   Library historians, from the publication of Justus Lipsius' Brief Outline of the History of Libraries in the late sixteenth century to the work of contemporary scholars, have dedicated themselves to discovering
not only the ways in which libraries influence their coeval
society, but also the ways in which society inhibits, encourages, or directs library growth.   The conditions which, most
historians agree, are important prerequisites for library
growth may be conveniently grouped under the following headings:

Social Conditions:  Under this heading might be cited
such positive influences as the rise of urban centers, which
in their myriad activities produce innumerable records and
require sophisticated information systems.   These needs
naturally encouraged library, or archival, development.   Another social factor of significance is education; a formal
system of education requires not only records and record
keeping, but also library facilities that will support the instructional system.   And, of course, the extent and nature
of literacy will have an obvious impact on library growth.
Finally, social conditions such as the stability of home life,
the availability of leisure time, the size of families, and the
size of the population at large, are all factors of significance
to libraries.

Economic Conditions:  Economic conditions are significant in many ways.   First, it is nearly axiomatic that
large-scale library growth is directly related to the economic
health or prosperity of a country.   Generally speaking, surplus wealth has had to be available in large amounts before
the resources necessary for widespread library development
become available.   Equally important is the fact that a well-
developed and prosperous economy rests upon a sophisticated
record-keeping system.   Libraries become essential "instru-
mentalities" of the economy; both as repositories for the
records of business and as the research facilities from which
future technological and commercial developments will be
mined.

Many historians have also noted that an economic
factor of real importance is the availability and cost of materials upon which written or printed records can be preserved.   The availability of an inexpensive and readily obtain-

able raw material is an essential prerequisite for large-scale library growth.   Finally, libraries will develop most rapidly when books are widely available and inexpensive; that is, when the book trade is well established.

Political Conditions:  Libraries and their contents are in serious hazard in times of strife and turmoil.   In contrast, conditions of political and social tranquility are conducive to widespread library growth.   At the same time, libraries are far more likely to develop rapidly and strongly when the governing establishment encourages their growth.   And finally, effective government generally requires access to great a- mounts of domestic and foreign information, which from the earliest of times has been gathered together and organized in libraries.

In summary then, libraries will flourish generally in those societies where economic prosperity reigns, where the population is literate and stable, where the government en- courages library growth, where large urban areas exist, and where the book trade is well established.   However, it should be noted that there are numerous cases in history, some to be discussed later, where these "favorable conditions" ap- peared to be inoperative.   In such cases one must look more carefully into the historical record in order to discover the motives of those who, for instance, encouraged library growth in times of financial depression or who inhibited library growth when conditions appeared to support widespread li- brary development.

Although early libraries were often associated with religious edifices, it cannot be assumed that the temple li- brary was the only, or even the most important, early form of library.   In fact, there seem to have been at least three, if not four, types of graphic collections that contributed to the general development of the early library form.   The first of these was the temple collection; the second the govern- mental archive; the third, organized business records; and the possible fourth, the collection of family or genealogical papers.   Where religious and temporal rule were in the same hands the first two types of collections sometimes merged; the second two were also close when family and business records came together.   In either case, the written records contained facts or information that were meant to be pre- served for future use, and for such use a logical order of arrangement was necessary wherever the number of items amounted to more than a dozen or two.

The temple collection will be considered first, since
this is the usual example of the proto-library.  A temple or
any other religious edifice of an advanced type presupposes
a formalized method of worship, a priesthood, and a hier-
archy of deities to be worshiped.   Usually there is a story
of creation and a genealogy of the gods to be remembered.
For generations, possibly for centuries, such a religious literature could be handed down orally from parents to children, or from priest to neophyte, but eventually it would become necessary to regularize this story and to provide for
an established, orthodox form of religious worship.   This
need might have been brought about through political change,
migration, the threat posed by other cults, or simply by the
growing complexity of the religious literature itself.   Perhaps the development of writing made such a religious stabi-
lization possible, or perhaps the need for such a stabiliza-
tion of religious practices helped to bring about the development of writing.   In either case, the temple collection began
with copies of the sacred laws, rituals, songs, creation stories, biographies of the gods and, later, the commentaries
of religious authorities on all of these.   The basic scripture
might be carved on stone, inscribed on leather, copper or
brass, or embossed on clay to be baked into imperishable
bricks.   Less important religious writings might be on the
common writing materials of a given time and place, such as
papyrus or parchment.

The theological collection was kept in a sacred place,
and presided over by a priest.   Only the most important of
the temple officials might have access to this library, and
probably only a few of them could read.   In most early societies, the scribe or the trained individual who could read and
write was a most important person, and often only a few of
the temple personnel belonged to this select group.   The
temple library may have been of the few, and by the few,
and for the few, but it preserved the most important literature of a given religion, which was a basic cultural heritage
for that particular group.   In Egypt, Palestine, Babylon,
Greece, and Rome, the temple collection certainly was among
the earliest and most important forms of the proto-library.

Next in importance were the government record collections, or archives.   To support the government, taxes or
tributes were necessary, and to make these sources of income reasonably accurate and honest, property ownership had
to be guaranteed and tax records compiled and kept.   Deeds
and property transactions had to be recorded and a graphic

representation of their legality filed in some government office.   Laws and decrees had to be published and preserved.
On a wider scale, agreements, treaties, and understandings
between rulers had to be put down in some permanent form.
Partnerships between kings and vassals were made and brok-
en, tribute was exacted from defeated powers, satellite gov-
ernors made their reports and pleas for aid in times of
stress.   Some of the earliest known records are such quasi-
diplomatic bits of correspondence between chief rulers and
their subordinates.   These were all official government records, and when they were preserved and arranged for future
use, they became government archives.   However, when codi-
fications of laws, accounts of military campaigns, genealogies
of rulers, and histories of reigns were added to these archival collections, the latter took on the aspect of a library,
and examples of such collections are known.   Since records
of military conquests and biographies of kings often included
as much fiction as fact, they added an element of literature
to an otherwise staid collection.   Governmental archives are
prominent among the early library forms.   They existed as
clay tablets, as papyrus or parchment rolls, even as copper
strips or bronze plates, but whatever their format they preserved an account of the major activities of governments, and
formed a basis for future histories.

   The civilization that had progressed enough to have
government and temple libraries was also more than likely to
have a rather advanced state of business and commerce.   Centers of government or of religious worship were usually in
relatively densely populated areas.   Such urban or semi-urban
areas developed along rivers, on harbors, or at junctures of
overland trade routes.   Advanced civilizations required something beyond barter and simple exchange of goods, and hence
some form of money became a necessity.   As business went
beyond the barter stage, records had to be kept.   Records of
property, inventories, purchases and sales, taxes and tributes
had to be preserved and arranged for ready use.   Reports
from and instructions to employees or agents in distant towns
had to be recorded and kept.   Such records, of course, formed
a business archive, but eventually the nature of the information included might be broadened.   Accounts of ocean voyages
or land explorations in search of trade, military and political
events affecting trade, natural disasters, manufacturing methods, or formulas for products--all these might well enter into the business archive which then took on more of the nature
of a library.   Whether archive or library, such collections
were familiar in the great trading houses of Egypt, Phoenicia,

and Babylonia, and later in Alexandria, Athens and Rome.
The business archive as an ancestor of the modern library is
not so obvious, unless we think of it as an industrial or "special" library.

The relationship between the family manuscript collection and the development of libraries may also be tenuous,
but it had a direct connection with the development of private
libraries and is a part of library history.    Some of the earliest known examples of written records relate to private matters.    Property ownership and inheritance are important factors in any organized society, and wills, deeds, sales forms,
inventories of cattle or of slaves form some of the earliest
surviving family records.    Genealogies indicating family line-
ages and relationships were often kept for generations.    Mar-
riages often involved dowries and marriage contracts were
vital records.    Letters to and from distant relatives and
friends also entered into the family collection of documents.
Not infrequently, recipes for favorite dishes or formulas for
making household products such as dyes and oils were kept.
Even plans for simple, homemade tools have been found in
the family "libraries" of Babylonia.    If the family were of an
upper class, religious scriptures and rituals or works of astrology and divination might be added to the collection.    Lists
of omens seem to have been a favorite family item in Babylonia.    Perhaps a king-list, a historical chronology, or even
the works of a local poet or storyteller might be added.    Finally, the family collection might become a genuine private
library with the addition of religious commentaries, tradition-
al epics and tales, and other writings of historical or literary content.    The family archive is thus the ancestor of the
private library, and by the time of the Greeks and Romans,
if not earlier, the well-stocked private library was not unusual.

One other factor in the early development of libraries
was the official or "copyright" collection of manuscripts.    As
literary works were produced and widely copied, assurance
of the accuracy, or purity, of the copied text was required.
Historical texts might vary slightly from copy to copy, and
so long as the actual facts were unchanged, little damage was
done.    But when poems and plays came to be written, the
author's original words were all-important to its literary value.    For this reason, in ancient Athens in the days of Sophocles and Euripides, official copies of plays were placed in a
public collection to guarantee that any person might have access to the correct texts.    Because plays and other literary

works could be pirated with ease, corrupted texts often circulated as readily as the original wording of the author.  When
correct texts were always available in an official library, all
other copies could be checked against the official one at any
time, and any question as to accuracy or authenticity could
always be answered.  Egypt had a similar practice in connection with religious scriptures.  The official, or orthodox,
scriptures would be kept under guard as a guarantee of the
authenticity or authority of their contents.  The Ark of the
Covenant of the early Hebrews is also an example of this.
Where such collections were large enough, arranged and available for use, they became early forms of public libraries.

Most important in the origin and early development of
libraries was the form of the graphic materials contained in
them because the arrangement and use of the library must
vary as the form of its contents varies.  In the course of
man's history he has experimented with almost every known
material in his search for the most suitable writing instrument and the most satisfactory writing surface.  Western man
has tried wood, stone, several metals, many types of hides
and leather, leaves, bark, cloth, clay and paper as writing
surfaces, and he succeeded fairly well on almost all of them.
For writing implements, he has tried chisels, brushes, sticks,
wooden and metal styluses, bird feathers and quills, in fact
almost any kind of pointed object that could be used with
paints or inks.  The ingenuity of early man was equalled only
by the variety of materials at hand.

Generally, however, three forms of writing surfaces
were most widely used in the ancient world, and most of the
surviving records are on one of these three.  The first of
these, and probably the most widely used in time and geographic area, was papyrus, which grew along the lower Nile
and throughout the Mediterranean area.  To prepare a writing
surface from the papyrus reed, the outer bark was removed
and the inner, soft pith was sliced into thin, narrow strips.
When these strips were placed in two layers, the top layer
perpendicular to the lower one, and pressed or pounded light-
ly while moist, a sheet of rough paper-like material was produced.  This sheet was then dried and polished with pumice
stone to form a good writing surface that would readily take
ink and still withstand ordinary handling.  Papyrus of various
weights and grades was produced, with the grade depending
upon the quality of the reed, the care with which it was made,
and the size of the sheets.  Some seven or eight grades were
denoted by different names, ranging from the hieratica, used

for the most important documents, down to the <u>emporetica</u>,
used mainly for wrapping paper.  Once the sheets were finished, they could be used singly for letters, short poems, or
documents; and for longer works, they could be glued side to
side to form a long strip.  The writing was usually done in
lines parallel to the length of the strip, forming columns or
pages perpendicular to the length.  A completed strip could
form a roll from ten to thirty feet in length, and from six to
ten inches wide.  Some rolls were wider and longer, apparently for special purposes.  The Harris Papyrus, for example,
is one hundred thirty-three feet long by seventeen inches
wide.  The end of a completed manuscript was glued to a cylindrical stick of wood, metal or ivory, and the strip wound
around the central core.  The complete roll might be encased
in a cylinder of pottery, metal, ivory or leather.  A note on
the contents of the roll and perhaps the seal of the owner
could be attached to the roll on a tab of wood, metal or ivory.
Such rolls could be ornate or plain, but the roll in this form
constituted the "book" of the Greek, Egyptian and Roman libraries.  Small collections or rolls might be kept in pottery
jars, but larger numbers were usually kept in niches or
"pigeon-holes" on the library walls.

     Very different in substance and appearance, but simi-
lar in form, was the parchment roll.  Parchment, or vellum,
its close relative, was the cured hide of the young sheep or
goat.  The hide was scraped clean of hair and fat and then
cured or tanned until it was thin and of almost translucent
whiteness.  The completed parchment was trimmed to page
size and also glued into long rolls.  Parchment was developed after centuries of using hides and leather in cruder
forms, but leather continued to be used for writing for special purposes, especially religious works and ceremonial
scrolls.  Both leather and parchment were more durable than
papyrus in ordinary usage, and parchment had the advantage
of being suitable for writing on both sides.  Papyrus, on the
other hand, was more porous, allowing the ink to show
through, and restricting the writing to one surface.  Parchment came into general use in the second century B.C., and
it and papyrus were equally popular for several centuries.

     The liquid used for a writing ink varied from time to
time and from place to place, but usually took one of two
forms.  The first and most widely used was a black ink made
by mixing lamp black in water with a thin solution of gum.
The second was a red ink made by mixing a red ocher or
iron oxide with water, also sometimes with a gum solution.

The ink was usually kept in a dried form and was mixed with water just before use.  The usual method of applying the ink to the writing surface was with a pencil-like wooden stick sharpened to a point, with the point then crushed into a brush-like condition.  Quills made from large feathers were not used until the Roman era, although hairbrushes, especially for finer, decorative work, were used in Egypt at a very early date.  The writing equipment of the Egyptian scribe included a rectangular palette with two shallow basins for the red and black inks, a deep bowl for water, and tubular case for his writing brushes.  For temporary work, the Egyptian student also used a writing board surfaced with gesso that could be wiped clean for reuse.

The third popular and widely used writing material in ancient times was the clay tablet, used in the cuneiform writing of the Mesopotamian Valley and neighboring areas.  It was used from Persia to the Mediterranean from the fourth millenium B.C. on into several centuries of the Christian era.  Essentially the clay tablet was just that--a tablet of soft, pliable clay of a firm consistency--suitable for taking impressions from a stylus of wood, bone, reed, or metal.  The clay was kept soft until used, then kneaded into the required size and shape.  If the writing took more than a short period of time, or if additional writing was to be added at a later date, the clay had to be kept moist, and this was usually done by wrapping it in a dampened cloth.  The usual clay tablet was pillow-shaped, about two or three inches wide by three or four inches long, and about one inch thick.  Some tablets were larger, reaching eight by twelve inches, and not all were rectangular; some were circular, triangular, cylindrical or cone-shaped.  The writing instrument, a stylus with a square or triangular tip, was held at an angle to the writing surface, and was used to make an impression rather than a continuous stroke.  This gave the writing the appearance of wedge-shaped dents with long tails; hence the name cuneiform or wedge-shaped, for this style of writing.  After the writing on the tablet was completed, it was left to dry; if it was to be kept permanently, it was baked in an oven.  Sometimes an outer sheath of clay was placed around the baked or inscribed tablet, and for legal documents the text might be repeated on the outside tablet.  If the outer envelope of clay was unbroken, the inner text could be considered intact and correct, thus giving a sort of carbon-copy to prevent tampering with texts.

The earliest writing on clay tablets was in vertical

columns, beginning at the top of the right-hand side of the
tablet and ending at the bottom of the left-hand side. Many
centuries later, the method of writing changed; it was done
in horizontal lines beginning at the top left-hand side and ending at the bottom right-hand side, as in the modern style.
Works of some length might require several, even dozens of,
tablets. A favorite method of keeping series of tablets together was in baskets, although sometimes they were merely
kept together on shelves. Each tablet was numbered separately, and a key word or text was prominently inscribed on
the end of the tablet. In some cases a lengthy text was
simply inscribed on a larger tablet. One of the larger ones,
containing the Annals of Sennacharib, was six-sided, about
one foot high and five inches thick. It was found at Nineveh
in 1830, and is now in the British Museum.

Since it is known that clay tablets were widely used in
Egypt along with the papyrus roll, it is likely that papyrus
and parchment were also used in Babylonia, particularly in
the later centuries before Christ. Because the climate in
Babylonia was humid, any papyrus or parchment would have
decayed long ago, but clay seals that were apparently originally attached to inscribed rolls have been found there.
Moreover, there are also illustrations to be seen on the
walls of excavated Babylonian palaces depicting scribes reading from a roll. There are also illustrations showing writers
using what was apparently a waxed wooden tablet for keeping
temporary records.

In the classical ages of Greece and Rome, the roll,
either of papyrus or parchment, remained the dominant form
for preserving written records, and it continued to be used in
Europe, especially for legal documents, into the modern era.
By the fourth century A.D., however, another book-form,
the codex, was becoming widely used. Basically the same as
our modern book, the codex took its name from the Latin
caudex, or trunk of a tree. The earliest form of the codex
was the diptych, which was two wooden or ivory leaves
hinged together on one side. The inner faces of these leaves,
coated with wax, could be inscribed with a sharp stylus. The
wax could be easily smoothed to make an erasure, and the
surface was ready for another writing. These wax diptychs
developed from the single wax tablet; hinges were simply
added on the side. The diptych could be used for sending
letters, computing accounts, preparing lessons, or for other
writing that did not need to be preserved. Eventually, more
than two leaves of metal, wood, or ivory were hinged to-

gether, and thus the modern book-form was approached.
When parchment, which folded easily, came into wide use as
a writing material, one large sheet folded like a diptych
formed a folio of two leaves or four pages.  When additional
sheets of parchment were folded, inserted and stitched along
the fold, a codex in the form of a small pamphlet or single
signature resulted.  Several of these signatures sewn, glued,
and bound together with leather or wooden covers became the
form the codex was to keep for hundreds of years.

The codex has generally been considered a product of
the Christian era, since the early Christians used this form
for their scriptures, but hinged, waxed tablets were used by
the Assyrians as early as the eighth century B.C.  In the
ruins of Nimrud, sixteen ivory tablets and several walnut tablets were found in 1953, each with evidence that it had at one
time been hinged.  One set of fifteen thin ivory leaves with
heavier covers and gold hinges was found, indicating that this
wax-tablet "book" had at least thirty pages.  It may have been
used as a student's workbook, or perhaps as an easier method of keeping current accounts.  One palace wall-illustration
shows a scribe using a similar tablet to record the number of
dead after a battle.

In summary, what began as a collection of records--
government, temple, business, or private--gradually grew into a library as other materials of historical, literary or in-
formative nature were added to it, and as its use grew beyond that of the individual who formed it.  Organized archives
existed in both Egypt and Babylonia before 3000 B.C., and
before 2000 B.C. there were institutions in both countries
that were libraries in the true sense of the word.  Libraries
developed as civilizations reached their peak, and declined
or were destroyed in periods of stress or conquest.  But
whereas individual libraries could be, and were, destroyed,
the idea of the library, once established, was indestructible,
and since the beginning of recorded history it has served a
vital purpose as the main communicative link in both time and
space.  A written record, on reasonably durable material,
can immortalize the ideas or actions of a given generation,
but only if those records are organized and preserved in library form will they seriously affect the development of generations to come.

## Additional Readings

There are few works that treat directly the origin
of libraries, although many of the general histories
of libraries consider the subject at least briefly.
The readings for this chapter include the basic general histories of libraries, several works on writing
and the alphabet, and a number of important works
on early libraries, literacy, and education.

Bowen, J.  A History of Western Education.  London, 1972.

Bushnell, G. H.   The World's Earliest Libraries.   London,
    1931.

Cippola, C. A.   Literacy and Development in the West.  Bal-
    timore, 1969.

Clark, J. W.   The Care of Books:  An Essay on the Develop-
    ment of Libraries and Their Fittings.   New York, 1901.

Dahl, S.   History of the Book.  New York, 1958.

Deringer, D.   Writing.  New York, 1962.

Deuel, L.   Testaments of Time; The Search for Lost Manu-
    scripts and Records.   New York, 1965.

Dunlap, L.   Reader in Library History.  New York, 1972.

Gelb, I. J.   The Study of Writing.  Chicago, 1963.

Guppy, H.   "Human Records; A Survey of Their History from
    the Beginnings," John Rylands Library Bulletin 27
    (1942):  182-222.

Hessel, A.   History of Libraries.  Translated with supple-
    mental material by Reuben Peiss.  New York, 1955.

Highet, G.   "The Wondrous Survival of Records," Horizon 5
    (1962):  74-95.

Irwin, R.   "Ancient and Medieval Libraries," In the Encyclo-
    pedia of Library and Information Science I:  399-415.

_____.   The English Library; Sources and History.   New
    York, 1964.

_____. The Heritage of the English Library. London, 1964.

Jackson, S. Libraries & Librarianship in the West; A Brief History. New York, 1974.

Lipsius, J. A Brief Outline of the History of Libraries. Second ed. Antwerp, 1607. Chicago, 1907.

Martis, W. A Palavra Escrita; Historia do Livro, de Imprensa, e da Biblioteca. Sao Paulo, 1957.

Milkau, F. Handbuch der Bibliothekwissenschaft. Leipzig, 1940. 3v. (vol. 3, Library History)

Mukherjee, A. K. Librarianship: Its Philosophy and History. London, 1967.

Olle, J. G. Library History: An Examination Guidebook. ı Second ed. London. 1971.

Possner, E. Archives in the Ancient World. Cambridge, 1972.

Richardson, E. C. The Beginnings of Libraries. Princeton, N. J., 1914.

Savage, E. A. The Story of Libraries and Book Collecting. London, 1913.

Smith, J. M. A Chronology of Librarianship. Metuchen, N. J., 1968.

Thompson, J. W. Ancient Libraries. Berkeley, Calif., 1940.

Thornton, J. L. The Chronology of Librarianship: An Introduction to the History of Libraries and Book-Collecting. London, 1941.

Vleeschauwer, H. J. de. "Encyclopedia of Library History," Mousaion (Pretoria) nos. 2-3, 1957; "History of the Western Library," ibid., nos. 70-74, 1963-64; "Survey of Library History," ibid., nos. 63-66, 1963.

Winger, H. W. "Aspects of Librarianship: A Trace Work of History," Library Quarterly 31 (1961): 321-35.

Wyss, W. V.   "The Libraries of Antiquity," <u>Living Age</u>
    316 (1923):  217-49.

## Chapter 2

## BABYLONIAN AND ASSYRIAN LIBRARIES

It is difficult to say whether the first library in the western world was located in Egypt or in Mesopotamia, but it is certain that in the civilizations emerging in those two areas in the fourth and third millenia B.C., writing produced "books" and these were preserved in sufficient numbers to form libraries. In the Mesopotamian Valley, inhabited successively by Sumerians, Babylonians, and Assyrians, the process that gave rise to libraries was certainly under way during those periods. Writing in pictographs had developed there possibly as early as 4000 B.C., and by 3600 B.C. the Sumerians in the lower valley were developing a cuneiform script from the pictographs. By about 3000 B.C. a cuneiform "alphabet" of about four hundred signs or characters was commonly used by scribes in government, temples and businesses. In the next few centuries, libraries, or at least well-arranged collections of records, were fairly widely established throughout the valley. Thanks to the durable qualities of baked clay, we know of these libraries. More than 200,000 clay tablets have been unearthed in the ruins of Mesopotamian towns, and since the cuneiform script has been deciphered, we can not only read the tablets, but we can also tell quite a bit about how they were originally collected and arranged into libraries.

The Sumerians in the lower valley were a non-Semitic people, but the upper reaches of the Tigris and Euphrates Rivers were inhabited about 2500 B.C. by a Semitic people known as Akkadians. About 2250 B.C., a Semitic leader, Argon I, united the whole valley into the old Babylonian Empire and built a powerful state that extended from the Persian Gulf to the Mediterranean. Culturally, however, the Babylonians built upon the Sumerian foundations, and the resulting civilization lasted some two thousand years. Under the rule

of Hammurabi (ca. 1700 B.C.) a high point was reached with
the publication of the famous Code of Laws, and the compila-
tion of historical chronicles and king-lists.  A thousand years
later, while the Mesopotamian Valley was ruled by the Assyrians, a series of progressive kings brought literature and libraries to an even higher degree of development, but after
625 B.C., conquest of the valley by Chaldeans, Persians and
Greeks in turn put an end to an era of history that was to be
unknown for the next two thousand years.  Not until the archeologist's spade exposed the myriads of clay tablets would
the western world again know the glories of the Sumerian-
Babylonian-Assyrian era.

However, while this civilization existed, the Mesopotamian Valley was one of the most enlightened and progressive areas in the world.  As the many ancient townsites of
the valley have been excavated and studied, the clay tablet
collections have unfolded a long and virtually continuous story
of library development.  One of the earliest finds in clay
tablets comes from the Red Temple at Erech.  This town
was in the lower valley of the Euphrates, and the tablets,
dating from about 3000 B.C., are in a pictographic script.
In another collection from the same area, but dated some
two hundred years later, the script is more advanced and appears to be partly pictographic and partly cuneiform.  At
Jemdet Nasr, near the site of the later Babylon, another
more advanced script has been found, dating from about
2700 B.C.  From Tello, near Lagash, a collection of almost
thirty thousand tablets, all in cuneiform, have been dated at
about 2350 B.C., while many more thousands have been
found at Nippur, south of modern Baghdad, dating from
around 2000 B.C.  More than a score of other collections of
clay tablets, apparently the remains of temple or palace libraries, have been found in the valley, along with many more
smaller collections that appear to have been private or business libraries or archives.

Although these surviving tablets are the sources of
much of our known history of Babylonia, there is remarkably
little history as such to be found among them.  About the
time of Hammurabi, an attempt was made to bring together
a complete history of the Mesopotamian Valley.  Chronologies
of the reigns of kings were compiled and the history of all
wars and international disputes was written down.  A religious history was also composed, giving the story of the
various gods, their temples and priests, half mythological
and half historical.  Unfortunately neither of these histories

survived, but, remnants of the political history, in the form
of lists of kings, were copied by the later Assyrians, along
with the story of how the histories were compiled.  These
king-lists, purporting to cover all the rulers of the valley
from before the Flood to Hammurabi, are questioned by modern historians, but they still form a basis for the study of
early Mesopotamian history.  Hammurabi's reign is also
noted for the codification of laws known by his name.  It was
not the first Babylonian code of laws, but it is the best
known, and it must have been compiled from a well-arranged
collection of works of law.  In fact, it presupposes an excellent legal archive or law library.  From the viewpoint of library history, the important thing is that in order to compile such histories or codes of laws the writers must have
had thousands of clay tablets to draw on, and those tablets
must have been well arranged and organized for use.

   There is undoubtedly a question as to how well organized the tablet collections of the Babylonians and Sumerians
were.  By the time of the Assyrians, however, we are on
firmer ground, since we are able to recognize the remains
of true libraries, arranged by subject matter, and available
through a primitive form of catalog.  Not only were the Assyrian libraries large and well organized, but they were apparently open to the reading public and well used.  Particularly under Sargon II, who died about 705 B.C., the Assyrians developed a palace library at Khorsabad that was a notable beginning.  Ruins of this library have been excavated;
in it, among hundreds of other tablets, was a king-list dating
from about 2000 B.C. to Sargon himself.  Sargon's immediate successors increased the size of the palace library, but
it was his great-grandson, Assurbanipal (ca. 668-627 B.C.),
who developed the library into one of the greatest of the ancient world.  Assurbanipal moved the royal capital to Nineveh and there in his palace accumulated a library of over
30,000 tablets.  Under his personal direction, agents were
sent to all parts of the Assyrian kingdom, which then extended from the Persian Gulf to the Mediterranean, and even to
foreign lands to collect written records of all kinds and on
all subjects.  Assurbanipal had his scribes taught to read
early Sumerian and Babylonian texts in order to translate the
ancient records into Assyrian.  He was particularly interested in religious texts, incantations, and verbal charms, but
his agents were instructed to bring back everything in writing.
He is reported to have asked Nabu, the Assyrian god of writing, to bless his library and to grant him the grace to erect
it.  Like the Alexandrian Library a few centuries later, the

library of Assurbanipal was open to scholars, both official
and unofficial.  In fact, many scribes and scholars were employed by the king to revise, compile, and edit the thousands of texts brought together in his library.

Assurbanipal's library was kept in many rooms in his
palace, and apparently there was some subject arrangement
by rooms.  One room, for example, was filled with tablets
relating to history and government, including agreements
with subordinate rulers, biographies of officials, and the
king-lists.  In this same room there were tablets of information on neighboring countries, copies of letters to and
from the royal ambassadors in other lands, and of orders
to military officials.  Another division of the library was
given over to geography, with descriptions of towns and
countries, rivers and mountains, along with lists of commercial products available from each area.  One division concerned laws and legal decisions, while still another was given
over to commercial records, including contracts, deeds, bills
of sale and the like.  Tax lists together with accounts of
tribute due from the nobility made up another division.  One
important room was given over to clay tablets containing legends and mythology, the basis of the religion of Assyria.
Included were the accounts of the Flood, lists of the gods,
their various attributes and accomplishments, and the hymns
of praise dedicated to them.  Rituals, prayers, and incantations made up an important subdivision of the group.  Still
other divisions of Assurbanipal's library were made up of
works in the sciences and pseudosciences--astronomy and astrology, biology, mathematics, medicine and natural history.
In all, the library must have contained about ten thousand
different works on about thirty thousand tablets, and it should
be pointed out that much of its contents consisted of copies
and translations of non-Assyrian works, drawn from their
predecessors in the valley and from their neighbors on all
sides.

The clay tablets inside the rooms of Assurbanipal's
library were kept in earthen jars, and the jars in turn were
kept in orderly rows on shelves.  Each tablet bore an identi-
fication tag, indicating the jar, shelf and room in which it
was to be found.  On the walls of each room, beside the door,
was a list of the works to be found in that room.  This
would correspond to a rough shelf list of the room's contents.
Moreover, something like a subject catalog, or a descriptive
bibliography, has been found on tablets that were apparently
kept near the door in each room.  These tablets include en-

tries giving titles of works, the number of tablets for each
work, the number of lines, opening words, important subdi-
visions, and a location or classification symbol.  The worn
condition of some of these "catalog" tablets indicates that
they were well used.

Assurbanipal took pride in his library and in having
collected it from all parts of the then-known world.  His official seal is an example of this pride.  On it, after invok-
ing the aid of his favorite god, Nabu, he says: "I have collected these tablets, I have had them copied, I have marked
them with my name, and I have deposited them in my palace."  That he meant them for the instruction of his subjects is also indicated, but from another source we learn
that he also controlled or censored the contents of the collection.  One of his scribe-librarians is reported to have
said: "I shall place in it whatever is agreeable to the king;
what is not agreeable to the king, I shall remove from it."
Censored or not, it is well for history that Assurbanipal's
library was compiled, for in it have been found many unique
sources for the earlier history of Mesopotamia.  The Epic
of Gilgamesh, for example, was preserved on twelve tablets
in Assurbanipal's library, as was a Babylonian tale of creation on seven tablets, and many other legends, epics and
hero-tales.  The remarkable thing is that the library survived as nearly intact as it did, and the reason for its survival is, oddly enough, probably due to a disaster.  When
Nineveh was destroyed in 612 B.C., the invading Chaldeans
and Medes apparently cared little for the clay tablets and
simply destroyed the palace containing them by pushing in
the walls with battering rams.  The collapsing walls buried
the tablet libraries beneath them and helped preserve them
until their discovery by archeologists in the nineteenth and
twentieth centuries.

Although Assurbanipal's library is the best known of
those in ancient Mesopotamia, and may well have been the
most spectacular in size and contents, it was far from being
the only major one.  In fact, from the many excavations in
the area, evidence of many more palace and temple libraries
has been found, with their approximate dating ranging from
2000 to 500 B.C.  Evidence is available that wealthy private
families also had libraries, and collections of business archives have been found.  However, it is in the ruins of palaces, temples and government buildings that the most useful
collections of clay tablets have been found.  In ancient Babylon itself, a municipal archive was discovered containing

several thousand tablets concerned with everyday city busi-
ness--taxes, deeds, contracts, marriage records, and court
decisions. A collection of over thirty thousand tablets was
uncovered at Lagash, apparently also a government archive.
One of the most interesting of the valley libraries dating
from about 1800 B.C. was found at Mari on the upper Euphrates in what is now Syria. This collection was partly archival but it took on the nature of a true library in that it
contained historical, literary and geographical works. In the
excavation of a palace at Nimrud, it was found that almost a
whole wing of the building had been given over to the storage
of records, including quantities of tablets concerning taxation
and trade, agricultural and administrative reports. Another
room of the Nimrud palace contained a series of treaties
made by an Assyrian king with princes of neighboring countries. In the ruins of Ur, a "Great House of Tablets" was
uncovered; this was a whole building devoted to housing records. It probably dates from the reign of Ur-Nammu, about
2100 B.C., and seems to have been a well organized law library or legal archive. One series of its tablets contained
a code of laws antedating Hammurabi's code by some three
hundred years, and also the records of a national court for
over a century.

Temple libraries were quite different in nature and
use from the government libraries. In content they included
histories of the gods, texts of formal rituals, hymns, incantations, invocations, and prayers, as well as the sacred epics
and scriptures. In addition, since Babylonian religion was
closely connected with science, or pseudoscience, the temple
libraries also contained works on agriculture, biology, mathematics, astronomy, and medicine. Near the above-mentioned
palace at Nimrud, there was also a temple library with tablets containing hymns, incantations, omens, and medical
texts. Assurbanipal also had a temple library apart from his
main library, and this, too, was entirely religious and
pseudoscientific in nature. As the temple was not only the
intellectual center of the community but also an economic factor in its large land-holdings and business enterprises, it
employed scores of non-religious workers and kept collections
of business records in addition to its theological writings.

One of the more important functions of the temple was
its school for scribes. The writing of cuneiform was a difficult process, and long years of study were necessary before
one could become proficient in the art. Students were trained
not only as priests and scribes, but also in other professions

such as astronomy, mathematics, medicine and accounting.
Tablets of practice work have been found, indicating how the
pupil progressed from the simpler cuneiform symbols to the
more complex ones and then on to the writing of complete
tablets.   In the "school library" there were textbook tablets
to show the student how to write, dictionaries, grammars,
and examples of business forms and letters.   There were
lists of place names, similar to a gazetteer, but also other
lists of plants, animals, minerals and commercial products.
Dictionaries of foreign language words translated into Babylonian were available for the scribe or student who was working with other current or ancient languages.   There were
even interlinear translations of important works in other languages.   There was a school for scribes in the temple at
Nippur, and from its surviving tablets comes a series of dia-
logues or debates between schoolboys on the art of learning.

        Physically, the Babylonian and Assyrian libraries were
quite different from anything resembling a modern library,
but this difference was largely due to the nature of the
"books"--the clay tablets.   Most of the tablet collections have
been discovered scattered among ruins, and it is difficult to
tell how they were originally arranged.   In a few cases, as
in Assurbanipal's library, it is possible to tell at least what
rooms or areas they were originally in, but sometimes even
this is difficult.   However, a few generalizations can be made
from the numerous collections that have been found.   It is
apparent that, whether in temple or palace, the tablets were
kept in a designated area, properly arranged, and supervised
by experienced personnel.   In some cases a few tablets have
been found in other offices, as if they were being consulted
by an official in his working quarters, or as if they constituted an individual's own private library.   Inside the regular
library rooms, the tablets have been found, at different times
and places, to be housed in various ways.   Some were on
narrow shelves, some in shallow bins, some in a pigeonhole
arrangement, some in baskets or clay jars.   Writing materials other than clay tablets, such as papyrus, animal hides,
waxed tablets, or even smooth wooden boards, were sometimes used, but these have not survived.   We know of them
through surviving illustrations and their being mentioned on
the tablets.   There are also great variations in the size and
shape of the surviving tablets, although the usual tablet seems
to have been about three by six inches in pillow form.

        Since the average clay tablet could contain only the
equivalent of two to three modern pages, it was necessary to

use several tablets for most works.  In these longer works,
the tablets were numbered consecutively and kept together by
means of a running "title" made up of the first word or
words of the text.  For example, the account of the creation
found in Assurbanipal's library begins with the words "Formerly that which is above...;" so the several tablets containing the story are labelled "Formerly that which is above,
No. 1," "Formerly that which is above, No. 2," and so on
for seven tablets.  In some collections there was a sort of
colophon on the first tablet, giving the owner, the scribe,
the first line or running title, and the number of tablets in
the series.  Sometimes the complete series of tablets would
be tied together with strings, or kept in separate baskets or
jars.  Shelving was apparently by a location symbol, although
related works in larger collections were kept together.  As
in Assurbanipal's library, finding lists or "catalogs" were often inscribed on the wall near the door, or on clay tablets
kept easily available.  Multiple copies were noted on the list,
with as many as six copies of favorite works being found in
some libraries.  One "catalog" of a collection at Agene,
which mainly consisted of works on astronomy and astrology,
advised the would-be reader to write down the number of the
tablet he needed and present it to the librarian who would
find it for him.

The librarian, or "keeper of the books," was of necessity a well-trained person.  First of all, he had to be a
graduate of the school for scribes, and then he had to be
thoroughly trained in the literature or type of records that he
was to keep.  After this, he served an apprenticeship for a
number of years, learning the trade of librarian and several
languages at the same time.  That the librarians must have
been polylingual is indicated by the numerous cases of works
in several languages being found in the same collection.  In
addition to serving as librarian, he was often called on to edit, transcribe, and translate works needed by higher government or religious officials.  He was variously titled "Man of
the Written Tablets," "Keeper of the Tablets," or "Master of
the Books."  One of the earliest Babylonian librarians known
by name was Amit Anu, who was "Tablet Keeper" in the royal
library at Ur nearly 2000 years B.C.  In the temple libraries
the librarian-scribe was a priest, often a high-ranking one,
while in the palace libraries he was often an important official.  In either case, he was usually of the upper classes,
often the younger son of a noble family.

The cuneiform script and the clay tablet were used for

more than three thousand years in the Mesopotamian Valley, and they were also widely used by peoples and civilizations outside that area.  One of these civilizations was that of the Hittites, who flourished to the north and west of Babylonia in what is now Turkey.  The remains of several libraries or archives have been found in the Hittite cities, particularly in their capital at Boghaz Keui.  The Hurrians, another non-Semitic people who lived in an area that is now a part of Syria, also employed clay tablets as a writing material.  The Hurrians may have used Babylonian as a diplomatic language, since at Nuzi, one of their main cities, a collection of tablets has been found that apparently was written by Hurrian scribes in Babylonian with many Hurrian words interspersed. Besides these neighbors of the Babylonians, various peoples around the eastern edge of the Mediterranean used clay tablets, including the Egyptians.  Even on the island of Crete and the mainland of Greece, the Minoans and Mycenaens made some use of clay tablets.  For business and diplomatic purposes, the clay tablet and cuneiform script apparently constituted something of an international lingua franca, and it is fortunate for the archeologist and historian that they were used.  Their durable qualities, far superior to that of other writing materials, make them one of our main sources for information on ancient history.

Whatever their other contributions to western civilization--and they were many--the chief claim of the Sumerian-Babylonian-Assyrian peoples to permanent fame lies in their contributions to communications.  They developed a method of writing; an economical, readily available, and relatively permanent writing material; and a system of arranging and using this recorded information in archives and libraries. Whatever the immediate purposes of the collection--commercial, legal, political, educational--the ultimate result was the preservation of the records of civilization's progress in this particular part of the world.  This, in the long run, probably contributed more to western civilization than Hammurabi's code of laws or the Assyrian war chariot.  With the exception of Hellenic Alexandria in the last three centuries B.C., and Rome in the first three centuries A.D., no region in the ancient world had such well-developed libraries as those of Babylonia and Assyria.  It can well be argued that the continuity of Sumerian-Babylonian-Assyrian civilization for three thousand years, despite many wars and conquests, can be largely attributed to its method of writing and its means of preserving records.  Thanks to these records, each civilization was able to build upon the past.

Moreover, it is quite obvious that without the remains of those libraries and archives we would know virtually nothing today of that three thousand years of history in the Mesopotamian Valley. Few periods in the history of western man so well demonstrate the cultural role of the graphic arts of communication and the practical value of well-organized archives and libraries.

### Additional Readings

Much of our information on ancient libraries comes from the archeologist, and so it is to works in this field as well as to writings on the history of libraries and culture in general that we must turn for knowledge of the Babylonian and Assyrian libraries. In addition to the following selected titles, there are a number of studies on individual collections of cuneiform tablets. Journals of archeology, ancient history, and linguistic studies often contain important articles on libraries and related subjects in the Mesopotamian area.

Awad, G. Ancient Libraries of Iraq. Baghdad, 1948.

Chiera, E. They Wrote on Clay: the Babylonian Tablets Speak Today. Chicago, 1938.

Condit, L. "Bibliography in its Prenatal Existence," Library Quarterly 7(1937): 564-76.

Dougherty, R. P. "Writing upon Parchment and Papyrus among the Babylonians and Assyrians," Journal of the American Oriental Society 48(1928): 109-35.

Fiore, S. Voices from the Clay: a Study of Assyro-Babylonian Literary Culture. Norman, Okla., 1965.

Kampman, A. A. Archieven en Bibliotheken in het Oude Nahije Oosten. Antwerp, 1942.

Kenyon, F. G. Ancient Books and Modern Discoveries. Chicago, 1927.

Kramer, S. N. From the Tablets of Sumer. Indian Hills, Colorado, 1956. (Reprinted: Garden City, N.Y., 1959, with title: History Begins at Sumer.)

Laessoe, J.  Peoples of Ancient Assyria, Their Inscriptions
and Correspondence.  New York, 1963.

Milkau, F.  Geschichte der Bibliotheken im Alten Orient.
Leipzig, 1935.

Rinaldi, G.  Storia delle Letterature dell'Antica Mesopotamia.
Milan, 1957.

Sayce, A. H.  The Archaeology of the Cuneiform Inscriptions.  New York, 1907.

Smith, G.  Ancient History from the Monuments: Assyria.
London, 1875.  Ancient History from the Monuments:
Babylonia.  London, 1895.

Weidner, E. F.  "Die Bibliothek Tiglatpilesers I," Archiv
fur Orientforschung 16(1952), 197-215.

Weitemeyer, M.  "Archive and Library Technique in Ancient
Mesopotamia," Libri 6(1956): 217-38.

## Chapter 3

## EGYPTIAN LIBRARIES

The earliest known libraries in Egypt were connected with palaces and temples, just as in Babylonia. Recorded history in Egypt is thought to go back at least to 3200 B.C., or roughly about the same time that writing and records began in Babylonia. The earliest form of writing by the Egyptians was pictographic, and many surviving examples of this writing have been found on inscribed monuments. Since this early pictographic writing was carved on stones, it is known by the Greek term hieroglyphic, which means sacred stone-writing. This form of writing had attained a classic form early in the third millenium B.C., and as it came to be written widely on papyrus, leather and other materials, it was modified into a cursive script known as hieratic. Both forms were used for more than two thousand years, and a third form was added by 700 B.C. This relatively late arrival was the demotic script, a kind of shorthand developed from the hieratic, and widely used in business and commerce. In time the stylized hieratic characters developed to the point where they could be used as a syllabary or even for separate sounds and letters, but they were used in this manner only in reproducing foreign names and words, and the writing of Egyptian continued with each word represented by one character, with or without a determinative. Thus the Egyptians came close to producing a phonetic syllabary and even an alphabet, but they conservatively adhered to their ancient forms instead.

With the advent of writing, records began to be kept. In both temples and palaces, special rooms were designated for the preservation of official manuscripts. Undoubtedly the archive preceded the library, and records of government, church, or business were kept in orderly arrangement long before the addition of history, literature, or theological works

brought the first real library into existence.  As in Babylonia, the early archives and libraries were under the direction
of specially trained scribes, and as early as the Fifth Dynasty
(ca. 2400 B.C.) there are references to a "House of Writings"
which was apparently a public archive.  Such titles as "Scribe
of the Archives," "Scribe of the Sacred Writings," and
"Keeper of the King's Records" can be found on the tombs of
men who were highly honored officials.  Apparently, until
about 2000 B.C. only a few people could read and write, and
the art practiced by the scribe was considered to be an almost mystical or sacred rite.  The fact that one early Phar-
aoh could read and write was considered significant enough
to record on his tomb-biography.  After about 2000 B.C. literacy became more common, and evidence is found of business records and of private libraries in the homes of wealthy
merchants and noblemen.

        Although we have reliable evidence that libraries did
exist in ancient Egypt, the archeological evidence for specific collections is much scarcer than in Babylonia.  Instead of
the thousands of tablets found in the Mesopotamian ruins, we
have only fragments of texts, tomb illustrations, and inscriptions from walls and monuments to rely on for the history of
Egyptian libraries.  There is, for example, evidence that
Khufu (Cheops), a monarch of the Fourth Dynasty (ca. 2600
B.C.), had a "House of Writings," and this practice continued under his successors.  That more than one such collection was kept can be gathered from the different titles assigned to them, such as "Archives of the Ancestors," "Hall
of the Writings of Egypt," and "House of Sacred Writings."
King Rameses II (ca. 1300 B.C.), also known as Ozymandias,
was reported to have a library of some twenty thousand rolls
in his palace at Thebes.  This room was designated "The
Healing Place of the Soul," so it was apparently a religious
or philosophical library rather than merely a government archive.  At least one of Rameses' librarians is known by
name, Amen-em-haut, whose bibliographic profession was
noted on his elaborate tomb.  As the governmental headquarters of Egypt existed at different places at different
times, evidence of various "royal libraries" have been found
at Memphis, Thebes, Heliopolis and other places.

        The palace library about which most is known was
that at Tell-el-Amarna (Akhetaton), a capital built by Amenhotep IV about 1350 B.C.  Here the remains of a library
have been found in a room designated as the "Place of the
Records of the Palace of the King."  This library consisted

of clay tablets--or at least all that has survived are the clay
tablets--written in Babylonian cuneiform characters.  As already noted, cuneiform was something of an international diplomatic language at various times in the ancient world, and
the collection of tablets at Tell-el-Amarna consisted mainly
of correspondence between King Amenhotep III (ca. 1400
B.C.) and various Egyptian vassal states and foreign rulers
in Asia Minor.  Although these letters were mainly diplomatic, much history can be obtained from them for this period
of the Eighteenth Dynasty, and much social and economic information as well.  They disclose, for example, that Egyptian doctors were much in demand at the royal courts of
Asia Minor.  It is quite probable that other records in this
library were kept on leather or papyrus and have failed to
survive.

     Evidences of Egyptian temple libraries are somewhat
more plentiful than for the palace collections, although it
should be pointed out that for the first few dynasties the
temple and palace were often the same building, since the
king was also a god.  The temple library apparently began
as a collection of sacred scriptures.  The Book of Thoth,
attributed to the Egyptian god of learning, was possibly the
nucleus around which such a collection began.  Books about
other Egyptian gods were added, along with writings of expo-
sition and comment about them.  In addition there were books
of ritual with instructions on how certain religious rites
were to be performed, together with hymns and incantations.
There were even sacred dramas, such as the Drama of Osi-
ris, a kind of passion play dating from about 1800 B.C., of
which only a fraction has been discovered.  Gradually the
temple libraries came to include much secular literature, especially science, since as in Babylonia, medicine and astronomy were closely connected with Egyptian religion.  Thus,
the Egyptian temple library was much more than an archive
of the church; it came to be a library in the fullest sense of
the word.

     Some temples, such as that at Abu Simbel on the upper
Nile, were communities in themselves.  In addition to the
fairly large staff of priests, the temple community included
farmers, tradesmen, skilled craftsmen, and a host of minor
officials and clerks, all engaged in the maintenance of the
temple and its lands and properties.  To keep up with all this
communal activity, a number of scribes kept records, taught
school, and served as "keepers of the books" in libraries
that contained not only theological works but also technical

writings, literature, historical annals, and practical texts in
many fields. In some of the temples there were apparently
two libraries, one a general library for the use of all who
could read, and another inner library of theological works for
the exclusive use of a select circle of high priests. In one
temple, called the "House of Life," there was a special
group of priests and scholars whose duties were to preserve
the religious traditions, compile the annals of the kings and
temples, and record important discoveries and technical advances. This group had its own library, a kind of copyright
collection of authentic religious texts kept separately to guarantee their validity and authenticity.

As in Babylonia, the temple was the scene of schools
for the training of scribes. In fact, most education, or at
least most formal education in writing and the literary arts,
was carried on in the temples, and these schools for scribes
had libraries of reference works and texts. To become a
scribe, the Egyptian boy began serious study at an early age
and then served many years of apprenticeship. He had to
learn as many as seven hundred different hieroglyphic characters in order to write proficiently, and many of those characters had two or more meanings, while many words could be
written in two or more ways. In addition to texts and grammars, dictionaries and business forms, these "school libraries" also contained works on history and literature as
well as books on ethics and moral living for the students.

Some of the Egyptian temples were particularly known
as centers of healing, and their library rooms contained collections that might easily be considered early medical libraries. In the "Hall of Rolls" at Heliopolis, long works
with lists of diseases and their cures were found. In the
temple of Ptah, at Memphis, remnants of books of medical
prescriptions were discovered, and in the temple of Horus at
Edfu, there were tracts on "the turning aside of the cause of
disease." Keepers of these medical books were given such
titles as "Scribe of the Double House of Life" and "Learned
Men of the Magic Library." One of the largest papyrus rolls
ever found is on medicine. This is the Ebers Papyrus, consisting of 110 pages of medical information and prescriptions,
and thought to have been written about 1550 B.C. Another
example, the Edwin Smith Papyrus (Egyptian papyri are often
called by the names of their discoverers or early owners),
was on both surgery and internal medicine, and covered both
diagnosis and treatment of diseases. One of the largest medical collections of papyri discovered was that of the Temple

of Thoth at Hermopolis where six intact works were found
along with fragments of others.   The scribe-priest who was
"Keeper of the Sacred Books" at this temple had an assistant, a woman librarian, with the title of "Lady of Letters,
Mistress of the House of Books."   There was also a medical school connected with this temple.

In addition to temple and palace libraries, the several thousand years of Egyptian culture also saw the growth of
private book collections ranging from a few rolls to fairly
large libraries in the homes of wealthy merchants or noblemen.   The private library, as indicated by fragments that
have survived and a few cases where remains of a whole collection have been found, varied to suit the taste of the collector.   It might consist almost entirely of family history
and genealogy, or business records, or the popular literature
of the period, including fiction and travel tales.   Again, it
might be a fairly general collection, representative of wide
interests and tastes.   The wealthier collector might have a
scribe to copy books for him, or he might purchase them
from public scribes and copyists.   His library might be
housed in a separate small room or closet equipped with special cupboards pigeonholed for rolls of papyrus.   In other
less wealthy homes, the rolls might be kept in a few jars,
and the jars themselves kept on shelves or the rolls might
be kept in leather cases.   Both cases and jars were often
highly ornamented.   The site of El-Lahun, excavated by
Flanders Petrie, revealed many private homes of a higher
class and remains of papyrus rolls were found in nearly
every one of them, indicating a high degree of literacy and
literary interests in this social group.   Not only were personal business files, family correspondence, legal papers,
and wills found in some quantity, but there were also many
examples of literature, history, theology, and even medical
and veterinary works.   Fate often played strange tricks on
the archeologists, however, since one fine example of a
papyrus roll, almost complete and in good condition, turned
out upon translation to be the equivalent of a grocery list for
a large household for a period of twelve days!

Although it is generally assumed that only the upper
classes could read and write with ease, it is interesting to
note the results of the excavation of a "workers' town" from
the period of Rameses II (1299-1232 B.C.), when the village
of Der El-Medina was constructed for workers who were
building a large project, probably a monument to the king.
The homes of these workmen and their families revealed

large numbers of papyrus scraps and even more ostraka, that is, scraps of limestone and broken pottery used for miscellaneous and less important writings. On these odd bits of written records were found bills, records of trades, payment of wages, contracts, law suits, work reports, letters, memoranda of all kinds, and many bits of literature and religious writings. Although such miscellaneous collections of scraps could not be considered evidence of private libraries, they indicate literacy among working people and also provide a wonderful picture of the economic and social life of this period. If not evidence of libraries, they represent the sources from which history is compiled and libraries are eventually formed.

Closely related to Egyptian libraries were those of the neighboring area of Palestine. In an area from which the Bible came, one would naturally expect a long history of preserved information that preceded and formed the foundation for such a lengthy scriptural text. For long periods of time much of that combination of history, literature, and mythology was preserved through memory and repeated orally from generation to generation. However, there is evidence in the Bible itself for the existence of collections of holy writings, similar to the Egyptian temple writings, going back at least to the days of Solomon. In the Hebrew Temple in Jerusalem, the Books of the Law, the writings of Moses, and those of the Prophets were preserved in a most secret place which was open to only a few priests. The Book of Joshua was added to this collection in due time, and still later the sermons and exhortations of the Prophets were included. All of this was preserved in and for the use of the Temple; it was also preserved for posterity. Much, if not all, of this first collection of sacred Hebrew writings was destroyed during the period of the Babylonian captivity. After the Hebrews returned from Babylon, Nehemiah reassembled the Books of Moses and those of the Kings and the Prophets to re-form the sacred library. He was aided in this task by Esdras, who some believe first edited the Pentateuch. This library was probably burned when Antiochus captured Jerusalem in the second century B.C., and may have been re-established a third time by Judas Maccabeus. There are various references in the Old Testament to this sacred collection of Hebrew writings. For example, Jeremiah speaks of the "book of the records of the fathers" that was kept in the Temple, and Ezra speaks of rolls being kept in a "scribe's chamber." In Second Kings, there is a note on a scribe being sent for the "Book of the Law" which was

kept in the House of the Lord.   In later pre-Christian years,
there were probably small collections of scriptures in all
synagogues, and libraries were maintained for the use of the
students in the schools for priests in the larger ones.   By
tradition, the Hebrew scriptures were usually preserved on
leather rolls.   Internal evidence in the Old Testament indicates that much of it was compiled from older written
sources as well as from oral tradition and this indicates that
organized collections of these sources were probably available to the scholars.

          Some early Biblical scholars thought there was a
"city of books" in ancient Palestine because that is a possible translation of the place-name Kirjath-sepher, and it
was assumed that one town either contained a number of libraries or at least was a center of the book-trade.   However, more modern research indicates that this was not the
case.

          As for actual archeological discoveries from the Pal-
estine area, only a few ostraka discovered in the ruins of
Lachish and a few other miscellaneous inscriptions have been
found.   None of these points to an actual collection that
could be called a library or an archive.   The Lachish ostraka, dating from about the sixth century B.C., are apparently remnants of a military correspondence relating to
one of the several sieges undergone by that hill town.   However, in the ruins of a city close to Palestine, Ugarit (modern Ras-Shamrah), on the Mediterranean coast, a temple collection has been uncovered that has all the earmarks of a library.   Actually, there were apparently two libraries, one
in the home of a high priest, and the other in the royal palace.   The Ugaritic city-society flourished about the thirteenth century B.C. and seems to have been closely related
to both the Hittites and Minoan Crete.   Clay tablets were
found in the palace library representing diplomatic correspondence, treaties, and laws.   In addition, there were some
history (including records of a military campaign), some
commercial texts, and a dictionary of Ugaritic and Sumerian.
Apparently this was the official library of a king named Nig-
med, and although it was on clay tablets and in a cuneiform
script, it was in the Ugaritic language.

          The library of the high priest was for the most part
a theological collection consisting mainly of works relating
to the religion and mythology of the Ugaritic people; but
there were also some epic poems, magic lore, and history,

with a few items that could be called scientific or medical.
There were also wordlists, or dictionaries, including bilingual ones.  It is interesting to note that among the religious
texts were portions similar in style and content to parts of
the Old Testament, and also long genealogical lists of kings
and priests.  The Ugarits apparently had borrowed their writing materials from both the Babylonians and Egyptians and
used both the cylinder seal and the stamp seal.

     The physical nature of the Egyptian libraries is a
subject about which comparatively little is known.  For example, it is apparent from excavations and from illustrations
found in tombs and on walls that the papyrus rolls were kept
in rooms on shelves or in pigeonholes but the method of arrangement of the rolls is not known.  Individual rolls were
kept in cloth or leather covers, and one or more of them
might be kept in a clay jar-like container with a cover.
More valuable ones were sometimes kept in metal containers,
often inlaid with jewels.  Where there were large numbers
of rolls, it seems fairly certain there was a system of arrangement because the "keeper of the books" was supposed
to be able to supply any requested book on demand.  In some
cases, as found in excavations, a list of the books in a library room was written or inscribed on the wall, and the
contents of the multi-roll containers were also listed on the
outside.

     Although papyrus was widely used over a long period
of time, other materials were also used for writing in ancient Egypt.  Clay tablets have already been mentioned, but
leather and other forms of animal hides were used before
papyrus was developed and they continued to be used for important writings.  Wax tablets, or simple wooden leaves with
a coating of wax, were used for temporary writings such as
lessons, letters, and accounts.  Incised inscriptions on stone
monuments and walls were among the most durable Egyptian
writings, but walls were also widely used for writings in ink
and colors.  In fact, virtually anything that would take ink--
flat stones, broken pieces of pottery (ostraka), and even un-
coated wood--was used for ordinary writing purposes.

     The librarian of ancient Egypt was an important and
highly educated person if we can assume that title for the
many "keepers of the books" and "masters of the rolls"
whose names have been found.  He was often of high political position or trained in other professions besides that of
scribe.  We know of some of these scribes from the "fu-

neral literature," the laudatory biographies that were frequently buried with the Egyptian dead.  The various titles of
the deceased and the accounts of his activities indicate that
the scribe-librarian was also an editor, if not an author.
He corrected, translated, amended, and criticized the material that passed through his hands--and probably censored
it, too.  Among the titles given to scribes in Egyptian fu-
neral literature are such designations as "Scribe and Judge,"
"Scribe and Priest," "Inspector of Scribes," "Keeper of the
King's Document Case," and simply "Royal Scribe" or
"King's Scribe."  Of course, not all of the scribes could be
considered librarians by any stretch of the imagination, but
enough of them were indicated as "keepers" of records to
warrant the assumption that many of them could be so designated.  Whatever his title, the Egyptian librarian was a
credit to his profession if he was even half as important as
his funerary biography reported him to be.

     Two other interesting sources of historically valuable
papyri should be mentioned.  In the Egyptian tombs, besides
the funerary papyri already noted, there was often placed a
copy of the so-called "Book of the Dead."  This work was
something of a guide-book for the deceased, designed to lead
him safely to a life after death.  Although the purpose and
theme were the same in each copy, the texts varied in
length and ornateness of form according to the importance
and wealth of the individual.  Hymns to the gods, prayers
and magical formulas were sometimes added to the document
to increase its value and effectiveness.  Sometimes literary
works were also found in the tombs, apparently favorite
books intended for use in the hereafter.  The third
form in which papyrus has been found in the tombs was
strictly utilitarian.  Rolls of papyrus were used as pillows
for the head of the corpse, papyrus sheets were used as
wrappings for the corpse, and wads of papyrus were even
used as stuffing for the eviscerated mummies.  In each case
where papyrus was used as wrapping or bulk, it was, of
course, unimportant waste from the standpoint of the em-
balmer, and it was usually just this--badly worn texts or
accumulated wastepaper.  But from the standpoint of the
Egyptologist, much information can be gleaned from such
sources, and occasionally genuine "finds" of historical or
literary value have been discovered in just this form.

     Another form of accidental or incidental preservation
of papyrus records has been in the junk piles or garbage
heaps surrounding ancient Egyptian towns.  Where the papy-

rus was covered with dry sand and separated from other organic matter, it has sometimes survived, but usually in fragments or badly torn.  However, from this source have come some of the most important pieces of information that we have on economic and social life of ancient Egypt.  Prices, taxes, wages, bits of local history and customs, even love letters and suicide notes have been found in this accidentally preserved form.  An example of such remnants of a significant private library found in a trash heap is the Oxyrhynchus papyri, uncovered in 1897 about one hundred miles south of Cairo.  The task of piecing together such bits of information is tedious, but is nevertheless rewarding.

Whatever its form the written material that has come down to us from ancient Egypt is only a minute fraction of the literature that flourished there before 500 B.C.  For more than two thousand years the civilization of Egypt remained relatively constant, using much the same tools, social forms and political and religious systems.  Particularly, they used the same writing forms and materials, and this consistency in the communicative arts undoubtedly aided in the permanence and relative lack of change in society.  Internal disorders and even defeat by more primitive peoples, such as the Hyksos (seventeenth century B.C.), did not bring permanent change to the well-established social and political systems, but the final defeat and end of ancient Egypt came with military conquest by more advanced and warlike rivals, the Assyrians, Persians, and Greeks.  First came the Assyrians who sacked Thebes about 661 B.C. and ruled Egypt for a century; then Egypt was dominated by the Persians for another century.  Finally, under Alexander the Great in 332 B.C., Egypt was conquered by the Greeks, and its subsequent culture was to be more Hellenic than Egyptian for several hundred years.  The result of these invasions was the near obliteration of ancient Egypt.  Palaces, temples, even tombs were sacked and razed.  The hieroglyphic, hieratic and demotic forms of writing were forgotten, to be replaced in turn, for the few who could read and write, by Greek, Latin, and finally Arabic.  Only the deeply entombed or virtually indestructible material survived, but from the written fragments a fairly reliable history of ancient Egypt can be written and if we know little of the libraries of that magnificent epoch of history, we know at least that they played a significant role in producing, prolonging and preserving the culture of what has been called "the cradle of western civilization."

Additional Readings

There are numerous works on the history and culture of ancient Egypt, and almost all of them
touch on the subject of Egyptian papyri. However,
information on Egyptian libraries as such is scattered and must be gleaned from many sources.
The works of the archeologist and Egyptologist
should be consulted, and the general works on ancient civilization, such as the Pauly-Wissowa
Real-Encyclopedie der Classischen Altertumswis-
senschaft, are also very valuable.

Baikie, J.   The Amarna Age: a Study of Crisis in the An-
      cient World.  New York, 1926.  (A study based large-
      ly on the Tell-el-Amarna tablets. )

_____.  Egyptian Papyri and Papyrus Hunting.  London,
      1925.

Breasted, J. H.   Development of Religion and Thought in
      Ancient Egypt.  New York, 1959.

Budge, E. A. W.   The Literature of the Ancient Egyptians.
      London, 1914.

Callmer, C.   "Antike Bibliotheken," Opuscula Archaeoligica
      3(1944): 145-93.

Cerny, J.   Paper and Books in Ancient Egypt.  London,
      1952.

Davies, N. M.   Picture Writing in Ancient Egypt.  New
      York, 1958.

Edwards, E.  Libraries and Founders of Libraries.  Lon-
      don, 1864.

Gardthausen, V.   Handbuch der Wissenschaftlichen Biblio-
      thekskunde.  Leipzig, 1920. 2v.

Grenfell, B. P. and Hunt, A. S.   Fayum Towns and Their
      Papyri.  London, 1900.

Hunt, A. S. and Edgar, C. C.   Select Papyri; Non-literary
      Papyri.  Cambridge, 1932.

Hussein, M. A. Origins of the Book; Egypt's Contribution to the Development of the Book from Papyrus to Codex. Leipzig, 1970.

Nichols, C. L. The Library of Rameses the Great and Some of its Books. Boston, 1909.

Porter, B. Topographical Bibliography of Ancient Egyptian Hieroglyphic Texts, Reliefs and Paintings. Oxford, 1927-1960. 5v.

Richardson, E. C. Biblical Libraries: a Sketch of Library History from 3400 B.C. to A.D. 150. Princeton, 1914.

————. Some Old Egyptian Libraries. New York, 1911.

Sayce, A. H. Aramaic Papyri Discovered at Assuan. London, 1906. 79p.

Sperry, J. A. "Egyptian Libraries: a Survey of the Evidence," Libri 7(1957): 145-155.

Vervliet, H. D. L., ed. The Book through Five Thousand Years. London, 1972.

Weitzmann, K. Illustrations in Roll and Codex; a Study of the Origin and Method of Text Illustration. Princeton, 1947.

Westermann, W. L. Zenon Papyri, Business Papers of the Third Century B.C., Dealing with Palestine and Egypt. New York, 1934-40. 2v.

Wilson, J. A. The Culture of Ancient Egypt. Chicago, 1951.

## Chapter 4

## GREEK LIBRARIES

In considering the history of libraries in Greece, it is usual to begin with those of the classical era, from the sixth century B.C. onward. However, it is now known that there was a literate civilization in Greece and the Aegean Islands almost a thousand years earlier, and that there were archives or collections of writings at Pylos and Mycenae on the mainland and at Knossos on Crete. This knowledge has come largely from the twentieth century excavations at those points and in the decipherment since 1950 of some of the inscriptions and tablets found there.

Since the late nineteenth century, clay tablets and inscriptions on stone and pottery have been collected in the vicinity of Knossos on the island of Crete. Some of the earliest of these inscriptions were pictographic, but from a later era, approximately 1400 to 1100 B.C., there were two types of linear inscriptions, using some pictographic signs but other apparently phonetic characters. These tablets were associated with the Minoan period of the island's history, when it was inhabited by a non-Hellenic people, and the period of its conquest by the Mycenaeans, an early Greek people. Later, examples of these two scripts, designated as "Linear A" and "Linear B" were found on the Greek mainland in the area from which the Mycenaeans came. For many years a mystery, Linear B was finally deciphered in the early 1950s by Michael Ventris and others, who discovered it to be an early form of Greek. The Linear A script remains very difficult to translate.

With this development, the Linear B texts took on new meaning, and hundreds of them have been studied. This form of writing seems to have been used almost exclusively for business purposes, or at least all of the surviving texts are on business and military subjects. Tablets have been discovered concerning land tenure, rations and equipment for soldiers, inventories of agricultural products and stock, lists of employees, and the like, but much social and economic history can also be gathered from them. The absence of literature, or even of much in the way of historical writing, is notable. Several possible explanations have been advanced for this absence. The first is that there was simply no literature at that period, or that all literature was then oral. Another explanation suggests that the literary and historical materials might have been kept in other places, either completely destroyed, or yet to be discovered. Probably the most logical reason is that any literary compositions of the Minoans and Mycenaeans may have been written on materials other than clay tablets (papyrus for example) that have decayed with time, whereas the cheaper materials used for business records have survived.

Both at Mycenae and at Pylos, special rooms have been found in the palaces with large numbers of clay tablets in them, some in jars neatly arranged in rows on shelves. This indicates a well preserved archive, with trained attendants. At Knossos many tablets were found, but they were so scattered that it was difficult to ascertain in what room or rooms they were originally kept. Clay tablets here were apparently only dried, rather than baked, and hence they are found usually in fragments. Elsewhere, the Linear B collections contained similar business and governmental information, ranging from the purely archival to the more usable "ready-reference" type of information in the form of commodity prices, sources of various goods, and even information on ship sailings and cargoes.

On a smaller scale similar collections of tablets have been found in the ruins of private homes, particulary at Pylos. Here, in what were apparently the homes of wealthy merchants, many scattered clay tablets have been found, indicating a highly literate business society. One of the homes seems to have been that of an oil merchant, and the tablets found there dealt with accounts and inventories of trade in oil and other goods, along with some business contracts and official papers.

By the twelfth century B.C., the Minoan-Mycenaean civilization had been overrun by the less-civilized Dorians from the north, and their literary culture disappeared. Sev-

eral centuries followed in which the peoples of Greece and
the nearby islands seem to have had little or no written language.  This period includes the era of Homer, when the
Iliad and the Odyssey were composed and transmitted as oral
epics for many generations before they were finally written
down.  By the seventh century, however, a literate society
again emerged, and once more the appearance of a written
literature was accompanied by the rise of archives and libraries.

Actually the libraries of classical Greece, which we
might date from the sixth century B.C. through the third
century A.D., have left us few physical remains.  Instead,
we must rely upon references in ancient Greek and Roman
literature for information concerning them.  The survival of
that literature is in itself fair proof that Greek libraries existed, but references to specific libraries are few and scattered.  Moreover, these references are sometimes contradictory.  For example, there are at least two accounts of the
ultimate fate of Aristotle's library.

Some time prior to the seventh century B.C., and
probably as early as the ninth, the Greeks obtained the alphabet from the Phoenicians and adapted it to their own language.
The first known Greek writers of note, with the exception of
the semi-legendary Homer, lived in the sixth century B.C.,
and some of their writings have come down to us.  Poetry,
philosophy, and science, as represented by Sappho, Thales,
and Anaximander, existed in this era.

If we are to believe the writer Aulus Gellius (second
century A.D.), Athens had a public library after 560 B.C.
Gellius says that the tyrant Pisistratus (605-527 B.C.) collected a large library and later gave it to the city of Athens,
where it was opened to the public.  The people of the city
added to the collection and took care of it for many years,
until the Persian conqueror Xerxes confiscated it when he
captured Athens in 480 B.C.  Continuing with Gellius's account, we learn that long after Xerxes had carried the library to Persia, that country was conquered in turn by King
Seleucus, who returned the books to Athens.  This makes an
engaging story, but one for which there is little corrobora-
tion elsewhere and which is generally doubted.  However, the
story may, like many ancient tales, contain a thread of truth
in its web of fiction.  From other sources we know that
Pisistratus was a builder of temples, a lover of music and
art, and that he caused a critical edition of the works of

Homer to be compiled during his period as ruler of Athens.
That he could and did compile a small library is not difficult to believe, but verification is difficult, and it is very
doubtful that he ever instituted a "public library" in anything
like the present sense of the term. Similar dubious evidence refers to a sixth century B.C. library at the court of
the tyrant Polycrates of Samos, and an early fifth century
B.C. collection in the palace of Hieros at Syracuse.

For the fifth century B.C., the library history of
Greece is still vague but on somewhat firmer ground. This
is the era of the development of prose writing, particularly
history and philosophy, and there is strong evidence suggest-
ing that Greek authors and scholars had access to substantial
library resources.

Moreover, there were now schools in the Greek cities,
and although the method of instruction was strictly lecture,
the teachers must have had some collection of written sources
to aid their excellent memories. Plato (427-348 B.C.), the
great philosopher and teacher of Aristotle, must have had a
private library of considerable size, although we have little
direct evidence to prove it. Plato was widely traveled and
well-read, and he must have had access to many volumes for
his education, writings and lectures. One source mentions
his purchase of books from one Philolaus of Tarentum, and
another has him buying books from the Greek colony of Syracuse in Sicily. What happened to these books after Plato's
death is unknown, although one writer notes that Aristotle
purchased some of them from his nephew, Speusippus. Aristotle went on to collect one of the largest private libraries of
ancient times. The two Greek historians, Thucydides and
Herodotus, must have had many written sources from which
to compile their works, and the latter particularly mentions
written records as one of the legitimate tools of the historian.

Aristotle (384-321 B.C.) founded a school of philosophy or lyceum known as the Peripatetic school. He taught
his followers, or pupils, while walking about in the grove of
the hero Lycus. His library of several hundred volumes was
acquired by purchase and gifts from his many followers, and
was apparently available for use to his pupils and friends.
Upon his death, this library was inherited by Aristotle's
teaching successor, Theophrastus of Lesbos. Theophrastus
formalized the Lyceum and built it into a school or university that was to survive for several hundred years. With

lecture rooms, quarters for teachers, and a colonnade for
walking lectures, Theophrastus' school was a model for others to come throughout the Mediterranean world. Theophrastus in turn enlarged the library and later bequeathed it to his
nephew Neleus. Neleus was not a successful teacher, and
in his later years withdrew from the school, taking his library with him to Scepsis in Asia Minor. His descendants,
apparently unlettered but aware of the value of the books,
saved them by burying them, according to the geographer
Strabo, to keep them out of the hands of the Attalid kings of
Pergamum who were building up their famous library. Finally, about 100 B.C., the mildewed and worm-eaten remnants of Aristotle's library were sold to Apellicon of Teos,
a minor Athenian military leader and book collector. Apellicon tried to restore the damaged volumes, but only succeeded in damaging them further when he made incorrect
"corrections" for missing fragments of pages, and otherwise
edited the works. After his death, Athens was captured by
the Roman general Sulla, who carried the library off to
Rome, where it eventually became a part of Tyrannion's library. Another account relates that Ptolemy II (285-246
B.C.) acquired Aristotle's library directly from Neleus and
brought it to Egypt to become a part of the great Alexandrian library. It is possible that both stories are partially correct, and it is quite probable that copies at least of Aristotle's library reached Alexandria eventually. In any event,
Aristotle's library goes down in history not only as one of
the greatest ancient private libraries, but also as an example
of an early academic library. Its complex wanderings,
many trials, and eventual preservation, provide us with some
insight into the remarkable ways in which books were transmitted from one generation to another.

The actual size and content of Aristotle's library are
unknown. It is reasonable to suppose that it contained many
of the sources he used in his own writings, and they alone
would make up a sizable collection. Also, it contained most,
if not all, of his own writings, estimated to have been at
least four hundred rolls. Since it is known that Aristotle's
friends and followers often sent him botanical and geological
specimens from their travels outside Greece, it is likely
that they sent him manuscripts as well, either copies of their
own writings or writings of others in which they knew he
would be interested. His library, in short, was large for
its time and as well-rounded in subject fields as his own
multifaceted writings.

Among other early Greek collectors of books who are reported to have acquired private libraries of note, a few deserve mention. Euripedes (480-406 B.C.), the poet and dramatist, was also a book collector. His plays show that he was well read, and it is assumed that he owned many of the books he used as background for his dramas. Euthydemus is reported as a collector of poetry and as the owner of a complete set of Homer's works. Larensis of Athens is supposed to have had the largest private library of the fourth century B.C. and to have had it well arranged and classified. Demosthenes (384-322 B.C.), the orator, had a select library, including many works copied in his own handwriting. Euclid of Megara (ca. 450-375 B.C.), the philosopher, was also mentioned for his collection of philosophic writings, as was Isocrates, his contemporary.

A library founded at Heraclea in Bithynia about 364 B.C. was reported to have been opened to the public by the ruler Clearchus. The Aegean islands, including Cos, Rhodes, and Cnidos, were known for their "public" libraries. Excavations on Cos revealed an inscription on the wall of a library enumerating donors of money and books. Frequent mentions of "100 drachmas and 100 books" indicate fairly wealthy donors. Apparently, "drives" for donations were in practice even in the classical era. Portions of a similar inscription have been found on the island of Rhodes, indicating a similar practice there. Still another inscription from Rhodes, and possibly from the same library, seems to be a catalog of a small library or a list of books in a gift collection. Other pre-Alexandrian libraries are mentioned as having existed at Corinth, Delphi and Patrae in Greece, at Ephesus, Smyrna, Soli, Mylasa, and Halicarnassus in Asia Minor, and at Syracuse in Sicily.

An interesting story is told of the formation of a second "public" library in Athens in the fourth century B.C. This collection came about because of the popularity of the plays of Aeschylus, Sophocles, and Euripides. When some groups of players began performing the plays of these authors with additions and corrections to the accepted texts, other playgoers objected. In order to make sure that only authentic versions of the plays were produced, official copies were deposited in a public collection. These could not be removed, but anyone could read and copy them. Thus we witness a faint glimmer of modern public library service; that is, the desire to provide people with ready access to the day's intelligence so that they can develop informed opinions on matters of public interest.

The most famous Greek library of all, indeed the
most famous of all antiquity, was not in Greece, but in
Egypt.  When Alexander the Great had conquered most of the
known world during his brief reign (336-323 B.C.), the glory
of Greece was spread far from the borders of the land itself.  Alexander's empire broke up after his death, but his
various lieutenants and successors imposed Hellenism, as
classical Greek culture is called, on much of the Mediterranean world.  In lower Egypt, after 305 B.C., a series of
rulers known as the Ptolemies created a nation that was
strongly Greek in population and culture.  Ptolemy I (Soter),
a tough-minded soldier-king, characterized by an unusual
sympathy for the life of the mind, attracted scholars and
scientists from all over the Greek world with his interest in
learning.

One of the scholars who was attracted to Alexandria
was Demetrius of Phalerum, who was driven from Athens in
307 B.C., and turned up about 297 at the court of Ptolemy,
where he soon became a court favorite.  Being familiar with
the school of Aristotle, then headed by Theophrastus in Athens, Demetrius may have suggested to Ptolemy the establishment of a school or "museum" with a well-stocked library to
add to the glory of his regime and make his name remembered for generations to come.  The term "museum" was
used to indicate a "house of the muses," or of the arts and
sciences.  Demetrius became the guiding hand of a Museum
established in the Brucheion or palace area of Alexandria,
which in time became something of a loosely organized "college" of scholars and students.  In the group of buildings
making up the Museum were lecture halls, study rooms, din-
ing rooms, cloisters, gardens, an astronomical observatory,
all connected by covered walks or porticoes, and in the
midst of the palace grounds were statuary and pools.  The
whole was dedicated to the gods of learning, and the director
was technically a priest but usually a scholar as well.  The
paid scholars who made up the staff of the Museum included
mathematicians, astronomers, geographers and physicians,
as well as historians, poets, writers and editors.

One of the major functions of the scholars seems to
have been that of revising, collating and editing the works of
earlier writers, beginning with Homer.  In fact, the division
of Homer's works into individual "books" is thought to have
taken place here, with each "book" being an appropriate
length to fill one roll.  Most of the scholars were Greeks,
but some were natives of other countries, particularly those

who could translate from their languages into Greek. Mane-
thos, an Egyptian, was employed to translate Egyptian works
and to compile a chronology of Egyptian history.  Also, according to tradition, seventy Hebrew scholars were engaged
to translate the Old Testament into Greek (the Septuagint) at
the Alexandrian Library.  Research, editing, and experimentation rather than teaching seem to have been the functions
of most of the scholars, but the presence of lecture halls and
students indicates an atmosphere of learning .

Demetrius apparently directed the organization of the
Museum Library and supervised its early acquisitions.  Upon the accession of Ptolemy II (Philadelphus), however, he
lost favor and was sent into exile.  Philadelphus was interested in the Library also, and other scholars took up where
Demetrius had left off, with Zenodotus of Ephesus serving as
librarian during a period of particularly rapid growth.  Philadelphus founded a second library at the Serapeum or Temple
of Serapis in the Egyptian section of Alexandria.  This smaller collection, sometimes called the Daughter library,  never
became as large as the Brucheion library, but it was apparently more of a public collection, used by ordinary students
and citizens.

To enlarge the Museum library, copies of all known
books in the city of Alexandria were added to the collection,
and since Alexandria was then the largest city in the world,
this must have been a large number.  In addition, agents
were sent to all parts of the known world in an effort to acquire other texts.  Ships arriving in the harbor of Alexandria
were forced to lend any books they might have aboard to be
copied.  Sometimes deposits were left for borrowed books until they could be copied and returned, but according to some
stories the deposits were sometimes forfeited and the origi-
nals never returned.

An important feature of the history of the Alexandrian
Library is the list of outstanding figures who served it as librarians, or who were at least connected with it as scholars.
There is some uncertainty as to which of the scholars known
to have been associated with the Library were actually librarians, but the following names are worth considering, along
with their estimated dates of activities with the Library:

| | |
|---|---|
| Demetrius of Phalerum | 290-282 B.C. |
| Zenodotus of Ephesus | 282-260 B.C. |
| Callimachus of Cyrene | 260-240 B.C. |

| | |
|---|---|
| Apollonius of Rhodes | 240-230 B.C. |
| Eratosthenes of Cyrene | 230-196 B.C. |
| Aristophanes of Byzantium | 196-185 B.C. |
| Apollonius the Eidograph | 180-160 B.C. |
| Aristarchus of Samothrace | 160-146 B.C. |
| Onesander of Cyprus | 100- 89 B.C. |
| Chaeremon of Alexandria | 50- 70 A.D. |
| Dionysius, son of Glaucus | 100-120 A.D. |
| Caius Julius Vasinus | 120-130 A.D. |

It is not known whether all these men were "head librarians," but their names are associated with the library during the periods indicated. Callimachus, in particular, was quite possibly only a scholar connected with the library, or perhaps an assistant librarian. Whatever their capacity, surely few libraries in western history could boast such a distinguished list of scholars in residence. Callimachus and Apollonius of Rhodes were poets, and Zenodotus, Aristophanes, and Aristarchus were critics, editors and Homeric authorities. Eratosthenes was a geographer and astronomer who taught that the earth was a sphere, and computed its circumference.

Callimachus was possibly the most important, at least from the point of view of library history, since he compiled a catalog of the famous Library. At any rate, to him is ascribed a work, of which only a few fragments remain, entitled "Tables of those who were outstanding in every phase of culture, and their writings." This work itself is thought to have been made up of one hundred and twenty rolls, but whether it was a catalog of the Library or merely an extended bio-bibliography is uncertain. Certainly it was something more than a mere bibliography, since the extant fragments give something of each author's life, his works, and even the number of lines of text in each work. Callimachus' catalog is usually called the _Pinakes_, from the word meaning tablets. Callimachus is also credited with devising the system of dividing longer works into "books" or parts in order to make the rolls more even in size and more easily handled and stored. That he was a classifier as well as a cataloger can be inferred from his division of his _Pinakes_ into eight major subject categories: Oratory, History, Laws, Philosophy, Medicine, Lyric Poetry, Tragedy, and Miscellany. Callimachus was unable to complete the gigantic task which he had begun, and his bibliographical work was carried on by succeeding librarians, particularly Zenodotus and Eratosthenes. Recent scholarship demonstrates that Callimachus was involved in a number of significant bibliographical

projects in addition to his famous <u>Pinakes</u>, and that he now
seems to fully merit the title of "father of bibliography."

The Alexandrian Library flourished for several hundred years, and for at least two hundred years it was of
tremendous importance in the cultural development of the
Hellenic world.  It drew scholars from great distances and
from almost all fields of knowledge.  Thousands upon thousands of rolls were bought, copied, stolen, and compiled for
its shelves until it contained, according to some estimates,
over 700,000 rolls.  It must be pointed out that this figure
may well be an exaggerated estimate, that many works were
present in several editions or copies, and that one roll was
probably only about one-tenth of an average modern book.
With all these factors considered, the Alexandrian Library
was still a tremendous collection and it must have contained
most, if not all, of the extant literature of the period.  In
addition to the volumes in the larger Museum Library, the
smaller collection in the Serapeum was reported to contain
over forty thousand rolls.

Some authorities think that the Alexandrian Library
may have had a stultifying effect on Hellenic literature, that
the desire of the scholar-librarians to collect and preserve
the record of Greek civilization consumed their energies to
such an extent that nothing remained to sustain creative
scholarship and writing.  Once the literature had been gathered, then scholarship took the form of editing, compiling,
and criticizing, rather than originating or composing new literature.  Indeed, many compilations came out of the Library.  A philologist named Didymus is supposed to have
compiled thirty-five hundred rolls of commentaries on famous works of literature in the Library.  Athenaeus, in the
second century A.D., said he studied fifteen hundred volumes
in the Library at Alexandria in order to compile his <u>Deipno-
sophistae</u> in fifteen volumes.

Unfortunately, the flowering of Alexandria as a cultural center was not to last forever.  After several Ptolemies
who were friends to literature and learning--as well as good
businessmen who provided funds for the Museum--Ptolemy
VIII (Cacergetes) came to the throne.  Having been forced to
leave Alexandria by his enemies, he returned in the course
of a civil war (88-89 B.C.) and burned much of the city.
The students and fellows of the Museum were at least tem-
porarily scattered, and Athenaeus reports that "great numbers of grammarians, philosophers, geographers, and physi-

cians [were roaming] the entire world, forced to earn their
living by teaching." Though never reaching its former
greatness, the Museum and its library were reconstituted
and survived for several hundred years longer.

After this period, the history of the Alexandrian libraries becomes even more uncertain.  Wars and civil strife
continued to plague Egypt, and conquerors came from many
directions.  To bring the story of the Library to its conclusion, it is necessary to go beyond the Hellenic era and into
several centuries of Roman domination.  In 47 B.C., when
Julius Caesar was conquering Egypt, the Library is thought
to have been at least partially destroyed.  This story is
based on the translation of a passage from the historian Dio
Cassius concerning a fire that spread from burning ships to
nearby wharves.  Possibly some stored volumes in warehouses were burned, but it is doubtful that the fire extended
into the Museum area.  However, the story claims that Mark
Antony gave Cleopatra some 200,000 rolls taken from the library at Pergamum to replace those burned by Caesar.  The
Library undoubtedly became less influential after the beginning of the Christian era, and at least some volumes were
taken to Rome to replenish libraries there.  As mentioned
above, Athenaeus used the Library in the second century
A.D., and the Emperor Hadrian visited it during his reign
(117-138 A.D.).  In 273 A.D., the Roman Emperor Aurelian,
conquering Egypt once again, burned much of Alexandria, including the Bruchion area, but it is possible that a library
and museum may have been rebuilt on a smaller scale.  The
Serapeum is thought to have survived until 391 A.D., when
it was destroyed by the Christian Bishop Theophilus because
of its presence in the pagan Temple of Serapis.  Finally,
anything left of a major library is supposed to have been destroyed by the Moslem conqueror Omar or his armies in
645 A.D.  According to one account the papyrus and vellum
rolls were used as fuel to provide hot water for the soldiers'
baths.  If a library was burned at this time, it was more
probably a Christian library established in a church or monastery on the original site of the Serapeum.

The two great libraries of Alexandria were by no
means the only ones in Greek and Roman Egypt.  The Temple of Horus, built at Edfu about 290 B.C., contained a magnificent temple library.  About 30 B.C., the Emperor Augustus established a library called the Sebasteum in his temple
in Alexandria, and there were doubtless other libraries in
the schools and temples, although direct proof of them is

lacking.  There is some evidence of private libraries during
this period, for in the ruins of a home identified as that of
Zenon of Philadelphia, a collection of business and personal
records were found along with fragments of literary and musical manuscripts.  Something of a professional or technical
library can be presumed from the scraps of papyrus found in
what were apparently the offices of engineers assigned to
reclamation work being done in the Fayum area of Egypt in
the third century B.C.  Other papyri found in the Fayum are
remnants of business, family, and local government records.
All government agencies under the Ptolemies kept extensive
records not only of laws but also of taxes, finances, and diplomatic affairs, according to scraps of records found in the
provincial townsites.  Under the Ptolemies, Egypt was a
prosperous and highly civilized nation, and Alexandria as
capital was one of the leading cities of the world.  Hence,
there must have been active government archives there in
addition to the important libraries.

Turning from Egypt to other areas under Greek influence during the post-Alexandrian epoch, there are several
other libraries of note.  In fact, as Alexander marched east
to India, he made use of the libraries and archives of the
countries he conquered by ordering the administrators he left
there to study the laws and records for the best means of
governing the new satellites.  Antiochus the Great, the Seleu-
cid king, established a library at Antioch on Orontes about
200 B.C., and opened it to scholars.  Antigonus Gonatus,
king of Macedonia, founded a library at Pella about 250 B.C.
Among all the libraries established by Alexander's successors, however, that at Pergamum was second only to Alexandria.  Attalus I, King of Pergamum, is probably responsible for the beginning of a library in his city, but it was
his son, Eumenes II (197-159 B.C.), who brought it to its
highest point.  Eumenes strove to match the library at Alexandria and was even accused of trying to tempt one of its librarians, Aristophanes of Byzantium, to come to Pergamum
from Egypt.  This library was also something of a school,
or group of scholars, similar to that at Alexandria, and the
grammarian, Crates of Malus, headed it for a while under
Eumenes II.  He was probably responsible for the early
growth of the library, but Athenodorus of Tarsus was also
its head for a while, and he was invited by the Roman Cato
the Elder to visit Rome and advise on the construction of libraries there.

Related to the library at Pergamum is the story of

the origin of parchment.  The Egyptians are supposed to
have cut off the supply of papyrus being sent to Pergamum,
to prevent its library from growing as large as that in Alexandria.  The librarians at Pergamum then developed a new
writing material, parchment (from the Latin Pergamene), as
a substitute for papyrus.  This is probably an exaggerated
tradition, since tanned and cured skins were used for writing in Egypt and Palestine for hundreds of years before Pergamum existed.  It is probable, however, that Pergamum
made greater use of parchment or even developed a finer,
whiter type of parchment that became famous throughout the
Mediterranean world and inspired the story.  It is also most
probable that the great majority of the rolls in the library
at Pergamum were of papyrus.

Attalus II (159-138 B.C.) continued to develop the library at Pergamum, which flourished for some time, but after his death it declined and in 133 B.C. Pergamum fell to
the Romans.  The library suffered some loss to the captors,
but it must have remained of considerable size if we are to
believe the story of Antony seizing 200,000 rolls from it in
43 B.C. as a gift for Cleopatra.  The Emperor Augustus
may have returned part or all of the gift to Pergamum, for
a library survived there for several hundred years.  According to a Russian tradition, Moslem conquerors carried some
of the Pergamum manuscripts to Bursa in Asia Minor, where
Tamerlane found them in 1402.  He in turn carried these
remnants of a classical library to Samarkand in Central Asia
where they remained until at least as late as the seventeenth
century, but all records of them are lost after that.

The ruins of the Temple of Athena in Pergamum have
been excavated, and from them we have our best example of
a Hellenic library.  The plan of the library may have been
adopted from that of Aristotle's in Athens, with the library
rooms located off a colonnade, in this case the north colonnade of the Temple.  The largest library room, some forty-
five by fifty-five feet in area, had a narrow platform about
three feet high around three sides.  Behind the platform the
walls had holes that could have held shelf brackets, or
served to anchor book cases.  Assuming pigeonholes for
rolls located on three walls, this room could have held only
about seventeen thousand rolls, indicating that other rooms
must have been used for library purposes at the time of its
largest size.  A bench kept the readers away from the rolls,
and may have provided a place where they could be unrolled
for examination.  In the middle of one end of this room was

the statue of the Greek goddess, Athena, to whom this temple was dedicated. Crates probably compiled a catalog of the Pergamum library, and he also may have carried its plans to Rome where libraries along similar lines were later established. Crates was in Rome as a member of the Senate about 160 B.C., and the Porticus Metelli, built about that time, was used as a model for temple libraries constructed under the Emperor Augustus.

In Greece proper, as distinguished from the Hellenic world resulting from Alexander's conquests, by the end of the third century B.C. libraries were common in all parts of the peninsula. After Alexander, Greece tended to become a quiet political area as his successors built empires elsewhere and the Romans gradually conquered the Mediterranean world. Instead of the center of an empire, Athens became and remained for several hundred years an educational center, famed for its scholars and schools. Public libraries became common not only in the larger towns and cities, but also in the smaller ones and in the inland areas. Apparently there was more than one in Athens, in addition to academic and private libraries. Polybius says that there were so many libraries in Athens that one scholar, Timaeus of Sicily, spent fifty years doing historical research in them. Polybius also reported that research could be carried on by any citizen in any one of Greece's major cities. Among academic libraries were those of the secondary schools, the general colleges or universities, and the special schools of philosophy and medicine. There are records of one secondary school, the Ptolemaion in Athens, where the students presented one hundred books annually to the school library as a graduation gift. On the university level, the institution sometimes termed the University of Athens was in operation about 300 B.C. and continued until after 500 A.D. Little is known of its library, but because of the scholars associated with it one can assume a notable collection. Such academic libraries must have been fairly common in all the cities of the Hellenic world, since fragments of textbooks and lesson sheets have been found in Egypt, on the island of Rhodes and elsewhere.

Private libraries also became common among the wealthier Greeks. Vitruvius, a first-century Roman writer on architecture, says it was always considered correct to have the library rooms of a mansion on the east side in order to have the best light for reading. Book collectors, of whom Apellicon of Teos has already been mentioned, became

common and books themselves were plentiful.  More than a
thousand authors are known to have written during the classical period of Greek literature and the collection of Greek
writers alone would have been a major occupation for a
wealthy bibliophile.  In addition to scholars and wealthy collectors, many political leaders amassed fair sized collections
of books, as evidenced by the Macedonian King Perseus whose
library was captured by the Romans in 187 B.C. and carried
to Rome as spoils of war.

In addition to public and private libraries there were
many specialized collections in ancient Greece.  The city of
Athens had its official archives, kept in the Metroon, or
Temple of the Mother of the Gods, and other cities quite
probably had similar collections.  Near Epidaurus was one of
the great medical schools, the Asklepieion, which flourished
from about 500 B.C. to later than 100 A.D.  It was a combined school and temple, with many buildings, accommoda-
tions for teachers, students, officials and visitors, ceremonial halls, baths, and a library.  The library was dedicated
to Apollo Maleates, and to Asklepios, the God of healing.
Other medical schools are known to have existed at Cos,
Cnidos, Pergamum, Rhodes, Cyrene, and Alexandria, and
each would have required a considerable medical library.
According to one tradition, the library on Cnidos was burned
at the order of Hippocrates because its students refused to
follow his teachings.  Special schools of philsophy, such as
the Sophists, the Stoics and the Epicureans, each had collections of their favorite writers.  The works of Epicurus alone
made up some four hundred rolls.  As late as 150 A.D.
there were still four major schools of philosophy in Athens.

Physically, the typical library in classical Greece was
usually associated with a school or temple, with special
rooms off colonnaded approaches to the temple itself.  Inside
the library rooms, the rolls were kept in pigeonholes or on
shelves on the walls.  Individual rolls, especially the more
valuable ones, were wrapped in cloth or some other protec-
tive covering, and an identifying tag was attached.  The writing material was largely papyrus, although parchment was
coming into wider use after 200 B.C.  Librarians during this
period were usually scholars, often outstanding ones, but it
is possible that some of the names associated with great libraries were administrators or advisers rather than librarians.  Be that as it may, the role of the librarian and
the library was important in Hellenic society and they played
a major part in creating and preserving the culture of that era.

In studying the history of libraries it is worthwhile to ask at this point: Why do we know so little about Greek libraries when such a relatively large amount of classic Greek literature has been preserved?  It is estimated that perhaps ten per cent of the major Greek classical writings have survived.  Why did so few of the writers, historians and compilers mention libraries if libraries were common?  Why do we have only fragmentary, incidental references to libraries in all the surviving pages of Greek literature?  There are two possible answers.  First, much that was written about libraries may have been lost.  Particularly, local history and religious history, two fields in which libraries might have been mentioned, are subjects on which very little has been preserved.  But the more probable answer is that libraries were considered so necessary to a well-ordered society that writers did not consider it of importance to mention them.  They could well have thought that libraries had always existed and would always exist.  Athenaeus, for example, writing about the great library at Alexandria, said: "And concerning the number of books, the establishment of libraries, and the collection in the Hall of Muses, why need I even speak, since they are in all men's memories?"

If our facts about Greek library history are few, the results in the preservation of Greek literature speak for themselves.  For the heritage of ancient Greece, with the exception of sculpture and architecture, has come down to us in the form of books preserved in Greek libraries.  If western library history began with the Egyptians and Babylonians, it reached its first "golden age" in classical Greece.

## Additional Readings

In the Hellenic era of ancient history, roughly 500 B.C. to 100 A.D., the information from archeological studies is supplemented by passages about libraries in the surviving classical texts.  However, this information is scattered and often contradictory.

Chadwick, J.  "The Organization of the Mycenaen Archives," Studia Mycenaea (1968):  11-21.

Davison, J. A.  "Literature and Literacy in Ancient Greece," Phoenix 16 (1962):  141-56, 219-33.

Dow, S. and Chadwick, J.  The Linear Scripts and the Tab-
    lets as Historical Evidence.  Cambridge, 1971.

Gardthausen, V. E.  "Die Alexandrinishe Bibliothek, ihr
    Vorbild, Katalog und Betrieb," Zeitschrift des Deutschen
    Vereins fur Buchwesen und Schriftum 5 (1922):  73-104

Goetze, B.  "Antike Bibliotheken," Jahrbuch des Deutschen
    Archaeologischen Instituts 52 (1937):  225-47.

Harvey, F. D.  "Literacy in the Athenian Democracy," Re-
    vue des Etudes Grècques 79 (1966):  585-635.

Irwin, R.  "Callimachus and the Alexandrian Library," in
    The English Library.  London, 1966.

_____.  "Hellas," in the Heritage of the English Library.
    New York, 1964.

Johnson, E. D.  "Ancient Libraries as Seen in the Greek and
    Roman Classics," Radford Review 23 (1969):  73-92.

Kenyon, F. G.  Ancient Books and Modern Discoveries.
    Chicago, 1927.

_____.  Books and Readers in Ancient Greece and Rome.
    Oxford, 1932.

_____.  "The Library of a Greek at Oxyrhynchus," Jour-
    nal of Egyptian Archaeology 8 (1922):  129-38.

Kleberg, T.  Bokhandel och Bokforlag i Antiken.  Stockholm,
    1962.

Parsons, E. A.  The Alexandrian Library; Glory of the Hel-
    lenic World:  Its Rise, Antiquities, and Destruction.
    Amsterdam, 1952.

Pfeiffer, R.  History of Classical Scholarship from the Be-
    ginnings to the End of the Hellenistic Age.  Oxford,
    1968.

Pinner, H. L.  The World of Books in Classical Antiquity.
    Leiden, 1948.

Platthy, J.  Sources of the Earliest Greek Libraries with
    the Testemonia.  New York, 1967.

Putnam, G. H.  Authors and Their Public in Ancient Times.
New York, 1894.

Reynolds, L. D. and Wilson, N. G.  Scribes and Scholars;
A Guide to the Transmission of Greek and Latin Literature.  Oxford, 1968.

Schmidt, F.  Die Pinakes des Kallimachos.  Berlin, 1922.

Turner, E. G.  Athenian Books in the Fifth and Fourth Centuries, B.C.  London, 1952.

_____.  Greek Papyri; An Introduction.  Princeton, 1968.

Westermann, W. L.  The Library of Ancient Alexandria.
Alexandria, Egypt, 1954.

Widman, H., "Herstellung und Vertrieb des Buches in der
Griechisch-romischen Welt," Archiv fur Geschichte
des Buchwesens 8 (1967):  545-640.

Witty, F. J.  "The Other Pinakes and Reference Works of
Callimachus," Library Quarterly 43 (1973):  237-44.

_____.  "The Pinakes of Callimachus," Library Quarter-
ly 28 (1958):  132-36.

_____.  "Reference Books of Antiquity," Journal of Li-
brary History 9 (1974):  101-19.

## Chapter 5

ROMAN LIBRARIES

    The libraries of ancient Rome were a direct inheritance from those of Greece, in types, organization, and contents. In fact, many of the actual manuscripts from the Greek libraries found their way into Roman collections. This cultural inheritance was a part of the general succession of the Roman world over that of classical Greece. From about 200 B.C., the Roman Republic gradually spread its military and political influence eastward and southward across the Mediterranean and westward and northward into Europe until by the beginning of the Roman Empire, about 30 B.C., the Roman world extended from Asia Minor to England. The conquering Roman legions greatly affected the cultures they overran, but they in turn were influenced by the material effects and cultures of those they conquered. Sculptures and manuscripts, architectural plans and educated slaves were carried back to Rome, along with more immediately valuable gold and jewels. Thus it was that Rome's first major libraries were acquired as spoils of war from Greece and Asia Minor.

    The earliest "libraries" of Rome were collections of historical records and laws, such as the <u>Annales Pontificum</u> that appear to have been brought together in eighty volumes about 120 B.C. These were strictly annals, brief accounts of major happenings in the Republic, and were kept in the official residence of the <u>Pontifex Maximus</u>, or chief priest. Even earlier than this, according to legend, the Twelve Tablets of Roman law were engraved on bronze and exhibited to the public about 450 B.C. Another early collection of public records was the <u>Libri Magistratum</u>, or Books of the Magistrates, recording their names and official actions over a long period of time. Some of these were recorded on linen, known

as the libri lintei, and were preserved in the Temple of
Moneta, the goddess of memory, on Capitol Hill. Just as
in Egypt and Babylonia, the early Roman temples had their
schools for priests and probably had collections of books as
well as copies of the formal religious works kept in the temple sanctuary. There were also a few private libraries in
the second century B.C., but there is little precise information about them.

The first notable Roman library of which we have recorded information was that of Paulus Aemilius. This Roman general, who was also a scholar, defeated King Perseus
of Macedonia in 168 B.C. While his victorious soldiers
ransacked the palace for everything of value, Aemilius himself claimed only the library, saying that he preferred it to
gold for the benefit of his sons. A few years later, Crates
of Mallos, then librarian at Pergamum, came to Rome as
an envoy to the Roman Senate. His public lectures and private discussions with citizens of Rome greatly stimulated
their interest in Greek literature and civilization, and the
Hellenization of Rome is frequently dated from his appearance in that city.

After Aemilius, it became common for the Roman
conquerors to bring home books as spoils of war. One particularly notable collection was that acquired by Cornelius
Sulla, the Roman general who took Athens in 86 B.C., and
seized the library of Apellicon of Teos. This is the private
collection that contained at least part of Aristotle's library.
Tyrannion served as librarian for Sulla's collection after he
carried it to Rome, and Andronicus of Rhodes is supposed
to have studied Aristotle's works there. Apparently Sulla
opened the library to his scholarly friends and became something of a literary lion in his later years. He passed the
books on to his son, Faustus, in whose home Cicero saw the
library in 55 B.C., but its later history is unknown. Luci-
us Lucullus, who had earlier fought under Sulla, became a
conqueror in turn and carried the Roman banner deep into
Armenia. He returned from his conquests with great quantities of books, including the library of the King of Pontus,
and set them up in his private library in Rome. After los-
ing political favor, Lucullus became a dilettante, opening his
library and gardens to visiting friends and scholars. Scipio
Aemilianus, conquering Carthage in 146 B.C., also found
libraries to be taken, but since they were largely in unknown
languages, he took only a few books on agriculture and allowed the remainder to be destroyed.

By 50 B.C., private libraries were becoming common
among the wealthy families in Rome, but the only public collections were the temple and government archives.   Julius
Caesar planned to establish a public library to equal or surpass the one at Alexandria, and to this end he appointed Terentius Varro (116-27 B.C.), a noted scholar and book collector, to gather together copies of the best-known literature
for a Roman public library.   Unfortunately, Caesar was as-
sassinated (44 B.C.) before his library plans could be accomplished.   Instead the first public library in Rome, like
so many of the private collections, came into being as the result of spoils of war.   G. Asinius Pollio, who had amassed
a fortune in his conquest of Dalmatia, used his wealth to
consolidate several collections already in Rome possibly including those of Varro and Sulla, to form a library in the
Temple of Liberty (Atrium Libertatis) on the Aventine Hill.
Public archives had already been housed there, but Pollio reorganized the collection, added the libraries he had acquired,
and opened the whole to the public about 37 B.C., making it
the first-known public library in Rome.

Beginning with Augustus, the Roman emperors took
over the task of building libraries in Rome.   Actually Augustus was responsible for two public libraries.   The first, in
the Temple of Apollo, was begun in 36 B.C., and dedicated
in 28 B.C.   It was divided into two separate collections, one
Greek and one Latin.   Pompeius Macer was the first librarian, and Julius Hyginus, a noted grammarian, also served
in that capacity.   Later enlarged by the Emperors Tiberius
and Caligula, this library on the Palatine Hill was one of the
two major libraries in Rome for several hundred years.   It
was damaged at least twice by fires but survived well into
the fourth century.   The second Augustan library was in the
Porticus Octaviae, a magnificent structure built in honor of
Octavia, the Emperor's sister.   Although the building was
constructed by orders of Augustus, it is thought that the library was founded by Octavia in memory of her son, Marcel-
lus, who died in 23 B.C.   Caius Melissus was the first librarian for this collection, housed in chambers over a prom-
enade.   Although damaged by fire in the reign of Titus about
80 A.D., the Octavian Library probably survived into the
second century.

The successors of Augustus maintained the tradition
of founding libraries.   Tiberius established one in his palace
on the Palatine Hill about 20 A.D., and his collection remained in existence into the third century.   Tiberius is also

credited with establishing a library in the Temple of Augustus, which was dedicated in 36 A.D. Since this temple also
had a statue of Apollo, there may be some confusion with
the Temple of Apollo established by Augustus, or with Tiberius' own palace library. The Emperor Vespasian established
another public library about 75 A.D., decorating it with
spoils captured in Jerusalem. Josephus, the Jewish historian, says that copies of the Books of Moses were deposited
there. This library was damaged by fire about 190 A.D.,
later restored, and survived into the fourth century. The
Emperor Domitian (81-96 A.D.) restored the libraries and
other public buildings damaged in the fires of Nero's reign,
and he is also credited with establishing a public library on
the Capitoline Hill. Hadrian is also given credit for establishing this library and little else is known about it.

Probably the greatest of the Roman libraries was the
Ulpian Library, founded by the Emperor Trajan in 114 A.D.
in his Forum. This collection may have been based on the
thirty thousand volume private library of Epaphrodites of
Cheronea and, like other Roman libraries, it was divided into Greek and Latin sections. Early in the fourth century,
this library was moved to the Baths of Diocletian. There
was a theater and lecture room along with the Baths, so that
it was more of a gentlemen's club than a public bath. This
move was apparently only temporary, possibly while the Forum was being repaired, since the library is reported to have
been returned at a later date. Trajan's Library was still in
existence in 455 A.D. when a bust of Sidonius Apollinarius
was placed there by the Emperor Avitus. The custom of
founding public libraries continued while Rome's power waxed
and waned, and there were reported to be no fewer than
twenty-eight or twenty-nine located in the city before the
fourth century. If so, we know little or nothing of twenty or
more of them. Some may have been in other public baths;
one may have been in the Temple of Esculapius or in a
school of medicine associated with it; others may have been
Christian collections begun as private libraries and opened to
congregations in the fourth century, or large private collections charitably opened to the public.

The Emperor Hadrian (76-138 A.D.) is also noted for
his library interests. At his palatial residence outside Rome
at Tibur (Tivoli), he maintained a private library of great
size and value modeled on a Greek library with covered walls
or colonnades leading off from the library rooms. Hadrian
also constructed a magnificent library in Athens, the remains

of which have been excavated.  It was a square enclosed by
a colonnade of 120 columns, with spacious rooms of alabaster
and gold, filled with paintings and statuary.  About its book
contents we know little, but we do know that in addition to
the library there were rooms for reading and for lectures,
and there was a central area from which books may have
been delivered to readers in a proper "circulation desk" atmosphere.  Hadrian is also credited with having revived or
established libraries at Ephesus and Pergamum, and with
founding an Athenaeum in Rome which probably included a library.

        The public libraries were by no means the only
sources of literature available to the wealthier Romans, since
private libraries were common for several hundred years at
the height of the Roman era.  That most of the Roman writers had access to well stocked libraries is apparent from
their writings, but it is often verified by references in their
correspondence and elsewhere.  Also, there is evidence that
other Romans, including physicians and lawyers, collected
books and built up sizable libraries.

        The writings of Cicero frequently mention his library
and those of his friends.  About 56 B.C. he wrote to his
friend Atticus:

                Mind you don't promise your library to anybody,
                however keen a collector you may find for it, for
                I am hoarding up all my little savings to get it as
                a resource for my old age.  If I succeed I shall
                be richer than Crassus and look down on any man's
                manors and meadows.

Cicero called his library "the soul" of his house.  At one
time he employed Tyrannion as librarian, and praised him
highly for the work done in arranging the books and in at-
taching title slips to them.

        Titus Pomponius Atticus was a book collector in his
own right, and also a prominent book dealer who counted
Cicero and other noted Roman literary figures among his
customers.  Atticus was also something of a book publisher
in that his servants made numerous copies of the works of
popular authors and presented them for sale.  Atticus' own
library was reputed to contain some twenty thousand rolls,
but was dwarfed by that of the writer Q. Sammonicus Seren-
ius, some two centuries later, who amassed over sixty

thousand volumes. The library of Sammonicus went eventually to the Emperor Gordian, who may have opened it as a public library.

Epaphrodites, a Greek secretary to the Emperor Nero, had a library of thirty thousand rolls. The two Plinys-- Pliny the Elder, the great naturalist, and his nephew Pliny the Younger, whose letters have been preserved--both had large personal libraries. Pliny the Younger also gave a public library to the temple in the town of Como (Comum), dedicating it to the young men of the community in the hope that it would turn them to literature instead of sports and gaming. Pliny may have aided in the founding of a library in Milan, although evidence of this is uncertain. Terentius Varro wrote a book, now lost, on libraries (De bibliothecis). Aulus Persius Flaccus, a poet of 34-62 A.D., had a relatively small library of only seven hundred rolls, but it was well selected. He left it in his will to his friend Cornutus. Silius Italicus, another poet who died in 101 A.D., was reported by Pliny the Younger to have become so wealthy from his writings that he had several villas, all furnished with large libraries, statues, and portraits. Herrenius Severus, a person of distinguished learning, asked Pliny to obtain for him pictures of his favorite authors to adorn his private library walls. Little is known about the personal library of Julius Caesar, but he is known to have carried his favorite works with him on his many travels.

Other private libraries must have been common, since Seneca (d. 65 A.D.) wrote that they had become as necessary in the homes of the wealthy as baths with hot and cold water. He deplored the buying of books by those who were not scholars, and asked:

> What is the use of having countless books and libraries, whose titles their owners can scarcely read through in a whole lifetime?... It is better to surrender yourself to a few authors than to wander through many.

A later author, Lucian, wrote an essay on "The Ignorant Book Collector," and asked:

> For what expectation do you base upon your books that you are always unrolling them and rolling them up, gluing them, trimming them, smearing them with saffron and oil of cedar, putting slip covers

on them, and fitting them with knobs, just as if
you were going to derive some profit from them?

Even Petronius in one of his satires introduces a
character, Trimalchio, who boasts of his Greek and Latin
library, but who displays ignorance of its contents.   While
the Roman villa libraries were frequently the subjects of
scorn in their own time, modern scholars credit them with
being the repositories of much of the classic Roman literature which survived the fall of the Empire.

Rome was by no means the only city in the Empire
to be graced with one or more libraries.   In fact, while
early Rome benefited enormously from the book collecting
ways of her conquering generals, Rome in the Imperial and
Christian eras developed a substantial publishing and book
trade of her own, and became the locus of a national book
distribution system.   Moreover, philanthropists from Rome
provided the means to establish libraries in many cities and
towns.   Augustus, having set the example by founding libraries in Rome, encouraged wealthy citizens to endow temples, libraries and schools throughout the provinces.

Other libraries were founded by the imperial government, possibly in attempts to Latinize the inhabitants of the
newly conquered territories.   In Tibur, just outside Rome,
there was a celebrated library in the Temple of Hercules.
Also, there were libraries at Como, Tortona, Ostia, Antium,
and Milan in Italy, and probably many others whose names
we do not know.   In Greece, the Romans established libraries at least in Athens, Corinth, Delphi, Patrae and Phi-
lippi.   There were Roman libraries at Durazzo (Dyrrachium)
on the Adriatic, and at Soli on the island of Cyprus.   In
Asia Minor there were Roman libraries at Ephesus, Halicarnassus, Antioch, Smyrna, at Prusa in Bithynia, and even in
a Roman colony in Jerusalem.   In Africa, there were Roman
libraries at Carthage and Timgad, and in the western Mediterranean at Massila (Marseilles) in France and Cordoba in
Spain.

At Timgad (Thamugadi), a Roman colony established
in North Africa, one Quintianus Rogatianus left funds for the
building of a library, and a magnificent structure was erected.   The remains of this building have been excavated, and
thus we know something of the plan of one provincial Roman
library.   It was about eighty feet square with a forecourt
surrounded by white limestone columns.   A central semi-

circular court had niches in the walls, apparently for cases
holding the rolls, and in the center was a statue, probably
of Minerva.   Rooms on each side could have served as reading rooms, and the entire structure is estimated to have
been able to house some 23,000 rolls.

   One interesting discovery of papyri from a site in
Roman Egypt has led to speculation concerning a library or
libraries there.   This discovery was at Oxyrhyncus, about
120 miles south of Cairo, where a Roman colony existed for
several hundred years.   Literally hundreds of pieces of papyri have been found there, largely in sandy trash heaps where
the dryness has preserved them.   Among them are parts of
papyrus rolls and codices, and of parchment codices.   The
contents include a variety of materials ranging from personal letters and business letters and contracts to government
records, fragments of classical literature, and excerpts
from the New Testament and early Christian writings.   It is
difficult to say whether this material came from libraries,
either private or public, but it is likely that some of it did.

   Another Roman library of note, and the only one of
papyrus and parchment rolls that has been uncovered in its
original location, was discovered in the ruins of the city of
Herculaneum.   This area was covered by ashes and lava
from an eruption of Vesuvius in 79 A.D.; it was excavated
in the eighteenth century.   From one private library about
350 rolls have been disinterred, most of them in Greek, but
a few in Latin.   The rolls were of papyrus encased in wood-
en boxes.   Additional fragments seem to indicate an original
collection of some three thousand rolls, and although charred,
some of them have been unrolled and translated.   Apparently
the collection was the private library of L. Calpurnius Piso,
and was housed in a room fifteen by thirty feet.   There
were some works of medicine, literary criticism and general
literature, but the majority were philosophic works of the
Sophist school, particularly by the philosopher Philodemus.
The Herculaneum papyri were first unrolled and read by Sir
Humphrey Davy in 1821.   Evidences of several other private
libraries have been discovered, and a temple room in Pom-
peii, also covered by the original eruption, was apparently a
public library.

   Contemporary with the Romans in Palestine was a religious group thought to have been the Essenes, a Hebrew
congregation dating from about 125 B.C. to 70 A.D.   The
remains of several libraries maintained by this group were

found in 1947 and later, in an area to the west of the Dead
Sea known as the Khirbet Qumran. Many rolls of papyrus
and several of thin sheet copper were found in several caves.
Remnants of more than six hundred rolls have been identified in these "Dead Sea Scrolls," most of them of a religious nature. Included were some books of the Old Testament, a collection of hymns, a manual of discipline and other religious works. Apparently the collection was a type of
master library maintained with a scriptorium where scribes
made copies of the religious texts for individuals or outlying
groups of the congregation. Many similarities have been
noted between the general religious philosophy of this Qumran group and that of the early Christians.

The later era of the Roman Empire saw a decline of
the great libraries of the ancient world, but it also saw the
beginnings of Christian libraries. The early Christians felt
the need to preserve and disseminate their scriptural literature and hence made good use of books and libraries. The
sayings of Jesus, the letters of Paul, and the early gospels
were kept by each congregation and guarded zealously at or
near the altar of each church. Paul himself refers, in 2
Timothy 4:13, to his own private library and requests that
books from it be brought to him. Bishop Alexander founded
a Christian library in Jerusalem before 250 A.D., and about
the same time Origen (ca. 182-251 A.D.) was establishing
his theological school and library at Caesarea. At Alexandria in Egypt there was a Christian library as early as 175
A.D. That city was the capital of Christian scholarship in
the third century, and Clement of Alexandria, who died about
215, quoted from 348 authors in his works, indicating access to a fairly sizable library. Origen had been a pupil of
Clement, and he in turn passed on his books to a pupil,
Pamphilus, who studied and taught at Caesarea for many
years. In 303 the Emperor Diocletian made a concerted effort to destroy all Christian libraries, and many perished,
but the one at Caesarea survived. Eusebius, writing in 330,
says that he used this library in writing his history of the
Christian Church. Jerome used it in the fourth century also, and Euthalius in the fifth; in fact, it may well have survived until the Persians captured Palestine in 614, when all
Christian records were destroyed.

With the recognition of Christianity by the Roman Emperor Constantine (ca. 288-337), the situation in the Christian churches improved considerably, and the remainder of
the fourth century saw the rapid spread of Christian churches

and the establishment of many Christian libraries. Eusebius
(265-340 A.D.), the church historian, studied and worked in
Pamphilus' library at Caesarea, and after the latter's death
built it into a learned collection of over twenty thousand volumes.   Jerome was born in Dalmatia, studied in Rome and
became a secretary to Pope Damasus.   He edited the Latin
Vulgate Bible, and wrote many commentaries on the scriptures, becoming one of the greatest Christian scholars of
all times.   In his later years he retired to head a monastery in Bethlehem and carried with him a large personal library.   In a letter written in 397, Jerome described his library and noted that it contained much history and philosophy as well as theology.   George, Bishop of Alexandria,
built up a library that was also both secular and religious.
When he was murdered in 361 by an anti-Christian mob, the
Emperor Julian secured his library and placed it in a temple
in Antioch.   Unfortunately it was burned a few years later,
according to tradition on the orders of Emperor Jovian to
please a whim of his wife.

   In the early Christian churches, the small collection
of scriptures and related books were kept to the left.   The
early Christians were among the first to use the parchment
codex instead of the papyrus roll as a book form.   This was
probably because the parchment was more durable and the
codex form more suitable for frequent consultation than the
more cumbrous roll.   For instance, when the papyrus rolls
that made up the library of Pamphilus in Caesarea became
worn in the early fourth century, they were recopied onto
parchment codices.   This was accomplished over a number
of years by two dedicated priests, Acacius and Euzoius.

   Turning from consideration of specific libraries and
types of libraries, it will be worthwhile to look briefly at
the physical nature of the Roman library, both public and
private.   As we have seen, most of the publicly owned libraries were connected with temples even though they contained public archives and general literature as well as religious works.   The temple libraries, in whatever part of
the Empire, usually followed the same general plan, being
adjacent to or over a colonnade leading to the main structure of the temple.   There were often two divisions of the library, Greek and Latin, with sometimes a third division for
archives.   There were rooms for the storage of books and
also rooms for reading, although the colonnades lent themselves to reading or discussing books while walking.   Some
of the libraries were associated with meeting rooms where

public readings of an author's works could be given.   Quite
often there was a statue connected with the library, as for
example that of a bronze Apollo, some fifty feet high, in the
Temple of Apollo in Rome.   On the walls above the books
were paintings, semi-reliefs, or sculptures of famous writers.   The organization, format and handling of the rolls were
similar to that in the Greek libraries, but the Romans added
the armarium or chest for keeping more valuable rolls.
Then, as the codex replaced the roll, the shelf replaced the
pigeon-hole, but the armarium continued to be generally used
for storing books well down into the Middle Ages.

Although books in the Roman public libraries did not
circulate outside the building as a general rule, it is apparent from several classical references that influential people
could on occasion borrow them for home use.   Marcus Aurelius, for example, writing to his friend Fronto about 145
A.D., tells him that there is no need for him to send to the
libraries of Apollo for certain volumes since he, Aurelius,
already has them out.   Instead he suggests that Fronto try
Tiberius' library, although he may have to bribe the librarian there in order to be permitted to take them.   Owners of
private libraries were also known to lend their volumes to
their friends, and there are references to such loans in the
letters of both Cicero and Pliny.   That the circulation of
books was a problem can be seen from the rules of an Athenian library of about 100 A.D., found on an excavated wall:

> No book shall be taken out, since we have sworn
> an oath to that effect.   It will be open from the
> first hour until the sixth.

Libraries in private homes varied in physical accom-
modations according to the wealth of the owner and the size
of the collection.   A few rolls might be kept in a container
of wood or lead, similar to a modern hatbox.   A larger collection would be kept in its own armarium.   As the collection became even larger, it would be kept in a special room
or apartment with armaria, desks and works of art.   A typical library in a rich private home would have been about
fifteen by twenty-three feet with several armaria in it.   The
single armarium would have been about three feet high by
five feet wide, and a medallion above it would indicate the
author whose works it contained, or perhaps a favorite author of the owner.   Such a library room has been unearthed
in Herculaneum.

The average Roman papyrus roll was about twenty
to thirty feet long, and about nine to eleven inches high.
The roll was usually wrapped in a linen cloth, particularly
if it was treasured, and tied with a string.  More valuable
rolls might be kept in envelopes or jackets made of parchment or leather, sometimes dyed in bright colors.  Considering the size of the roll and the dimensions of excavated
Roman libraries, the average temple collection must have
been about twenty to forty thousand rolls, unless others were
stored elsewhere.  The armaria themselves were divided into nests (nida) by both horizontal and vertical shelves for
rolls, or by horizontal shelves only for codices.  Sometimes
the armaria were built into the walls, but usually they were
separate, movable pieces of furniture.  Pliny notes that he
had an armarium built into the walls of his bedroom.

The early Roman librarian was often a highly educated slave or prisoner of war from Greece or Asia Minor,
like many early teachers and scholars.  Later on in Roman
history, the librarian was a native scholar, often an author
as well.  Still later, however, the position became more
that of a civil servant.  Titus Atticus (109-32 B.C.), scholar and friend of Cicero, noted that all his librarians were
slaves.  Tyrannion, librarian for Cicero, was captured by
Lucullus on the Island of Rhodes about 72 B.C., and brought
to Rome.  He soon obtained his freedom and set himself up
as a teacher of Greek.  Later he became wealthy as a book
publisher and seller, and was a friend and confidant of both
scholars and statesmen.  He advised Cicero and Sulla on the
building up of their collections and helped catalog Cicero's
library.  Terentius Varro served as librarian, or at least
as book collector, for Julius Caesar.  He was a man of
great learning, a writer of history, satire, and poems.  Andronicus of Rhodes, an Aristotelian scholar, is supposed to
have cataloged the library of Sulla.

Under the Emperors, the several libraries in Rome
seem to have been administered by a central library chief
known as the procurator bibliothecarum.  About 100 A.D.,
this post was held by Dionysius of Alexandria, a noted grammarian, who also served as secretary to the Emperor.  Under Hadrian it was held by C. Julius Vesinus, a former tutor who later became administrator of the Museum in Alexandria.  About 250 A.D. the position was held by Q. Vettur-
ius Callistratus, according to an inscription discovered in
Rome.  Under this director of libraries, each library had
its own librarian (bibliothecarius or magister).  Library staff

members were numerous, many of them slaves and some of
them women.   Lesser library positions carried the titles of
librarius, vilicus, and antiquarius, with probably other titles
at different times and places.   The librarius seems to have
been a worker of various duties, from cataloger to copyist,
and from translator to clerical worker.   The vilicus was a
general attendant, somewhere between custodial and clerical.
The antiquarius was the scholar-librarian, historian and pa-
leographer.   Generally speaking, the librarians of Rome did
not equal in importance those of Alexandria or Pergamum in
their more prosperous days.   Instead, the administrative positions became political appointments or civil-service jobs,
while the actual library work was done by well-educated but
less important assistants.   The work in the larger libraries
became highly specialized with many types of work and varying degrees or ranks of service.   Closely allied with the librarians were the booksellers, who often doubled as publishers in their production of multiple copies of popular texts.
Many of them aided in the selection and acquisition of desired works for the libraries, particularly the private ones.
Often the public libraries produced their own texts by copying others.

That the books within the Roman libraries were arranged according to general subjects is known, but just what
those subject classifications were is uncertain.   Certainly
they were divided into Greek and Latin, and apparently all
the works of a single author were kept together under his
major subject.   The works in the various schools of philosophy were separated, as were those of different religious
groups.   Catalogs of two types were known, and sometimes
both were used.   The first type was a sort of classified catalog, or shelf list, arranged just as the rolls themselves
were stored.   The other was a bibliographical catalog, arranged by author but giving titles or first lines, lengths of
works, and sometimes biographical information about the author.

While the Romans did not invent censorship, it is obvious that they did vigorously control the kinds of reading
material made available to the people.   The Emperor Augustus was a builder of libraries, but he also controlled their
contents.   He ordered the works of Julius Caesar removed
from the public libraries and did the same for the works of
the poet Ovid.   The latter was not only subject to censorship, but was also banished to the Black Sea area for the
later years of his life.   The writings of the Christians were

suppressed by most of the Emperors before Constantine, but
later, when Christian bishops came into power in certain
areas, they in turn sometimes suppressed non-Christian writings.   In doing so, they destroyed many works of classical
authors now known to us only through excerpts or bibliographical notes in later writings.   For example, while the Emper-
or Diocletian attempted to suppress all Christian libraries in
303, the Emperor Theodosius I in 391 tried to destroy all
"heathen" libraries.   Under his direction, the Temple of Serapis in Alexandria was reported to have been destroyed
along with most if not all of its library.   A Christian church
replaced it with a small collection of Christian works.   The
Emperor Julian also tried to destroy Christian texts, but
founded libraries of classical works at Antioch and Constantinople.   Justinian in 529 preserved Roman law and Christian
theology, but ordered classical works at the Academy in Athens confiscated, and forbade the teaching of Greek philosophy
there.   In the same century, Pope Gregory I is reported to
have suppressed the works of Cicero and Livy, not because
of their contents, but because young men were reading them
when they should have been reading the Bible.   Gregory is
also accused of having ordered the burning of the Palatine
Library in Rome, but this is generally discredited.   Between
the activities of the Christians and non-Christians in burning
books, and the later censorship by the Moslems after the
seventh century, many works of classical authors that might
have otherwise survived, were lost forever.

The great libraries of the classical world were, one
and all, destined to be destroyed.   Some of them met their
end in accidental fires or natural disasters, such as those of
Rome and Herculaneum.   Many more were destroyed in wars,
internal conflicts and barbarian raids.   The northern hordes
who swept down on Rome and Greece in the fifth and six centuries had little or no respect for learning, and books were
just so much papyrus or parchment to them.   Athens' last
great library, that of the Academy, was destroyed in 529.
Just when the last classical library in Rome disappeared is
uncertain, but it is doubtful that more than one or two of
them survived the fifth century, and none came through the
sixth.   Finally, it should be noted that a large number of
Roman libraries simply decayed and disappeared as a result
of neglect and disuse.   Political disturbances, rulers uninterested in books and learning, economic disasters--all contributed to an atmosphere in which libraries were closed and
books deteriorated.

Ammianus Marcellinus, writing about 378, reported
that the libraries of Rome were even then like tombs, closed
forever. This was possibly a premature judgment, for some
of them are known to have been open after that, but in general he was right. The days when Rome's great libraries
were popular were over. The great period of Roman literature and learning had passed; the classical era was gone,
and the Dark Ages had begun. But in many corners of the
western world the sparks of learning were still alive in the
sixth century. The Eastern Empire was still alert and libraries were growing there, with many books flowing east-
ward from Rome. Also, on the western fringes, in Spain,
France and even England, private libraries were still being
collected and used, and in Italy itself the monastic system
that was to preserve learning throughout the Middle Ages was
already beginning.

### Additional Readings

Many of the readings already cited in Chapters 3
and 4 contain information on libraries in the Roman era, and these may be supplemented by the
numerous fine studies of Roman archeology, literature and culture, many of which contain references to Roman libraries. The following titles
refer more specifically to Roman libraries and
the book trade.

Boak, A. E. R.   The Archive of Aurelius Isidorus in the
    Egyptian Museum...   Ann Arbor, 1959.

Boyd, C. E.   Public Libraries and Literary Culture in An-
    cient Rome.   Chicago, 1915.

Clift, E. H.   Latin Pseudepigraphia; A Study in Literary At-
    tributions.   Baltimore, 1945.

Cramer, F. H.   "Bookburning and Censorship in Ancient
    Rome," Journal of the History of Ideas 6 (1945):   147-
    96.

Cross, F. M.   The Ancient Library of Qumran and Modern
    Biblical Studies.   London, 1961.

Davis, D. G., Jr.   "Christianity and Pagan Libraries in
    the Later Roman Empire," Library History 2 (1970):
    1-10.

Deuel, L. "Rolls and a Villa [Herculaneum]," in his Testaments of Time. New York, 1968.

Kleberg, T. "Bibliophiles in Ancient Rome," Libri 1 (1950): 2-12.

_____. "Book Auctions in Ancient Rome," Libri 23 (1973): 1-5.

Langie, A. Les Bibliothèques Publiques dans L'Ancient Rome et dans l'Empire Romain. Fribourg, 1908.

Norman, A. F. "The Book Trade in Fourth-Century Antioch," Journal of Hellenic Studies 30 (1960): 122-26.

Pedley, K. G. The Library at Qumran: A Librarian Looks at the Dead Sea Scrolls. Berkeley, Calif., 1964.

Reichmann, F. "The Book Trade at the Time of the Roman Empire," Library Quarterly 7 (1938): 40-76.

Roberts, C. H. "The Codex," Proceedings of the British Academy 40 (1954): 169-204.

Skeat, T. C. "The Use of Dictation in Ancient Book Production," Proceedings of the British Academy 42 (1956): 179-208.

Van der Valk, M. "On the Edition of Books in Antiquity," Vigiliae Christianae 11 (1957): 1-10.

# PART II

## MEDIEVAL LIBRARIES

## Chapter 6

## BYZANTINE AND MOSLEM LIBRARIES

Of all the libraries of antiquity, those in Constantinople came nearest to surviving intact through the Middle Ages. In particular, the Imperial Library, founded by Constantine the Great in the fourth century, varied in size and importance with the fortunes of the Byzantine Empire, but in one form or another it survived until the capture of the city in 1453 by the Ottoman Turks.

The background of Byzantine history is both Greek and Roman. The site of the city of Constantinople on the European side of the Straits of the Bosporus between the Mediterranean and the Black Sea was known to the Greeks as Byzantium. After the Emperor Constantine had won control over both the Eastern and Western Roman Empires about 325, he established his capital at this spot and renamed it Constantinople. In the course of time, the Western Empire declined and was overrun by barbarians from the North, but the Eastern or Byzantine Empire continued to exist, at times powerful and at other times weak, but always culturally effective for more than a thousand years. Essentially, the Byzantine culture was more Greek than Roman, more Eastern than Western. Its role in Western civilization is due to its effect on the Balkans and Russia, and to its preservation of many of the Greek and Latin classics. In general, more Greek writings than Latin were preserved in Constantinople, as Greek was the dominant language in the Eastern area. A thousand years after Constantine, in the fourteenth and fifteenth centuries, copies of these manuscripts found their way to Italy and western Europe, heralding the dawn of the Renaissance. In founding Constantinople and in adopting Christianity as a state religion, Constantine made his name one of the most remembered of all the Roman emperors.

An imperial library in the Eastern Empire had been established by the Emperor Diocletian at Nicomedia, his capital, before 300, but little is known about it. Constantine founded an imperial library at Constantinople sometime after 330 and before 336. His agents searched for Christian books throughout the Empire for his library. He also collected the writings of the Greek and Latin secular writers for his library, but it apparently grew quite slowly since there were reported to be only about seven thousand books in the library at Constantine's death in 337. A generation later, the Emperor Julian tried to overthrow Christianity and he may have ordered the destruction of some Christian works in the library, but he also established a library of classical literature in Antioch and gave his own book collection to the imperial library in 362. Theodosius II (401-450) is credited with enlarging the library to about 100,000 volumes, but it declined again under Leo I. His successor Zeno (474-491) saw the library partially destroyed in a fire, and rebuilt it with copies of works gathered from other libraries. The library at this time probably contained over 100,000 volumes, with more codices than rolls.

In the fifth century, the library of the Academy, a university or school of philosophy, was founded under Theodosius II (408-450) in Constantinople. This school flourished for several centuries, particularly under the Emperor Justinian (527-565). Under Leo the Isaurian (717-741), both university and imperial libraries suffered in the Emperor's fight against the worshipers of idols or icons. Books containing religious pictures were sometimes destroyed by the "iconoclasts," who regarded them as heathen. The Academy ceased to exist in the late eighth century, and the imperial library declined to some 35,000 volumes, but in the ninth century a university was re-established. This institution was staffed with a noted group of scholars headed by Leo the Mathematician, and its library played a large role in the Byzantine "renaissance" that was to come in the eleventh century.

The Emperor Justinian is noted in library history for two reasons. First, it was he who closed the last surviving classical school, then at Athens, in 529 because he felt that the curriculum there was contrary to the teachings of the Christian Church. A more positive accomplishment under Justinian was the codification of Roman law. This work, done by a commission of scholars appointed by the Emperor, involved the study and condensation of some two thousand

volumes of legal works, going back nearly a thousand years
in Roman history.  The Justinian Code, with its Digests and
supplementary works, form the Corpus Juris Civilis, the basis of all civil law in western Europe through the Middle Ages
and into the modern era.  Around this work there grew up in
Constantinople a school of law which was formalized into a
legal university in the eleventh century.  To compile Justinian's Code, a well-organized law library must have been
available, and undoubtedly a library was provided for the law
students throughout the history of the school of law.  In 1045,
the Emperor Constantine VII is recorded as having ordered
that the law library contain "all the books useful and necessary for the teaching of law," and that it be administered by
a "devout" librarian.  The value of the legal work of Justinian's era, and its effect on the legal and juristic history of
the western world, can scarcely be over-emphasized.

Besides the libraries of the Emperor and the university, there was usually a third major library in Constantinople, the library of the Patriarch, the head of the Eastern
Church, and it, too, fluctuated in size and importance
throughout the long history of Byzantium.  Constantine the
Great is reported to have also started this library with a gift
of fifty volumes, elegantly inscribed on parchment.  In time,
a school or college grew up under the direction of the Patriarch, distinct from the Imperial University.  This school, although taught by religious scholars, usually educated the administrators and higher civil servants of the Empire, while
religious leaders themselves were educated in the monasteries.  Whether this school made use of the library of the
Patriarch or had its own library is uncertain, but it is known
that some of the Patriarchs had private libraries of their
own.

Monastic life flourished in the Eastern Empire even
earlier than it did in the West, and many monasteries were
founded in Asia Minor and Greece before 500.  For several
centuries these monasteries followed the laws of monastic life
laid down by St. Pachomius of Egypt (d. 346) which encouraged study but did not insist on the formation of libraries.
About 825 at Studium, a monastery near Constantinople, the
Abbot Theodore produced a new set of monastic regulations
that emphasized the scriptorium and the library, and outlined the duties of the librarian.  After this, each monastery
was encouraged to form a library of its own.  The monastic
libraries on the Greek peninsula of Mt. Athos are particularly notable for their longevity, some of them surviving down

to the modern era.   Religious works were the texts usually
preserved in the monasteries, but some secular works were
also found there.   Since some monastic orders provided hospitals and even taught physicians, their libraries also contained medical and scientific works.   An example of one of
the most important texts to survive in a Byzantine monastery
is the Codex Sinaiticus, one of the earliest extant manuscripts
of the Bible, now in the British Museum, but originally
found at the monastery of St. Catherine on Mt. Sinai.

The period from 850 to 1100 saw a renaissance in
Byzantine learning and literature.   This rebirth of interest
in knowledge and learning stimulated a revival of the university, and encouraged the work of a number of significant authors, although their works for the most part consisted of
compendia or anthologies rather than original productions.
In the ninth century, the scholar and patriarch Photius compiled his Bibliotheca (or Myrobiblion) which was a summary
or digest of some 280 earlier works, many of them now lost.
Whether he had all of the works mentioned in his own library or not, he must have had access to an excellent collection.   Included in the works discussed were many theological titles, but also much Greek history and literature with
some works in the arts and sciences.   Arethas of Caesarea,
a tenth century follower of Photius, had a private library of
which something is known from his surviving letters.   He
owned copies of Euclid, Lucian and Aristides, as well as
Aristotle and Plato, and wrote commentaries on some of the
classic authors.   One volume of his library has survived and
is now in the Bodleian Library at Oxford.

Suidas, a tenth century encyclopedist, also culled from
many sources in compiling his Lexikon, a dictionary-encyclo-
pedia of general knowledge.   Among the few examples of literature as such, John Geometres' tenth-century poems are
as filled with references to classical authors as the works of
his prose-writing contemporaries.   An eleventh-century poet,
John Mauropous, expressed his feeling for his library in a
couplet:

> Living among my books like a bee among flowers
> Nourished on words like a grasshopper on dew.

Outside of Constantinople, most of the major cities of
the Byzantine Empire contained, at different times, one or
more libraries in monasteries, schools and churches.   Since
the Empire itself expanded and contracted several times dur-

ing its thousand year history, so the fortunes of its various
provincial cities also fluctuated considerably. Libraries under Byzantine control are mentioned at Caesarea, Berytus
(Beirut), Thessalonika and Athens, among others. Eustatius,
Archbishop of Thessalonika in the twelfth century, quoted
from more than four hundred authors in his writings, indicating access to a good library. On the other hand, when
Michael Acominatus became Archbishop of Athens in 1175,
he noted that the city had no libraries at all, and that his
two chests of books constituted the largest collection of literature in the city. When the Norman Crusaders overran
much of Greece in the late twelfth century, they took books
from both private and public collections as spoils of war,
and possibly initiated the flow of manuscripts from East to
West.

Besides authors and religious leaders, other Byzantine
figures owned private libraries of note. The emperors usually had personal libraries in addition to the imperial library, and Valens, in the fifth century, hired both Greek
and Latin scribes to produce a library for himself and his
children. In the same period, most of the twenty-eight pro-
fessors at the Academy were reported to own personal libraries. Tribonian, the legal scholar who headed Justinian's
committee for codifying Roman law, placed his two thousand-
volume library at the disposal of the Committee. In 620, a
scholar by the name of Tychicus was reported to possess a
large library, a fact recorded by a government official who
evidently coveted the library for his own.

At various times during its long history, Byzantine influence extended from Ceylon to Paris and from Spain to Moscow. Charlemagne, for example, obtained copies of books
from the imperial library at Constantinople for his palace library at Aachen. Monasteries in Armenia borrowed books
from Constantinople, and copies of them are still preserved
in the Miasnikian State Public Library in Erevan. The Moslems, close neighbors and frequent enemies of Constantinople
for eight hundred years before its fall, borrowed not only literature but art, education, political science and philosophy
from the Byzantines. Their influence was strong in Sicily
and southern Italy, where an eleventh-century monastery library contained Greek classical authors that were virtually
unknown in the rest of Western Europe. The Serbian Empress Elizabeth in the thirteenth century obtained a Greek library from Constantinople. Basil Lapu, Prince of Moldavia
in the next century, also had a library containing classical

Greek authors.  Thus it can be seen that the great writings
of the classical era, particularly those of Greece, were
never completely lost to the Western World.  They were always available to the Byzantines, and to those western peoples in cultural and diplomatic contact with the Eastern Empire.  However, during most of the Middle Ages these contacts were few and tenuous, and for all practical purposes,
scarcely significant.

Unfortunately, the glory of Byzantium that had with-
stood wars both external and internal for many centuries
gradually came to an end after 1200.  Norman invasions of
the Greek peninsula in the late twelfth century presaged that
end, and when Constantinople itself was captured in 1204,
the city was almost completely destroyed.  Some of the invaders realized that the books in the public and private libraries were valuable, and so began a trade in manuscripts
with eager Italian buyers.  Many more were probably destroyed than sold, and so it is not unreasonable to assume
that greater damage was done in the destruction of Constantinople by the Christians in 1204 than by the Turks in 1453.

After the fall of Constantinople, the capital of Byzantium was removed to Nicaea, where Emperor John III (1222-
54) re-established the imperial library.  In the thirteenth
century, Nicaea became a center of culture, with schools,
churches, monasteries and hospitals the equal of any in the
western world.  From Nicaea, the Byzantines began a return
to power, recapturing Thesalonika from the Normans in
1246, and returning to Constantinople in 1261.  There, Emperor Michael Paleologus reinstated the imperial library in
a wing of the palace.  The last two centuries of Byzantine
history are an anti-climax because the once great empire was
gradually reduced until it was little more than the city of
Constantinople by 1450.  Pressed on all sides by enemies
such as the Italians, Serbs, Bulgars and Turks, and troubled
with dissension and lack of leadership, the Eastern Empire
finally fell to the Ottoman Turks in 1453 and a great era in
Eurasian history was ended.

Oddly enough, while Constantinople was weakening po-
litically between 1260 and 1450, it was experiencing a revival in literature and learning.  In schools, libraries, monasteries and hospitals, Constantinople was far ahead of either
the declining Moslem world or pre-Renaissance Europe.
This, of course, came to an end when Mohammed II led his
conquering forces into the city.  Churches and monasteries,

homes and palaces alike were sacked and everything of value
was taken.  Many books were undoubtedly destroyed, but
some of the Turkish soldiers realized that they were potentially valuable and hundreds were saved and sold.  At first
it was reported that volumes of Aristotle and Plato sold for
a penny each, but soon after the conquest their value rose
as the Italian traders resumed their traffic in manuscripts
and other treasures.  It is impossible to say just how many
libraries and how many volumes were in existence in Constantinople in 1453, but it is known that despite the large
number of books destroyed, traffic in Greek manuscripts remained a profitable business for more than a hundred years
afterward.

The significance of Constantinople in Western civilization is great, not because of its own art and literature--al-
though that was prodigious if not original--but because it preserved so much of classical literature through the Middle
Ages when it was virtually lost in the West.  Of the Greek
classics known today, at least seventy-five per cent are
known through Byzantine copies.  The flow of manuscripts
from East to West had begun even before 1200, but it
reached its high point in the fourteenth and fifteenth centuries.  For some traders, manuscripts were the most valuable single item of trade, and the effect of this literary trade
on the West was the rebirth of interest in classical literature, history and philosophy which we call the Renaissance.
In this sense, it was the decline of Byzantium that provided
the impetus to the end of the Middle Ages in Europe and the
birth of the modern era.

Constantinople was not the only center of culture in
the Eastern Mediterranean during the Middle Ages.  Close
neighbors and long-time enemies of the Christian Byzantines,
the Moslems, sprang into prominence in the seventh century.
In a few decades after 622, when the Moslem era began, the
religion of Islam swept the Arabic world and its fringes
from Persia to Morocco.  The Moslems came close to Constantinople on several occasions, but were unable to capture
the city until 1453.  Under the inspiration of the Islamic religion, the Arabs developed both a military power and a literary culture that was to flourish for several hundred years.

Before the coming of the Prophet Mohammed, however,
there was little literature or literacy among the Arabic peoples.  Instead, an oral literature of tales and poetry was
handed down from generation to generation, much as in

Homeric Greece. The first major item of written literature
among the Moslems was the Koran itself. This collection of
sayings of the Prophet came to represent both the "Bible"
and the philosophical base of Mohammedanism. To know the
Koran and its teaching became the duty of all Moslems, and
hence literacy became all important and schools began to be
organized. To teach the Koran, scholars and priests were
necessary and higher institutions of education were started,
many of them connected with the churches or mosques. The
result of all this was a stabilized Arabic language that was
suitable for a secular as well as a religious literature. Another fortunate development aided the expansion of Arabic
literature and learning. This was the use of paper as a
writing material, much cheaper and more available than
parchment or papyrus. An economical writing material
meant that more copies of literary works could be produced
and that reading material of all kinds could reach a wider
audience. The technique of manufacturing paper came to the
eastern Moslems from China by way of central Asia about
800, and the knowledge of the process spread gradually
through the Moslem world, reaching Spain about 950. Paper
could be made from a variety of fibrous materials, but the
best varieties were produced from linen or cotton rags.

Although Mohammedanism spread largely through the
strength of its military power, and some Moslem leaders
were known to have held that no book was necessary except
the Koran, the world of Islam in general was a book-loving
society. Seldom in the history of the world have books been
held in such high esteem, at least among the upper classes.
Along with studying the Koran, the devout Moslem was encouraged to copy it and make it available to others, so the
craft of the scribe became popular in the Arab world, and
thousands of copies of the Koran were produced, many of
them in beautiful scripts and bindings.

The first center of the Moslem world was Damascus,
where the Umayyid dynasty ruled from 661 to 750. These
rulers promoted learning and established a royal library that
also included the archives of the church and state. About
690, the archives were separated from the literary and religious works, the latter forming a palace library, and the
former being relegated to a House of Archives. For the
palace library, which was open to use by serious students
and scholars, copies of books from all parts of the known
world were obtained. Works of alchemy, medicine and astrology were included as well as literature, history and
philosophy, and, of course, works on the Moselm religion.

A footnote to early Moslem culture concerns the Nestorian Christians who were driven from Syria by the Emperor Zeno about 485. These Christians fled to Persia, where at Nisibis they built up a strong center of Greek culture, complete with libraries of the classics. They attracted scholars from Greece, including some of the faculty of the school at Athens that was closed by Justinian in 529. Thus the Moslems found, deep in the mountains of Persia, a treasure house of Greek science and philosophy that they soon had translated into Arabic. In fact, most of the surviving Greek literature was translated into Arabic by 750, and Aristotle, for example, became so widely studied that literally hundreds of books were written about him by Arabic scholars. The Moslems also obtained Greek works from Constantinople through regular trade channels, and captured others in their various wars with the Eastern Empire.

The great period of Moslem literature and learning came under the Abbasid rulers, or Caliphate, from about 750 to 1050. These Caliphs moved the capital of the Moslem world to Baghdad, and during this era the power and influence of Islam spread from Persia around the south shore of the Mediterranean to Spain and even Southern France. Actually Spain and Morocco never recognized the rule of the Abbasids, and their areas of control varied considerably in periods of internal and external conflicts, but culturally the area that accepted Islam became unified. The early Abbasid Caliphs, adopting a religious philosophy that encouraged learning and debate, promoted the establishment of universities and libraries throughout their realm. Early beginnings were made under Al-Mansur (754-775), and Harun al-Rashid (785-809) of Arabian Nights fame, but it was Al-Mamun the Great (813-833) who brought the "House of Learning" or university at Baghdad into prominence. With libraries, laboratories, subsidized scholars, a translating service and even an astronomical observatory, this institution attracted scholars from Spain to India. Its books were culled from the accumulated scholarship of a dozen languages, and its faculty spoke as many or more. The libraries were open to scholars from all over the world, whether their interests lay in religion or science, poetry or medicine. Scholarly relations were maintained with all civilized countries of Europe, Asia and Africa, and contact with western Europe was relatively open, particularly during the periods of peace. Interchange of ideas between East and West continued throughout the Abbasid era, and it is quite possible that during these years the Islamic world received more from the West than it transmitted. In later years this trend was to be noticeably reversed.

By 900, Baghdad was a center of learning that rivaled
if it did not exceed Constantinople. Its schools and libraries
were models for similar institutions throughout Islam. It
was said that Baghdad alone had over one hundred booksellers in 891, and that at the height of its cultural glory it had
some thirty public libraries. Other university and public libraries were located all the way from Bokhara and Merv,
deep in the heart of Asia on the land route to China, through
Basra and Damascus, Cairo and Algiers, to Morocco and
Spain in the west. A geographer, Yakut al-Hamawi, who
visited Merv in 1228, found no less than twelve libraries
there available to the public. Ten were endowed libraries
and two were in mosques. One had over twelve thousand
volumes in codex form, and another had been in existence
since 494 A.D. Yakut noted that the lending policies of the
libraries in Merv were so liberal that he was able to have
over two hundred volumes to work with in his rooms at one
time.

Under the rule of the Seljuk Turks in the latter eleventh century, Moslem education in the East became more
purely theological, but also during this era a more formal
university was established at Baghdad. This was the Niza-
miyah, founded about 1065, basically a theological seminary,
but with other courses also formally taught. It had board-
ing facilities for students, student scholarships, endowed pro-
fessorships, and other characteristics of a modern university. A noted hospital was connected with this institution,
and both university and hospital had libraries. Though its
buildings were ransacked and its students and faculty scattered, the university managed to survive the Mongol conquests and was still in operation in the fifteenth century.

In Egypt, the Fatimid Caliphs during the tenth to
twelfth centuries built up a center of culture in Cairo that
was to rival any in the world at that time. The Caliph al-
Aziz (975-996) protected poets and scholars and established
a royal library for their use. Catalogs of this and other
libraries in Cairo were compiled, along with subject bibliographies of the known branches of knowledge. Established in
Cairo in 972, the mosque-university El Azhar still survives
to the present day.

It was reported, although it was possibly an exaggeration, that the libraries of Cairo, at the height of the city's
cultural development in the mid-eleventh century, contained
over a million volumes. In 1068, a revolt against the

Fatimid ruler Al-Mustansir resulted in the sacking of the
royal palace and the dispersal or destruction of its 200,000
volume library.  According to one reporter, manuscripts
were used for lighting soldiers' fires, and leather bindings
of rare volumes served as repairs for their boots.  However,
the library must have been rebuilt, for when Saladin came into power in 1173 he found it to contain over 100,000 volumes.
At an earlier date, a Cairo library was reported to have had
its own staff of librarians, administrators, binders, calligra-
phers, servants and guards, supported by rentals from property with which it had been endowed.  It was supposed to
contain over 2,400 copies of the Koran, most of them individual works of calligraphic and book-binding art.  Science,
particularly astronomy, art and architecture flourished under
the Fatimids, and literally hundreds of volumes were written
by its scholars with the aid of its libraries.  Unfortunately
the combination of Mongol conquerors and Christian Crusaders was to end this Egyptian renaissance abruptly.

Another place in which Moslem scholarship and learning reached high levels was Spain, where the followers of
Mohammed prevailed for several centuries.  The Moslems
entered Spain after 711, and in Cordoba, Seville, Toledo and
other cities they built an advanced civilization that outshone
anything in western Europe during the same period.  At Cordoba, for example, there was a noted Moslem university, as
well as several other large libraries including the royal library,
reputed to contain over 400,000 volumes.  Its catalog alone
consisted of forty-four volumes.  Under Al-Hakim II (961-
976), this library was reported to have given employment to
over five hundred people, including many agents sent to all
parts of the world to buy books.  Al-Hakam gave his own
private library to the royal library at Cordoba which had
been founded about 850 and greatly enlarged under the rule
of Abd-al-Rahman III (912-961).  Elsewhere in Moslem Spain
there was a total of seventy libraries in the tenth century,
several in Toledo.  In addition to the royal library, these included libraries in universities in Cordoba, Seville, Malaga
and Granada, among others, and in numerous mosques.  Private libraries flourished in Moslem Spain, and it was said
that Cordoba was the greatest book market in the western
world in the tenth century.  Sicily also came under Moslem
influence during the ninth and tenth centuries, as did Sar-
dinia and Corsica.  From these islands, as well as from
Spain, western Europe received translations of classical writings preserved by the Moslems.

Probably at few times in the history of the world have
private libraries reached such size and elegance as under the
Moslems.   The wealth brought by conquest, tribute, and
trade developed among them an elite and highly literate upper class.   Since bigamy was practiced, and even encouraged for those who could afford it, large families were the
rule among the nobility, and among them many younger sons
pursued learning and scholarship as a career.   Next to war
and conquest, these became the most honored professions,
and the collecting of libraries both for use and for show, became common among the wealthy.   Many of these private libraries reached remarkable size, according to the references
we have to them in the works of geographers, historians and
biographers.   The library of one Baghdad scholar of the
tenth century was reported to require four hundred camel
loads to move it when he took it from one residence to another.   So numerous were these private libraries that one
writer has estimated that, as of 1200, there were more
books in private hands in the Moslem world than in all libraries, public and private, of western Europe.   It was not
uncommon for wealthy bookmen to leave their libraries to
the people, and to endow these libraries, thus ensuring their
continued growth and usefulness.

One interesting thing about the Moslem libraries is the
wide variety of subject matter they contained.   With the exception of religious works of other faiths, the Moslems gathered, copied, and translated everything they could, in all
subjects, of all times, and in all available languages.   Greek
and Latin classics, Sanskrit philosophy, Egyptian history,
Hindu epics, and medieval French love-poems--all were to
be found somewhere in the Moslem libraries, along with biography, science and pseudo-science from all times and
places.   Though most of these libraries were subsequently
destroyed, from surviving catalogs and isolated volumes we
find evidence of all these and other subjects as well.   For
example, the library at Fez in Morocco contained the works
of the Roman Livy and the Greek Galen, among others.   The
library at Damascus contained all the known works of Aristotle.   A library at Gaza, between Egypt and Palestine, contained many Egyptian papyri, some in hieroglyphics.   The
Justinian Code of Laws was present in many Moslem collections, indicating the respect that was felt among the Arabs
for this great legal collection, even though it differed sub-
stantially from their own laws.

Of course, the major holdings of many Arabic li-

braries, particularly those in the mosques, related to the
Moslem religion.   Copies of the Koran were numerous, and
commentaries on it filled thousands of other volumes.   All
members of Mohammed's family, both his immediate ancestors and descendants, were subjects of biographies, often
more fanciful than accurate.

Unfortunately, we have little accurate information concerning the physical conditions in the Moslem libraries.   The
usual book-form was the codex, either of parchment or some
other animal skin, or of paper.   Rolls were by no means
unknown, particularly in the earlier centuries, and in the
eastern areas the exotic Asiatic accordion-shaped volumes
and even the Hindu palm-leaf olas were occasionally seen.
As for library arrangement, there are references to the custom of placing different subjects in different rooms in the
larger libraries, and even of having "subject specialists" in
charge of them.   In smaller libraries, the books were kept
in chests with a list of the contents on the outside.   In the
larger libraries, the staff list might number hundreds when
copyists, binders, illuminators, and other employees were
added to those whom we would usually consider as librarians.   The latter were often scholars, writers or poets,
multilingual, and well paid by patronizing rulers or nobles.
However, library administrators are also mentioned, indicating that the management of these large enterprises often
called more for a business man than for a scholar.   This
was particularly true in the endowed libraries where profit-
making businesses were involved.

The larger libraries seem to have been cataloged as
a matter of normal procedure, and the catalogs took the
form of manuscript volumes.   References are found to catalogs which filled as many as twenty, or even forty, volumes.
These catalogs were apparently arranged by subject, but
items were arranged by the order of acquisition within each
subject class.   Since shelving was by subject in room or
chest, the catalog was thus something of a classified accession list, but it apparently served its purpose and was widely used.   Many of the Moslem libraries included not only
rooms for reading, but also rooms for meetings and smaller
rooms for discussion and debate.

Particularly in the wealthy private libraries, but also
in some of the public ones, the arts of illuminating and binding reached a high level among the Moslems.   Calligraphy
itself was an art, and the cursive Arabic script lent itself

to beautiful productions.  The use of fine vellums, often dyed
with exotic colors, and of different colored inks, together
with ornate, heavily tooled and embossed leather bindings,
produced some of the most beautiful books the world has ever
known.  Such fine works were, of course, exceptions, but
the book itself was thoroughly appreciated and widely used.
Although few Moslem libraries were public in the modern
sense of the word, most of them, even large private ones,
were available to serious scholars.  Even outside circulation
of books was not unknown, and in many cases extra services
were provided, such as free writing materials, copyists and
translators.

Some of the results of the scholarship in these libraries and schools can be seen in the writings of representative Moslem authors.  In 987, Muhammad al-Nadim produced a multi-volumed Index of the Sciences, a bibliography
of books in Arabic on all branches of knowledge, with biographical notes on the authors.  Some idea of the great loss
to world literature in the destruction of Arabic libraries can
be obtained when it is noted that not one in a thousand of the
books al-Nadim described is presently known to exist.  Another tenth-century writer, Muhammad al-Tabari, wrote a
history of the world in 150 volumes, saying that he had consulted over ten thousand source volumes in writing them.
The Egyptian scholar and astronomer Ibn al-Haytham, one
of the early eleventh century, wrote over one hundred volumes on mathematics, astronomy, philosophy, and medicine.
Even greater writers, although not so prolific, were the Arabic authors whose works reached the medieval European
world.  Averroes (Ibn Rushd), who lived in Spain in the
twelfth century, brought the works of Aristotle back to western Europe with his text and commentaries which were translated into Latin.  Before that, the only works of Aristotle
known to western Europe were excerpts translated by Boethius about 500 A. D.

Unfortunately, the story of Islamic libraries is too
similar to that of their predecessors in the classical era,
for they, too, ended in wholesale destruction.  Many Moslem libraries suffered in civil wars and in the decline of interest in learning under various rulers at different times.
Religious dissension often resulted in conquests that brought
on destruction of books relating to the history and beliefs of
particular Moslem sects.  When Saladin, a Sunnite Moslem,
conquered Egypt in 1175, a country where the Shi'ite Moslems had been in power, he is reported to have destroyed

whole libraries and distributed the finer works to his victorious followers. After 1100, reactionaries gained control in most of the eastern Moslem world, and the fortunes of Moslem libraries declined sharply. Those that survived tended to center on theology. Learning continued to flourish in North Africa and Spain for two more centuries, but here, too, there was a noticeable decline after 1300.

Not the least important in the destruction of Islamic libraries were the depredations of the Christian crusaders from the eleventh to the thirteenth centuries. In Syria, Palestine, and parts of North Africa, the Christians destroyed libraries as enthusiastically as the barbarians in Italy a few hundred years earlier. When Spain was reconquered from the Arabs, the great Islamic libraries at Seville, Cordoba and Granada were destroyed or were carried away by their retreating owners. As late as 1499, Granada was the scene of a bonfire of Arabic manuscripts. In the next century, however, Philip II, in building the Escorial Library, appreciated the value of Arabic sources and brought together all that he could find in Spain, plus others purchased in Morocco. He acquired for this library over four thousand Arabic manuscripts relating to the history of Spain.

Fire and flood also took their toll of Moslem libraries, and one particularly large one at Medina was destroyed in 1257 by a fire caused by lightning. The greatest destruction, however, resulted from the raids of the Mongols in the thirteenth century. From the mountains and steppes of central Asia came the hordes of Genghis Kahn, conquering and destroying everything before them. In the first great sweep to the Caspian Sea and northern Persia, the cities of Bokhara, Samarkand, and Merv were destroyed along with many smaller towns. Samarkand had been a Moslem city for over five hundred years, and its schools and libraries were well endowed and well used. The libraries of Merv were justly famous, but all were destroyed along with many of the scholars who were using them. These depredations took place about 1218 to 1220, and after that the Mongols withdrew. In 1258, however, they returned in greater force under the command of Hulagu Khan, and this time they reached and destroyed Baghdad. In one week, libraries and their treasures that had been accumulated over hundreds of years were burned or otherwise destroyed. So many books were thrown into the Tigris River, according to one writer, that they formed a bridge that would support a man on horseback. Students and scholars were considered particularly useless to the victors and they were killed by the hundreds.

The Mongols also destroyed at this time one of the strangest libraries in history. This was one built up by the sect known as Assassins at Alamut and reputed to contain much concerning magic and murder, but also some fine works in philosophy and science. After destroying thirty-six public libraries and hundreds of private ones in Baghdad, the Mongols under Hulagu swept on through Syria, virtually wiping out the ancient city of Damascus. Finally, the Moslems of Egypt were able to stop the Mongols in 1260, and they gradually fell back to the Caspian area. Although they did not long maintain their hold, the Mongols destroyed so much in wealth, books, and lives that the glory of Islam was forever dimmed. It is ironic that Hulagu himself, in his later years, became a devotee of learning, and estabished a library and astronomical observatory at his home at Maraghah in northwestern Persia. The fourteenth century saw a cultural renaissance of sorts in Eastern Islam, but this in turn was ended by the invasion of Tamerlane in 1393. Between foreign invasions and internal dissension, the Arabic peoples for the most part sank back into a state of widespread illiteracy that continued down to the twentieth century. Before that happened, however, there had flourished in Islam for nearly a thousand years one of the world's truly great civilizations.

But what was the effect of that Moslem civilization on the western world and particularly on the libraries of the western world? Since much of the literature itself was lost, the effect was not as great as if the libraries had been preserved. However, the Islamic libraries, almost as much as those of Constantinople, were the connecting link between the learning of classical Greece and the cultural development of western Europe. One point of contact in particular was Spain. As early as 953, John of Gorce was sent to Cordoba by the German Emperor Otto the Great. Gorce learned to read Arabic and returned to Germany with his saddlebags filled with Arabic manuscripts, including some translations from Aristotle and some Arabic works of science. In 1070, Daniel of Morley, an English scholar, visited Toledo and returned to England with copies of Arabic scientific works. Roger Bacon, English scientist and philosopher of the thirteenth century, received much of his learning from Arabic sources. Gerard of Cremona, who died in 1187, spent most of his life in Toledo and translated over seventy scientific works from Arabic into Latin. When the Christian Spanish captured Toledo, they found a wealth of Arabic books and, although many were destroyed, others were kept and translated into Latin. The Christian King Alfonso X of Castile had been taught by Arabic teachers, and when he founded the University of Salamanca in the thirteenth century, it was largely modeled on the Moslem universities, even using translations of the same textbooks. Thus, even before 1250, works of Arabic science and translations and commentaries on the Greek classics had reached western Europe either through Spain or through Sicily and southern Italy. The works of Galen and Hippocrates, Greek physicians, enlarged upon by their Arabic successors, became the textbooks of the earliest European medical schools at Naples, Bologna, Padua and Paris. Without the knowledge gained from the Moslem world, it is likely that the cultural development of modern Europe would have been considerably delayed.

Although the Christian Crusades resulted in the destruction of some Islamic libraries, they also resulted in contact, social and commercial as well as military, between western Europe and the eastern Mediterranean, and through that area with the whole of the exotic East from Arabia to China. This contact resulted in an expansion of trade and in the development of new tastes in western Europe, both literary and culinary. With the trade in fine fabrics, rare metals, and tasty foods came the trade in manuscripts that flourished for hundreds of years. Commerce led to economic development, interest in explorations, and the eventual discovery of America. Economic stability helped in the development of nationalism, and laid a foundation for the rediscovery and growth of such ideas as liberty and democracy. But it was in the books that came from Constantinople and from the Moslem libraries and booksellers that western Europe rediscovered the ideas and ideals of the classical world, and with them came the intellectual ferment that marked the beginning of the Renaissance and heralded the dawn of modern history. Thus, in any study of library development in the West, it is necessary to remember that for a thousand years much of the best in our literary heritage was preserved in the East--in the libraries of Byzantium and Islam.

## Additional Readings

The best source materials on Byzantine and Moslem libraries are found in publications in Greek, Russian and the Middle Eastern languages. Ma-

terial in English is scarce, but more is available
in Italian, French and German library and historical journals. The following readings will provide an introduction to the subject.

Bashiruddin, S. "The Fate of Sectarian Libraries in Medieval Islam," Libri 17 (1967):  149-62.

Buksh, S. "The Islamic Libraries," Nineteenth Century 52
(1902):  125-39.

Husset, J. M. The Church and Learning in the Byzantine
Empire, 867-1165. London, 1937.

Irwin, R. "The Byzantine Age," in The English Library.
London, 1968, pp. 42-63.

Khoury, J. "Livros, Bibliotecas e Bibliofilos Entres os
Arabes," Bolletin Biblio (Rio de Janeiro) 18 (1952):
57-74.

Lewin, B. Den Orientaliska Boken:  Skrift Och Bokvasen in
Islams Varld. Stockholm, 1951.

Mackensen, R. S. "Arabic Books and Libraries in the Umai-
yad Period," American Journal of Semitic Languages
and Literatures 52 (1935-6): 245-53; 53 (1935-6): 239-
50; 54 (1937): 41-61.

_____. "Background on the History of Moslem Libraries,"
Ibid. 51 (1934-35): 114-25; 52 (1935-36): 22-33, 104-10.

_____. "Four Great Libraries of Medieval Baghdad,"
Library Quarterly 2(1932): 279-99.

Nicholson, R. A. A Literary History of the Arabs. Cambridge, 1930.

Padover, S. K. "Byzantine Libraries," in The Medieval Library, ed. by James Westfall Thompson. Chicago,
1939, pp. 310-29.

Pinto, O. "Libraries of the Arabs during the Time of the
Abbasids," Pakistan Library Review 2 (1959):  44-72.

Sutton, K. M. "The Byzantine Background to the Italian
Renaissance," American Philosophical Society Proceedings 100 (1956): 1-76.

Vasiliev, A. A.  History of the Byzantine Empire.  1928.
    Madison, Wisconsin, 1961.

Vleeschauwer, H. J.  "History of the Western Library:  the
    Byzantine Library to Justinian,"  Mousaion 74 (1964):
    187-220.

Von Grunebaum, G. E.  Medieval Islam:  a Study in Cultur-
    al Orientation.  Chicago, 1953.

Wilson, N. G.  "The Libraries of the Byzantine World,"
    Greek, Roman and Byzantine Studies 8 (1967): 53-80.

## Chapter 7

## MONASTIC AND CATHEDRAL LIBRARIES

The ravages of conquest and the advent of a barbaric age placed all learning in real jeopardy. With increasing rapidity those concerned with the life of the mind were fleeing the strife-torn cities, and books and learning quickly passed into the church. For nearly a thousand years the typical European library was to be the small collection of manuscripts, laboriously copied and jealously guarded, in the many monasteries scattered from Greece to Iceland. Instead of the magnificent temple library, with its thousands of rolls in vaulted marble rooms, the library of the Middle Ages was more often a collection of a few hundred codices kept in a bookchest or two in the corner of a monastery chapel. This decline in books and libraries was typical of the general cultural decline that took place in most of western Europe after the fall of Rome. The remarkable thing is not that so much of classical learning was lost, but that so much was preserved in the most trying of circumstances.

Fortunately for western civilization, the links with the past were never totally lost. Even before the end of the old order there was the beginning of the new, or at least of the institution that was to preserve a part of ancient culture throughout the dark ages. That institution was the medieval monastery. Monasteries were already being established in Egypt, in Palestine, and possibly in neighboring areas by the third century A.D., and the idea of the monastery library already existed in those areas. Like the early Christian churches, the monasteries treasured their small collections of scriptures, epistles and commentaries and gave them an honored place in their chapels.

The exact origins of monasticism are obscure. The

earliest known Christian monasteries seem to have been in
Egypt, although the idea did not originate there.  Isolated
religious communities had been known before Christ, and the
recent discoveries in the Qumran caves of Palestine indicate
such a development more or less contemporary with Christ.
The early monasteries have some relation to the hermit, the
dedicated Christian who fled the populated areas in order to
live alone to meditate on his sins and to avoid committing
more.  Perhaps some of these attracted followers and established religious communities, or perhaps the monasteries
began as dedicated religious groups, but at any rate separate
settlements for men and women were established at an early
date and the rise of Christianity is closely associated with
the rise of monasticism.

One early Egyptian monastery of which we have some
record was founded by St. Pachomius (292-345 A.D.) at Ta-
bennisi in upper Egypt.  St. Pachomius had only a small
collection of religious works which he guarded zealously.
Among the rules he formulated for his monastic group were
several relating to the use of books, but in general they
were restrictive.  The books were to be kept in a cupboard
built into the monastery chapel wall and all were to be
locked up each night.  During the daytime, each monk was
allowed to use one book at a time, but it had to be used in
the chapel area only and could not be taken to any other
part of the monastery.  From Pelusium, another Egyptian
monastery, we have the letters of the monk Isidore (ca. 390-
450).  These letters indicate that the monks there were ac-
quainted with Greek and Latin literature as well as with the
religious texts.

Monasticism spread to western Europe by the end of
the fourth century with early monastic groups around Rome,
and an important monastery at Lerins, on the Mediterranean
coast of France, was established by St. Honoratus about
410.  As the civilized world began to crumble under the
raids of the northern barbarians, small groups of devoted
Christians withdrew to remote island or mountain areas to
worship in relative security.  Of all these, one of the most
significant was founded by Magnus Aurelius Cassiodorus
about 540.  Cassiodorus had been secretary to Theodoric,
the Ostrogothic ruler of Rome from 489 to 526, and had
hoped to found a university in Rome similar to the Museum
in Alexandria.  He failed at this because of the uncertain
conditions of the time, but when he at last retired from public office he used the wealth he had acquired to begin a

monastery at Vivarium in southern Italy.  His own private
library became the nucleus of the monastery book collection,
and he spent the remainder of his long life in study and de-
votion.

Cassiodorus had a strong respect for learning and a
reverence for books in general, so his library included many
works of classical Latin authors, with a few Greek ones, as
well as religious texts.  Not content with merely collecting
and copying other writers, he also did some effective writing
of his own.  His most important writing, from the standpoint
of library history, was the Institutiones Divinarum et Saecu-
larium Litterarum, a lengthy guidebook for everyday living
in a monastery.  Along with detailed instruction for a religious routine, the author told how manuscripts should be
handled, corrected, copied and repaired, and included what
amounted to an annotated bibliography of the best literature
of the time.  Cassiodorus is also credited with having introduced the idea of intellectual as well as manual labor into
the duties of the monks, and hence is largely responsible for
the origin of both scriptorium and monastic libraries.  Under
his direction, a few Greek works were obtained and translated into Latin, and thus he helped enlarge the small amount
of Greek literature available in western Europe for the next
five hundred years.  Cassiodorus was a link between the classical and medieval worlds; as a child he had a classical education; as a man he saw the remnants of the old world fade
away; and as an elderly scholar he aided in the foundation of
the monastic system that was to keep learning alive through
the Middle Ages.  Historians once believed that Cassiodorus'
great library found its way to the monastery at Bobbio after
its owner's death.  However, recent research indicates that
the books were sent to Rome and dispersed by booksellers
there.

Contemporary with Cassiodorus, but much more influential in the long run, was the work being done at the monastery of Monte Casino by St. Benedict and his followers.
St. Benedict (ca. 480-543), finding life in Rome too worldly
for his tastes, withdrew to the mountains south of the city to
live as a hermit.  His religious sincerity attracted followers,
and in 529 a monastery was founded that was to be the parent house for the Benedictine Order, the oldest and one of
the most significant of the several monastic orders.  From
Monte Cassino, monks went out to establish other monasteries in western Europe, and with them went the Rules of
St. Benedict for the conduct of life in the monastery.  Under

these _Rules_, which were to serve as the essential guide to monastic life for centuries to come, the reading and copying of books was made a regular part of the monastic routine. St. Benedict evidently viewed the copying and reading of books as a spiritual rather than an intellectual task; as a mental treadmill designed to keep the minds of his monks free of worldly thoughts. But his more liberal followers, perhaps influenced by the _Institutiones_ of Cassiodorus, took a more positive attitude toward books and reading. As the Benedictine order spread, each new monastery constructed contained its library and scriptorium, thereby assuring the preservation of many classical works.

The monastic idea spread gradually throughout Europe, but many of those in northern Europe and even in northern Italy were established not by monks from Vivarium or Monte Cassino, but by missionaries from Ireland as a result of Roman occupation of the British islands. The Romans had conquered the southern part of England by 50 A.D., and that area remained under Roman domination for some four hundred years. Roman towns and villas similar to those in the provinces of southern France and Spain grew up, and a cultured society existed side by side with the less civilized Britons. England was never completely converted to Christianity under the Romans, but the natives of Ireland were Christianized under the teaching of St. Patrick and others in the fifth century. By the sixth century, Ireland could boast of many monasteries, and from them missionaries went out to England, Scotland, France and other parts of Europe. St. Columba (Columcille, 521-597) left Ireland to found a monastery on the island of Iona off the coast of Scotland, and from this point Christianity spread to Scotland and northern England. St. Columban (Columbanus, 543-615) established monasteries at Luxeuil in Burgundy, at St. Gall in Switzerland, at Wurzburg and Salzburg in Germany, and at Tarantum and Bobbio in Italy. In each of these monasteries, as in the monasteries in Ireland and Britain, books and learning were emphasized, beautiful manuscripts were produced, and secular works as well as religious were included in the libraries.

The monastery and its library first came to England through the efforts of St. Augustine of Canterbury, who was sent there as a missionary by Pope Gregory about 597. Augustine brought with him a small collection of Christian texts, and other books were later obtained from Italy, along with the _Rules of St. Benedict_, to form a small library at Canter-

bury.  Benedict Biscop, in the seventh century, founded the
twin monasteries of Wearmouth and Jarrow in northern England, and built up excellent libraries there.  He made at
least five trips to Rome, each time obtaining books for his
monasteries from sources in Italy and southern France.  The
Venerable Bede (673-735) was a student of Benedict Biscop,
and made good use of the libraries in writing his Ecclesiastical History of England.  Coelfried, successor to Biscop,
continued to build up the libraries of the twin monasteries,
and one of his students, Egbert, founded a library at the cathedral school at York.

In France, a monastery of great importance was that
at Corbie, established by monks from Luxeuil about 660.  A
celebrated school was established at this monastery, and its
library and scriptorium were among the best in western Europe.  In Germany, St. Boniface, an English monk, was establishing monasteries in the eighth century, including those
at Fulda, Heidenheim and Fritzlar.  Libraries at each of
these monasteries are known to have existed in the eighth
century, and a catalog compiled at Fulda between 744 and
749 still survives.  The works of the Irish monks stand out
in the seventh and eighth centuries, otherwise a bleak era for
books and libraries.  It was a period of decline in Italy and
southern France as the centuries of invasion by the European
barbarians was followed by an era of conquests by the Moslems.

One bright cultural spot in the seventh century was
Christian Spain.  Despite the fact that much of the population
was illiterate, there were cultural centers in the larger
cities, and several religious groups that served as schools
or training corps for priests.  One of the foremost Spanish
scholars of this era was Isidore, Bishop of Seville from 600
to 636, who not only collected a library of the best-known
literature of his day, but also culled from it to form an early
version of an encyclopedia.  Just how many books he owned
is uncertain, but they must have numbered several hundred,
since he kept them in fourteen bookcases, or armaria.  Each
case was dedicated to a particular author.  Seven cases were
inscribed with the names of religious writers, such as the
Sts. Augustine, Ambrose, and Jerome, while others were
dedicated to literary figures, historians, and writers of sacred and secular law.  Over each case there was a poem to
the author, and for the whole collection, Isidore wrote a descriptive poem that included the following passage:

> Here sacred books with worldly books combine;
> If poets please you, read them; they are thine.
> My meads are full of thorns, but flowers are there;
> If thorns displease, let roses be your share.
> Here both the laws in tomes revered behold;
> Here what is new is stored, and what is old...
>
> A reader and a talker can't agree;
> Hence, idle chatterer; 'tis no place for thee!

In his encyclopedia, the Etymologiae, Isidore also provided an early instance of library history by recording all that he could discover on the libraries of the classical era.

The late eighth and early ninth centuries saw the development in western Europe of what is known as the Carolingian Renaissance, under the rule of the Emperor Charlemagne (786-814). Charlemagne himself was seriously interested in learning, knew Latin and even a little Greek, but it was the scholars who flocked to the relative security of his realm, who gave the era its literary significance. He invited learned men from all of Europe to come to his court, and among them was the English scholar Alcuin (735-804). Alcuin had been educated at the cathedral school at York and came to France in 782 to supervise the palace school at Aachen. He sent back to England for books to be copied and with the encouragement of the Emperor he and his followers established schools and monasteries throughout western Europe.

A most significant outgrowth of this new intellectual activity was the increased demand for books, which stimulated production on a large scale and insured the preservation of much of the Latin literary heritage. Later, as Bishop of Tours, Alcuin set up an outstanding library and scriptorium there. For a half century or so literature and learning flourished, and significant libraries were built up at Corbie and Lyons in France, St. Gall in Switzerland, and Fulda in Germany, among others. Probably the largest of them all was the palace library at Aachen, where Charlemagne filled his shelves with richly bound volumes, and even exchanged books with the Eastern Roman Emperor at Constantinople.

The Carolingian revival was dependent upon the security and wealth of Charlemagne's empire for its nurture, but in the ninth and tenth centuries the empire was challenged and eventually devastated by constant attacks by Norsemen,

Huns, and Saracens, and once again learning in most of
northern and western Europe broke down.   The Danish and
Viking invasions, which had begun in the late eighth century
and continued for some two hundred years, destroyed many
monasteries and libraries.   The coastal areas of England
and France were particularly affected, but many secluded
monasteries were also damaged by isolated raids or local
wars.   The Abbey at Tours, for example, was ravaged six
times in a little over fifty years.   In 867, the Danes overran much of northern England, and York was ransacked.   Its
books were scattered and its priests and scholars killed or
driven away.   A library established near Hamburg in the
early ninth century was destroyed by Vikings, even though it
had been established primarily for the purpose of carrying
Christianity to them.   Moslems continued to be a threat to
the Mediterranean coasts of France and northern Italy, and
the same general area was visited by the Huns around 900,
with more destruction of churches and monasteries.   The
early Irish culture that gave rise to the missionaries Columba and Columban was ended in two centuries of Viking
raids and conquests from about 850 to 1050.   All over western Europe the story was much the same, but where monasteries were not destroyed they often suffered from stagna-
tion and neglect.   Only an occasional well-managed or well-
located institution managed to thrive throughout the troubles.
One of these was Cluny, founded in France about 910, which
not only thrived but led a temporary revival in monastic cultural activities.

     The various orders of monks had different ideas con-
cerning books, libraries and literary labors.   The Benedictines, liberally interpreting the rules of their founder, were
foremost in the development of monastic libraries and in the
copying and distribution of manuscripts.   The Benedictine
rules concerning libraries were enlarged and clarified, particularly for their monasteries in England, by the Constitu-
tiones of Bishop Lanfranc, issued in the eleventh century.
Among the other orders, the Carthusians and Cistercians also adopted library and reading rules, although they were not
as interested in secular works as were the Benedictines.
The Augustinians generally collected only a few books but
prized them highly, while the Franciscans at first would own
no books at all.   Later, in the thirteenth century, the Franciscans began to collect books for their libraries, and the
parent house at Assisi developed a comparatively large library within a few years.   For all orders, the monastery
was generally accepted as a center of learning, and the say-

ing was common that "a monastery without a library is like
a castle without walls." Convents for nuns were equally active in collecting and preserving both religious and secular
literature, and several nuns became well known in literary
fields. St. Paula, who headed a convent in Palestine in the
fourth century, was a scholar in Hebrew and Greek as well
as Latin. The nun Melania, who founded a convent near
Carthage about 420, had earlier gained a living by transcrib-
ing manuscripts, and the library of her convent was noted
for the beauty of its books. Gertrude, Abbess of Nivelle in
seventh-century Belgium, was active in building up the library there, while St. Hroswitha in tenth-century Germany
not only collected a library at her convent, but also wrote
religious poetry and drama.

Throughout the early Middle Ages, Rome remained a
source of supply for books needed by the growing monastic
collections of France, Germany and England. The early
Popes attempted to maintain libraries at their headquarters,
and churches and monasteries in and around Rome continued
to have significant book collections. According to legend,
either St. Peter founded the papal library or St. Clement did
so in 93 A.D. Since most of the early Christian congregations maintained collections of scriptures, and since these
collections were often augmented by religious commentaries,
lives of the martyrs, church records, and accounts of missionary activities, it is probable that a central collection of
Christian literature existed in Rome even before the Church
was recognized. However, the first known library for the
Church at Rome was that of Pope Damasus in the late fourth
century. Damasus is reported to have built a structure to
house the library near the theater of Pompey in the Campus
Martius and to have modeled it after the Temple of Apollo.
An inscribed stone has been found that reads:

> I have erected this structure for the archives of
> the Roman Church; I have surrounded it with porti-
> cos on either side; and I have given it my name
> which I hope will be remembered for centuries.

Pope Hilary (461-468) is credited with establishing two
small libraries for the use of laymen and pilgrims, placing
in them approved copies of the scriptures and other religious
works. Pope Agapetus, about 535, hoped to establish a
school of theology and literature at Rome with the help of
Cassiodorus. Agapetus endowed the school with a library for
the use of scholars, but in that troubled era it is doubtful

that either school or library ever materialized.  Pope Gregory I (590-604), himself a prolific writer and collector of
manuscripts, was active in building up the papal library and
in making it useful to those who needed it.  He maintained
contact with religious officials and groups from Constantinople to Spain and both loaned and borrowed works to be
copied for church collections.  In the seventh century there
was a papal library in the Lateran Palace where the Pope
resided, and when the Church Council of 640 met there, the
library was so well organized that the librarian was con-
gratulated by the Council for being able to find any book at
any time it was needed by a member of the Council.  It was
also noted that this librarian could translate Greek into Latin at sight, apparently an unusual scholarly ability at this
time.  As late as 855, Rome was still a source of manuscripts, but in the following centuries its churches and libraries suffered considerably in wars and political troubles.
In the tenth century, there was still a papal library, but it
was housed for safety in a specially built tower, the Turris
Cartelaria, where it was little used.  This collection is last
mentioned by Pope Honorious III, who died in 1227, and its
contents were apparently scattered or decayed from neglect.
From 1309 to 1377, the headquarters of the Pope was at
Avignon in France, and here there was a library for the
clergy, and also one for a clerical university established by
Pope Boniface VIII in 1303.  The modern history of the papal library, however, begins with the establishment of a collection in the Vatican by Pope Nicholas V in the fifteenth
century.

The tenth and eleventh centuries marked another low
period in the development of libraries and literature in western Europe except for a few bright spots, such as Cluny in
France and St. Gall in Switzerland.  There was a decline of
interest in the classics and many monks were even illiterate
and allowed the books in the libraries to go untended.  The
works that were copied were largely theological, and probably there were fewer volumes in all European libraries in
1100 than there had been in 900.  Southern Italy was an exception because of its contacts with Byzantine sources which
provided it with Greek manuscripts and kept alive its interest in the classics and even in medicine and law.  Especially significant was a rebirth of interest in intellectual affairs
at Monte Cassino, the first of the Benedictine monasteries,
where many important Latin classics, notably the works of
Tacitus, Seneca, and Varro were copied and probably saved
from extinction.  While conditions improved somewhat in the

monasteries generally, by the twelfth century intellectual
life, and the accompanying books and libraries, were beginning to move back toward the city, first to the cathedrals
and soon thereafter to the university centers.

The cathedrals, which were the headquarters churches
for bishops or archbishops, were far more than merely
large churches; they were also religious schools where training for the priesthood took place and often secular training
at a lower level as well. In some cases, the cathedrals
were in the direct charge of some monastic order, as in
England where seven were run by the Benedictines. Others
were directly under the Pope, in charge of appointed bishops. Almost all their income came from church-owned lands
or from gifts of wealthy patrons. They were usually located
near the growing towns and cities and hence were more available to the average student than the more isolated monasteries. Although they had existed since the days of Alcuin,
if not earlier, they became more prominent in both religion
and education after the tenth century.

The cathedrals and their schools had book collections
from the first, but they often differed from the monastic libraries in several ways. Designed for educational rather
than inspirational reading, the cathedral libraries generally
contained more secular books than the monastic collections.
They usually had more consistent means of support, and
hence grew steadily and maintained current writings more often than the monastery libraries. The book collections came
in time to be larger, more complete, and better organized.
Some of the better-known cathedral libraries were those at
York, Durham, and Canterbury in England; at Notre Dame,
Orleans and Rouen in France; at Bamberg and Hildesheim in
Germany; and at Barcelona and Toledo in Spain. There were
sometimes three book collections in a cathedral organization:
the main collection, largely theological; the service books;
and the school library, containing most of the secular literature. As of the eleventh century, all together would contain
only a few hundred volumes. Durham's cathedral library had
only about six hundred volumes in 1200, but included among
them were a few medical works. The cathedral at Rouen in
1150 had even fewer volumes, but one-third of them were
classical. Canterbury, one of the largest cathedral libraries, possessed about five thousand books in 1300, but
this was exceptional. The thirteenth century saw a rapid increase in the number of books available, and in the size of
all major libraries. The cathedral libraries were never as

numerous as those of the monasteries, and in general they
were not as important in the cultural history of western Europe, but they served as a bridge, both chronologically and
culturally, between the monasteries and the universities, and
also brought together the cultural resources that their material wealth could afford.

The monastery or cathedral library up to the thirteenth century was usually only a small collection of a few
hundred volumes or less.  It was kept in a book chest or a
small closet in the monastery cloister rather than in a specific library room or building.  Later it was connected with,
or close by, the scriptorium where the monks copied texts
as a part of their regular duties.  At St. Gall in Switzerland,
in the ninth century, the books were kept in an attic room
directly over the scriptorium.  A common word for library
in the early Middle Ages was armarium, which was literally
the book chest where the books were kept.  The librarian, or
person who supervised the books, was known as the armar-
ius.  Other terms for librarian were bibliothecarius and cus-
tos librorum, or keeper of the books.  At Fulda, in Germany, the librarian was facetiously called "clavipotens frater,"
or "brother with the power of the keys" to the books.  Early
monasteries strove to have a library containing at least one
book per monk, but once this ratio was achieved their collections usually grew slowly.  St. Gall had four hundred volumes in 841; Cluny had only 570 in the twelfth century; Bobbio had 650 about the same time, and as late as the thirteenth century, the monastery at St. Pons de Tomières in
France had only three hundred.  With respect to size of libraries, it should be pointed out that the average volume was
large and often contained two or more different works.  Many
of them were florilegia, or selections from many authors,
giving a wide sampling of literature in a relatively small
space.  Acquisitions for the medieval library came by copying in the scriptorium, by gifts, and by occasional purchases.
Gifts came from entering monks, who often brought with
them any books they might own, and from visiting dignitaries,
wealthy patrons, and neighboring scholars.  Many volumes
came as bequests on the death of their owners.  Since the
leather-bound parchment codices were very durable, more
books were lost through wars, fires and neglect than through
excessive use.

The average monastery or cathedral library contained
mainly religious volumes.  The core of the collection was
the Bible, often in large script and in many volumes.  Next

in importance came the works of the early church fathers
with later commentaries on them, the lives of the martyrs
and saints, and the service books of the church.  Finally,
there were Latin textbooks and grammars, a few of the Latin classics, and perhaps a few works of local literature and
history.  Greek authors were unknown in most of western
Europe, except a few in Latin translation, but they were still
known in southern Italy.  At the monastery of St. Nicholas,
near Otranto, both Greek and Latin were taught from the
eleventh to the fourteenth century, and monastic collections
in nearby Sicily also contained Greek works.  By the twelfth
century the average monastic library would have been enlarged both in numbers and in range.  All of the earlier
works would still be present, and there would also be more
and better editions of the Latin classics, some civil and canon law, works of the medieval writers from Boethius onward, and even some science, poetry, and drama of the later
writers.  Local authors would be more prominent in each
collection, and works in the local language would be added
to the majority in Latin.  In format, the books of the twelfth
century were almost entirely parchment codices.  Papyrus
had gone out of use and paper had not yet reached most of
Europe.

Interlibrary lending was not unknown in the Middle
Ages.  Books were loaned to be copied and also just for
reading, usually between neighboring collections, but sometimes between libraries as far apart as France and Greece
or England and Austria.  One English library, of the Priory
of Henton, loaned twenty volumes in 1343 alone.  In ninth-
century Germany, when texts were very scarce, the three
monasteries of Fulda, Wurzburg and Holzkirchen inter-
changed their texts regularly for copying.  Books were also
rented and pawned.  Ordinarily the books were to be loaned
only to the residents of the monastic community, and then
only one at a time.  In some monasteries, the books could
be used only in the daytime and in the vicinity of the book-
presses.  In others, they were loaned for the year and could
be taken to the reader's living quarters or study carrel.  Occasionally books were loaned to outsiders, such as neighboring church leaders or rulers, but then some collateral was
usually required, either a book or books of equal value, or
a deposit of money.

When the size of the medieval library warranted it,
the books were roughly classified by subject, and sometimes
by size or acquisition.  At first the division might be be-

tween theological works and secular ones; between Latin
works and those in other languages; or between textbooks
and more serious tomes.   The religious works might be subdivided into Scriptures, commentaries, biographies and service books.   The secular works, particularly in the cathedral
libraries, might be divided according to the teaching subjects of the trivium and the quadrivium (grammar, rhetoric
and dialectic; arithmetic, geometry, music and astronomy).
In some libraries, these divisions were designated by letters
and these letters were prominently inscribed on the book-
chests.   Such a broad classification system apparently sufficed as long as the collections were small, but later in the
Middle Ages more complicated schemes were planned, if not
actually used.   Catalogs of the collections, probably more
for inventory purposes than for reader use, were kept from
the earliest days.   These catalogs were in reality merely
lists of books, some arranged by author, some by title, and
others by a catchword from the title or first line, or combinations of all three.   Almost none were in alphabetical order.   Such lists have survived from the eighth century onward, and are fairly numerous for the later Middle Ages.
Some of these were originally kept on strips of parchment
tacked to the side of the book chest, while others were kept
in codex form.   Those of the later centuries were longer,
more carefully prepared, and had some logic to the arrangement.   In the early fifteenth century, John Boston of Bury,
an Augustinian monk, compiled a sort of union catalog of
books in all the monasteries of England.   He visited hundreds of monasteries, listed the major works in them and
then combined them into an alphabetical catalog with locations by numbers.

The librarian, or custodian of the library, was usually one of the monks assigned by the abbot or bishop.
Sometimes the position rotated; sometimes an older or in-
capacitated monk would be given the task.   However, since
the duties were simple, owing to the small size and infre-
quent use of the collection, the position of librarian was usually combined with some other duty.   In English libraries,
the position of keeper of the books was often combined with
that of the cantor or sub-cantor (precentor or succentor)
who were also responsible for the direction of the choir and
the teaching of singing.   Rules for one of these libraries
read:

> Let not a book be given to anyone without a proper
> and sufficient voucher, and let this be entered on
> the roll.

The same rules reminded the librarian that he should know
his wares:

> Thou must have full knowledge of what is given to
> thy charge. The first duty of a librarian is to
> strive, in his time, as far as possible, to increase
> the library committed to him. Let him beware
> that the library does not diminish, that the books
> in his charge do not in any way get lost or perish.
> Let him repair by binding books that are damaged
> by age. Let him know the names of the authors.

In some cases librarians were held personally responsible
for the safety of the books in their charge and had to replace
any that were lost or damaged. Most of the medieval librarians are unknown but a few became famous. Alcuin, for
example, was librarian at York for a few years after 780.
He described the contents of his library in a long poem which
began:

> There shalt thou find the volumes that contain
> All the ancient fathers who remain;
> There all the Latin writers make their home
> With those of glorious Greece transferred to Rome...

Toward the end of the Middle Ages, in the fourteenth
and fifteenth centuries, there were many physical changes in
the monastic and cathedral libraries. The number of books
increased, in most cases from a few hundred to a few thousand. The armaria, or book chests, had given way to book
closets and then to small library rooms. By the fifteenth
century, some religious institutions were constructing separate library buildings. The library of Christ Church, Canterbury, constructed in the early fifteenth century, was a long
room sixty by twenty-two feet, built over a chapel. At Rou-
en, France, a cathedral library building completed in 1424
was constructed of masonry, twenty-five by one hundred-five
feet. At York, the cathedral library finished in 1421 had
two floors, books upstairs and a study downstairs. As the
number of books increased, they were taken out of the book
chest and put onto combination desk-shelves, arranged in the
long, narrow rooms so as to catch the most of natural light.
Candles or lamps were usually forbidden in the library rooms
for fear of fire. Sometimes the collections were divided into two parts, one for general public use, the other for more
restricted use. The custom of chaining books to the desks
began not with the most valuable ones, but with the ones

most used.   Later, after the coming of the printed book,
many manuscript volumes were chained simply for safekeeping.   Various devices were employed to make the books
more readily available, such as the book-wheel and the circular desk.   The book-wheel was something like a water-
wheel with a number of books arranged on it so that a reader standing in one position could consult as many as a dozen
different volumes in succession without moving from his original position.   The circular, hexagonal, or octagonal desk
was a similar arrangement on a horizontal plane.   Here the
reader usually had to walk around the desk to consult the
several books arranged on its top, but in a few instances
these desk tops were also attached to axles so that the books
could be rotated into a position in front of the reader.

Monasticism flourished and declined at various times
and places in western Europe, but generally speaking its libraries represented the heart of western learning for over a
thousand years.   Then, as the cathedral libraries grew and
as the universities developed and emerged as full-blown educational centers, the monasteries declined and their cultural
significance faded.   Their importance lasted for varying
times in different countries, but for the most part they had
declined or disappeared by the seventeenth century.   Where
they remained, their libraries were of little significance outside the monastery walls.

In England, for example, the monasteries were closed
under Henry VIII in the sixteenth century, and their libraries were destroyed or scattered.   It is estimated that
the eight hundred or more monasteries must have contained
at least 300,000 volumes at the time of the confiscation of
monastery properties.   Of these, less than two per cent are
known to have survived.   Even private libraries were destroyed by Protestant reformers seeking to wipe out all evidence of the Roman Catholic Church.   Some of the finer
manuscripts that were taken from the monastery libraries
ended up in booksellers' hands, but many of the ordinary ones
were used for candle lighters, pot cleaners, and even for
scrubbing boots.   Agents of the king secured a few of the
finer works for his own private library, but the great majority were lost forever.

In Germany, the peasant uprisings in 1524-25 resulted
in great losses to monastic libraries, and French libraries
suffered in the religious wars in that country between Catho-
lics and Huguenots a century later.   In the eighteenth century

it was the libraries of Austria and Scandinavia that suffered, to be followed by others all over Europe in the French Revolution and Napoleonic wars.  Besides these disasters, many individual monasteries were lost in fires and floods.  Others were neglected or even abandoned as the fortunes of various orders and individual monasteries declined.  Poggio Bracciolini, the Italian manuscript hunter of the early fifteenth century,  found priceless manuscripts moldering in an attic at St. Gall.  In other cases, as the monasteries declined or ceased to exist, their libraries were transferred to other collections, church, municipal or university, and it is usually these that have survived.  The library of the Abbey of Cluny, justly famous in the tenth and eleventh centuries, had dwindled to just a few manuscripts by the eighteenth century, and these were housed in the local town hall.  Fortunately, they were eventually turned over to the Bibliothèque Nationale in Paris.

Fortunately, the end of the monasteries and the destruction of their libraries came after the invention of printing, so that most of the significant texts were in print, and few if any unique sources were lost.  But even if other forces had not led to the decline of the significance of monastic libraries, the coming of printing would have.  The ready availability of books by the hundreds and thousands meant that many types of libraries and educational institutions would become available.  Nevertheless, the role of monastery libraries in the preservation of Western culture cannot be denied.  When all other civilizing forces were destroyed or in decline, they kept the love of learning alive, and their little libraries often sheltered the only copies of the works of such great classical writers as Cicero, Varro and Tacitus.  The golden chain of learning wore remarkably thin, but it did not break.

## Additional Readings

Material on Medieval libraries is quite plentiful, especially in German, French and Latin.  The items listed below are mainly in English, and represent the best and generally most recent treatments of the subject in that language.

Beazley, M.   "The History of the Chapter Library of Canterbury Cathedral," Trans. of the Bibliographical Society 8 (1904): 113-85.

Beddie, J. S.  Libraries in the Twelfth Century:  Their Cata-
    logs and Contents.  Boston, 1929.

Bischoff, B.  Die Suddeutschen Schreibschulen and Bibliothe-
    ken in der Karolingerzeit, ed. 2.  Leipzig, 1960.

Cassiodorus Senator, Magnus Aurelius.  An Introduction to
    Divine and Human Reading.  ed. by L. W. Jones.  New
    York, 1946.

Chambers, R. W.  "The Lost Literature of Medieval Eng-
    land," The Library 5 (1925): 293-321.

Clark, J. W.  Libraries in the Medieval and Renaissance
    Periods.  Cambridge, 1894.

Connolly, B.  "Jesuit Library Beginnings," Library Quarterly
    30 (1960), 243-62.

Edmunds, S.  "The Medieval Library of Savoy," Scriptorium
    24 (1970): 318-27; 26 (1972): 269-93.

Hobson, A.  Great Libraries.  New York, 1970.

Hughes, H. D.  A History of the Durham Cathedral Library.
    Durham, 1925.

Humphreys, K. W.  The Book Provisions of the Medieval
    Friars, 1215-1400.  Amsterdam, 1964.

_____.  The Library of the Carmelites at Florence at the
    End of the Fourteenth Century.  Amsterdam, 1964.

Irwin, R.  "Cassiodorus Senator," in his The Heritage of the
    English Library.  New York, 1964, pp. 119-131.

Jackson, S.  "Cassiodorus' Institutes and Christian Book Se-
    lection," Journal of Library History 1 (1966): 89-100.

James, M. R.  "The Library of Bury St. Edmunds Abbey in
    the 11th & 12th Centuries," Speculum 47 (1972): 617-45.

Ker, N. R.,  "Cathedral Libraries," Library History 1 (1967):
    38-45.

_____, ed.  Medieval Libraries of Great Britain:  A List
    of Surviving Books.  ed. 2.  London, 1964.

Kibre, P. "Intellectual Interests Reflected in Libraries of the Fourteenth and Fifteenth Centuries," Journal of the History of Ideas 7 (1946): 257-97.

Knowles, D. The Evolution of Medieval Thought. New York, 1962.

Laistner, M. L. W. Thought and Letters in Western Europe; A.D. 500 to 900. London, 1931; Ithaca, N.Y., 1957.

Morgan, F. C. Hereford Cathedral Library. Hereford, 1958.

Ogilvy, J. A. A. Books Known to Anglo-Latin Writers from Aldhelm to Alcuin (670-804). Cambridge, Mass., 1936.

O'Gorman, J. F. The Architecture of the Monastic Library in Italy, 1300-1600. New York, 1972.

Phillips, D. R. The Romantic History of the Monastic Libraries of Wales from the Fifth to the Sixteenth Centuries... Swansea, 1912.

Putnam, G. H. Books and Their Makers during the Middle Ages. New York, 1896. 2 v.

Reynolds, L. D. and Wilson, N. G. Scribes and Scholars; A Guide to the Transmission of Greek & Latin Literature. Oxford, 1968.

Savage, E. A. Old English Libraries: The Making, Collection and Use of Books during the Middle Ages. London, 1911.

Streeter, B. H. Chained Libraries; A Survey of Four Centuries in the Evolution of the English Library. London, 1931.

Streeter, E. C. "Medieval Libraries of Medicine; 500 A.D. to 1500 A.D.," Bulletin of the Medical Library Assoc. 10 (1921): 15-20.

Thompson, J. W., ed. The Medieval Library. Chicago, 1939.

Wilson, R. M. "The Medieval Library of Titchfield Abbey," Proceedings of the Leeds Phil. and Literary Society 5 (1940): 150-77, 252-76.

Wormald, F. and Wright, C. E., eds.  The English Library
    Before 1700: Studies in Its History.  London, 1958.

## Chapter 8

THE RISE OF THE UNIVERSITY, THE RENAISSANCE,
THE INVENTION OF PRINTING, AND
THE GROWTH OF LIBRARIES IN EUROPE TO 1500

## The Rise of University Libraries

In the long drama of western civilization, the role of
the monastic libraries, and even of the libraries of Constantinople and Islam, was that of preserving the cultural remains of the classical era.  The monastery libraries were
largely concerned with theology and saved secular works only incidentally, but they did collect and preserve in addition
many of the works of the medieval writers.  The Byzantine
libraries were used as sources by commentators, encyclope-
dists, codifiers, and compilers of epitomes and summaries,
but not very much as sources for original works.  The Moslem libraries were somewhat better employed, and particularly in the sciences their users improved upon the Greeks
and turned over to western Europe works far advanced in
mathematics, medicine, and astronomy.  But for libraries
to be a great cultural influence, they must be used; their
doors must be open to large numbers of scholars and students, so that the information contained in their volumes can
be disseminated to the largest possible proportion of the
population.  Although the cathedrals with their attendant
schools put their libraries to work to a certain extent, it
remained for the medieval university to develop libraries
that would not only preserve the heritage of the past, but
would also open it up to general use.

Although there were a few schools that could be called
institutions of higher learning in the early Middle Ages, it
was not until the late twelfth century that the university as
such emerged.  However, long before there was anything

like an organized institution, there were groups of students
who gathered around a teacher to learn what he had to teach.
Many students wandered from town to town and from country
to country in search of the best teachers.  In some towns
where there were several good teachers, the students would
be forced to organize themselves into groups to protect themselves and to obtain better terms from the townspeople and
teachers.  In turn, the teachers organized for their own purposes, and these student and teacher "guilds" formed the nucleus of the early university.  The word university came
from the Latin universitas, which at first meant any organized guild or corporation, while the term used for the combination of students and teachers at first was studium generale.
For many years there was no prescribed curriculum nor any
specific courses or degrees.  Gradually, however, rules and
regulations were adopted, charters were obtained from king
or Pope, and formal universities were recognized.

Although institutions for higher learning were known
in ancient times, and in medieval Constantinople, it is probable that the immediate inspiration for the early universities
in western Europe came from those in Moslem Spain.  Christian students had attended these institutions long before there
were any established in the rest of Europe.  These students
brought back books that included Latin translations of Arabic
versions of the Greek classics, the philosophy of Aristotle,
and the medicine of Galen and Hippocrates, as well as the
works of the Moslem scientists themselves.  By the early
twelfth century, there were schools of medicine at Salerno
and Bologna in Italy, where the teaching was almost entirely
from Latin translations of Arabic texts.  But there is also a
link between the cathedral schools and the early universities.
At Paris, there had developed before 1200 three strong theological schools at Notre Dame, Saint-Victor, and Ste. Geneviève, and each of these was more or less directly an outgrowth of a cathedral school.  Some historians have traced
a direct connection in the development of higher education
from the schools of Charlemagne's era to the university at
Paris, but many of the links are tenuous, and the specific
origin of that university, like that of several others, is uncertain.

At Salerno, no university as such developed from the
earlier medical school, but at Bologna in 1158 the group of
teachers and students was officially recognized by Emperor
Frederic as a university.  By 1150, the theological schools
in Paris were approaching university status, and in 1167 a

group of English students there withdrew to form their own
school in England--a school that was the beginning of Oxford
University. In 1179, the schools at Paris set up requirements for the title of master, along with a regular organization of chancellor, masters, and students, with a system of
lectures and examinations. It was thus in fact a university,
but the status came officially in 1200, when Emperor Philip
August granted a charter. Two other European universities
date from the twelfth century: Reggio in northern Italy,
formed by students withdrawing from Bologna; and Montpelier
in France, where a school of medicine was joined by a
school of law in 1160. By 1300, there were sixteen other
embryo universities established in western Europe, including
those at Naples and Padua in Italy, at Orléans and Toulouse
in France, at Salamanca and Seville in Spain, at Cambridge
in England, and at Lisbon-Coimbra in Portugal.

For many years the universities did not have libraries as such. The teachers or masters had small book
collections of their own, and these were sometimes lent to
favored students. The students copied the lectures and thus
secured textbooks, or bought or rented them from booksellers. The booksellers (stationarii) became numerous around
the universities, and their bookstocks were essentially rental
libraries for the use of the students. The booksellers eventually formed guilds of their own, and both the university officials and the guilds took pains to insure that the texts of
books sold or rented to the students were authentic. Probably the earliest "libraries" in the universities, other than
the stocks of the booksellers, were those of the student
groups or "nations." These groups sometimes lived or ate
together or at least had headquarters where books were com-
munally owned and used. Sometimes fees were collected to
pay for the purchase or copying of texts for the student library, and there were often gifts from departing students and
interested patrons. At Bologna, the libraries of the nations
were cared for by student librarians with the title of con-
servateur des libres, and it is probable that similar practices existed at other universities. At Oxford and Cambridge
the student groups evolved eventually into "colleges," each
with its own faculty, curriculum and, later, its own library,
but on the continent they continued as little more than board-
ing groups or fraternities. In most European universities,
central libraries are a relatively modern development, but
the schools and colleges comprising the universities began developing libraries by the fourteenth century. Whatever the
nature of book collections around the universities, whether

bookseller, student library, or college library, they were
usually quite small before the advent of printing.

The growth of the libraries at the University of Paris
and at Oxford will perhaps give a representative picture of
early university library development.  At Paris, the earliest
definite information we have about a library comes in 1250
with the endowment of a college there by Robert de Sorbonne.
As a part of his endowment, Sorbonne gave his personal library to the school, along with funds for its upkeep.  Other
gifts of books came to this collection, and its catalog of
1289 listed over one thousand titles.  Appended to this catalog is a physical description of the Sorbonne Library which
provides us with some insight into the nature of the medieval
university library.

The library room was long and narrow, twelve by
forty feet, lighted by nineteen small windows on each side.
There were twenty-eight desks in the room.  The more valuable books were chained to the shelves, but the chains were
long enough to reach the desk.  According to the catalog,
the books were arranged in major divisions, including those
of the trivium and quadrivium, plus theology, medicine and
law.  Only four titles were in French, the remainder in Latin.  Another catalog compiled in 1338 listed some seventeen
hundred titles in the Sorbonne Library, indicating that growth
was slow.

Rules for the use of the Sorbonne Library in the early
fourteenth century are also revealing.  Books were to be
used only in the building in which the library was housed,
and if taken from the library room, they had to be returned
before the end of the day.  If anyone other than a student or
teacher took a book from the library, he had to leave a deposit of equal value.  Somewhat later, the library was divided into two sections, one of permanent reference and another of second copies and works of less value which were
allowed to circulate.  The reference books, many of them
chained, were known as the small library, while the circulating collection was known as the great or common library.

In the fourteenth century and after, other colleges at
the University of Paris formed libraries of their own, including one for the Faculty of Medicine, formed in 1391.
Many of them were initiated with donations of private libraries, including some given by former faculty members.
Over the years, more than fifty different colleges and

schools connected with the University formed libraries, and it was not until the nineteenth century that the University as such achieved a central library. When this was done it was formed with the Sorbonne Library as a nucleus.

Although Oxford was recognized as a studium generale before 1200, it was not until 1214 that recognition by the Pope gave it full standing as a university. Robert Grosseteste (ca. 1168-1259), Bishop of Lincoln, gave a small library to the Greyfriars at Oxford in 1253, and there was a small library for the general use of the scholars in St. Mary's Church, but most of the college libraries at Oxford were not begun until the fourteenth century or later. For example, Merton College dates from 1274, but its library was not formally begun until 1377; University College may have had a collection of books for the use of its students as early as 1280, but an organized library is not noted there until 1440; for Balliol College the corresponding dates are 1282 and 1431. Oriel College was founded in 1324, and as late as 1375 owned only one hundred volumes. However, in 1444, this College removed its books from their ancient chests in the chapel hall and housed them in an entirely separate library building. New College, founded in 1380, was the first Oxford College to begin with a library of its own, and after that date most of the colleges began with their own libraries.

The New College Library is one for which we have some early information. The founder of the College, William of Wykeham, Bishop of Winchester, gave sixty-two volumes for the chapel library, and three hundred-twelve for a common or circulating collection. Of this latter group, an early inventory showed one hundred thirty-six volumes of theology, thirty-four of philosophy, fifty-two of medicine, fifty-three of canon law, and the remainder of civil law. Each fellow at New College could borrow two books at a time and keep them for periods up to a year. He also had a key to the library so that he could use other books there during the day. The books for general reference were chained, and an inventory was taken of all books once a year.

In 1345, Richard de Bury, Bishop of Durham, and a noted bibliophile, planned the formation of a college at Oxford to be endowed with his own private library at his death. Five Benedictine monks were to be placed in charge of the library, and all student-monks were to have the right of borrowing books for use in their own rooms. Duplicate copies of books could be borrowed by anyone in the university com-

munity, providing that a deposit was left in their place.
Durham College was founded by Richard's successor, but unfortunately the library was apparently sold to pay Richard's
debts, and few if any of his books were ever received by the
College.

The general university library at Oxford had a complicated early history and did not emerge as an effective collection until the fifteenth century.   About 1320, Thomas Cobham, Bishop of Worcester, erected a building at Oxford with
a lower floor to be used as a church and an upper floor to
be used for an oratory and a general library for all the colleges.   Before the library could be organized, Bishop Cobham died, and his books ended up in the Oriel College Library.   In 1367, Bishop Cobham's books, having been forc-
ibly removed from Oriel by the university chancellor, were
placed for general use in a room above St. Mary's Church.
Some of the books were sold at this time to obtain funds for
the care of the remainder by the chaplain.   The small collection drifted until 1411, when a new Chancellor, Richard
Courtenay, took the library under his supervision and guaranteed pay for a chaplain to act as librarian and to keep the
library open five hours each weekday.   With this stimulus,
the collection grew and with many gifts from Humphrey,
Duke of Gloucester, and others, the general library moved
into a new location in the 1480s in the new Divinity School
Building, where it was known as "Duke Humphrey's Library" in honor of its chief donor.   Humphrey, the younger
brother of King Henry V, was a learned man himself, and
his personal library was probably the finest in England for
its time.   Among his gifts to Oxford were finely bound copies
of the Greek and Latin classics, as well as contemporary
French and Italian works.   This was the collection that was
to be destroyed in the "reforms" of Edward VI in the sixteenth century.

Elsewhere in Europe more than seventy-five universities were established before 1500, ranging from Seville in
Spain to Uppsala in Sweden and from Catania in Sicily to
Aberdeen in Scotland.   All followed, in general, the organizational pattern of Paris and Oxford, and some type of library was present in all.   On the continent, however, the
formation of central university libraries was often delayed
for several hundred years after the formation of separate
college or institute libraries; in fact, the central library is
still not a major entity in some European universities.   The
fifteenth century saw a few universities with separate library

buildings, including Heidelberg in 1442 and Vienna in 1475. The universities in central Europe developed a different type of library in the faculty collection, as distinct from the college or student libraries and the common or university library.

Unlike the monastery libraries, where acquisitions were gained by copying, the early college libraries grew largely through donations. Numerous instances can be cited of gifts of books to the colleges from kings, nobles, bishops, and merchant collectors. Besides those already mentioned, notable examples would include gifts of books in 1336 to Balliol and Merton Colleges at Oxford from Bishop Stephen Gravesend; gifts of eighty books in 1350 to Trinity College, Cambridge, by Bishop William Bateman; and gifts of two hundred fifty volumes to New College, Oxford, in 1387 by Henry Whitefield. On the continent, university libraries received similar gifts, as when Bishop Matthias of Worms gave ninety books to Heidelberg in 1410, and Johannes Sindel bequeathed two hundred volumes on medicine and mathematics to Prague in 1450. Endowed funds were also given to universities for the purchase of books or the upkeep of libraries, and there is evidence that library fees were collected from students in some cases. Collections remained small, however, as demonstrated by Heidelberg's 396 volumes in 1396 and 840 in 1461, or Cambridge's Queen's College with 199 volumes in 1472. Not until printed books became common did the library book stocks reach into the thousands.

The physical condition of the early university libraries strongly resembled the contemporary monastery collections. The manuscript codices were kept in book chests in the twelfth and thirteenth centuries. By the late thirteenth and early fourteenth centuries they came out of the armaria onto a desk-shelf combination called pulpitum. Each of these could hold about eighteen or twenty books, frequently chained but removable to a lower, slanted desk-shelf. At Queen's College, Cambridge, there were 192 volumes on ten desks and four half-desks. In another library, there were 988 books chained to fifty desks. By the fifteenth century, separate library buildings were being erected--usually long, narrow rooms lighted by many tall windows. The shape of the room was designed to make as much use of natural light as possible, but it was also probably influenced by the fact that prior to being placed in separate buildings, libraries had often been housed in rooms over arcades or open corridors. Inside the rooms, the book-desks were located between the

windows, so that the light fell directly on the reading shelf.
Book-stalls or carrels were being used by the fifteenth century, with tall bookcases of four to six shelves providing
separate booths for readers.

The contents of the medieval university library varied
considerably from place to place, but there was some uni-
formity.  Most of the books would be in Latin, with a few in
the local language, and even fewer in Greek.  Religious
works would be predominant, including the Bible, the church
fathers, theological commentators, lives of the saints, service books, and canon law.  The classics would come next,
followed by the medieval writers, with some history and local literature.  Philosophy, mathematics, medicine and astronomy, largely in translations from the Arabic and Greek,
were more in evidence in later years.  Finally, civil law,
based largely on Justinian's code, and a few standard textbooks in logic and grammar would round out the collection.
By the fourteenth and fifteenth centuries there would be more
local material and also more science than in the earlier
years, but otherwise the collections would vary little from
1200 to 1450.  As in the monasteries, the books were
shelved roughly by subject, and the end of a shelf usually
contained a list of the books shelved within.  Local classification systems were devised in some cases, but usually they
were little more than a location symbol, referring to desk,
shelf and book number.  The catalogs or booklists were arranged more or less alphabetically, but sometimes indis-
criminately by author, title, catchword, or size.  One library even arranged its inventory list by the first word on
the second page, whatever it might be.

Some of the rules and regulations for the use of university libraries sound familiar, but others appear foreign
to us now.  In some cases, students could take out the circulating books for a month, or even as long as a year; in
other cases, only teachers and advanced students were allowed to remove books from the library.  Some books could
be taken out if a deposit were left.  In one university library, a few books were considered so valuable that they
were kept under triple locks, so that three different officials
with separate keys would have to be present before the books
could be seen.  In fifteenth-century Oxford, "only graduates
and people in religious orders who have studied philosophy
eight years shall study in the library of the University...."
The same regulations required an oath "that when they enter
the common library for the sake of study they will handle

the books they consult decently and not inflict any harm on
them by tearing out or ruining layers or single pages of the
book...." At the Sorbonne in Paris there was a fine for
students who left books lying open, and at the University of
Angers in 1431 there was a fine for keeping books over
thirty days.

Book selection policy at Cambridge was probably similar to that at other medieval universities:

> No book is to be brought into the Library or
> chained there, unless it be of suitable value and
> utility, or unless the will of the donor has so di-
> rected; and none is to be taken out of it unless it
> so happens that there already be a considerable
> number on the same subject, or that another copy
> in better condition and of greater value to take its
> place has been acquired.

Duplicate books were sometimes sold, and on occasion valuable volumes of little direct use to the students would be
sold so that more usable titles could be acquired. Library
books were sometimes pawned, officially or unofficially, or
even taken for debts owed by the college or its masters.
Interlibrary lending between universities seems to have been
even less common than between monasteries, and often college libraries of the same institution would zealously guard
their unique items to prevent their copying by another.

Librarians did not emerge as a professional class in
the early universities. Instead, the keeper of the books was
usually a minor faculty member or even a student. Where
the colleges were connected with religious orders, the books
were in the charge of one or more monks. At Oxford, and
probably elsewhere, books were left to the care of the chaplain. Sometimes the librarian was a scholar well-versed in
the contents of the volumes he guarded, but he was more often a "keeper of the books," charged with their physical
care rather than with the responsibility of mastering their
contents. In fact, rules concerning the librarian and his duties were often more strict than those imposed upon users
of the library. In some cases the library caretaker was
personally responsible for every book in his charge and li-
able for their costs if any were lost or damaged. Inventories were usually made annually, and often carried out in
the presence of a high college official.

The early university library was in many ways a direct outgrowth of the monastery and cathedral libraries, but it varied from them in one important aspect: it was a working library. There are frequent references to heavily used volumes in the early college libraries, to books that were badly worn and frequently mended, and to the need for replacements. The emphasis of the libraries was on the maintenance of books for use, and not on the keeping of volumes for rarity alone. In this sense, the medieval university library might be called the earliest modern library. In the use of these libraries, in the education of the thousands of students who flocked to the early universities, the medieval world was given a new society of learned men. These "graduates" for the most part did not remain secluded in monasteries or dedicated to theology, but were trained in civil and canon law, in medicine and philosophy, and they went out into the world and made their knowledge known to others. From the universities and their modest book collections came the learning that was to pave the way for the Renaissance in western Europe. If it was the monastery libraries that preserved knowledge for a thousand years, it was the university libraries that put that knowledge to use, and in doing so ushered in the modern era and put an end to the Middle Ages.

## The Great Book Collectors and the
## Rescue of the Ancient Classics

Although monastery, cathedral, and university libraries were the most significant centers of learning during the Middle Ages, there were also private libraries worthy of notice. These libraries were of lasting importance for several reasons. First, they added materially to the amount of literature available at any given time and place, supplementing the institutional libraries. Second, by means of gifts and bequests, they frequently became parts of the institutional libraries, and added considerably to their value. Finally, in the case of the private libraries of the feudal nobility, they often formed the nuclei of future municipal, state and national libraries. Frequently they were more finely bound, more handsomely written, less worn, and better preserved than their counterparts in the more public collections.

The fate of the many Roman private libraries that existed prior to 500 is worth considering, since it seems likely that at least some of the thousands of manuscripts in the

villas of the nobility would have survived.  Some of them did
survive as gifts to monastic and church collections, and in
isolated family libraries of Italy, Spain and southern France.
Certainly a good percentage of the extant Latin literature survived in western European collections, although some of it
was literally lost for decades or even centuries.  Early
manuscripts were worn out, and those that have come down
to us are copies of copies, so that textual examination, comparison and criticism are necessary to obtain anything close
to the correct original.  But although some of the contents
of the late Roman private libraries have survived, most of
them were destroyed as definitely and finally as those of the
Roman temples themselves.

Though they were rare--at least, modern evidence of
them is scarce--private libraries existed in western Europe
even in the darkest periods of the Middle Ages.  A private
library of secular literature in southern France in the fifth
century, including many of the Latin classics, is described
in a letter of Rusticus, Bishop of Narbonne from 430 to 461.
He depicts what was apparently a provincial Roman villa,
equipped with bookcases adorned with portraits of orators and
poets.  Apollinaris Sidonius, writing at Toulouse in the same
century, shows acquaintance with a sizable library of sources.
The private library of Isidore, Bishop of Seville, accumulated in the seventh century, has already been mentioned, but
other Spanish contemporaries of Isidore also had significant
collections.

Many other church officials, bishops, archbishops and
cardinals, contributed to medieval library history, either in
their own collections or in the libraries they built in their
institutions.  The Bishop of Passau in the tenth century re-
putedly prized his library, although it included only fifty-six
books.  Philip d'Harcourt, Bishop of Bayeux in the twelfth
century, gave a hundred volumes of his personal library to
the cathedral at Bec in Normandy.  Richard Gravesend,
Bishop of London (1280-1303), owned eighty volumes, including three Bibles, works of the church fathers, canon law,
and some works of secular history.  John of Salisbury willed
his library to the cathedral at Chartres in 1180, while Roger
de Thoris, Archdeacon of Exeter, gave his books to the
Greyfriars there in 1266.  Even parish priests found it possible to own a few books, and Geoffrey de Lawath of St.
Magnus in London had a library of forty-nine volumes in the
thirteenth century, including some medical works along with
theology and grammar.  Usually the books owned by religious

figures were theological, but there were often evidences of interest in literature and practical subjects as well.

The development of book collections in Italy from the ninth to the twelfth century shows an interesting contrast. While northern Italy lagged behind France and Germany in the collecting of libraries during this period, the southern part of the peninsula, along with Sicily, was undergoing a miniature renaissance of its own. Both in the monasteries and at the courts of the rulers there was an atmosphere that encouraged learning and scholarship. This was true despite the almost constant strife, with Italians, Normans, Spanish, Moslems and Byzantines warring for control of the area. Greek was taught in the monastery schools; libraries were gathered which included Greek works, translations from the Arabic, and Hebrew as well as Latin. Duke Sergius of Naples in the ninth century collected a small library and presented it to the cathedral there. His son, Duke Gregory, could read both Latin and Greek in an era when the latter language was almost unknown in the rest of Europe.

Some women among the medieval nobility were well educated and became scholars and book collectors. A few nuns and abbesses were noted for their interest in books during the early Middle Ages, but after the twelfth century it was the wives and daughters of noblemen and rulers who turned to collecting libraries. Clemence of Hungary, wife of Louis X of France, had a library of her own in the early fourteenth century. Jeanne d'Evreux, wife of Charles the Fair (1322-28), owned a library, largely religious but containing some secular works in French. Jeanne of Burgundy and Blanche of Navarre, both wives of Philip VI (1328-50), brought books of their own to be added to Philip's library. Queen Isabel, wife of Charles VI (1380-1422), had so many books that one of her ladies-in-waiting had to serve as her personal librarian. Margaret of York, English wife of Charles, Duke of Burgundy in the fifteenth century, brought a small library of English works with her in 1468, and joined with her husband in continuing to build up the library of the ducal house of Burgundy. A scholar in her own right, she commissioned the translation of Boethius's Consolation of Philosophy from Latin into French, and brought William Caxton from England to learn the art of printing in Bruges. He later became the first printer in England. Margaret, Countess of Richmond, was another English lover of books in the fifteenth century. She had a "fine library, stored with Latin, French and English books," some bound in velvet with silver

clasps.  Other examples of noble women book collectors are
not difficult to find, and their scholarly activities indicate
that they read their books as well as collected them.  The
subject content of their collections was in general similar to
those of contemporary men--heavily theological, but ranging
widely into philosophy, history and literature, both classical
and contemporary.

The Jewish minority in western Europe produced many
scholars and book collectors.  Under the Moslems in Spain
and Sicily, the Jews flourished in a tolerant atmosphere, and
many scholars, lawyers, and physicians emerged among
them.  The Jewish Bible, together with the core of literature built up around it, formed the basis of many Jewish
book collections, but others went far beyond this theological
center and built up large libraries of secular literature.

Jews in the north of Europe were not so wealthy as
those in the Mediterranean area, so that they were often
hard-pressed to acquire even the necessary books for their
synagogues.  However, one French Jew, Juda Ibn Tibbon of
the twelfth century, left a library notable for its contents if
not for its great size.  Tibbon left his books to his son
with concise instructions on how to handle them:

> Arrange them all in good order, so that thou weary
> not in looking for a book when thou needest it....
> Write down the titles of the books in each row of
> the cases in a separate notebook and place each in
> its row, in order that thou mayest be able to see
> exactly in which row any particular book is with-
> out mixing up the others.  Do the same with the
> cases.  Look continually into the catalog in order
> to remember what books thou hast.  When thou
> lendest a book, record its title before it leaves the
> house; and when it is brought back draw thy pen
> through the memorandum....

Tibbon (1120-70) was a philosopher and scholar who translated books from Arabic into Latin.  His motive in building
his library was to make it so complete that he would never
again have to borrow a book.

In addition to the nobility and clergy, the professional
man of the Middle Ages was sometimes a collector of books.
Also, some of the skilled craftsmen, particularly those connected with churches and monasteries, were readers and

owned a few books.  Physicians were particularly interested
in books and often went beyond medical treatises in their collecting.  Johannes Sindell, physician to Emperor Frederick
III, left two hundred books at his death in 1450.  In Austria
in 1453, Dr. Johannes Polzmacher gave his library to a
monastery near Vienna.  It was strong in both civil and canon law as well as classical literature.  Herman Schedel
(1410-1485), a Nuremberg physician, began collecting books
in Greek, Latin, Italian and German, and on his death his
cousin, Hartman Schedel (1440-1514), also a physician, took
over the library, broadened its contents to include art and
archeology, and built it into one of the largest and most valuable collections of its time.  The Schedel library passed
later into the hands of the Fugger family, and eventually became a part of the Royal Library in Munich.  Most physicians and lawyers of the later Middle Ages had small collections of professional books, and a few acquired collections
on other subjects.

Two famous medieval book collectors left us works
concerning their collecting activities which discussed books
they owned or wanted to own.  One was Richard de Fournival, Chancellor of Amiens in France, who wrote his Biblion-
omia in the thirteenth century.  In this somewhat fanciful
work he described a "garden of literature" in which different
tables were covered with manuscripts on different subjects.
His largest subject area was philosophy, but medicine, law,
and theology were also included in his "garden."  There is
some doubt as to whether the work describes an actual book
collection or is merely imaginary.  Also, there is some
doubt that it was actually written by Fournival, although it is
usually ascribed to him.  However, it is an excellent account of literary interests of the period and most of the manuscripts described  are known to exist or to have existed
at one time.

The other bibliophile was Richard de Bury (1287-
1345), teacher, officeholder, and later Bishop of Durham.
He was an ardent book collector from his earlier years, and
when he later became a diplomat in the service of Edward
III of England, he visited libraries, scriptoria and booksellers
in many parts of Europe.  He bought many books and others
were given to him, particularly after he became a bishop.
He respected and would accept books in almost any form and
on almost any subject.  His Philobiblon (or The Love of
Books) was completed about 1344, but it was not printed until 1473, and since that date it has appeared in many editions.

Basically, it is a book in praise of books, but it also tells
how the author collected his library, and thus gives an elaborate picture of the book world of his day.  Some of his
chapter headings were:  "That the treasure of wisdom is
chiefly contained in books"; "That it is meritorious to write
new books and to renew the old"; "Of the numerous oppor-
tunities we have had of collecting a store of books"; and finally, "That we have collected so great a store of books for
the common benefit of scholars and not only for our own
pleasure."  De Bury noted that books were the storehouses
of wisdom, and he says of them:  "There everyone who asks
receiveth thee, and everyone who seeks finds thee, and to
everyone that knocketh boldly it is speedily opened."  One
other notable quote from the Philobiblon shows the author's
basic belief:  "All the glory of the world would be buried in
oblivion, unless God had provided mortals with the remedy
of books."  Richard de Bury's books were supposed to have
been given on his death to the Priory of Durham at Oxford,
but instead they were probably sold to pay his many debts.
Some estimates indicate that Richard de Bury may have possessed as many as fifteen hundred volumes, a very large library for his time, but whatever the number, it is certain
that it was the most notable private library in fourteenth
century England.

The most important private libraries in Europe before
1500, however, were the libraries of the Italian scholar-
bookmen who figured prominently in the Renaissance.  The
Renaissance was ruled by a central concept--humanism--
which permeated all areas of intellectual life, but was essentially literary in nature and was firmly grounded upon the
study and imitation of classical literature.  Scholars everywhere grew increasingly committed to the classical spirit,
and many determined to devote their lives to seeking out,
recovering, editing, translating and critically analyzing the
works of the ancients.

The movement, basically secular in nature, was
spearheaded by men of the world, most of whom were fanat-
ical book collectors.  As scholars have frequently noted,
their insatiable appetites for the works of the classical authors led to the accumulation of many very important private
libraries, and stimulated the growth of a book trade which
contributed to the breakdown of the Church's monopoly on
learning.  In time, humanism even gained some influence
within the Church, and several noted book collectors of the
late Renaissance were ecclesiastics.

From the fourteenth century through the sixteenth,
Italian merchants, princes and religious leaders, either in
collaboration or in competition, succeeded in bringing to
light the majority of the Greek and Latin classics now known
to the western world.  Some of these classics were discovered in Italy itself, in monasteries, church libraries, or in
private hands.  Still others were found or rediscovered in
the, by then, neglected monastery libraries of France,
Switzerland, and central Europe.  But of more importance
were the volumes brought to Italy from Constantinople,
Greece, and the Moslem countries.  For centuries these had
been lost to western Europe and might have been lost forever if they had not been rescued at that time.

Petrarch (1304-74) was one of the earliest of these
Italian book collectors.  He collected manuscripts from all
parts of Europe and devoted himself particularly to the classic Latin authors.  While the reputation of some of his pre-
cursors--such as the Paduan judge and lover of classical
poetry, Lovato Lovati--has grown in the light of recent research, Petrarch remains the unrivaled champion of the
early Renaissance.  His rare qualities as book collector and
scholar aided him in the quest for the classic Latin authors,
and he built the finest private library of his day.  He had
hoped to see his library made available to the public after
his death, but his plans never materialized and his books
were scattered.

His contemporary and follower, Boccaccio (1313-75),
also played a leading role in the rescue of the ancient classics.  While less the scholar than his mentor, Boccaccio
wrote widely in a popular vein and did much to stimulate interest in classical literature.  It was Boccaccio the book collector who is believed to have been responsible for unlocking
the riches of the library at Monte Cassino, and for spiriting
away a number of major works, most notably those of Tacitus, Apuleius, and Varro, to his home in Florence.  Upon
his death, this magnificent collection of books was given to
the monastery of San Spirito in Florence.

A third Florentine completes the triad of great Renaissance book collectors from that city.  Coluccio Salutati
(1331-1406) had studied with Petrarch when the latter was
an old man, and he knew Boccaccio well.  Coluccio stands
as the humanist who passed the torch from one generation
of humanists to another, and several of his disciples were
leading figures in the "Great Age of Discovery,"  in the

first half of the fifteenth century.  By 1400 the popularity of
the ancient texts, and the unprecedented recognition awarded
to those who recovered them, stimulated an enormous interest in the recovery of the classical writers, and many Venetian, Florentine, and Genoese ship captains considered
manuscripts to be valuable cargo for their return trips from
the eastern Mediterranean.  In 1408 Guarino of Verona returned from a visit to the East with a collection of fifty
Greek manuscripts for which he found a ready sale.  The
Sicilian book collector, Giovanni Aurispa, brought in over
two hundred Greek manuscripts in the year 1423 alone, a
feat which amounted to the "transplantation of an entire literature to new and fertile soil."  Francesco Filelfo, who
went to Constantinople in 1420 as a member of the Venetian
legation there, brought home with him about forty Greek volumes, many of which were unknown in Latin translation before that date.  The quest for manuscripts led not only to
works in Greek but to Hebrew as well.  Giovanni Pico della
Mirandola, a Christian Hebrew scholar, owned more than one
hundred Hebrew works, and his student and friend, Johann
Reuchlin, acquired thirty-six more in the same language.

It is noteworthy that much of this collecting was done
by individuals rather than by universities, church, or governmental agencies.  Many of them were merchants or religious personnel, but the greatest collectors were the Italian
princes and their agents.  Several men became famous for
their ability to locate and obtain manuscripts for pay.  Janus
Lascaris (ca. 1450-1535), for example, obtained many manuscripts from the East, first for Louis XII of France and
later for the Medici family in Italy.  Many of these came
from the monasteries of Greece, including Mount Athos and
others on the Aegean Islands, and among them were scores
of previously unknown works.  Vespasiano da Bisticci made
a profession of obtaining and copying manuscripts, and aided
in the building up of several of the famous Italian collections.
Poggio Bracciolini (1380-1459) was a collector famous for his
discoveries of unknown manuscripts in European monasteries.
He is most noted for uncovering lost works of Lucretius and
Quintilian.

One important religious collector was Cardinal Bessarion (ca. 1400-1492), a Greek by birth but a long-time
resident of Italy.  He translated many classical Greek works
into Latin and tried to build up the largest Greek library in
the world.  He had agents searching Greece and Asia Minor
and was responsible for rescuing several hundred manuscripts.

In 1468 he gave his library to the city of Venice on condition that it be suitably housed and open to the public.  This
library eventually was built and became the Biblioteca Marciana, or Library of St. Mark.

Among the most important Italian collectors were the
members of the Medici family.  Cosimo de Medici (1389-
1464) hired Vespasiano da Bisticci to collect books for him.
At one time, Vespasiano employed forty-five copyists and in
twenty-two months produced some two hundred books, all
elegantly inscribed and bound, for the Medici library.  Cosimo's library contained the Bible in several copies, religious
commentaries, works of the church fathers, the medieval
writers, and also many classical works in philosophy, history, poetry and drama.  In addition to the works he obtained himself, Cosimo also acquired a library of eight hundred volumes collected by Niccolo di Niccoli of Florence.
Tomaso Parentucceli, later Pope Nicholas V, was at one
time Cosimo's librarian.  Cosimo was himself a scholar who
read Latin well and had some knowledge of Greek, Hebrew
and Arabic.  Drawing on his collections, he began several
libraries including one in the Convent of San Marco at Florence and another in the Abbey at Fiesole.

Most of Cosimo's volumes, however, remained at his
death in the family library, and this collection was greatly
enlarged by his grandson, Lorenzo de Medici (1449-92).
Lorenzo the Magnificent, prince, poet and patron of the arts,
had Janus Lascaris as one of his book-collecting agents, and
built up a noble library of religion and the classics.  He allowed scholars to use his library, and even permitted other
collectors to copy his treasures.  Nearly half of his books
were in Greek and languages other than Latin, and he was
one of the first to permit printed books on his shelves.  After his death, the Medici family library led a precarious existence, first in the Convent of San Marco, later in Rome,
and finally in 1521 back in Florence.  Eventually it was
housed in the Biblioteca Laurentiana, a building designed especially for it by Michelangelo.

Federigo, Duke of Urbino (1444-82), was another of
the ardent fifteenth-century Italian collectors.  He had a series of rooms in his palace filled with books, and invited
artists, scholars and writers to use them.  He loved the
classics, but also added to his library the standard church
literature and contemporary authors.  For many years he
maintained a large staff of copyists, and Vespasiano da

Bisticci also served him for a time as librarian and book-
buyer.  At his death in 1482, his collection included seven
hundred seventy-two manuscripts, of which seventy-three
were Hebrew and ninety-three Greek.  The library room in
his palace measured forty-five by twenty feet, and the books
were kept in eight presses, with seven shelves each.

The development of the Vatican Library in Rome during the later Middle Ages can be considered along with private libraries since it was largely the result of the activities of a few individuals.  Pope Nicholas V (1447-55) who,
as Tomaso Parentucelli, had been librarian to Cosimo de
Medici, was responsible for the rebirth of the Vatican Library.  The library collected by the Popes at Avignon had
been dispersed, and after the return of the papacy to Rome
no serious attempt had been made to rebuild the collection.
When Nicholas became Pope, he found only some 350 volumes in various states of repair, and to this he added his
own private library.  Then he proceeded to add to it with
all the resources at his command and with his own wide
knowledge of the book world.  He sent papal agents all over
Europe seeking manuscripts as gifts or for copying.  The
papal librarian, Tortelli, helped to build the collection and
translated Greek works into Latin.  By the time of his
death, Nicholas had built the Vatican Library to over twelve
hundred volumes and made it one of the finest in Italy.

The papacy for the next few years was more concerned with the war against the Turks than with the papal library, but Pope Sixtus (1471-84) not only enlarged the library but remodeled a building for it.  In 1475, it included
2,500 volumes, about one-third Greek and two-thirds Latin.
In 1484, an inventory of the library in its new quarters
found it housed in four rooms and containing some 3,500 volumes.  The four rooms consisted of a public Greek library,
a public Latin library, a rare book collection of "biblioteca
secreta," and the Pope's private library.  The humanist
scholar, Bartolomeo Platina, was librarian in the Vatican
after 1475.  He cataloged and classified the library, keeping
strict records of all use, and opened it to all serious scholars.  Although the primary purpose of the library was to
collect and preserve works on the history and doctrine of the
church, from the days of Nicholas V onward it also contained
an increasing number of secular works.  Although he probably exaggerated a little, the contemporary Vespasiano da
Bisticci was able to say of the new Vatican Library that:
"Never since the time of Ptolemy had half so large a number of books of every kind been brought together."

The Emergence of the National Libraries

      Though many of the libraries of the late medieval
bookmen went into public collections or were scattered, a
significant few went to form the beginnings of future national
libraries.  The kings of Naples, beginning with Charles I
(1220-85), built up a notable library in that city.  This royal collection grew in size and usefulness for some two hundred years.  In 1485, however, when the French captured
Naples, most of the royal library was carried away as
spoils of war to join other collections in forming the French
royal library.  More specifically, however, the French national library began with Charles V, who took a small collection left by his father and installed it with many additions
in the Chateau du Louvre in 1367.  With Gilles Malet as librarian, the French royal library grew to nearly a thousand
volumes scattered through three rooms of the palace.
Though largely theological, the library also contained many
other subjects, including history, law, French literature, and
science.  There were some works translated from the Arabic.  Actually, earlier kings of France had owned books
from before the days of Charlemagne, but most of these,
like his, were dispersed at the death of the collector.  In
the wars with the English in the early fifteenth century, part
of the royal French library was captured and carried to England by the Duke of Bedford, but in 1461, Louis XI re-established a library in the Louvre.  In 1472, the library of the
Duc de Berry was added to this collection, and still later a
part of the collection of the Dukes of Burgundy.  About 1500,
Louis XII moved the royal library to Blois, where the Orleans family already had a magnificent collection, and added
to it the libraries he had captured in Italy.  Not until 1595
was the royal library to return permanently to Paris.

      In England, the kings had also been haphazard collec-
tors of books since the days of King Alfred the Great in the
ninth century.  He not only collected books, but translated
Latin works into Anglo-Saxon, including the writings of Bede
and Boethius.  After Alfred, various English kings made
small palace collections of books, often gifts unopened, but
these were considered private property and never became the
base of a national library.  Not until the eighteenth century
was England to acquire one in the British Museum.

      In Austria, the national library had its beginning in
the early fifteenth century when Emperor Friedrich V ordered
all books and archives belonging to the government to be

brought to a central location and organized.  Books from
Constantinople came to this collection as the Byzantine Empire disintegrated, but the library was still not very large
when, in 1497, Emperor Maximilian I officially established
an imperial library with Conrad Celtes, the humanist poet,
as the first librarian.  Elsewhere in Europe, the library
of the Dukes of Burgundy, augmented by those of some of
the Austrian princes, survived intact until the nineteenth century when it formed the basis for the national library of Belgium.  Several German principalities began their libraries
with the collections of their rulers before 1500, and in Spain
the union of Aragon and Castile in the late fifteenth century
made the foundation of a Spanish national library possible.

One of the most famous of the European royal libraries in the fifteenth century was that of King Matthias
Corvinus of Hungary (1440-90).  Matthias had agents throughout Europe buying and borrowing volumes for his library.  In
that library, which occupied a wing of the palace at Buda,
he had twenty or more copyists, illuminators, and bookbind-
ers producing beautiful volumes in Latin, Greek, Arabic and
Hebrew for him.  In 1476, he married Beatrice of Aragon,
herself an ardent book collector, and between them they
gathered a library that for its time was unusually large and
beautiful.  It was housed in a wing of the palace and divided
into two collections, one Latin and the other Greek and Oriental.  Various reports credit Matthias with having up to
fifty thousand volumes, but it is doubtful that he could have
had over a tenth of that number.  After his death, his books
were gradually dispersed and any that were left were probably taken by the Turks when they captured Buda in 1526.
Many individual items from the Corvinus library have survived, however, and they now form some of the most treasured items in modern European libraries.

All told, the fifteenth century was remarkable from
the standpoint of library development, and much of this progress came through the efforts of individuals rather than organizations.  Two events helped to shape this development.
The first was the coming of the Renaissance, with its emphasis on humanism and the recovery of classical philosophy
and literature.  Cause and effect are closely intertwined
here, since the building of book collections undoubtedly helped
to bring on and spread the Renaissance.  The second event
was the development of printing from movable type, which
occurred about the middle of the fifteenth century.

Printing and Libraries

This analysis of the growth of libraries in Europe
prior to 1500 cannot conclude without at least brief reference
to the invention of printing from movable type.  Bacon, in
his Novum Organum, announced that three inventions unknown
to the ancients had changed the "appearance and state of the
whole world," and they were "printing, gunpowder and the
compass."

Scholars are just beginning to extend their work on
the history of printing beyond questions of origins and development to the far more complex matters related to the impact, influence, and consequences of the invention of printing.  The development and spread of the press from its point
of origin in mid-fifteenth-century Germany is best left to histories of printing.  However, it is important to note that
each major development in the book arts has had a measur-
able impact on the history of libraries.  This influence is
particularly obvious in the case of printing.

The most dramatic consequence was the marked increase in the output of books, coupled with a substantial de-
crease in the amount of labor necessary to produce them.
Such a combination of developments meant that throughout
Europe books were much more readily available to people
and generally at a much lower cost.  This fact had the result of making more books much more readily available to
libraries of all kinds, and contributed to the rapid increase
in the size of libraries and a concomitant growth in complexity.  In a way the invention of printing may be said to have
given birth to modern librarianship, in the sense that the
ever-increasing size of library collections made possible by
the printing press stimulated the emergence of a profession
charged with the responsibility of organizing and directing
these at once large, complex and valuable national resources.

Additional Readings

This list of additional readings is quite selective
and deals almost exclusively with the history of
libraries.  For a treatment of the history of the
development of libraries within the context of the
development of the press and reading tastes, see
Elmer D. Johnson, Communication: An Introduction to the History of Writing, Printing, Books

and Libraries. 4th ed. Metuchen, N.J., 1973.
This work contains extensive bibliographies.

Avanzi, G. Libri, Librerie, Biblioteche nell' Umanesimo e
Nell Rinascenza; Cataloghi e Notizie. Rome, 1954-56.
3v.

Bernard, S. "The Rape of Books from the Abbey of St.
Gallen," Downside Review 85 (1967): 35-8.

Berthoud, J. "The Italian Renaissance Library," Theoria
(U. of Natal), 26 (1966): 61-80.

Connell, S. "Books and Their Owners in Venice, 1345-
1480," Journal of the Warburg and Courtauld Institutes
35 (1972): 163-86.

De Bury, R. The Philo-biblon. With an Introduction by
Archer Taylor. Berkeley, 1948.

Delhaye, P. "L'organization Scolaire au XII$^e$ Siècle," Tra-
ditio 5 (1947): 211-68.

Delisle, L. Reserches sur la Librairie de Charles V...
Charles VI. Paris, 1907. 2v. [reprinted Amsterdam,
1967].

Deuel, L. Testaments of Time... New York, 1965. [Book
One: A Renaissance Prelude.]

Eisenstein, E. L. "Some Conjectures about the Impact of
Printing on Western Society and Thought," Journal of
Modern History 40 (1968): 1-56.

Fava, D. Lexioni di Biblioteconomia e Bibliografia. Milan,
1946. [Contains several essays on the libraries of the
Italian Renaissance.]

Garrod, H. W. "The Library Regulations of a Medieval
College," The Library 8 (1927): 312-35.

Geanakoplos, D. J. Greek Scholars in Venice: Studies in
the Dissemination of Greek Learning from Byzantium
to Western Europe. Cambridge, 1962.

Ghellinck, J. de. "Un Evêque Bibliophile au XIV$^e$ Siècle:
Richard Aungerville de Bury," Revue d'Histoire Ec-
clesiastique 18 (1922): 271-312; 482-508.

Jones, W. R. "Bibliothecae Arcanae: The Private Libraries of Some European Sorcerers," Journal of Library History 8 (1973): 86-95.

Kelly, T. Early Public Libraries; A History of Public Libraries in Great Britain Before 1850. London, 1966. [Chapter 1 on Medieval libraries.]

Kibre, P. The Library of Pico della Mirandola. New York, 1936.

Poulle, E. La Bibliothèque Scientifique d'un Imprimeur Humaniste au XVe Siècle...Arnaud de Bruxelles... Geneva, 1962.

Rhodes, D. E. John Argentine, Provost of King's, His Life and His Library. Amsterdam, 1967.

Rouse, R. "The Early Library of the Sorbonne," Scriptorium 21 (1968): 42-71.

Taylor, A. Renaissance Guides to Books; an Inventory and Some Conclusions. Berkeley, 1925.

Thompson, J. W. The Medieval Library. Chicago, 1939. [Part III: the close of the Middle Ages and the Italian Renaissance.]

Ullman, B. and P. A. Stadter. The Public Library of Renaissance Florence: Nicolo Niccoli, Cosimo De'Medici and the Library of San Marco. Padova, Italy. 1972.

Vleeschauwer, H. J. de. Libraria Magna et Libraria Parva dans la Bibliothèque Universitaire de XIIIe Siècle. Pretoria, 1956.

Wormald, F. and C. E. Wright, eds. The English Library before 1700. London, 1958.

# PART III

# MODERN LIBRARY DEVELOPMENT IN THE WEST

Chapter 9

EUROPEAN LIBRARIES:
Expansion and Diversification to 1917

## European National Libraries

The growth of libraries in Europe since 1500 has been
enormous as compared with the pitifully small collections
available during the Middle Ages. The primary cause of
this remarkable growth was, of course, the development of
printing, which produced more books and cheaper books than
could have been imagined a century earlier. Ready access
to books also contributed to an increase in literacy levels;
a development that stimulated demand for books and encouraged the rise of a substantial book trade. Before 1500 a
great book might be available in a hundred manuscript copies,
and read at most by a few thousand people; after that date,
it could be available in thousands of copies and read by hundreds of thousands of people. It has been estimated that in
the sixteenth century more than one hundred thousand different books were printed in Europe alone, and assuming an
average of a thousand copies each, that would mean a hundred million available to Europeans during that century. The
power of the printed word increased a hundredfold the power
of the written word, and never again were Europe and the
western world to suffer from a lack of graphic communication for the conveyance of facts and ideas.

Of all the libraries of modern Europe, the most outstanding have been the national libraries, those rapidly growing collections dedicated to preserving every book and manuscript which in any way related to the national heritage.
Sometimes these collections developed at the expense of other
libraries. They may not always have been as influential as
some other libraries, notably those of the great universities,

141

but they benefited from the spirit of nationalism and often
survived and even flourished while other libraries suffered
in wars or depressions.  Generally speaking, they had per-
manency and economic security if not generous budgets and
well-trained staffs.  Their collective success and survival
have meant much to the total history of libraries in the western world.

The French national library in Paris, the Bibliothèque
Nationale, ranks among the finest of European libraries.  Its
development through a series of royal family libraries down
through the sixteenth century has already been traced.  After
sojourns in castles at Blois and Fontainebleau, the royal library was returned to Paris during the reign of Henry IV
(1589-1610).  In 1537 it had received the "right of deposit"
of one copy of each book printed in France, and was thus assured a steady supply of new acquisitions at minimal expense.
For some years the royal library was housed at the College
of Clermont in Paris, but by 1622 it was installed in an old
mansion on the Rue de la Harpe.  In that year its first
printed catalog was issued, listing some six thousand titles.
This catalog was divided into two main divisions, manuscript
and print, and each of these was subdivided by language.
Under Louis XIV (1643-1715), and particularly under his
Prime Minister, Jean Baptiste Colbert, the royal library
grew rapidly.  With Nicholas Clement as librarian, the collection was reclassified according to a system of twenty-
three main divisions based on the letters of the alphabet.
By the 1720s the library was forced to move to a site on the
Rue Richelieu, where it soon contained some eighty thousand
printed volumes and sixteen thousand manuscripts.  These
quarters have been enlarged, extended, remodeled, and virtually rebuilt over the years, but the site has remained the
same down to the twentieth century.

Throughout its history the Bibliothèque Nationale has
been favored by the accession of thousands of major works,
including many whole libraries.  Some of these have been
purchased, others were donated or acquired by more direct
means.  One of the earliest collections added was made up
of some eight hundred manuscripts collected for Catherine de
Medici, and acquired under the librarianship of J. A. de
Thou in the early seventeenth century.  In 1662 the library
of Raphael Trichet du Fresne, containing some twelve hundred volumes, was purchased.  In 1670 the medical library
of Jacques Mentel, almost ten thousand volumes, was acquired, and in 1672, agents of the library returned from the

Near East with some six hundred thirty manuscripts in Hebrew, Syriac, Coptic, Turkish, Persian and Greek.  One of
the most exotic acquisitions was a gift of forty-two volumes
in Chinese from the Emperor of China through a returning
French missionary.  In 1728 the greater part of the library
of former Minister Colbert was purchased, and about the
same time a collection of medieval manuscripts was donated
by Archbishop Roger de Gaigneres.  The library of Aimar
de Ranconnet, first president of the French Parliament, was
confiscated when he was imprisoned for political reasons in
1559.  In addition, book-dealers throughout Europe sent
books and manuscripts for consideration, and diplomats in
foreign countries sent back gifts and purchases, so that the
royal library grew constantly in numbers and value.

The late eighteenth century saw a rapid growth at the
expense of other French libraries.  In 1763, for example,
when the Jesuits were expelled from Paris, their libraries
were seized and the more valuable works added to the royal
library.  After the beginning of the French Revolution in
1789, the library suffered at first from lack of interest and
funds, but it soon was designated the "Bibliothèque Nationale"
rather than the "Bibliothèque Royale," and thousands of volumes from the libraries of the fleeing nobility were added to
it.  Later on, libraries from monasteries, cathedrals and
church schools were seized, and all books that were not duplicates were placed in the national library.  The unwanted
volumes were destroyed or sent to public libraries throughout France.  Thus, while the Revolution resulted in the
breaking up of many private and religious libraries, it also
brought many treasures into the Bibliothèque Nationale and
aided in the establishment of municipal libraries.  Moreover,
it brought with it the ideas and ideals of national library
planning, national bibliographies, and library service for all
the people.  Still later, the armies of both the Revolution
and the Empire under Napoleon seized libraries in other parts
of Europe and added choice volumes to their national library.

Thus, in the nineteenth century the Bibliothèque Nationale was one of the foremost libraries in the world.  By
1818 it contained nearly a million volumes; by 1860, a million and a half; and by 1908 there were more than three million printed volumes.  Concomitant with the ever-increasing
size of the collections was the ever more pressing problem
of reorganization to cope with the rapid growth.  In 1739 the
librarian, Abbé Jean-Paul Bignon, a tireless bureaucrat who
was both Royal Librarian and President of the Academy of

Sciences, divided the library into four main collections: theology, canon law, civil law, and belles lettres. In 1840 a complete reorganization was begun and in that year the author catalog alone totaled eighty-nine volumes. In the 1850s the library building was virtually rebuilt under the architectural guidance of Henri Labrouste. The late nineteenth century found the library under the able direction of Leopold Delisle (1874-1907) who, although he was a medievalist at heart and strongly interested in manuscripts and paleographical studies, did much to modernize the library and make it available to scholars from all over the world.

Equal to the Bibliothèque Nationale in international importance is the British Museum, which, now a part of the new British Library, remains the national library of Great Britain. This library is not as old as that of France, since the early royal book collections were usually dispersed upon the deaths of their owners, but it has grown rapidly in its two centuries of existence. Although based in part on royal collections, the British Museum has been largely the result of the amalgamation of many private libraries. As early as 1556, the scholar and scientist John Dee suggested to Queen Mary that a royal library should be collected from the scattered manuscripts of the monasteries closed by Henry VIII, but nothing came of the suggestion. Again, a century later, John Dury in his The Reformed Librarie Keeper made a similar suggestion, and in 1694 Richard Bentley's Proposal for Building a Royal Library was even more specific. Perhaps as a result of Bentley's suggestion, the first elements of the British Museum began taking shape in 1700. In that year, the valuable manuscript library of Sir Henry Cotton, together with housing, was bequeathed to the nation by its owner and accepted by William III. In 1707 Queen Anne allowed the royal library to be housed with the Cottonian library, but the two were moved several times, suffered from a fire in 1737, and were never available to the public.

The achievement of a truly national library for England came in the 1750s. In 1753 Sir Hans Sloane, royal physician and a notable book collector, directed in his will that his library and museum be sold to the government for a modest sum on condition that it be suitably housed and maintained. After much debate in Parliament, the collection was purchased and a sum appropriated for a building. Sloane's library contained over fifty thousand volumes, but it was overshadowed by another contemporary private collection, that of Robert Harley, which contained as many books plus thousands of pamphlets and manuscripts. Unfortunately, at Harley's death much of his library was sold, but the manuscripts were acquired by the government. To these collections, King George II, in 1757, added his own private library, and the British Museum was formally opened to the public in a rambling mansion known as Montague House on 15 January, 1759. The title of Museum was appropriate, since the Sloane collection included many thousands of geological and botanical specimens, but over the years the library has far surpassed the museum in general significance.

Although several minor collections were added to the library in the eighteenth century, the book collection as a whole grew only slowly until after the Napoleonic wars. In 1817 a major accession came in the purchase of the Charles Burney library of some thirteen thousand volumes and five hundred early Greek and Latin manuscripts. Most important in the Burney library, however, were the files of seventeenth- and eighteenth-century British newspapers, bound chronologically and indexed by Burney himself. In 1823 the library of George III was added to the Museum, literally doubling the size of its printed collection. Plans for a new building were begun, and a first wing of this structure was completed in 1828, at which time the library had over 200,000 volumes. The new building was planned originally as a huge quadrangle surrounding an open court, but in the 1850s the Museum was converted into a solid square by making the center court into a bookstack surrounding a circular reading area.

The British Museum has had many outstanding librarians and directors, but probably the most significant was Sir Antonio Panizzi, who came to the staff as assistant librarian in 1831. His energy and interest led him to the position of Keeper of the Printed Books in 1837, and under his administration the library earned the reputation of being the best administered in the world. He supervised the move into the new building in 1838, the building of the central reading room and stacks in the 1850s, the preparation of the first complete catalog and the accompanying catalog rules, the enforcement of the deposit law, the obtaining of special funds from Parliament for the enlargement of the collection, and the beginning of the printed catalog. Finally, in 1856, he was rewarded with the title of Principal Librarian, and he filled this position until his retirement in 1868. His leadership in library affairs was widely acknowledged, and he must be considered the most influential librarian of his time.

There are also national libraries in Scotland and
Wales.  The National Library of Scotland, renamed in 1925,
was formerly the Advocate's Library, founded in Edinburgh
in 1682.  Originally a legal library, it began at an early
date to specialize in Scottish literature and history.  In 1709
it was granted depository rights for all books published in
Great Britain, and under the librarianship of the historian-
philosopher, David Hume, it grew to a collection of some
thirty thousand volumes by the mid-eighteenth century.  By
1900, gifts of books and funds increased it to nearly a half-
million volumes.  The National Library of Wales, in Abery-
stwyth, founded in 1873, was based on two large private libraries, those of Sir John Williams, a Welsh surgeon, and
Edward Owen, a Welsh language scholar, and on the library
of the University College of Wales.  The library concentrates
on Welsh language and literature, containing virtually everything published in Welsh or about Wales since the invention
of printing.  In a building of its own since 1916, the Welsh
National Library also serves as the library of the University
of Wales and as a regional library for Wales in the National
Library System.

Possibly the largest national library in the world today is that of Soviet Russia, the Saltykov-Shchedrin Library
in Leningrad, formerly the Imperial Russian Library of St.
Petersburg.  Like the British Museum, this collection had its
beginning in the eighteenth century, and like the Bibliothèque
Nationale it owes its origins to the spoils of war, in this
case a captured Polish library taken by the armies of the
Empress Catharine.  This library had been built up by the
Counts Andreas and Joseph Zaluski before 1740.  It was
largely western European in language and origin, but it contained a few Russian works and almost everything printed in
Polish.  In 1740 the Zaluski library was formally turned over
to the Polish government and a few years later it was opened
to the public as the Polish National Library.  When Warsaw
was captured by the Russians in 1794 and Poland was divided
between Prussia, Russia and Austria, the national library
went to the Russians as spoils of war, with its two hundred
fifty thousand books and ten thousand manuscripts.  After the
death of Catharine, the library remained inactive until Count
Alexander Stroganoff was appointed its director in 1800.  He
added to it the various small collections owned by the Russian
government and organized it into an effective library collection.  An early acquisition was the Dubrovsky collection of
manuscripts, obtained by a Russian agent in Paris during the
French Revolution.  Many of these had been originally in the

Abbey of St. Germain des Prés, and before that in the monastery at Corbie. At Stroganoff's death in 1811, A. N. Olenin became director of the imperial library and it was officially opened to the public. Since the original Polish collection had contained only a few books in Russian, the defect
was remedied in 1810 by a legal deposit law that gave the
library two copies of every book published in Russia. With
a relatively meager budget, Olenin greatly increased the size
of the library through exchanges, purchases and gifts, and
at his death in 1843 he left a scholarly collection that was
really a national library.

Count M. A. Korf, librarian from 1849 to 1861, was
responsible for the next period of growth for the Russian
Imperial Library. During his administration he added some
350,000 printed volumes and 11,000 manuscripts, as well as
large number of prints, photographs, musical scores and
maps. He also remodeled the library building and completely reorganized the book collection, dividing it into departments on the general plan of the British Museum. More important for the library, Korf advertised it and brought it to
the public attention so that it not only grew in size but in
use and public esteem. By 1860, it was second only to the
Bibliothèque Nationale in all the libraries of Europe. Growth
was steady, if not spectacular, during the remainder of the
nineteenth century, and a new building was completed in 1901.

Another late comer in the national library field in
Europe was the German Imperial Library in Berlin. In 1661
the private library of Frederick William, the Great Elector
of Prussia, was opened to the public, but it was housed in
an almost inaccessible wing of the palace and was not very
large. Before his death, Frederick William had built this
collection to more than 20,000 volumes, all cataloged and
classified by its librarian, Christoph Hendreich. In 1699
the legal deposit system was adopted, which aided the growth
of the library in Prussian-printed works. Under Frederick
William I of Prussia the library grew to about 75,000 volumes by 1740, and under Frederick the Great to about
150,000 volumes by 1790. The library was moved to a new
building in 1780, and after that date the book collection grew
fairly rapidly through the purchase or donation of several major private libraries.

In 1810 the library was placed under the Prussian Department of Culture and thus divorced from the direct control of the King. Growth of the collection was henceforth

more systematic, and until 1831 the national library served
also as the library of the University of Berlin.  From 1817
to 1840 Frederich Wilken was head librarian, and his administration was characterized by remarkable growth of the collection to over 300,000 volumes.  The political unification of
Germany in the 1870s brought new importance to the former
Prussian National Library, which now became the German
Imperial Library.  Since there were other and larger libraries in the new Germany, such as the former national libraries of Bavaria, Saxony and Hanover, the Imperial Library
concentrated on building up its collections of foreign publications from all parts of the world.  By 1890 the library contained over 800,000 volumes, and by 1909, when it moved
into a new building, it had over 1,250,000 works, including
one of the finest collections of incunabula in the world, and
more than 33,000 manuscripts.

There are other state libraries in Germany that in
many respects are also "national" libraries.  For example,
the Bavarian State Library at Munich has a longer history
and at times has been larger than the Prussian State Library.
Formed in the sixteenth century from the library of Duke
Albrecht V of Bavaria, this collection grew with such acquisitions as the Schedel Library from Nuremburg and the J. J.
Fugger collection from Austria.  Many Bavarian monastic and
church libraries were taken into the State Library in the nineteenth century, making it one of the treasure houses of Europe for manuscripts and incunabula.  By the twentieth century it contained over a million volumes.

The Austrian National Library in Vienna also has a
long and interesting history.  Although the "Hofbibliothek"
was founded as such in 1493, it later added two collections
that were even older.  These were the libraries of the University of Vienna, begun in 1364, and of the town of Vienna,
dating from 1466.  The Emperor Maximilian I was largely
responsible for the founding of the national library, but the
royal family continued to build up and maintain various private palace libraries as well.  In the eighteenth century, during the reign of Maria Theresa, some of the royal collections
came into the National Library, adding to those already given
by Emperor Leopold in 1665.  As the library grew, it was
housed in various quarters in Vienna, but in 1623 it was ac-
commodated in a wing of eight rooms in the Hofberg Castle.
Under Charles VI, in 1726, a building was constructed for it,
and although soon found to be inadequate, it was made to
serve with new wings and additions until it was completely

rebuilt early in the twentieth century. The Austrian National
Library has had a long line of illustrious librarians and directors over the years. In the sixteenth century, many important manuscripts were obtained from Austrian monasteries,
in addition to a portion of the library of King Matthias Corvinus of Hungary. Hugo Blotius, as librarian under Maximilian II, greatly enlarged the collection, cataloged it for the
first time, and secured the law of legal deposit to gain for
the national library a copy of each book published in the Empire. In the seventeenth century, part of the valuable Fugger
family library was purchased, adding at one time over fifteen
thousand volumes. About the same time, the library of the
scientist and astronomer Tycho Brahe was acquired. The
eighteenth century saw a new influx of books and manuscripts
from monastery libraries, especially when the Society of
Jesus (Jesuits) was dissolved in central Europe in 1775. The
French Revolution and the Napoleonic conquests threatened
Austria's libraries, and treasures from the National Library
were removed from Vienna several times to avoid capture by
the French. The nineteenth century saw a decline in rate of
growth for the library, partly due to lack of space, but there
was better organization of the collections and greater appreciation by the public. Johann Karabacek, director of the library from 1899 to 1917, saw the library through the rebuilding period and into new quarters, and completely reorganized
and modernized its routines. After World War I, the Imperial Library was renamed the National Library for the new
and smaller Austria, but its holdings in manuscripts and rare
books continued to make it one of the most valuable collections in Europe.

Italy, like Germany, has several national libraries,
including two with the title of National Central Library, at
Rome and Florence. The National Central Library at Florence originated in 1747, with its main book collection the
thirty thousand-volume library donated by Antonio Magliabecchi to the city in 1714. Magliabecchi, a noted bibliophile
and one-time librarian for the Duke of Tuscany, left his
books for the good of the "poor people of Florence." During
the latter half of the eighteenth century, books from several
suppressed monasteries were added to the collection, and during the nineteenth it continued to grow with major gifts and
bequests. By 1859, it contained nearly one hundred thousand
volumes and over three thousand manuscripts, but the nature
of the collection was more that of a rare books museum than
of a public library. After the formation of the Kingdom of
Italy in 1861, the Florence Library was united with the Pala-

tina Library formed by the Grand Duke of Tuscany, and the
resulting collection became the National Library. Growth was
rapid after this date, and by 1930 it contained over two million printed works, twenty-two thousand manuscripts, and
many thousands of letters, music scores, maps and ephem-
era.

The Victor Emmanuel Library at Rome is also designated a National Central Library, and there are six other national libraries located at Bari, Milan, Naples, Palermo,
Turin and Venice. The library in Rome opened in 1876 with
much of its original collection of books seized from monasteries and religious houses closed in 1873. Closely connected with the Victor Emmanuel Library is the Biblioteca
Casanatense, an endowed collection of some three hundred
thousand volumes, strong in medieval history and theology.

The National Library at Milan dates from 1763, when
a private library of Count Carlo Pertusati was purchased by
the government and placed at the service of the public. It
enjoyed the sponsorship of Empress Maria Theresa of Austria and received several large gifts through her interest.
In the nineteenth century it grew steadily, concentrating its
acquisitions in the fields of Italian drama and the history of
Lombardy. The national library in Venice is the famous
Biblioteca Marciana, originally begun with the collection donated by Cardinal Bessarion in 1468. Although it contains
only about eight hundred thousand printed volumes, its manuscript collection of some thirteen thousand volumes is invaluable and includes some of the rarest early medieval codices
in existence. The national library at Turin is one of the
most recent to be so designated, having been formerly a university library formed in 1720. It is housed in an eighteenth-century palace remodeled for library purposes. At
Naples the national library was founded in 1804 and based
on the private collection of Cardinal Seripando. Housed in
a former royal palace, it contains today over one and a half
million volumes and ten thousand valuable manuscripts. Collectively, the national libraries of Italy form both a cultural
heritage and asset that will rank with the national libraries
of any of the western nations.

In Spain and Portugal the national libraries are also
of relatively modern growth. That of Spain dates from the
Royal Library of Philip V, founded in 1712. The king himself gave eight thousand volumes to start the collection. It
grew slowly at first, having only thirty thousand volumes by

1750, but later it received many important gifts, including
some complete libraries, and by 1874 it had over three hundred thousand volumes.  In the 1880s, the Spanish government purchased the library of the Duke of Osuna, with thirty-
two thousand books and twenty-seven hundred manuscripts,
and added it to the National Library.  In Portugal, the National Library at Lisbon was founded in 1796, largely from
the contents of suppressed monasteries.  For this reason, its
collection, even in the twentieth century, is heavily theological, although it is also strong in Portuguese history and literature.

　　The smaller nations of northern Europe all have national libraries, as do those of eastern Europe and the Balkans.  In many ways their histories are inextricably linked
to the great wars that swept Europe in the twentieth century,
and thus they are better treated in Chapter 11 of this work.

　　The national libraries of Europe collectively represent
a magnificent cultural heritage in graphic form.  By definition their role is nationalistic in nature, and these libraries
are devoted to collecting, organizing, and preserving the
graphic records and artifacts reflecting the history of their
respective countries.  They are frequently the most impressive libraries in their respective countries and national librarians like Abbé Bignon in France and Antonio Panizzi in
England must be ranked among the most influential librarians
of all time.

　　The focus of the national libraries has insured their
existence in even the most difficult of times.  They have benefited from the copyright privilege, which provides that one
copy of every book copyrighted in their respective countries
shall be deposited in the national library.  Furthermore, they
have generally been the beneficiary of substantial government
support, and they have been able to demand large-scale philanthropy unknown to most university and public libraries.

　　Their administration has generally reflected their
principal goal--to collect and preserve their cultural heritage.
Thus, great emphasis was placed on the acquisition and organization of materials.  This explains why national libraries
have become known as great research libraries and bibliographic centers, while at the same time earning a reputation
for conservative use policies and a general aloofness from
other library affairs.

Nevertheless, it should be emphasized that by the on-
set of World War I, the first of two wars that were to drastically affect the European library scene, the great national
libraries were well established and could boast the most magnificent collections in Europe.

## European University Libraries Since 1500

By 1500, the universities were well established in
Europe.  Although they differed widely in organization from
country to country and even from institution to institution,
the universities were on the whole a powerful cultural influence in the era that represents the bridge between medieval
and modern.  Libraries also differed considerably from university to university.  In some there were major central or
university libraries; in some the college libraries were all
important, with little or no central collection; in others the
emphasis was on faculty or departmental libraries.  In any
case, the early university communities depended heavily on
the "stationers," or booksellers and book-renters who gathered around every campus.

After 1500, the size of libraries increased considerably.  One reason for this, of course, was the invention of
printing, which made available large numbers of cheap books.
Another reason was the availability of books and manuscripts
from the libraries of suppressed monasteries.  From the
sixteenth century through the nineteenth, in various parts of
Europe at different times, monasteries were closed, and in
many cases their literary treasures eventually found their
way to the shelves of university libraries.  Much of the material thus received was theological, rare and scholarly, but
the important point is that it was preserved in working libraries where it could be put to use.

At the University of Paris, the most important and
the largest of the college libraries was that of the Sorbonne.
From about 2,500 volumes, mostly manuscript, at the end
of the fifteenth century, the Sorbonne collection grew slowly
through periods of successive prosperity and decline paral-
leling the fortunes of the University as a whole.  By the beginning of the French Revolution in 1789, it contained some
25,000 printed volumes and 2,000 manuscripts.  In 1792 the
University was closed, and in 1795 its library was seized
and divided, with the printed volumes going into public libraries and the manuscripts to the Bibliothèque Nationale.

When the University of Paris was reopened after the Napoleonic era, a new Bibliothèque de la Sorbonne was established,
and in 1861 its name was changed to Bibliothèque de la Uni-
versité.  Since then its growth has been steady, so that by
1900 it was approaching a million volumes in all of its departments.  In 1897 the Sorbonne Library was moved into
new quarters with a reading room seating three hundred persons and two stack rooms of five floors each.

        Besides the Sorbonne, which now serves as the library
of the college of arts and sciences, there are the libraries
of the colleges of law, medicine and pharmacy, the Bibliothèque Ste. Geneviève, and the newly created science library,
the Bibliothèque d'Orsay.  The library of the Faculty of Medicine dates from the late fourteenth century, and its holdings
by 1500 numbered only about eleven hundred volumes.  In
1509 the system of chaining the most used volumes to the
reading desks was adopted and was used for nearly three hundred years.  During the French Revolution, the medical library profited to some extent because it was combined with
the library of the Royal Society of Medicine, and the entire
collection moved into a new building to serve the medical college.  By 1900 it contained about 180,000 volumes and was
one of the best medical libraries in Europe.  The library of
the Faculty of Law was formed in 1772 and included some
eighty thousand volumes by 1900, while that of the Faculty of
Pharmacy was not begun until about 1882, but owned fifty
thousand volumes by 1900.

        The oldest library now under the University is that of
Ste. Geneviève, dating from the twelfth century.  Originally
the library of the Abbey of Ste. Geneviève, it remained small
until the sixteenth century.  Numbering some forty thousand
volumes by 1710, it was then a semi-public library, noted as
being open to "all honest men who requested admittance."
Apparently the librarian at that time had staff problems much
as modern librarians do, since he reported that a gift of
books received seventeen years earlier had still not been cataloged.  Though it lost some of its rarer manuscripts during
the French Revolution, Ste. Geneviève's library survived as
a whole, and by 1860 its holdings had grown to more than
160,000 volumes and 5,000 manuscripts.  After years of
separate administration as a government-owned library, it
was placed under the administration of the University of Paris
where its strong collections of history and social sciences
make it a most valuable part of the university library system.

There are some thirty other major college and university libraries in Paris, and several hundred scattered
throughout France.  Most of the early French universities
were church-related and did not survive the Revolutionary
era, so that most modern institutions date from the nineteenth century, particularly the 1870s during the era of the
Third Republic.

Down to the nineteenth century there were really only
two universities in England, Cambridge and Oxford.  The libraries of these two venerable institutions were already centuries old by 1500, but the religious troubles of the following century severely crippled them.  When Henry VIII ordered the dissolution of the monasteries and religious orders
in 1537, it marked the beginning of one of the most tragic
episodes in the history of libraries.  Henry, irritated with
the church in Rome and jealous of the wealth and influence
of the church in England, ordered the monasteries closed
and had their properties divided among the King's friends.
As was so often the case in history, the valuable libraries
of the monasteries suffered destruction simply because they
were housed in an institution under attack.  Consequently,
thousands of invaluable and irreplaceable books and manuscripts were wantonly destroyed.  At first, the university libraries benefited to some extent, with acquisitions from
some of the closed monastery collections, but later their
contents, too, were "censored" and were nearly erased altogether.  Many books were seized by agents of the King and
sold as waste paper, although some volumes found their way
to collectors on the continent and a few were saved by bookmen in England.  In the 1550s, Edward VI's Royal Commis-
sioners almost completely destroyed the remainder of the libraries at Cambridge and Oxford.  At the latter, even the
library shelves were removed and sold.  After this purge
of libraries, about the only ones left in England were those
of the older cathedrals.  A contemporary writer, John Bale,
approved the end of the monastic orders but deplored the destruction of the libraries:

> If there had been in every shire but one single li-
> brary, to the preservation of those noble works,
> it had been well.  But to destroy all without con-
> sideration is and will be unto England forever a
> most horrible infamy.

The central library at Oxford was reborn between
1598 and 1602 when the indefatigable Thomas Bodley refur-

nished it with two library necessities: stacks and books. Bodley had traveled on the continent many times, both as a private citizen and as a governmental envoy, and he knew the best sources of books and manuscripts. Thomas James was selected as the first librarian of the new library that was to become known as the "Bodleian." James issued the first printed catalog of the library, numbering about two thousand titles, in 1605. When Bodley died in 1613, he endowed the library further and its growth since that date has been continuous. Some of the college libraries at Oxford had survived the purges of the mid-sixteenth century, others were reconstituted, and as new colleges were formed, each of them began with a library of its own. Wadham College was founded in 1612, with a library formed the following year. Pembroke College, founded in 1624, was fortunate in having a library from the beginning. The Bodleian Library moved into a new, separate library building in 1612, and several of the college libraries also acquired new quarters, either in separate buildings or in wings or halls of classroom buildings. By 1620 the Bodleian claimed sixteen thousand volumes, and by 1700, nearly thirty thousand. During the seventeenth century, it had obtained two important gifts, a collection of thirteen hundred manuscripts given by Archbishop Laud and a library of eight thousand volumes donated by a lawyer, John Selden. In 1714 a physician, John Radcliffe, endowed a library of science and medicine at Oxford with a building of its own. In the mid-nineteenth century, this library and building were given to the trustees of the Bodleian and became a part of the main library. By 1900 the Oxford University libraries contained over 800,000 volumes and 41,000 manuscripts.

Although the Cambridge University libraries fared better in the sixteenth century than those at Oxford, the central library there still had only 300 printed books and 150 manuscripts in 1582. Moreover, Cambridge had no benefactor such as Sir Thomas Bodley. After the Restoration of Charles II in 1660, Cambridge received some royal attention and the library received several notable gifts and bequests from the King's friends. Henry Lucas left a collection of four thousand volumes to Cambridge in 1666, and Bishop Tobias Rustat gave £1,000 for the purchase of books. In 1755, Cambridge moved its library into a new building, and though its growth was not spectacular until the latter half of the nineteenth century, it contained nearly a million volumes by 1900. The college libraries at Cambridge also grew steadily, several of them acquiring separate buildings in the seventeenth century.

By the late nineteenth century, Trinity College, in a building designed by Sir Christopher Wren, boasted a library of over ninety thousand volumes, but the other college libraries were smaller.  They, too, have received many significant collections over the years, most notably the Samuel Pepys library given to Magdalene College.

Although Oxford and Cambridge were for centuries the only universities in England, other universities were established in Scotland and Ireland.  The University of Glasgow, founded in 1453, had a notable library almost from the beginning, while St. Andrews University, founded about the same time, dates its central library from 1610.  The library at the University of Edinburgh was founded in 1583, largely with funds and books donated by Clement Little, a wealthy merchant-lawyer.  A fourth Scottish university, at Aberdeen, was founded before 1500, but its earliest library records date from the 1630s and its collection never equalled the others in size or importance.  In Ireland, the library of Trinity College in Dublin began with a gift of books by the English Army after a victory over the Irish in the Battle of Kinsale in 1601.  By 1604 this collection contained four thousand volumes, and it grew steadily to become in time the most important library in Ireland.  James Ussher, later primate of Ireland, directed the early growth of the collection, and on his death in 1655 willed his own library of seven thousand volumes and six hundred manuscripts to it.  Other major gifts were received over the years, and by 1900 it contained over three hundred thousand volumes and two thousand manuscripts.

In Germany, several university libraries had been established before 1500, including those at Cologne, Erfurt, Freiburg, Greisswald, Heidelberg, Leipzig, Munich, Rostock and Tübingen.  They were followed in the sixteenth century by Marburg, Würzburg, Königsberg, Wittenberg, and Jena.  Small at first, but supplemented by additional college and institute libraries, they were often formed or enlarged by books acquired from the suppressed monasteries.  Leipzig University's library, for example, was started in 1543 with books taken from a closed Dominican monastery.  The religious wars of the sixteenth century spelled disaster for some libraries, but benefited others.  The seventeenth century brought the Thirty Years' War, when many German libraries were ravaged by invading armies, and by 1700 both universities and libraries had reached a low ebb.  However, the eighteenth century brought better conditions, with Göttingen's

University library growing from 12,000 volumes in 1737 to
150,000 in 1800, for example. Especially important was the
closing of the Jesuit institutions, which resulted in the trans-
ferral of many books to the universities in the 1770s.

Although the French Revolution and Napoleonic wars
brought more disruption to the German universities, they
soon overcame these handicaps. Not only did the central collections increase in size in the nineteenth century, but the
same was true for the many separate college, faculty, and
institute libraries. By 1875 the university libraries at Göttingen, Heidelberg, Leipzig, Breslau and Strassburg contained from 300,000 to 400,000 volumes each, and were
among the best research libraries in the world. Not only
were their book collections excellent, but their librarians
were recognized leaders of the emerging library profession
and provided influential examples for librarians of other
places and later eras to follow. New ideas in librarianship
either originated in German libraries or were quickly adapted
to German needs. After the unification of Germany in the
1870s, the university libraries continued to flourish and new
buildings were soon required to accommodate the rapidly increasing bookstocks.

In Italy, where the medieval university began and
flourished, the period since 1500 has seen less progress than
the auspicious beginnings promised. Although fifteen strong
universities existed in 1500, and several new ones were added in the sixteenth century, a period of decline soon set in
and very few were added before 1900. In most Italian universities, central libraries were not begun until long after
the universities' establishment, and in a few cases none ever
were established. Instead, institute and departmental libraries were forced to provide most library service in the
Italian university, many of which are large and valuable.
Padua did not have a central library until 1629, and Bologna
not until 1712, but later universities, such as those at Mes-
sina and Sassari, had central libraries from the beginning.
Most of the collections have grown more from gifts than from
planned purchases, and this partly explains the lack of popularity of the central collections.

Italian university libraries probably suffered less from
wars in the sixteenth and seventeenth centuries than those of
northern Europe, but their growth was slow. Even by the
nineteenth century, collections usually numbered fewer than
100,000 and in many cases, although these constituted valuable

research materials, they were of little use to the average
student.   Lack of staff, crowded quarters and poor organization also added to Italy's library problems.   Unification
of the nation in the 1860s brought increased emphasis on
education, and most of the universities were taken over as
state institutions.   Steady growth was the rule for their libraries in the early twentieth century, and there were few
losses in World War I.

        In Russia, university libraries are quite a different
story.   There, universities were late in beginning and grew
only slowly until the twentieth century.   Since the Russian
Revolution, however, the university libraries have grown
tremendously, both in size and numbers, and they constitute
today an important part of the overall library program in
the Soviet Union.   The oldest university in Russia proper is
the University of Moscow, founded by M. V. Lomonosov in
1755.   The Universities of Vilnius and Lvov, now in the Soviet Union, but formerly in Lithuania and Poland, were
founded in 1570 and 1681 respectively, and in the nineteenth
century others were founded at St. Petersburg, Kazan,
Kharkov, Kiev, Dorpat and Odessa.   University libraries
were small in the early nineteenth century, but the central
collections were usually supplemented by both student and departmental collections.   Moscow University Library grew
most rapidly, receiving over a hundred major gifts of private
collections.   The University of Kazan Library was fortunate
in having the mathematician Nikolai Lobachevski as librarian
from 1825 to 1835, and he made of it the best-organized library in Russia, complete with full catalog and his own classification system.   In 1834, the library was moved to a new
building and shortly afterward a card catalog was initiated--
one of the earliest in Europe.

        The development of Russian university libraries in the
late nineteenth century is readily illustrated by the rapid
growth of their book collections between 1876 and 1910.   During that period, Moscow University Library grew from some
150,000 to over 300,000 volumes, and other collections grew
as follows: St. Petersburg, 50,000 to 125,000; Dorpat (now
the University of Tartu), 125,000 to 400,000; Odessa, 40,000
to 250,000; and Kazan, 100,000 to 242,000.   By the beginning of World War I, there were thirteen major universities
in Russia with some 3,000,000 volumes in their libraries
for their 43,000 students.   This does not generally count the
books available in libraries other than the central collections.

Poland's university libraries go back well into the fourteenth century, when the University of Cracow was founded in 1364. Called the Jagellonian University since it was organized in 1400 by Ladislas Jagellon, this university has played a prominent role in the history of Poland. Copernicus studied there in the fifteenth century. Although other early universities were established in Lvov and Vilna, now in the Soviet Union, Cracow University remained the major institution of higher education in Poland down to the nineteenth century. A university was established in Warsaw in 1808, and several others were added when Poland was recreated as an independent state in 1918.

Scandinavian universities, like their neighbors in Germany, are strong combinations of both the old and the new. Fortunately, however, their libraries have not suffered as much from wars as those more exposed on the continent proper, and their growth has been more steady over the years. Probably the oldest university in this area is that at Uppsala in Sweden. The University of Uppsala was founded in 1477, and although there was no central university library before 1620, there were the local cathedral library and the libraries of the university student groups or "nations." There were eventually to be thirteen of these student groups, one for each province of Sweden, and there was considerable competition between them in building up libraries. The central library began with a gift by King Gustavus Adolphus of his private library. In the Thirty Years' War, the libraries of several German monasteries were captured by the Swedish armies and presented to the library at Uppsala. With the gift of a private library by the Count Magnus Delagardie in the later seventeenth century, the library at Uppsala reached some 30,000 volumes before 1700. Most of the contents were in Latin until after 1692, when copyright deposit privileges for all books published in Sweden were granted to the University. The student libraries continued to function through the nineteenth century, and by 1900 they contained anywhere from 2,000 to 30,000 volumes each, greatly supplementing the central library.

European university libraries evolved steadily during the period treated here. Originally small collections supporting rather limited academic programs, they came by 1900 to represent the "heart of the university"--collections designed to play a major role in the university's newly defined objective of seeking the truth through original research. The invention of printing and the development of an extensive

and well-organized book trade greatly facilitated the collection of books and other materials.  As collections grew, those
charged with the responsibility of managing the library found
more and more of their time being absorbed in matters relating to the acquisition, organization, and use of their materials.

Books, now readily available, and no longer guarded by "bibliomaniacs," came to be viewed as instruments
to be used rather than simply artifacts to be preserved
or guardedly consulted.  The chained libraries of the early
1600s, where the books were chained to their respective
locations, gave way in time to libraries where both faculty
and students could consult the library's resources in the
building, and in some cases even remove the books from
the library.

The burgeoning size of the collections, and the increased use fostered by liberalized circulation policies, required librarians to spend more and more time considering
questions related to the housing and organization of their collections.   Library organization was generally based on the
provision of a shelflist, or accessions list, as an inventory
record, and the publication of a printed subject catalog for
the use of patrons.  By 1900, the growing size of libraries,
and the increasingly insistent demands of readers for improved access to collections, had given rise to the card cata-
log--usually divided into an alphabetical author catalog supplemented by a classed or topical catalog.

Classification schemes were studied and the latter part
of the nineteenth century witnessed a number of major developments, many of them emanating from the United States.
By 1900 many university libraries could boast their own buildings, but a significant feature of the European scene remained
the existence of a number of more or less autonomous departmental or institute libraries on each campus; European university libraries rarely evidenced the centralization so common to their American counterparts.   Most significant, however, was the emergence of the university as a major center
for research and the education of scholars; a development that
placed increasing responsibilities upon university libraries to
meet the research needs of their patrons.

The Emergence of Public Libraries

 While academic libraries underwent a rather steady
development from "houses of treasures" to utilitarian research centers all over Europe, little of this sort of consistency of development can be discovered for public libraries
during the same period.

 One problem was the different ways in which "public"
was defined in Europe, and for that matter in America, during the period under discussion.  In some countries "public"
simply meant "not private," while in others it came to mean
something more like the modern American and English usage:
open to all on an equal basis, supported by public tax funds,
and administered as a public trust.

 Furthermore, the student of library history must remember that governments have frequently taken a very pro-
nounced interest in public libraries, and their interest has
rarely been altruistic in nature.  That is, they have usually
become involved in public library affairs because they saw
the library as playing a potentially positive role in the process of government.  Again, this involvement was provoked
by widely varying considerations in different European countries.  In many, especially the totalitarian nations, the purpose has been to selectively disseminate information thought
conducive to the continued welfare of the State.  In others,
especially those favoring a democratic political style, the
emphasis has been on the free flow of information.  As a result the development of public libraries in Europe projects
a complex and diverse picture upon the historical canvas.

 Before considering this development, it is necessary
first to define what we mean by "public library."  Certainly
the national libraries were publicly owned in the later centuries, although they may have begun as private libraries of
kings or nobles.  Also, many of the universities, and almost
all of them in later years, were owned by the governments,
so they were public in ownership at least, and many of them
were open to general use.  On the other hand, many private
libraries were open to the public, or at least to individual
scholars.  What we mean today by the public library is the
general library that is not only publicly owned but which is
open to any citizen who desires to use it.  More particularly,
we mean by the public library the municipal or regional circulating library.  In this restricted sense, the public library
does not appear on the European scene until the late nine-

teenth century, and in many respects it is a twentieth-century development.  However, public reference libraries were available in most large cities of Europe throughout the period covered, and no consideration of public library history in Europe can be complete without noticing them.

These public reference libraries began in many ways, but usually as a gift of a private library, through the transfer of a monastery or cathedral library to public use, or as a professional collection.  No matter what its origin, the growth of such libraries between 1500 and 1900 was usually slow.  Where progress was made in times of peace and prosperity, collections were often destroyed or dispersed in times of war.  The libraries were usually poorly housed (although a few of them were in architecturally elegant surroundings) and had inexperienced or uninterested "library keepers" rather than librarians in charge of them.  Hours of opening were few and the contents were of such a scholarly nature that few people used them.  A few librarians saw in the public library something more than an antiquarian collection, but they were rare.

The history of public libraries in France is typical. In the sixteenth century, a number of town libraries were established in the larger cities but they were usually little more than reference collections in the city halls.  Lyons, for example, had a "Bibliothèque de la Ville" in 1530, and Aix-la-Chapelle in 1556.  These were often theological collections given by, or taken from, local monasteries or churches, and were poorly housed and little used.  Paris had several semi-public collections such as the Mazarine Library, and others connected with churches and colleges, but before the French Revolution there was little in the way of public library service elsewhere in France.

The period from 1789 to 1815 saw a social and economic revolution in France accompanying the French Revolution and the Napoleonic era, and the effect on libraries and educational institutions was tremendous.  In 1789, shortly after the Revolution began, all religious libraries were declared national property and the books and manuscripts were confiscated.  In 1792, there was a general confiscation of books belonging to the nobility or other citizens who had fled France after the Revolution began.  It is estimated that as many as eight million books were confiscated and gathered into general book deposits at several points in France.  Although many were lost or damaged in this process, several

hundred thousand of the more valuable volumes ended up in
the Bibliothèque Nationale, while the remainder were set
aside for new district libraries to be established throughout
France. Most of these libraries were established, at least
in name, but the books assigned to them often languished in
warehouses for years, and even when opened the libraries
were poorly managed and rarely used. In some cases the
books were sold and the funds put to other use. By the
1820s the larger French cities had municipal libraries fairly
respectable in size, but they were usually poorly housed.
Amiens, for example, had forty-six thousand volumes housed
in an upper floor of the courthouse, and Rouen had forty
thousand volumes on the second floor of the city hall.

In the 1830s France experimented with the idea of
public libraries for adults located in the public schools, but
this idea did not catch on, and the majority of adults continued to read books purchased or obtained from lending libraries. The subscription library, begun in England by the
eighteenth century, had its counterpart in France, but it was
not very successful outside of Paris and the larger cities.
After 1850, a few publicly supported "popular" libraries were
opened in Paris. By 1908 there were some eighty of these.
There was no central public library, but the collections
were centrally supervised. Most contained only a few thousand volumes and were housed in rented rooms or in unused
areas of municipal buildings. They were open only a few
hours each week and reached only a small portion of the
public.

In 1904 a new stimulus to public library service in
France came with the activities and writings of Eugene Mor-
el, who attempted to introduce in France the American and
English conception of the public library. This resulted in
some increase in the numbers and use of the popular libraries, as for example in the Department of the Seine, outside of Paris, where some fifty communal and village libraries were formed before 1914. They were, however, directed almost entirely toward recreational reading and
reached only a few adults. Shortly before World War I, a
survey of public libraries in France showed that the library
situation there was deplorable. Unfortunately, the war came
before any improvements were made.

Across the Channel in Great Britain, the development
of public libraries has been unlike that in France. The sixteenth century began with the great loss of libraries brought

on by the closing of the monasteries and the dispersal of their collections.  The seventeenth century saw the revival of the university libraries and the growth of a few notable cathedral and private libraries, but little was done in the direction of public library service.  Several municipally owned libraries were founded in the seventeenth century, but they could hardly be called public libraries in the modern sense of the word.  Most of them were the result of books left to the towns upon the death of prominent citizens.  Norwich, for example, had a collection given to the town in 1608, and some of the original volumes are still in the Norwich Free Public Library.  In 1615 a city library was opened in Bristol through gifts and efforts of Dr. Toby Matthew and Robert Redwood.  Leicester dates its public library from 1632, and the Chetham Library in Manchester was a gift of Sir Humphrey Chetham in 1653.  The contents of these early libraries were heavily theological or classical, were not allowed to circulate, and hence were little used.  In some cases they were stored away for years at a time.  In the late seventeenth century, some parish churches made small gift collections available for public use, and the private grammar schools made primitive beginnings toward library collections.

        In the eighteenth century a few publicly owned libraries were added, but the three major additions to library service were the parochial libraries, the subscription or social libraries, and the circulating libraries.  The first were largely the work of one man, Dr. Thomas Bray, who, late in the seventeenth century, had taken part in the formation of the Society for the Propagation of the Gospel in Foreign Parts.  This group was mainly interested in providing ministers for the English colonies in America, but Dr. Bray went further and attempted to supply those ministers and their parishes with books for religious training and inspirational reading.  Finding that many English parishes were in need of the same support, Dr. Bray and his associates founded similar church libraries in parishes throughout England.  These parochial libraries were almost entirely theological, small, and suffered more from neglect than from over-use.  However, they provided the local ministers with some professional reading, and possibly a few of the parishioners with some rather heavy fare.

        The commercial circulating libraries were entirely different.  They were established by booksellers, usually on a purely commercial basis.  Edinburgh is said to have had

a circulating library as early as 1725, and others were definitely in business in London and other large cities before
1750.   These "libraries" would be called rental collections
today, but they provided the general public, or all who could
afford the small fees, with popular reading matter.   By
1800, most of the larger towns in the British Isles had circulating rental libraries, and some of them remained profitable down into the twentieth century.   Rental fees at these
collections were usually small, not over a shilling per month.
William Lane of London was one of the most enterprising of
the circulating library founders.   He established chains of
bookstores with circulating collections in them, and then published books, fiction and popular nonfiction, to fill them.
Charles Edward Mudie established Mudie's Circulating Libraries in the nineteenth century, and had at one time over
25,000 subscribers in London alone.   These libraries, with
their blatant appeal to the romantic and erotic interests of
the lower and middle classes, were labeled "evergreen trees
of diabolical knowledge" by the playwright Sheridan, and drew
increasing criticism from conservative members of elite society who feared that they would contribute to the corruption
of the morals of the masses.   Paperbacks and public libraries virtually replaced the commercial circulating libraries in the twentieth century, but the "two-penny library"
was still popular in the early 1900s.

       The latter part of the eighteenth century saw the de-
velopment of the subscription library, a natural extension of
earlier and more informal "book clubs."   A group of the
more well-to-do readers of a community would form a "lyceum" or "reading society" with a library for the use of
members only.   Shares in the library were frequently sold,
and fees were paid by the month or year.   The quality of the
reading matter was generally more serious than that of the
circulating libraries.   The Society Library of Dumfries,
Scotland, was begun around 1745, and the Liverpool Lyceum
about 1758.   By 1800 the subscription libraries were common.   They were usually housed in rented halls or rooms,
with a keeper on duty at certain hours, but by the mid-nineteenth century many had acquired their own buildings.   Some
of them grew to respectable size and provided a large part
of the "public library" service available before 1850.   One of
the most famous and successful of the subscription libraries
is the London Library, established in 1841 and boasting Car-
lyle among its founders.   At the turn of the century it contained over 500,000 volumes and still thrives today.   Another
interesting survivor is the Leeds Library, founded in 1768 and
limited to 500 subscribers throughout its long existence.

For the benefit of the workers and small tradesmen
who could not afford the subscription libraries, benevolent
individuals and groups formed "mechanics' institutes" that included in their programs libraries of vocational and inspirational reading matter available at small rental fees.   Fiction
and more popular non-fiction volumes were later added.
Probably the first of these libraries was the Birmingham
Artisans' Library, formed in 1795.   The Glasgow Mechanics'
Institute, formed in 1823, not only had a library but conducted classes and later became a recognized educational institution.   Other mechanics' libraries were founded at Edinburgh, 1821; Perth and Liverpool, 1823; and Aberdeen and
London, 1824.   The idea spread to the smaller towns, and
by 1850 there were reported to be nearly seven hundred in
the British Isles.   Some of them lasted only a few decades,
but many were eventually to become public libraries, or their
books were given to local public libraries after the passage
of the Public Libraries Act.   The role of the subscription libraries and the mechanics' institute libraries as forerunners
of the free public library cannot be overlooked.   They demonstrated the desirability of relatively large and readily ac-
cessible libraries to large numbers of people.   At the same
time, the inadequacy of voluntary support for library service
was becoming readily apparent to library advocates.   The
audience of the mechanics' institute libraries was limited,
but it probably included a majority of those who would have
been interested in using a free public library, and they
helped in promoting the idea of library service and in providing a ready-made reading public when free libraries were
established.

Modern public library history began in Great Britain
in 1847, when Parliament passed an act appointing a Committee on Public Libraries to consider the necessity of establishing libraries through the nation.   That famous committee, ably presided over by William Ewart and vigorously supported by public library pioneer and library historian Edward
Edwards, reported in 1849; noting the poor condition of library service then available, it recommended the establishment of free public libraries in all parts of the country.   The
Public Libraries Act, passed in 1850, allowed cities with
populations exceeding 10,000 to levy taxes for the support of
public libraries, and subsequent laws extended the act to
Scotland and Ireland and to smaller towns.   In 1870 the Public School Law, which made communities responsible for the
establishment and maintenance of free public schools, increased the number of readers and consequently the demand

and need for free public libraries.  By 1877 more than
seventy-five cities had taken advantage of the Library Act to
establish free lending libraries, and by 1900 the number had
passed three hundred.  Andrew Carnegie's philanthropy provided library buildings for many of the municipal libraries,
and in fact the buildings were sometimes better than the collections they housed.

Although public libraries in Great Britain were relatively poorly supported and understaffed until after World
War I, they met a definite need, and as generations of school
children accustomed to public library service grew up, both
use and support of the public libraries increased.  Fortunately, the growth of public libraries came at a time when
many large private libraries were being broken up, and many
of the latter were bought by or given to public institutions.
In this manner some of the public libraries in the larger
cities, although founded late in the nineteenth century, came
to have collections that rival many of the older collections
on the continent and compare favorably with university and
research libraries.

Since 1500 Germany has been the home of some of
the world's greatest libraries, but although many of them
have been owned by the government and open to limited public use, they have not been public libraries in the modern
sense.  Probably one reason has been that Germany was divided into a number of small kingdoms and principalities until 1870, and each of these governmental units tended to promote one large "national" library rather than several smaller
public ones.  Also, library tradition in Germany has always
been directed toward the scholarly research library, whether
university or public, and the English-American idea of a
popular circulating library has been slow to win acceptance.

Municipally owned libraries, however, had an early
beginning in Germany.  Several had already been established
before 1500, but after that date town libraries were established in Ulm (1516), Magdeburg (1525), Lindau (1528), Hamburg (1529), Augsburg (1537), Eisleben (1542), Luneberg
(1558), Grimma (1569), and Danzig (1580).  These "libraries"
were usually small collections of theological works, poorly
cared for and little used.  Martin Luther, in 1524, urged
that public libraries be established to encourage the spread
of Protestantism, and many small collections were instituted
in churches and town halls.  In the seventeenth century there
was little progress in German public libraries, and those

already established were often neglected.  During the Thirty
Years' War, which caused great loss of life and property,
many libraries changed hands, but the small public collections were hardly worth taking as spoils of war.  More royal libraries were established in Germany during this century,
and although they began as private collections they often
ended up as public reference libraries.

Eighteenth-century Germany saw the development of
what were then the greatest libraries in Europe, in the royal or court libraries and in the universities.  Concentrating
on scholarly materials, these libraries secured and preserved large numbers of books, pamphlets and manuscripts
on all subjects.  As monasteries were closed or declined
and lost interest in their libraries, their books and manuscripts were frequently obtained by the scholarly libraries
and thus preserved for future generations.  Many magnificent
private collections were also bequeathed or given to the
court and university libraries.  The scholarly reference library became the standard in Germany during this century,
and popular libraries for the general reading public were
never seriously attempted.

In the nineteenth century, a beginning toward popular
circulating libraries was made.  The town of Grossenhain,
for example, opened a library for the circulation of books to
the general public in 1828, and about the same time systems
of village libraries were begun in Saxony and Wurtemburg.
In the 1840s, an attempt was made to open popular libraries
(Volksbibliotheken) in Prussia, and by 1850 four such libraries were opened in Berlin.  After 1870 the Society for
Extension of Popular Education promoted popular libraries,
and a few were established with support from both the Society and the local government.  Some industries established
popular factory libraries for their employees.  A public circulating library was opened in Kiel in the 1890s, and by
1900 there were twenty-eight popular libraries in and around
Berlin, ranging in size from three to ten thousand volumes
and appealing largely to the workers.  In 1907 the Berlin
Municipal Library was formed to act as a central library for
the many popular libraries already functioning, and it grew
steadily until the coming of World War I.  Little attention
was paid to public library service for children, although there
was a public children's library in Berlin.  Elsewhere in Germany before 1914, small popular libraries were established
by educational and charitable organizations, but it was difficult to obtain municipal support for them.  In Hamburg,

where the Stadtsbibliothek was a valuable reference library
of over 600,000 volumes, a separate Volksbibliothek was established only in 1899.

By the mid-twentieth century the Russians were probably the most library-minded people in the world if their library statistics can be believed.  However, this has not always been the case.  As of 1500, Russia was not far removed from its period of Mongol control and was still deep
in medieval feudalism, far behind even eastern Europe in cultural progress.  Russia had experienced neither a Renaissance nor a Reformation and was easily two hundred years
behind western Europe in general development as of 1800.
Public libraries in the modern sense of the word were unknown until late in the nineteenth century, and even church
and monastery libraries were scarce.  Odessa had a municipal library founded in 1837, there was one in Kazan in 1866,
and in Kharkov by 1886.  These were the non-circulating, research type of public collection.  Some semi-public society
libraries were also opened in the larger cities, while in rural areas, by the 1890s, public schools were maintaining
small collections of books for adult readers.  The library at
Kazan, for example, was supported by a private organization
although it was open as a public reference library until the
1920s, when it became the basis for the national library of
the Tatar Republic.  In 1880 the Russian government statistics reported 145 public libraries throughout the nation, containing together almost a million volumes.  By 1905 the figure reported had increased to five thousand free public libraries, but it was noted that many of them had very few
books, some as few as fifty volumes.  By 1915 there were
reported to be eight hundred public libraries in Russia large
enough to be in charge of a full-time "library keeper," with
more than twenty thousand smaller book collections at the
community level.  The municipal library in Odessa at this
time had some 200,000 volumes, while that at Kiev had over
600,000.  Obviously, the idea of public library service in
Russia is not solely Communist, but neither was censorship
and state control.  Both of these enemies of free libraries
were strong under the Czars, and freedom of speech and
press were only slightly greater before 1917 than after.

Elsewhere in the Soviet-dominated world the library
pattern is much the same, but development has usually been
on a slower and smaller scale than in Russia.  In Poland,
for example, the eighteenth-century nobles began to collect
private libraries, many of which became large and valuable.

Some of them eventually became parts of public collections, but the dismemberment of Poland in the 1790s set back cultural development, and for more than a century the Polish people were minorities in Russia, Germany and Austria. The larger Polish cities, such as Warsaw, Poznan and Lublin, established public reference libraries toward the end of the nineteenth century, often with the aid of societies interested in the preservation of the Polish language and culture. Warsaw's public library, for example, was formed by a library society in 1907, and was not officially converted into a municipal library until 1928.

In Bulgaria and Rumania there was even less in the way of public libraries before the twentieth century. About 1860, public reading clubs were started in Bulgaria as a part of the general resistance movement to Turkish domination, and after independence was achieved in 1878, some of these grew into small public libraries. The largest public collections before 1900 were those in Sofia and Philoppopoli, with about 25,000 volumes each.

In Rumania modern library history began in 1831 with the establishment of a public library in Bucharest. Progressive library legislation was included in the general reform laws passed in 1864, but library development was slow until after 1900. From then until 1945, public libraries were centered in the few larger cities, but these were of the scholarly reference type rather than circulating collections.

Italian libraries are a different story. The great Renaissance libraries, private and public, led the way for all European libraries into the modern era, but unfortunately library progress slowed considerably in Italy after the sixteenth century and did not keep up with northern Europe. Many of the large private collections ended up in libraries open to the public, but they were often museums of books rather than public libraries. Some such public reference libraries were established in the seventeenth century, but more in the eighteenth and nineteenth. Although these collections sometimes contained valuable manuscripts and rare books, they were usually short of funds and poorly staffed, so that their public services were almost nonexistent. In the late nineteenth century some of them became more conscious of serving the public and opened reading rooms. By 1900 Bologna's public library had some 200,000 volumes, with others at Brescia, Ferrara, Padua and Palermo, for example, being only slightly smaller. The suppression of monasteries

in the 1860s added to the bookstock of many of these "biblioteches communales."

Popular reading rooms and circulating libraries in
Italy are more a product of the twentieth century. By 1908
there were some three hundred small "biblioteches communales" and "biblioteches popolares" and in that year a
Federation of Popular Libraries was established to promote
public libraries. Some progress was made, but World War
I intervened, and even in the 1920s the popular libraries
were usually housed in wings of public buildings or in upstairs rooms over stores or offices.

In northern Europe, Belgium and the Netherlands have
libraries that resemble those in both England and Germany.
Like Germany, both Belgium and Holland had important research libraries belonging to the cities during the seventeenth and eighteenth centuries. However, they were not circulating libraries and in many cases were hardly ever open
to the general public. Amsterdam's municipal library, for
example, dates from 1578, and one in Antwerp was founded
in 1609. In the latter half of the nineteenth century, popular libraries were established in the larger towns, but they
were more often used by children than adults and were open
only a few hours a day. Their bookstocks were usually only
a few thousand volumes. Belgian libraries suffered much in
both World Wars, and rebuilding after them was difficult.
The public library at Dendermonde, for example, was founded
in 1850 and contained about 28,000 volumes when it was destroyed in 1914 by the German armies.

The libraries of the Scandinavian countries are considered last not as a matter of accident or even of geography. They may well be considered almost in a separate
category because their public libraries are probably the best
in Europe. The reason for this is partly the relatively compact population of the countries, but also the manner in
which the Scandinavian peoples approach the problem of libraries and the enthusiasm with which they have advanced library service in the last century. They combine the fervent
appreciation of the value of books that is so noticeable in the
Communist countries with the freedom of the press and the
freedom to read that is the earmark of the western democ-
racies, and the result is effective library service.

In Denmark modern public libraries date from the
1880s when Andreas Steenberg began a campaign for public

libraries operated along American lines. A municipal free
library was established in Frederiksberg in 1887, and other
public libraries followed, so that by 1909 there were some
fifty public libraries in the country, with about seven hundred branches and stations. A central public library that
was established in Aarhus in 1902 had about 200,000 volumes by 1910, and this library came to operate as a central clearinghouse on public library matters and as an ad-
visor for small public libraries elsewhere in Denmark. In
1905 an association for promoting public library service was
formed, and this group did much to sponsor and develop library service in villages and rural areas.

Norway's modern public libraries also began in the
nineteenth century, in many cases with small private reading societies and lending libraries. Later, parish libraries
were organized, often supported by private gifts and administered by the clergy. A few Norwegian public libraries
date from the late eighteenth century. The Deichmann Library in Oslo, for example, was founded in 1780 as a privately endowed free library. In 1898 it was reorganized
along modern lines by Haakon Nyhuus, who had received library training in the United States. A public library was
opened in Arendal in 1832, and one in Bergen in 1874. In
1901 a national commission to study the use and needs of
public libraries resulted in the appointment of a national library inspector and in the passage in 1905 of a public library law. By 1910 there were some eight hundred public
library outlets in Norway, mostly small village libraries
with a few larger ones in the major towns. Traveling book-
boxes brought popular reading to fishermen and workmen in
more sparsely populated areas, and supplementary reading
to the children in the rural schools.

There were some public libraries, or at least publicly owned book collections, in Sweden prior to 1800, but
neither these nor a movement for public library service in
the 1830s achieved much in the way of public circulating libraries. In the 1840s there was government aid for small
public collections in the schools, and privately sponsored libraries were also opened to the public subject to inspection
by district school inspectors. The 1850s brought the establishment of small public libraries similar to those in England, and more of the privately sponsored or society libraries. Some industries, particularly in the lumbering
areas, provided small popular libraries for their employees.
By 1900 Sweden had some 7,500 library outlets in schools

and public collections, and central county libraries were being formed to supervise the many small libraries.  Grants
of government funds for the support of public libraries as
such came in 1905, while the first modern children's library
was established in 1911.

In summary then, public library development in Europe between 1500 and 1917 was erratic, characterized by
some three and one-half centuries of indifference and less
than a century of active interest.  The nature and extent of
public library development in the various parts of Europe
varied greatly, and was to become even more confusing with
the rapidly changing political situation which developed out of
the two World Wars.  Nevertheless, by 1914 most European
nations had arrived at the point where they agreed that some
form of publicly supported library service was desirable.

Governments cited a number of reasons for this consensus, including the need to provide a harmless form of
recreation for the masses; the need for controlling the
sources of information available to the people; the need to
compete effectively with the circulating libraries and their
high circulation of "unhealthy" fiction; or the need to provide
the free access to information required if a democratic republic was to function properly.  But once the consensus on
the need for public libraries was achieved, a number of other factors influenced the extent to which libraries were developed in the various European nations--most significantly,
the economic resources available, the extent of literacy,
the political stability of the country, and the commitment of
the government to libraries.  The ways in which these factors, plus the horrible destruction of two World Wars, conspired to influence public library development in Europe after 1917 will be discussed in a later chapter.

## Private Book Collectors and the
## Rise of European Libraries

Our attention in this book must focus increasingly on
the ever more complex and extensive development of "public
libraries"--that is, those libraries publicly owned, or at
least open to the public with or without restrictions on their
use.  However, the strictly private library is also a part of
library history and must be briefly considered, if for no
other reason than the significant role the private collector
and the fruits of his labors played in the foundation of many
of the great libraries discussed in this chapter.

Several points deserve mention. The private collector with means often had a better chance to build up a well-rounded library or a definitive subject collection than did a public library. With no "public" to serve, the private library could be built to a point nearing perfection and maintained at that point without fear of loss or wear. Unfortunately, the death of a book collector often resulted in the sale or dispersal of his library; only rarely did a family maintain an ancestral book collection through several generations. When the private library was dispersed, it might be given or sold to a public library, or it might find its way into the hands of other collectors. Eventually, however, many of the finest private libraries were obtained and preserved intact in public hands.

While the medieval book collector was most often a member of the nobility or clergy, many of the great collectors after 1500 were wealthy merchants or professional men. However, book collection has not been the monopoly of any one group, and people from all walks of life have been ardent bibliophiles. The development of printing undoubtedly broadened the field of book collecting; with the lower cost of the printed book, virtually every educated man was in a position to collect a small library and most of the writers and thinkers of the period did so. At least part of the stimulus for book collecting came with the Renaissance as it spread northward from Italy, and although it may be said that modern learning relied most heavily on the books in publicly owned libraries, it certainly was encouraged by the widespread availability of books in private libraries.

As we have already demonstrated, great book collectors played a major role in the development of many of Europe's most significant libraries. What, for instance, might have been the nature of the British Museum collections without the addition of the Cotton, Sloan, and Harleian libraries. It is difficult to imagine the great national libraries achieving such significance without the acquisition of the many private collections that became available to them either through purchase, confiscation, or benefaction. The debt owed by society in general to private collectors of books and manuscripts can hardly be overestimated. Although their range of interest is often narrow and their holdings are for years removed from the public view, the end results of their collecting have proven to the benefit of all mankind. Whether donated or sold as a unit to a public or research library, or split up and resold to other collectors, books have not been destroyed. Moreover, they are often kept in far better condition in private libraries than they would have been in public ones. Without the prodigious efforts and costly collecting, and even the personal vanity of the book collector, many of our most valuable literary treasures would have most certainly been lost.

## Additional Readings

The following list of readings represents only a small portion of the literature dealing with the four centuries of European library history treated in this chapter. The works cited do, however, represent some of the best and most recent work available, and the serious student will find them good guides to the more specialized literature. Those preferring to make a detailed review of the literature on European libraries should see James G. Olle, Library History, Second edition, London, 1971, which is very useful for the English scene, and each issue of Library History (London, the Library Association) contains a detailed essay on recent publications on European library history.

Aitken, W. R. A History of the Public Library Movement in Scotland to 1955. Glasgow, 1971.

Allred, J. R. "The Purpose of the Public Library: The Historical View," Library History 2 (1972): 185-204.

Altick, R. D. The English Common Reader: A Social History of the Mass Reading Public, 1800-1900. Chicago, 1957.

Assmann, K. Sächsische Landesbibliothek Dresden, 1556-1956. Leipzig, 1956.

Bostwick, A. E. Popular Libraries of the World. Chicago, 1933.

Burton, M. Famous Libraries of the World. London, 1937.

Bužas, L. Geschichte der Universitats-Bibliothek München. Weisbaden, 1972.

Chapman, M. "American Ideas in the German Public Libraries: Three Periods," Library Quarterly 41 (1971): 35-53.

Clarke, J. A. "Abbe Jean-Paul Bignon, 'Moderator of the Academie and Royal Librarian'," French Historical Studies 8 (1973): 213-35.

_____. "French Libraries in Transition," Library Quarterly 37 (1967): 366-72.

_____. Gabriel Naudé, 1600-1653. Hamden, Conn., 1970.

_____. "A Search for the Principles of Book Selection, 1550-1700," Library Quarterly 41 (1971): 216-22.

Cushing, G. F. "Books and Readers in 18th Century Hungary," East European Review 47 (1969): 57-77.

Dana, J. C. and H. Kent, eds. Literature of Libraries in the 17th and 18th Century. New York, 1907.

Danton, J. P. Book Selection and Collections: A Comparison of German and American University Libraries. New York, 1963.

Darnton, R. "Reading, Writing, and Publishing in Eighteenth-century France: A Case Study in the Sociology of Literature," Daedalus 100 (1971): 214-56.

Davis, D. G. "Problems in the Life of a University Librarian: Thomas James, 1600-20," College and Research Libraries 31 (1970): 43-49.

Edwards, E. Free Town Libraries: Their Formation, Management, and History in Britain, France, Germany and America. London, 1863.

_____. Lives of the Founders of the British Museum... London, 1870.

Ellis, A. Library Service for Young People in England and Wales, 1830-1970. Oxford, 1971.

Esdaile, A. J. K. National Libraries of the World: Their History, Administration, and Public Services. London, 1957.

Finlayson, C. B. and S. M. Simpson. "The Library of the University of Edinburgh: The Early Period, 1580-1710," Library History 1 (1967): 2-23.

Fischer, H. "Conrad Gesner (1516-1565) as Bibliographer and Encyclopedist," The Library 21 (1966): 269-81.

Griest, G. L. Mudie's Circulating Library and the Victorian Novel. Bloomington, Ind., 1970.

Hamlyn, H. M. "Eighteenth Century Circulating Libraries in England," The Library 1 (1946): 197-222.

Harris, M. H. "David Hume: Scholar and Librarian," Library Quarterly 36 (1966): 88-98.

Harrison, K. C. Libraries in Scandinavia. Second Edition. London, 1969.

Hartmann, K. J. Geschichte der Göttinger Universitats-Bibliothek. Göttigen, 1937.

Hassenforder, J. Development Comparé des Bibliothèques en France, en Grande-Bretagne et aux Etats-Unis dans la seconde moitié du XIXe Siècle (1850-1914). Paris, 1967.

Hobson, A. Great Libraries. New York, 1970.

Irwin, R. The English Library: Sources and History. London, 1966.

_____. The Heritage of the English Library. London, 1964.

Jackson, S. L. "Bodley and the Bodleian; Collections Use and Administration," Library Quarterly 39 (1969): 253-70.

_____. "Highlights of Continental Librarianship, 1680-1787," Journal of Education for Librarianship 11 (1971): 344-50.

_____. "Pioneer Librarianship Thinking in the Early Nineteenth Century," International Library Review 3 (1971): 67-76.

_____. "Tax-supported Library Service to the People: Why Was 1876-1877 the Nodal Point?" _International Library Review_ 4 (1972): 417-21.

Kaufman, P. _Libraries and Their Users_. London, 1969.

Kelly, T. _Early Public Libraries: A History of Public Libraries in Great Britain Before 1850_. London, 1966.

_____. _History of Public Libraries in Great Britain, 1845-1965_. London, 1973.

Martin, H. J. _Livres, Pouvoirs et Société à Paris au XVII$^e$ Siècle (1598-1701)_. Geneva, 1969.

Miller, E. _Prince of Librarians, The Life and Times of Antonio Panizzi..._ London, 1967.

_____. _That Noble Cabinet: A History of the British Museum_. London, 1974.

Minto, J. _A History of the Public Library Movement in Great Britain and Ireland_. London, 1932.

Montgomery, J. W. "Luther and Libraries," _Library Quarterly_ 32 (1962): 144-47.

Mumby, F. A. and I. Norrie. _Publishing and Bookselling_. London, 1974.

Munford, W. A. _Edward Edwards, 1812-1886: Portrait of a Librarian_. London, 1963.

_____. "George Birkbeck and Mechanics Institutes," in _English Libraries, 1800-1850_. London, 1958, pp. 33-58.

_____. _Penny Rate: Aspects of British Public Library History_. London, 1951.

Neveux, P. L. "Origines de nos Bibliothèques Provinciales," _Revue des Bibliothèques_ 39 (1932): 140-71.

Newman, L. M. _Leibniz (1646-1716) and the German Library Scene_. London, 1966.

Norris, D. M. _A History of Cataloging and Cataloging Methods, 1100-1850.   London, 1939.

Paunel, E.   Die Staats-Bibliothek zu Berlin .... 1661-1871.
    Berlin, 1965.

Predeek, A.   A History of Libraries in Great Britain and
    North America, tr. by Lawrence Thompson.   Chicago,
    1947.

Reichmann, F.   "Three Hundred Years of the Prussian
    State Library," Library Quarterly 32 (1962): 225-30.

Riberette, P.   Les Bibliothèques Françaises Pendant la
    Revolution (1789-1795).   Paris, 1970.

Serrurier, C.   Bibliothèques de France, Description de
    leurs Fonde et Histoire de leur Formation.   The Hague,
    1946.

Trenkler, E.   "History of the Austrian Nationalbibliotek,"
    Library Quarterly 17 (1947): 224-31.

Varma, D. P.   The Evergreen Tree of Diabolical Knowl-
    edge.   Washington, 1972.

Wehmer, C.   "History of German University Libraries,"
    Library Trends 12 (1964): 496-506.

Wormald, F. and C. E. Wright, eds.   The English Library
    before 1700: Studies in Its History.   London, 1958.

## Chapter 10

# LIBRARIES IN AMERICA TO 1850

## Latin American Library Beginnings

Long before the establishment of the Jamestown Colony in Virginia or the arrival of the earliest settlers on the St. Lawrence, there was already a highly developed Spanish culture in parts of Latin America. A number of the earliest explorers of that area are known to have packed a few precious books among their belongings when making the hazardous journey to the New World. However, by far the most bookish of the early settlers were the churchmen--especially the Jesuits and Franciscans--who lived and worked in parts of Latin America as early as the middle of the 16th century.

Scholars have provided us with detailed studies of the rather extensive development of libraries in colonial Latin America, and their work clearly demonstrates the way in which the private collections, just as in Europe, came in time to form the nucleus of the first university and public libraries. For instance, in 1767, when the Jesuits were expelled from Latin America, their many fine libraries eventually found their way into the university and national libraries.

The eighteenth century, however, represents a troubled time for most parts of Latin America, and we have been able to discover scant evidence of a "public" library development during this period. It seems clear that books were available in libraries, and for sale, at the universities in Peru, Argentina, Guatemala, and Cuba, but specific details are difficult to discover. Thus Latin American library history for the most part begins with the nineteenth century and the end of colonialism.

Most of the Latin American countries which achieved independence formed national libraries early in their existence, partly as a matter of national pride.  These collections were often made up largely of sequestered private or religious libraries and, once gathered together in some public building, they were largely forgotten.  Throughout much of the nineteenth century they remained more like museums than libraries.  Brazil's national library was founded in 1810, but as late as 1900 it had only about 200,000 volumes. Chile's national library dates from 1813, and Argentina's from 1810, while Uruguay claims 1816, Venezuela 1833, Peru 1821, and Mexico 1833, as the dates of their earliest national collections.  Some university libraries claim eighteenth-century beginnings, such as those of the University of Havana, 1728, and the Central University of Quito, 1787. The early nineteenth century saw more universities established, and also a trend toward public libraries, especially in the larger colonies.  Brazil established state libraries, in the 1850s and 1860s, notably those at Aracaju for Sergipe State in 1851, and at Curitiba for Parana State in 1857. These remained generally small, and often combined functions of archives and library at the same time.  Emphasis was largely on preservation rather than use, and lack of interested librarians kept the nineteenth-century Latin American library poorly organized and uninviting.  Foundations were being laid, however, for a few significant libraries of the future, especially in the national collections.

Private Libraries in the United States

In the nineteenth century the Rev. John Milburn reflected that:

> Men must have bread before books.  Men must
> build barns before they establish colleges.  Men
> must learn the language of the rifle, the axe and
> the plough, before they learn the lessons of Gre-
> cian and Roman philosophy.

What the Reverend Milburn failed to note was that while bread was considered vital for the preservation of the body, a few books were often viewed as equally vital for the preservation of the soul.  It is clear that many pioneer families would have deemed it foolish in the extreme to set out for a strange and faraway country without their Bibles, hymnals, and prayer books.  Furthermore, while the rifle, axe, and

plough were essential tools of the farmer and hunter, books
were considered equally essential tools by the many lawyers,
doctors, preachers, and educators who settled in early
America.

It is also obvious that while books were considered
necessities by many pioneer families, people did find it im-
perative to institute certain economies when they moved to
the new world, or when they followed the sun toward the
progressively retreating American frontiers of the eighteenth
and nineteenth centuries.   Thus we should not be surprised
to find that the libraries found in the English colonies of
America were generally small and "purposive" in nature.

Small private libraries existed from the very first in
the Pilgrim and Puritan colonies in Massachusetts.   Of the
Pilgrims, the Rev. William Brewster left a library of over
four hundred volumes when he died in 1643, many of them
obtained after he came to the New World.   Governor William
Bradford owned some eighty volumes; the Plymouth minister
Ralph Partridge had almost as many, and even Captain Miles
Standish owned some fifty books.   Most of the Pilgrims'
books were religious, but there was also some history, travel and political science, a few literary titles and classics,
and a few practical works such as those on agriculture and
military science owned by Standish.   Governor Bradford's
library contained some works in French, while William
Brewster owned some volumes in Latin and a Hebrew grammar.   Of seventy wills of Plymouth citizens still extant for
the period 1620 to 1690, only twelve failed to mention books.

Among the Puritans on Massachusetts Bay, the ministers and doctors usually had small private libraries, ranging
from a dozen volumes to as many as several hundred.   Governor John Winthrop brought a collection of both legal and
religious works, but its size and specific contents are not
as well known as those of some of his followers.   In 1669,
the Reverend Benjamin Bunker left about eighty volumes of
religious works, while his contemporary, Jonathan Mitchell,
left one hundred eight volumes of religion, seventy-four of
classics, and eleven of science, mostly medicine.   Other
professional men of seventeenth-century New England usually
had small book collections at least, but this is also true of
many merchants, farmers, skilled craftsmen, and even fishermen.   Generally, the smaller the number of books owned,
the more religious their nature, and the owner of a single
volume usually possessed a Bible.   Wills and inventories

of estates are the most readily available sources of information concerning colonial book possessions, but wide acquaintance with books is also apparent in the surviving letters,
speeches and papers of the early settlers.

The largest library in mid-seventeenth century New
England was probably that of Governor John Winthrop, Jr.,
of Connecticut.  As early as 1640 this collection numbered
over a thousand volumes, and after his death in 1676 it was
preserved and enlarged by his son and grandson.  Remnants
of the collection given to the New York Society Library in
the nineteenth century indicate that it was cosmopolitan in nature, with books in Latin, French, Dutch, Italian, Greek and
Spanish as well as English, and on subjects as varied as religion, history, travel, philosophy, law, and literature.

In the latter years of the seventeenth century, the
largest New England private library was that of Cotton Mather, the author and minister.  His father, Increase Mather,
had owned some 675 volumes in 1664, but many of them were
lost in a fire in 1676.  Cotton Mather's library contained
about 2,500 volumes by 1700, and before his death in 1728
it had reached some 4,000 volumes.  Both of these libraries
were largely theological, but the son's in particular contained
many volumes of history, geography, and philosophy, with a
few titles in scientific fields.  Since he wrote over four hundred books and pamphlets himself, it is easy to see that he
not only collected books but made good use of them as well.

Although the libraries mentioned were exceptional in
size, small collections were not unusual in the New England
home.  To aid the buyers of books, there were booksellers
in Boston by the 1670s, and both before and after that date
many New Englanders ordered books from England.  In addition, itinerant book hawkers visited the smaller towns, carrying a few books in their packs and taking orders for others.

Seventeenth-century Virginia also had its private libraries, especially in the homes of government officials,
lawyers, ministers and planters.  Surviving wills show that
blacksmiths, carpenters and ship captains also owned books.
Robert Hunt, Oxford graduate and chaplain with the first colony in 1607, brought books with him which were burned in a
fire in 1608.  John Wingfield, one of the earliest arrivals at
Jamestown, brought books with him, and John Pory, Secretary to the Colony a decade later, spoke highly of his books
as "being in solitude the best and choicest company." Thomas

Bargrave, a minister, left his library for the use of a proposed Indian school in 1621, and James Lobe, a former
ship's surgeon, left in his will a "cedar chest full of books."
Some women also left libraries, although the collections may
have been made by their husbands.  Mrs. Sara Willoughby
left a library in 1673 that was largely religious in nature,
but included Aesop's <u>Fables</u> and a practical title:  <u>Directions</u>
<u>for Planting Mulberry Trees</u>.  Toward the end of the seven-
teenth century, larger book collections could be found in Virginia.  In 1690, William Fitzhugh's library was kept in a
room which he called his "Study of Books," and it contained
works on history and medicine as well as law.  Ralph Wor-
meley, the Secretary of the Colony who died in 1701, left
375 books, quite general in nature, while the Presbyterian
minister, Francis Makemie, left a library of 992 titles, some
of them "handsomely bound."  Wills mentioning books, sometimes by list of titles, sometimes merely as "parcels of old
books," are numerous for the period after 1650, and one
writer estimates that there must have been a thousand book
collections worthy of being called private libraries in seventeenth-century Virginia.  Subjects included in the libraries
ranged from theology to farming and from the classics to almanacs.  They indicate a high degree of literacy among at
least a part of the population, but it should be pointed out
that probably half of the adult population, as of 1700, was illiterate.

     In the eighteenth century the private library became
more common, particularly among professional people, government officials, and large plantation owners in the South.
In New England there were such noted private libraries as
that of Thomas Prince, a Boston minister whose avocation
was the study of New England history.  He formed an important library of books and manuscripts relating to New
England and deposited them in the Old South Church in Boston before his death in 1758.  These books later became the
property of the Boston Public Library.  In Newport, Rhode
Island, the minister and lawyer, Abraham Redwood, built up
a private library that later formed the nucleus of the Redwood Library in 1745.  James Franklin had a small library
in his Boston newspaper office around 1725.  It was stronger
than usual in the relatively contemporary English drama, poetry and essays.  In the middle colonies, John Sharp of New
York built up a large collection of books which he gave to
the city in 1713 for public use.  It was largely theological
and there is little record of its use until it became a part
of the New York Society Library in 1754.  The Reverend

Alexander Innes left a sizable collection of books at his death
in 1713, and these were donated to the Anglican churches of
New Jersey and New York. Samuel Johnson, an early president of King's College in New York, built his library around
English literature, the classics and history. One of the finest private libraries in New Jersey was that of Richard
Stockton, a signer of the Declaration of Independence. Because of his patriotic activities he was a marked man for the
British and his home and library were destroyed in 1777.

Probably the most important private library of the
middle colonies was that of James Logan of Philadelphia.
This Quaker gentleman, who had served as lieutenant governor and as chief justice of Pennsylvania, collected more than
three thousand volumes before his death in 1751. His library
was strong in mathematics, astronomy, and science in general, but it also included many of the classics and works of
history. Logan hoped to make his library available to the
public and before his death a building was erected for it,
with books circulating to serious readers "under certain circumstances." Logan was one of the most outstanding scholars of the colonies, reading Greek, Hebrew and French, and
as much at home in Latin as in English. The Loganian Library was closed during the Revolution, but in 1792 it was
joined with the Philadelphia Library Company. Benjamin
Franklin also had a notable private library of his own, in addition to his activities in connection with other libraries. He
bought books frequently on his trips to Europe, usually books
that he wanted to read or use. At the time of his death in
1790, Franklin owned more than four thousand volumes, including a wide range of topics. Willed to his grandson,
Franklin's books were scattered, with many of them coming
on the market in 1801, when they were sold by a Philadelphia
bookseller. Fortunately, many of Franklin's volumes were
recognizable as such, and about a thousand of them can now
be located in various libraries.

Thomas Chalkley gathered a small library on the history and doctrines of the Quakers, which he donated in 1742
to help form the Friends' Library. This specialized collection was to become the most important library on the Quakers
in America.

In the South, the largest private library of the later
colonial period was that of William Byrd II of Westover, Virginia. Byrd's father had built up a large estate and had
started to collect books, but it was the son who, before his

death in 1740, enlarged the library to nearly four thousand
volumes. Byrd was a planter, lawyer and public official, as
well as a writer, and his library reflected the cultural level
and interests of the well-to-do planter. Almost a fourth of
the collection was made up of works of history, with another
fourth in classical literature, and about ten per cent each in
English literature, law, and science. There were a number
of volumes in French and Latin, and theology was represented by a few works of the church fathers, some volumes
on the Church of England and some current books of sermons. For at least a few years Byrd had a librarian in
charge of his books. This was William Proctor, who also
served as tutor for the Byrd children. Byrd's library was
well-used, not only by his family, but by numerous friends
as well. Other Virginia planters also had libraries numbering in the hundreds of volumes. The large plantation owners
were not alone in acquiring books, most ministers, lawyers
and doctors had at least small professional collections, and
many farmers and merchants owned more than the usual Bible
and almanac. In the smaller collections, as evidenced in
wills, inventories and sales, books of practical value such
as those on farming, surveying or law joined with sermons
and inspirational works to make up the majority.

As conditions in the more heavily settled regions of
the colonies became more stable, books became more readily
available. Bookstores were established throughout the New
England and Middle Atlantic colonies, and some few were established in the South, although the latter region, due to persistent transportation problems and lack of towns of size, acquired most of its books direct from English dealers. After
the obvious difficulties encountered by bookmen during the
Revolution were behind them, sizable libraries were built
throughout the colonies.

At the same time, each generation of pioneers experienced essentially the same problems in acquiring and building libraries as they followed the frontier west. First on the
eastern slope of the Alleghenies, then in the Ohio Valley, and
then in the Mississippi Valley, and finally in the far west,
settlers were forced to work hard and long to establish themselves in their new homes. Such hard work left little leisure
for reading, and the hard financial times left little money for
the purchase of books. Nevertheless, an examination of wills
and probate court records relating to the estates of these pioneers reflects a situation similar to that which we have described on America's first frontier. Many of the early pio-

neers owned books; most of the book collections were small
and religious in orientation; the professional men almost always owned a collection of books relating to their work; and
in a few cases really large and impressive libraries were
collected under the most difficult of conditions.

Not to be ignored in this discussion of private libraries is the development of the privately owned book collection that in size, value, and arrangement warrants the
name of library. A collection of books in itself, no matter
how large, is not necessarily a library, but when those books
are well selected, arranged in some logical order, cataloged
or not, but usable by the owner and/or by others, then they
constitute a library and deserve recognition as such. The
United States has been fortunate throughout its history in having a sizable number of citizens who collected and preserved
books, and doubly fortunate that many of those book collections have ended up in publicly available libraries. Just
when a collection becomes a library is debatable, however.
The United States Census of 1870 reported a total of 107,673
private libraries in the nation, admitting that its figure was
incomplete. Since the average size of these "libraries" was
only about 235 books, and since there was no way of indicating just how many of the books were in reality texts, pamphlets, children's books or catalogs, this figure tells us little.
Time and place, as well as number of volumes and their nature, must be considered in determining a library worthy of
note. For example, three hundred books in frontier St.
Louis in 1805 is notable; the same number in Boston at the
same date is not, unless the collection consisted of extremely rare works.

Many of the private libraries built up in the colonial
period were dispersed or destroyed during the American Revolution. Libraries of patriots were destroyed or scattered
by the actions of the British and Tories, as in the case of
Joseph Hooper of Massachusetts, whose five hundred-volume
library was burned with his home. In Philadelphia, private
libraries were scattered when British soldiers occupied the
abandoned homes, and the same thing happened on Southern
coastal plantations occupied by the enemy. On the other
hand, many libraries belonging to wealthy Loyalists were confiscated and sold by revengeful patriots, particularly toward
the end of the war. But the coming of peace after the Revolution, together with pride in a new nation, encouraged the
collection of private libraries, particularly of Americana,
and by the early nineteenth century many notable collections
had begun.

The early Presidents all had private libraries of some
size, and this custom was apparently followed by many other
state and national leaders.    President Thomas Jefferson, who
was to gain a reputation as the greatest bibliophile to ever
occupy the White House, inherited a small library from his
father, but a fire in his home in 1770 destroyed this collection.    Although he mourned the loss, Jefferson noted that
this group of books was easily replaced, since it was largely
composed of legal works and texts.    He immediately began
building up another library that numbered 2,640 volumes by
1783, and 6,487 when he sold it to the Library of Congress
in 1815.    Between 1815 and his death in 1826 he collected
yet a third library of nearly a thousand volumes.

The first half of the nineteenth century witnessed the
activities of several important book collectors who concentrated on books in the general field of Americana--history,
travel, biography and literature.    One of the earliest of these
was John Allan of New York (1777-1863), who amassed a notable collection of Americana and also collected early illustrated works and examples of early American printing.    His
library was sold in 1864 for almost $38,000.    Isaiah Thomas
(1749-1831), historian of printing, collected a library of early
Americana, including many early newspapers.    This collection went to the library of the American Antiquarian Society,
which he had helped to establish in 1812.    John Carter Brown
(1797-1874) is one of America's best known book collectors,
since his library was kept intact and passed on to Brown University in 1900.    As a relatively wealthy man, he was able
to acquire many rare items and on occasion to purchase
whole collections.    It was particularly strong in early Americana, travels and explorations; at the time of its first catalog in 1865, it contained some 5,600 titles, many in several
volumes.    The Brown Library was later increased by his
widow and sons and has grown considerably since becoming
the property of the university, so that today it is one of the
finest collections of Americana in existence.    Peter Force,
editor and historian, began collecting books in the 1820s, and
became such an avid collector that he often mortgaged his
property in order to increase his library.    Centering his interest on American history, he collected books, pamphlets,
broadsides, newspapers, periodicals and manuscripts until he
owned more than sixty thousand items in all.    In 1867 his
heirs sold this collection to the Library of Congress, thereby
more than doubling that library's holdings in its field.    James
Lenox (1800-1880), able to retire from business at the age of
forty, spent the latter half of his life building his immense and

valuable library.  In 1870, convinced that his library was
too large for any individual to own, he gave to the people
of New York both his books and his large collection of paintings, and later a building to house both.   Although he subsequently gave more books and funds for book purchases, his
original gift contained some fifteen thousand volumes.   Much
of his library was Americana, particularly before 1850, but
he also had a large collection of Shakespeareana, English literature, and Bibles.   Not all of the book collectors of the
early nineteenth century were in the Northeast, however.  Almost every portion of the country had its ardent collectors
and many of their libraries have fortunately been preserved.


## College Libraries

The history of the college library in America stretches
back into the 17th century nearly as far as that of the first
private collections.   Indeed, America's first college could be
said to have begun with a collection of books.   Harvard had
been founded in 1636, so that young men could be trained for
the Puritan ministry without returning to England, and it acquired its name in 1638 when the Reverend John Harvard
gave the college some 280 books and a small endowment.
Other gifts of books followed, including one of forty volumes
from Governor John Winthrop in 1642, but the college library
grew only slowly.   Its holdings were largely theological, and
even in 1723, when the first catalog was printed, it contained only 3,500 volumes.   In addition to about two thousand religious works, there were titles in history, geography,
classics, science, and languages, in that order.

In 1764, when Harvard College was more than a century and a quarter old, the library contained fewer than five
thousand volumes, and in that year it was burned with almost
all of its book collection.   After this tragedy, friends of the
college came to its aid and the Massachusetts Legislature
voted funds to replace the burned building.   In addition, a
popular subscription raised more money for the purchase of
books, and with many gifts the library was back to its former size by 1775.   Something of the nature of a colonial college library can be gathered from the library rules at Harvard in 1765.   The librarian was required to keep the library room open and heated only on Wednesdays, and only
junior and senior students could take books from the library.
If these rules sound strict, they were an improvement over
the earlier ones which allowed only the seniors to have li-

brary privileges.   After 1765 Harvard boasted an "undergraduate library," which was a collection of duplicates and
more popular works set aside for the use of students.   Perhaps the real intent of this move was to restrict student use
to a smaller and more replaceable collection, preserving the
majority of the library for faculty use.

A college and a college library were planned for the
new colony of Virginia as early as 1620.   A collection of
books was gathered in the colony and others were sent from
England to provide a library for "Henrico Indian College,"
to be established near the present site of Richmond.   The
Indian uprising of 1622 put an end to these charitable plans
and Virginia did not acquire a college until William and Mary
was founded in 1693.   This founding was largely the result of
the determination of the Reverend James Blair to provide for
the training of Anglican ministers in the college, and he ap-
propriately became its first President.   A few hundred books
were gathered for the use of the college before 1700, but
most of these were destroyed in a fire in 1705.   The library
was reestablished with a few gifts, but the private library of
the Reverend Blair provided most of the reading for the first
few decades.   In 1742 the will of Governor Alexander Spots-
wood gave the college about two hundred volumes, and the
next year, upon the death of Blair, his library, or most of
it, officially became the college library.   Even so, it is
doubtful that the college owned more than two thousand volumes before the Revolution.   Younger faculty members usually "kept" the library a few hours per week, and for some
years only clerks were in attendance.   No books circulated,
and apparently only the faculty used the college library to
any extent, while students generally relied on their texts and
lecture notes.

New England's second college also began with a collection of books.   The eleven ministers who organized a society
for the formation of Yale College in New Haven in 1700 each
donated a few books, and in the next decade other donations
increased the collection to nearly a thousand volumes.   In
1714 the Reverend Elihu Yale, for whom the college was
named, gave three hundred books to its library, and in 1733
the Reverend George Berkeley of London sent a gift of some
one thousand volumes, including many valuable folios.   By
1742 the Yale library contained some 2,500 volumes, and the
college president, Dr. Thomas Clap, in that year began to
reorganize and catalog the collection with the aid of a tutor.
He divided the library into sections, roughly according to

size, and numbered each book in each section, giving to each
a fixed location.    Next he drew up three catalogs, or booklists:   one alphabetically by author, one arranged as the
books on the shelf, and a third by broad subject matter, using about twenty-five headings.    By 1765 Yale's more than
four thousand volumes were still heavily theological, although
there were many volumes on history, classics, philosophy,
and mathematics.    Literature and science were neglected,
and there were few books published in America, and in fact
few titles published after 1725.

          Among other colonial colleges, the College of New
Jersey was begun about 1750, but its library had only some
twelve hundred volumes as late as 1764.    Governor Jonathan
Belcher of New Jersey gave his library in 1757, some 475
volumes, and other gifts came from friends in America and
in England.    When Dr. John Witherspoon became president
of the college in 1768, he added three hundred volumes to
the library, but it still contained fewer than two thousand
when it was virtually destroyed by British soldiers during the
Revolution.    The University of Pennsylvania (then the Academy)   had its library beginnings about 1750 also, but despite
the enthusiastic support of Benjamin Franklin, and library
fees charged to students, its book collection was not very
large before the Revolution.    King's College (later Columbia
University in New York) was begun in 1757, and its major
library patron was a Reverend Bristowe of London, who donated some fifteen hundred volumes.    Joseph Murray of New
York, one of the college's founders, also left it his library
and an endowment, so that by 1764 the collection was large
enough for the appointment of its first librarian, who was also the professor of mathematics.    Columbia's library, too,
suffered at British hands during the Revolution, but some of
the pilfered volumes were later restored.    Rhode Island College (later Brown University in Providence) began about
1765, with some books collected by the Reverend Morgan Edwards, but still had only some 250 volumes in 1772.    Other
gifts were received, however, and the collection grew slowly.
Fortunately, the Rhode Island students also had access to the
volumes in the Providence Library Company, founded in 1753.
In 1766, Queens College (later Rutgers) was founded in New
Brunswick, New Jersey, but apparently its library, prior to
the Revolution, consisted largely of the books belonging to
its faculty.    The last colonial college was Dartmouth, where
classes started about 1770 and where a library was begun
several years earlier.    Eleazar Wheelock, who founded the
college as a school for Indians, had begun to round up books

as early as 1764.  Fortunately, Dartmouth in New Hampshire
was little disturbed by the Revolution, and with other gifts
being received, a librarian was appointed in 1779 to arrange
and administer some twelve hundred volumes.  In general,
colonial college libraries were small, made up almost entirely of gifts, managed on a part-time basis by an instructor,
open only a few hours weekly, and little used, especially by
the students.

The few college libraries formed during the colonial
period suffered during the Revolution; in fact, higher education in general was set back seriously by the conflict leading
to independence.  Still another decade of uncertainty was to
follow the Peace of Paris in 1783, but by the 1790s there
was a definite improvement in colleges and college libraries
and a few new colleges were begun.  Growth was slow, however, for most college libraries until after 1850, and the
colonial tradition of opening the library only a few hours a
week, with close restrictions on the use of books, was hard
to outgrow.  Not until after the Civil War, and indeed not
until the late nineteenth century, did modern libraries really
begin to develop in the nation's colleges and universities.

Though forced to move from Cambridge to Concord
during the early part of the Revolution, Harvard College
saved its library and even added to it with funds allocated
by the new state legislature and with books confiscated from
fleeing Loyalists.  It revived during the 1780s, and a foreign
visitor, Francisco de Miranda of Venezuela, described it as
"well arranged and clean ... contains some 12 thousand volumes, English generally, although not badly selected."  By
1790, it had reached the place it was to keep as the nation's
preeminent academic library.  The printed catalog of that
year shows a strong emphasis on theology, but an increased
interest in English literature and more titles by eighteenth-
century writers.  History, travel, and philosophy were important but there was very little in the field of science.  The
only periodical was the Gentleman's Magazine.  By 1827
Harvard's library totaled over 25,000 volumes, and by 1840,
when it was moved into a building of its own, it contained
40,000 volumes exclusive of pamphlets.  The building was a
bequest of former Massachusetts Governor Christopher Gore
(1758-1829), and although it was constructed with the expec-
tation that it would meet the needs of the college for a century, it was outgrown in less than twenty-five years.  By
1856 it contained 70,000 books and 30,000 pamphlets.
Much of this growth came through gifts, and some of the

more important ones are worth mentioning.  In 1818, the library acquired the American history collection of the German
historian, C. D. Ebeling, totaling about three thousand volumes relating to America, with some ten thousand maps and
charts forming the most complete cartographic collection on
America then in existence.  The libraries of two Presidents,
John Adams and John Quincy Adams, came in part to Harvard, and over a period of many years Senator Charles Sum-
ner gave some thirteen hundred volumes, fifteen thousand
pamphlets (many very rare), and some two hundred fifty valuable maps.  All told, between 1780 and 1840 more than a
thousand noteworthy gifts of books were received, not counting the many gifts and bequests of funds for the library endowment.

Besides its main college library, Harvard also had
several significant departmental and special libraries before
1860.  The Law School Library had its beginning in 1817,
when Governor Gore presented his own library to the school.
Many other gifts were added, and in 1863 this collection
alone had thirteen thousand books.  The Divinity School Library dates from 1825, and by 1863 this collection, augmented by some four thousand volumes from the religious
library of Professor Gottfried Lücke of Göttingen, also totaled over thirteen thousand volumes.  The Library of the
Phillips Astronomical Observatory began in 1847, and before
the Civil War there were also libraries in the Museum of
Comparative Zoology and the Lawrence Scientific School.  Besides these, there were also student society libraries, such
as those of the Procellian Club, the Hasty Pudding Club, the
Christian Brethren, and St. Paul's Society.

About Yale's library in 1784, Señor Miranda was not
complimentary.  He noted that it was "nothing special: two
or three thousand volumes."  However, with numerous gifts
of funds and books, the library grew slowly from 4,700 volumes in 1808 to 21,000 volumes in 1850, and 78,000 in
1875, not including pamphlets.  There were also several special libraries, including the Law School Library founded in
1845, and the Theological Seminary Library.  Two student
society libraries, the Linonian and the Brothers in Unity libraries, were actually begun before the Revolution.  In 1860,
the Linonian had twelve thousand volumes; the Brothers in
Unity was somewhat smaller.  The Yale Library moved into
a new building in 1846, after having been housed previously
in rooms or wings of several college buildings.

Several other New England colleges were formed in
the half-century after the Revolution, and in general they followed a familiar pattern.   The gift of a small collection of
books started off the college library, and later gifts of endowment funds and books provided a little growth.   Only
about the middle of the nineteenth century did much support
for the library come from the college authorities, with the
appointment of a regular librarian and a definite budget.
Williams College in Massachusetts began in 1793, and a year
later its library had fewer than four hundred volumes.   By
1876 it could boast of only 17,500 volumes, with an additional 10,000 in two society libraries.   Wesleyan University in
Middletown, Connecticut began its library in 1833, based on
the collection of Thomas Chapman of Camden, New Jersey.
In 1868 Isaac Rich of Boston gave funds for a library building, and a few years later this building housed 26,000 volumes, an excellent collection in the 1870s.   Bowdoin College
Library in Brunswick, Maine began with the college, but received its real start in 1811, with the gift of some four thousand volumes from James Bowdoin, the son and namesake of
the Massachusetts governor of the 1780s.   Bowdoin College
was particularly fortunate during its first half-century, and
its library reached some eighteen thousand volumes by 1875.
Amherst College Library began with a single case of books
in 1821, but with gifts of books from friends and subscription drives among the alumni, the library grew to some
thirty thousand books by the 1870s.   In that decade, Amherst
was fortunate in having as assistant librarian a young man
named Melvil Dewey, who was recataloging the library with
what he called the decimal system of classification.

In 1800 the Dartmouth College Library numbered only
three thousand volumes, and at one time it was reduced to
selling rare volumes in order to purchase new and more usable ones.   After its student society libraries were added,
the Dartmouth Library reached some fifty thousand volumes
by 1875.   Brown University began its post-Revolutionary existence with a library that consisted of about five hundred
old, moth-eaten and mildewed volumes that had been stored
during the war.   With several major gifts of books and funds
from the Brown family of Newport and other alumni and
friends, it reached some 45,000 volumes by 1860, housed in
the Doric architecture of Manning Hall.

In the Middle Atlantic States, the University of Pennsylvania Library was one of the foremost in the antebellum
era.   Beginning its post-Revolutionary period with a gift of

books from the King of France, a series of fairly large gifts increased its holdings steadily until, by 1860, it had some twenty thousand volumes. There were also medical and law libraries on the campus as well as two student society collections. Other college libraries in Pennsylvania before 1850 included Dickinson College in Carlisle, founded in 1783; Washington and Jefferson College in Washington, founded in 1802; and Allegheny College at Meadville, founded in 1820. Each of these remained small in size and had only seven to eight thousand volumes as late as 1875, although each was fortunately supplemented by one or more student society libraries. In New Jersey, Rutgers College Library remained small, reaching only seven thousand volumes by 1870, while Princeton (still the College of New Jersey) was more fortunate in reaching thirty thousand volumes by 1875. Princeton's library was burned almost completely in 1802, but numerous gifts, including $1,000 for books given by President James Madison, an alumnus, aided in its growth over the years. In 1873 Princeton's library moved into a new octagonal stone building with a book capacity of 100,000 volumes, donated by John C. Green of New York City.

In New York, Columbia College library developed with a relatively small central collection and several departmental libraries. With the gifts of the private libraries of several of its presidents, and of such notable New Yorkers as Supreme Court Justice John Jay, the central library totaled some sixteen thousand volumes by 1860. The reason for the slow growth of college libraries during this period can be seen in Columbia's library book budget: about $175 in 1825 and only $500 as late as 1862. As late as 1870 Columbia added only 325 volumes, including fifty bound periodicals.

In the South Atlantic States, the colonial college of William and Mary was joined after the Revolution by the state colleges of North Carolina, South Carolina and Georgia. In Williamsburg, the college that had provided colonial Virginia with both political and intellectual leadership suffered a decline after the Revolution and grew only slowly. After 1825, the new University of Virginia in many ways replaced William and Mary, and its library, as planned by Thomas Jefferson, became one of the finest in the nation. Jefferson personally selected the first consignment of books for the University library and spent the last year of his life (1825-1826) working with them. He died soon after the University was formally opened, but his effect on the institution was long felt. President James Madison also gave the Univer-

sity of Virginia Library a large gift, including some 2,500
volumes and $1,500 in cash.  Another large donation came
in 1838 when Christian Bohn of Richmond gave the Library
about four thousand books and fifteen hundred engravings.  It
had been housed almost from the beginning in the Rotunda
Building, also designed by Jefferson, one of the most hand-
some college structures in the south.

North Carolina's University Library at Chapel Hill began in 1795 with a small collection including fourteen volumes
donated by the Governor of the state, William R. Davie.  Other donations followed, and in the 1820s the college president
sent to England to purchase almost a thousand volumes for
the library, along with apparatus for a chemistry laboratory.
In 1850 the library moved into a separate building constructed
in the form of a Greek temple, and at that time it numbered
about seven thousand books.  The library of the University of
South Carolina at Columbia began shortly after the founding
of the University in 1805.  Though most gifts to the library
were relatively small, the State did give more support than
most contemporary publicly owned college libraries received,
and the book collection grew steadily.  In its own building after 1841, the main library was supplemented by a student society library of 1,250 volumes.

West of the Appalachian mountains, the first "college"
to be established was Transylvania University at Lexington,
Kentucky, in 1798.  It grew only slowly at first, but after
1820 it became a full-fledged university with law and medical
schools.  In that year $14,000 was raised for the library
and other equipment, with the result that a collection of some
four thousand volumes was soon gathered.  Most of the college libraries of the Ohio and Mississippi valleys date from
the second quarter of the nineteenth century.  St. Louis University Library began in 1829, and by 1875 had seventeen
thousand volumes, with an additional eight thousand in the student society libraries.  The Indiana University Library began
in 1829, with a collection of books purchased by its first
president.  Gifts were scarce, but small appropriations were
occasionally available and state and federal documents helped
fill the shelves.  The first catalog was printed in 1842.  A
fire destroyed most of the library's five thousand volumes in
1854.  Marietta College, in Ohio, founded in 1835, raised
some $8,000 in subscriptions from friends and alumni in
1850 to add to the college library, and by 1870 it had some
fifteen thousand books, with another ten thousand in the society libraries.

Thus by the middle of the nineteenth century, hundreds of colleges had been established in the country, with libraries which varied greatly in both collection size and the nature and extent of services. However, some few generalizations do seem to be justified. In his now famous Notices of Public Libraries in the United States (1851), Charles Coffin Jewett described the Nation's college libraries in the following way:

> Our colleges are mostly eleemosynary institutions. Their libraries are frequently the chance aggregations of the gifts of charity; too many of them discarded, as well nigh worthless, from the shelves of donors.

He noted that this was not true of all of our libraries, but sadly, it aptly characterized most of them.

No matter where it was located, the typical college library before the Civil War was small, usually under 25,000 volumes, and was made up almost entirely of gifts, with little or no direct financial support from the college administration. Open to students only a few hours per day or even per week, its bookstock consisted almost entirely of old books, reference works, and standard editions. Little attempt was made to keep the library attractive or inviting to students, and in fact the student was not expected to use it very much. If the collection was housed in a separate building, that structure was usually classic in design and little fitted for library purposes.

Generally, a member of the faculty was charged with the responsibility for supervising the library, a task one was expected to assume with no reduction in other duties and no increase in pay. One is not surprised to find that these new "librarians" were often reluctant recruits who approached their duties with distaste and impatience. Consequently, hours when the library was open for use were short; rules were strict and inflexible; and the librarian was often viewed with mixed emotions of fear and disgust by the students. Some few librarians, like Charles Coffin Jewett of Brown, were dedicated and informed professionals, but such men were rare indeed in antebellum America.

While questions relating to the acquisition and organization of library materials were beginning to garner some attention from professionals like Jewett, most librarians

found that they could deal with the small collections under
their charge with a minimum of imagination and effort.  If
the collection was classified, it was usually by a locally devised system, and the only catalogs were printed or manuscript lists kept by author, location number, and/or broad
subject.

College libraries, with their small and inadequate collections, limited hours, and prohibitive circulation policies
were of little use to the college student.  Fortunately, students had recourse to the literary society libraries that developed on most college campuses in the first half of the
nineteenth century.  These societies were primarily debating
societies and their interests ranged across all areas of academic and public concern.  As these debates were expected
to be learned, as well as  rhetorically correct, the students
immediately recognized the need for substantial libraries
from which to mine their material.

Since the college library of the antebellum period offered little support for the contemporary and popular reading interests of the society members, the societies quickly
developed libraries which in many cases rivaled or far ex-
celled their respective college libraries in size and usefulness.  At Brown, for instance, the leading society was the
Philermenian, founded as the Miskosmiam Society in 1794,
and reorganized and renamed in 1798.  The members of the
Philermenian gathered for fortnightly meetings to listen to
debates, hear their fellows read speeches and poems, and
judge declamations.  In 1798, the society began to collect a
library, and by 1821 it contained 1,594 well-selected volumes.  In 1833 the Philermenian Society library and the library of a rival group--The United Brothers--contained in
aggregate some 5,600 well-used volumes, and their collections eclipsed by far in usefulness and value the 6,000 volumes in the university library.

## Predecessors of the Public Library

Probably the first attempt at a public library in the
colonies came in 1656, when Captain Robert Keayne, a merchant of Boston, willed his book collection to the town for a
public library, stipulating that the town build a suitable building to house it.  Boston at least partially met this condition,
building a Town House with a room for the books, but it is
doubtful that they were used much.  A catalog was made in

1702, a few other books were added, and the collection met its end in a fire in 1747.

In 1656 Governor Theophilus Eaton left some ninety-five volumes to the town of New Haven for the use of a proposed college. The college never materialized, and the town council, after worrying over the books for several years, finally sold them to a minister in 1689. They had been kept in the town schoolhouse during the intervening years, so they might be considered a public collection, whether or not used. Concord, Massachusetts, was also concerned in 1672 with "some bookes that belong to the towne," but how many there were, or how they were used, the records fail to say. Although evidence of publicly owned book collections is scarce, that of publicly used church libraries in the era around 1700 is firm. The King's Chapel Library in Boston, for example, was founded in 1698 with books given by the Bishop of London, and several colonial New England wills refer to ministerial libraries being left to churches for the use of the public.

The Reverend Thomas Bray, the Anglican clergyman who sponsored parish libraries in England, was particularly interested in establishing libraries in the colonies, and between 1695 and 1704 he was responsible for establishing some seventy libraries in America. Bray divided these libraries into three types: 1) the five provincial libraries, which were large libraries established in the major city of each province; 2) thirty-nine parochial libraries, which were smaller collections given to Anglican parishes; and 3) some thirty-five layman's libraries, which were distributed to ministers, and which contained books that were loaned or given outright to the residents of the area. The provincial libraries were the largest of the three types, and the most significant collections were established in Annapolis and Charleston.

Early library laws in Maryland and South Carolina were passed by the provincial legislatures to secure and maintain the Bray libraries. At least one of the Bray collections, sent to Annapolis, Maryland, was intended as a general public library and contained some eleven hundred volumes. It was maintained by the provincial government in the State House from 1697 until 1704, when it was burned. Some surviving books were united with those of a local school and survived into the twentieth century as a prized collection of the St. John's College Library.

Other parish libraries stemming from the activities of Bray and his associates were formed in New York, Pennsylvania, North Carolina and South Carolina. A collection of books sent to Bath, North Carolina in 1700 numbered 166 bound volumes for the use of the ministers and some 800 books and pamphlets for the use of the general public. Oddly enough, the books for the use of the ministers were more general than those for the use of the public, since the latter were almost entirely theological or inspirational. A Bray library sent to Charleston led to the passage of a legislative act in 1700, placing a minister in charge of the library and giving detailed instructions concerning its use. With such an auspicious beginning it seemed likely the parish libraries would grow and eventually become active public services, but no provisions were made for adding new books, and after the death of the Reverend Bray, interest in parish libraries declined and most of them disappeared. A few books originally in the parish libraries have survived in public or church collections, and they serve as a reminder of a library venture that preceded by two centuries the rise of the public library.

As conditions grew more stable in the colonies, and as the people gained increased leisure for recreation and study, many bookish individuals began to cast about for a way in which the increased demand for books might be satisfied. The solution--the social library--seems to have been the child of the fruitful mind of one of America's greatest intellects, Benjamin Franklin.

His voracious appetite for knowledge and his desire to improve himself and others led him to organize his now famous Junto in Philadelphia in 1728. The group's purpose was to nurture honest and decorous debate and thought, and to contribute in any way possible to the betterment of mankind. The club, made up of twelve young Philadelphians of primarily humble origins, was dedicated to the ideal of the search for truth. Franklin expressed this basic belief in intellectual freedom when he wrote that "when Truth and Error have fair Play, the former is always an overmatch for the latter."

In their search for knowledge and understanding his friends in the Junto were constantly frustrated by their lack of books. In an attempt to solve this problem Franklin suggested in 1730 that the members of the Junto all bring their books to the little room where the group was then meeting and by thus "clubbing our Books to a common Library, we should ... have each of us the Advantage of using the Books of all the other Members, which would be nearly as beneficial as if we owned the whole." However, the experiment was short-lived because some of the members felt their books were not being properly cared for, and also because of the inconvenience of the arrangement.

But the intelligence of "clubbing" as a means of providing increased access to books was readily obvious to Franklin, who in 1731 "set on foot my first Project of a public Nature, that for a Subscription Library." This library, founded in 1731 and chartered in 1742 as the Library Company of Philadelphia, was the first established in this country--in Franklin's words, "Mother of all N. American Subscription Libraries now so numerous." He was especially proud of these libraries and was confident that his library was imitated by other communities and that "These Libraries have improved the general conversation of the Americans," and have made the "Common Tradesmen and Farmers as Intelligent as Most Gentlemen from other countries." Scholars have been skeptical of Franklin's claim that the Library Company spawned all the other social libraries of the period, but recent scholarship has demonstrated convincingly that Franklin's creation was indeed very influential in the establishment of other libraries throughout the Colonies.

Once established, the social library form became a popular means by which local communities could supply their reading needs. This library type, which definitely represents a significant predecessor of the public library, came in the years after 1731 to take on a number of different forms, all grouped for convenience under the label "social libraries." However, for our purposes, it would be well to pause for a moment to consider the term's various mutations. Franklin's Library Company of Philadelphia was what is known in legal terms as a joint stock company; that is, each member of the library company owned one or more shares in the corporation, and his shares could be bought and sold like stock in any company.

This "proprietary" form became the basic model for the creation of social libraries, but in time other social libraries came to need support beyond the original funds derived from the sale of stock in the company. Thus they began to collect annual fees in addition to requiring purchase of stock, and in time even allowed individuals who were not shareholders in the corporation to "subscribe" to the library (thus the origin of the label "subscription" library) on a year-to-year basis, or for even briefer periods of time.

A third major refinement of the original proprietary library form was the athenaeum, an organization founded along social library lines but which emphasized the provision of scholarly newspapers and magazines as its essential service, while also sponsoring frequent cultural and recreational programs as another aspect of its activities. Furthermore, the athenaeum was frequently the most expensive--stock ranged as high as $300 a share as compared to an average among social libraries of $1 to $4--and thus was the most aristocratic of the social library forms. The first, established in Boston in 1807, remains the most impressive of them all, and provided the model for many more, including those still in existence in Salem and Philadelphia.

Finally, a further development of the social library form came in the early nineteenth century when interested individuals established what were known as "mechanics' " and "mercantile" libraries. Ray Held, in his history of libraries in California, attempted to classify social libraries by who used them, and concluded that one could divide social libraries into two groups: 1) those established by individuals who intended to make personal use of them; and 2) those established by individuals who intended them for the use of others. The mechanics' and mercantile libraries fall into the latter group, and represent the rise of libraries founded by benevolent leaders for the use of the "people." In this case, wealthy businessmen and industrialists supported the establishment of mercantile and mechanics' libraries throughout the industrialized cities of America in order to "promote orderly and virtuous habits, diffuse knowledge and the desire for knowledge, improve the scientific skill," and generally make the mechanics working in America's factories, and the mercantile clerks training for management of her commerce, effective citizens and productive workers.

The organization of the social library was usually very simple. In the smaller ones, there was little or no attempt to arrange the books except in general classifications, but in the larger collections more serious attempts were made at cataloging, ranging from simple manuscript accession records to printed alphabetical or classified lists. Housing for the collection might be in a public building, a member's home or business, or, for larger collections, in a separate rented

or owned building.   Hours of opening ranged from a few
hours one or two days per week to fairly regular schedules
of eight to ten hours daily.   An attendant, volunteer or paid,
charged books and checked on their return in the smaller
collections, but the larger ones had more or less full-time
"librarians."   As early as 1793, a pamphlet had been written
to advise the book selectors for social libraries on the best
methods of obtaining books and the best books to be chosen.
This was the Selected Catalogue of Some of the Most Es-
teemed Publications in the English Language Proper to Form
a Social Library, written by Thaddeus Mason Harris, who
had served for a short time as a librarian at Harvard.   His
booklet was one of the earliest American works on book selection, and as such it is interesting.   He divided all books
into three classes:   memory, reason and imagination.   The
first class included all phases of history, biography, and
travel; the second, science, philosophy, and religion; and the
third, poetry, drama, fiction and art.   In all, he recommended only eighty-one titles, but these were well selected
for the time and purpose.   Ordinarily, the smaller social libraries bought only a few new books each year, but collectively they made up a major book market, so that the book
publishers and dealers soon came to offer them special dis-
counts to secure their trade.

        The social library proved a very efficient means for
meeting the growing reading appetite of America's rapidly increasing population.   However, it was characterized by a
fatal flaw--the principle of voluntary support--and as Jesse
H. Shera has noted, "the shifting sands" of voluntary support
were proving inadequate to the task of supporting the widespread and efficient library service so desired by library advocates throughout the nation.   Especially troublesome was
the tendency of social libraries to fail during hard financial
times.   The depressions of 1819, 1837, and 1857 all pressed
severe economic deprivation upon the nation, and people were
forced to withdraw support from all sorts of cultural and recreational activities, including social libraries.   As a consequence, many American communities lost their library service every time the region experienced difficult financial times.
Such instability was simply unacceptable to those who believed
that libraries were essential, for whatever reason, to the
success of the Republic.   Their efforts to discover a form
of support which would be capable of bringing stability and
energy to library service led them eventually to the idea of
supporting libraries with public tax funds.

Thus the many variations on the social library model first formulated by Franklin and his young friends in Philadelphia constitute a significant chapter in the unfolding story of the rise of the public library. Indeed, when the public library was established in the latter half of the nineteenth century, it either absorbed the local social library or, in many cases, actually found its origins in the gift of the collection belonging to the social library. At any rate, social libraries had very limited futures once public libraries were established in their respective communities, and only the most unique, or those boasting the most impressive of traditions--like the Library Company of Philadelphia--are still in existence.

The nation's social libraries were generally promoted as serious sources of knowledge for those who desired to improve themselves. They did not, at least openly, cater to the public taste for romance and popular fiction, choosing instead to purchase only the best nonfiction and some few classic works of fiction. The public's voracious appetite for romance was filled by libraries designed as commercial ventures and aimed at stocking only the most popular and exciting of the new fiction. These libraries, called "circulating" libraries, made their first appearance just prior to the American Revolution.

Maintained usually by printshops or bookstores, these "libraries" made available rental books for a small fee, either a book at a time or a number of books over a given period of time. Possibly the first of these rental collections was opened by William Rind in Annapolis, Maryland, in 1762. He proposed to allow his customers the use of two books at a time for an annual fee of twenty-seven shillings. His venture was unsuccessful and it was discontinued in 1764. However, the idea caught on and by 1765 or a little later, there were rental collections in Boston, Philadelphia, New York and Charleston. One in Boston, begun by John Mein, was particularly ambitious and published a catalog of some twelve hundred titles available for rent at the rate of twenty-eight shillings a year for all that one could read, one volume at a time. Unfortunately, Mein was a Loyalist, and as the Revolution approached he was forced to leave the city. In New York, Samuel Loudon's circulating library offered some two thousand titles to discriminating readers in the early 1770s, and some of his most popular volumes were poetry. The circulating library was to have its greatest success in the half century after the Revolution, and it should

be noted that most of the enterprises that rented books also
sold them. Booksellers were common in the larger towns
before 1775, with Philadelphia having at least twenty-five different sellers of books advertising before that date. Their
basic bookstock usually consisted of primers and other textbooks, prayerbooks and dictionaries, with the local laws and
almanacs being regular items. Besides these, the average
buyer could find sermons, current political tracts, and some
literature, but the heavier works found in most private libraries were probably ordered from England.

While the purely commercial circulating library increased in numbers after the Revolution, its cultural importance was probably negligible when compared to the social libraries. For one thing it was restricted, as was the bookstore of which it was usually a part, to the larger towns.
It depended upon a reading public somewhat different from
that of the social library--more on the casual reader than
the serious one. It was usually small, but in a few cases
in old, established stores it sometimes reached several thousand volumes. Caritat's Circulating Library in New York
City, opened in 1797, had over five thousand volumes in its
catalog of 1804, including more than a thousand titles of fiction. Even more than the social library, the circulating library reflected popular reading tastes, but unfortunately
there are few surviving records of the bookstocks of those
commercial ventures, much less any counts of their actual
use. An interesting example of a circulating library was the
"Book Boat" that flourished on the Erie Canal for a generation after 1830. Going from Albany to Buffalo and back, the
boat would tie up at a wharf for a few hours or even a few
days at a time, and rent its literature, varying from sermons
to joke books, at two cents an hour or ten cents a day. The
rental collections were less important in the general development of public libraries than the social libraries, but they
provided a needed service and they have left their descendants in the public library pay collection and the drugstore
rental shelf.

While the social and circulating libraries must be considered significant predecessors of public libraries in this
country, it is important to note that another significant fore-
runner of the public library was the school district library.
Writing in his Third Annual Report for 1839, Horace Mann,
then Secretary of the Massachusetts Board of Education,
stated the credo for such libraries--a credo that was to be
utilized again (in a slightly different form) by the founders
of America's first public libraries:

> After the rising generation have acquired habits of
> intelligent reading in our schools what shall they
> read? for, with no books to read, the power of
> reading will be useless; and with bad books to read,
> the consequences will be as much worse than ig-
> norance as wisdom is better.  What books, then,
> are there accessible to the great mass of the chil-
> dren in the State, adapted to their moral and intel-
> lectual wants, and fitted to nourish their minds
> with the elements of uprightness and wisdom?

It was this question that prompted educators, intellec-
tuals, and eventually legislators to seek for a way in which
such reading might be furnished to adults as well as children, and one solution was to establish libraries associated
with the school-districts so common to the seaboard states.

This type of library apparently originated in New York
state but spread widely throughout New England and the Middle West.  New York's Legislature passed an act in 1835
that made it permissible for school districts to levy taxes
for school libraries.  This law brought little response, but
a second one passed in 1838, which provided state funds to
match local levies for books, was more successful, and in
three years more than 400,000 books were placed in the
schools of the state.  This idea grew until by 1850 there
were nearly 1,500,000 books in New York's school libraries.
However, without proper staff and quarters many of the
books were lost or allowed to deteriorate.  The interest in
the libraries was high at first but soon declined, and state
laws later allowed the library funds to be spent for other
purposes.  In Massachusetts, a school district library system was established in 1837, and 2,084 such collections were
reported there by 1850.  In all, they contained only about
100,000 volumes, or an average of about fifty books each,
and here again the movement was hardly a success.  Connecticut followed Massachusetts in 1839, and Rhode Island in
1840, and in a few cases in these states the collections
eventually became working school libraries.  Several Middle
West states, including Michigan, Indiana, and Ohio, passed
school district library laws before 1850, but in general they
were not very successful.

The school district libraries were a failure partly because of their contents and partly because of the way in
which they were handled.  They usually consisted of textbooks, general works, and a smattering of inspirational lit-

erature, with little attention paid to their selection.  The
majority were above the reading level and beyond the interests of all but the most advanced students, and though they
were theoretically available to the adults of the community,
they were not widely used.  Several publishing firms took
advantage of the school district library laws and compiled
sets of works, poorly selected, printed and bound, but sold
on commission through local representatives.  These sets
often took up the entire funds available, and their drab appearance and dry contents did little to promote their use.
For lack of adequate quarters in the school buildings, the library books were often stored in the homes of teachers or
school board members, and an investigation of the New York
school district libraries in the 1850s found many of the books
molding in closets, cellars and attics.  In a sense, the
school district library was an attempt at both public and
school library service, and in both it was a failure.  It was
premature, poorly supported, and consequently unsuccessful,
but it established the precedent of public support for library
services and paved the way for better school and public libraries at a later date.

Another form of library service to children which deserves notice is the Sunday School library--perhaps the most
numerous and least known library type in nineteenth-century
America.  Practically every church, especially in the North
and West, could boast a small collection of books designated
as the "Sunday School" library.  At times they represented
fairly substantial general collections, but more often they
contained only religious and inspirational works.  Where other sources of reading material were not available, especially
in frontier areas, they were frequently consulted by children
and adults alike; but the specialized nature of the collections
and their general neglect soon lead to their decline.

In addition to the school-district and Sunday school libraries, children did have access to books through several
other kinds of libraries.  One source of reading for children
came in the form of the libraries attached to the many private schools and academies established in the country prior
to the Civil War.

Some academies were established during the colonial
period, but little is known of their libraries.  The Boston
Latin School, for example, is supposed to have been founded
in 1635, but nothing is known of its library until the nineteenth century.  There was definitely a library there in 1844,

when the Boston Latin School Association was formed to support it, and by 1875 it had some five thousand volumes.   In
New York City, Public School No. 1 had a small collection
of books in 1810, and by 1820 the city was appropriating $50
per year for library books in each school.   In Virginia, the
state legislature chartered Rumford Academy in 1804, with
authority to promote a lottery to raise funds for a library,
but apparently it was not successful.   In frontier Missouri,
St. Louis Academy boasted a library in its 1818 advertise-
ments, and the Academy of the Sacred Heart had a library
in 1827.   Abbott Academy at Andover, Massachusetts, was
established in 1829 and had a well-organized library by 1842,
but in 1875 it still contained only fifteen hundred volumes.
The academy movement was strong in New England and the
Middle West by 1825, and in the South by 1850.   In Ohio,
there were no fewer than 171 academies and institutes founded
between 1803 and 1850.   In most cases, little is known of
their libraries, but from the remains of a few that have survived, or where printed catalogs are available, it is apparent they were often gift collections, poorly selected and seldom used.   Moreover, the academy libraries were usually
cared for by a faculty member, and any organization or cataloging was usually haphazard.   Hours of opening were few
and emphasis on reading other than textbooks was usually
lacking.   However, many of the teachers in the academies
often had book collections of their own which were more per-
tinent to the needs or interests of the students than the
school libraries, and usually available to the students.   Also,
in the stronger academies, there were often literary society
libraries that were small but well-used.

Besides the academies, there were also a few public
libraries offering books particularly for children in the early
nineteenth century.   The library founded by Caleb Bingham
at Salisbury, Connecticut, in 1803 was specifically designated
for children from nine to sixteen years of age, although it
seems to have been used generally by adults as well.   In
1804 Dr. Jessey Torrey started a library for young people
in connection with the New Lebanon, New York, Library Society.   Some of the subscription libraries contained books for
children, and there is evidence of a Children's Library Society in Louisville, Kentucky in 1810, and in Richmond, Virginia in 1823.   The West Cambridge, Massachusetts Juvenile
Library was started in 1835, but it was only open a few hours
each Saturday.   Three books per family could be taken out
for thirty days.   The apprentices' libraries, YMCA libraries, and the Sunday School libraries each provided some

service for children and young people.  The apprentices' libraries were usually available to boys over eleven or twelve,
as were the YMCA libraries, and the Sunday school collections tried to win juvenile readers with sentimental stories
of unbelievably good little girls and boys.  Circulating rental
libraries also contained some titles of interest to older children, but books available to children in public collections before the Civil War were generally scarce.


## The Emergence of Special Libraries

In a sense many of the libraries discussed to this
point could be defined as special.  However, in modern usage we tend to consider special libraries to be relatively
small collections with carefully defined clienteles, and with
an explicit and sharply focused mission.  Given these characteristics it is possible to survey the first two centuries of
American library history and identify examples of libraries
that might legitimately be labeled "special."

For instance, the Pennsylvania Hospital Library in
Philadelphia, probably the first medical library in the United
States, began in 1763.  Similarly, the Library of the American Philosophical Society, founded in 1743 in Philadelphia,
may well be the oldest special library of any type in the nation, unless the parochial libraries sent over around 1700 by
Dr. Thomas Bray for the use of Anglican ministers could be
so considered.  Since there were few libraries of any type
antedating these, it may be said that special libraries have
as venerable a history as any others in the United States.

Early theological libraries were almost always associated with colleges and schools of divinity.  Apparently, the
oldest strictly theological collection was that of St. Mary's
Theological Seminary, founded in Baltimore in 1791.  There
was also a Presbyterian Theological Seminary in Beaver
County, Pennsylvania, established in 1794.  It began with a
library of some eight hundred volumes collected by the Rev.
John Anderson.  By 1825 twenty-one more theological libraries, most of them in seminaries, had been established,
and by 1875 there were over one hundred twenty.  The library of Andover Theological Seminary, Andover, Massachusetts, although larger than average, is typical of the growth
of the theological collection.  The seminary was founded in
1807, and opened in 1808 with a small library which grew
slowly from gifts and purchases until by 1875 it possessed

over 34,000 volumes, not including some 12,000 pamphlets.
Besides several large gifts, in 1858 Andover was able to
purchase the library of Dr. C. W. Nieder of Berlin, containing some four thousand rare and valuable works. The seminary library issued a printed catalog in 1819, and another in
1838, with a supplement in 1849. From 1818 to 1866 it occupied a room in the college chapel, but in 1866 it moved
into a separate building that had been donated by three Andover citizens. The majority of theological libraries were
smaller than that at Andover and ranged during the nineteenth
century from two to fifteen thousand volumes in size. In
addition to the strictly theological libraries, there were also
strong theological collections in most of the early college libraries. Harvard's Divinity School, for example, began its
own library in 1825, and owned seventeen thousand volumes
by 1875. Also many churches had small libraries, although
they were usually more like study collections for the ministers than actual libraries.

The legal profession was an early developer of special libraries. Since his tools of trade were law books, the
colonial student of law usually added to his textbooks the
provincial laws and legal handbooks and thus developed a
small private law library out of necessity. Some of these
were undoubtedly used by other lawyers, as were also those
in the offices of provincial officials. These could hardly be
considered special libraries, however, and it was not until
after 1800 that the first law libraries emerged. Philadelphia's Law Association Library opened in 1802, and Boston's
Social Law Library in 1804. As their names indicate, they
were extensions of the social library concept to groups of
lawyers, enabling them to buy collectively more law books
than they could afford individually. County law libraries,
semi-public in nature, were established in New York and other Northeastern states by the 1840s. Sometimes they were
initiated by public legislation, as in Massachusetts, and at
other times by local law associations. Still another type of
law library in the nineteenth century was that of the law
school, or law department in a college. Harvard University's
Law School Library was founded in 1817, and contained over
fifteen thousand volumes in 1875. In that year, twenty-one
other law schools reported libraries, most of them less than
ten thousand volumes in size.

Historical libraries were popular in the nineteenth
century, and these also varied considerably in size. The
Massachusetts Historical Society was probably the earliest

to be formed, having been chartered in 1791, but it was followed by several others in neighboring states early in the next century.  By 1850 most of the states had historical libraries, a few receiving government funds and the remainder depending upon supporting societies.  In either case, acquisitions consisted largely of gifts, free government publications and exchanges with other historical groups.  Some towns and counties supported local historical societies, but in most of these the libraries were small and neglected.  By 1875 there were some eighty historical society libraries from Maine to California and from Alabama to Wisconsin, varying in size from only a few hundred volumes to the New York Historical Society's sixty thousand.  The Rhode Island Historical Society Library in Providence is typical of historical libraries prior to 1875.  The Society was organized in 1822 and had about 150 members, with a $5 admission fee and $3 annual dues.  Beginning with a few gift volumes, its library contained about six thousand volumes and thirty thousand pamphlets by 1870.  The collection was primarily on the history of Rhode Island, secondarily on New England and the remainder of the United States.  Many of its volumes were obtained by exchange of its publications with similar societies in other states.  The Society owned its own building but had no paid employees, and its library, with volunteer "librarian," was open only to members and their guests for a few hours each week.  Some historical societies were sponsored by, or related to, religious organizations.  The Friends' Historical Society of Philadelphia and the Presbyterian Historical Society of the same city are examples.  Each of these had libraries of several thousand volumes in the 1860s.  Although most of the historical libraries were poorly financed, their collections often contained many valuable volumes, and their publications made notable additions to the published historical literature of the United States.

Somewhat akin to the historical libraries were the scientific society libraries that developed in the larger cities during the early nineteenth century.  From its colonial beginnings, the library of the American Philosophical Society in Philadelphia grew only slowly, but its additions in science and philosophy were almost invariably valuable.  By 1875 it contained some twenty thousand volumes and about as many pamphlets.  Also in Philadelphia was the Academy of Natural Sciences, founded in 1812 and by mid-century proclaimed as one of the best in its field, with thirty thousand volumes and thirty-five thousand pamphlets.  The Franklin Institute was founded in the same city in 1824, as a group particularly

interested in the physical sciences, and its library was only
a little smaller than the other two.  In Boston, the American Academy of Arts and Sciences (founded 1780) and the
Boston Society of Natural History (1831) each had libraries
of more than ten thousand volumes by 1875, while the Massachusetts Horticultural Society (1829) had a library of about
twenty-five hundred volumes.  In New York there were such
scientific libraries as those of the American Geographical
Society, founded in 1852, and with ten thousand volumes in
1875; and the New York Academy of Sciences, founded in
1818, with only thirty-five hundred volumes at the later date.
In 1885 New York City had at least thirty-three special libraries of note, including nine medical and hospital libraries,
six law libraries, eight scientific libraries, four theological
libraries, two historical libraries, and one insurance library.

        Special medical and hospital libraries were fewer and
smaller than those in other subject fields in the nineteenth
century, possibly because the literature in the field of medicine was relatively small.  After the Pennsylvania Hospital
Library, five other medical libraries were begun before
1800, and by 1860 there were twenty-three medical libraries,
varying in size from one thousand to ten thousand volumes,
most of them in the Northeast.  In New York the Hospital
Medical Library was begun in 1796, and by 1875 had over
ten thousand volumes, while the Academy of Medicine Library there had accumulated only three thousand volumes
since its founding in 1846.  Philadelphia's College of Physicians Library, dating from 1789, had 18,750 volumes in
1875, and was, next to the Library of the Surgeon General's
Office in Washington, the largest medical library in the
country.  Elsewhere, there were libraries of hospitals, medical schools, and societies in almost every state by 1850,
although most of them were small.


## Libraries Serving Government

        As the national libraries in Europe are among the
major libraries of the world, so in the United States the nation's greatest library is a government agency, the Library
of Congress.  Originally intended as the reference library
for the national legislative body, this institution has had a
long and varied history, but it has emerged in the twentieth
century as the national library in all but name.  The Library
of Congress is not the only major library operated by the
United States government, and besides the federal libraries

there are also many important ones belonging to the various
states.  Altogether, the government libraries in the United
States represent a major portion of the library resources
available to the American people.  They are designed primarily for the use of government officials and employees,
but many of them are also open to the general public, and
directly or indirectly, their valuable resources are available.

The history of the Library of Congress begins with
the history of the United States.  The new government, from
1776 on, made use of several book collections in New York
and Philadelphia, particularly those of the New York Society
Library and the Philadelphia Library Company.  A few
books were owned by the Continental Congress and its successors, but no definite move toward an actual library came
until after the government moved to the new capitol at Washington, D.C. in 1800.  In that year, Congress appropriated
funds for the purchase of books, and a first order for 740
volumes was placed in London.  In 1802 a room for the
Congressional Library was set aside in the new Capitol, and
President Thomas Jefferson appointed the first librarian,
who was also serving as Clerk of the House of Representatives.  Jefferson also aided in the selection of this first library, but it had grown to only about three thousand volumes
by 1814.  In that year, during the war with Great Britain,
the Capitol was burned by an invading army and the embryo
Library of Congress was destroyed.  After the war there
was considerable debate as to how the library could be reconstituted, and former President Jefferson solved the problem by offering to sell his excellent private library to the
government.  After much debate the offer was accepted, and
in 1815 the collection of 6,500 volumes was purchased, giving the nation a library that was much superior to the one
that had burned.

George Watterson was appointed as the first full-time
librarian of Congress, and temporary quarters were found
for the new library until 1824, when permanent quarters
were completed in the new Capitol.  By this date, Congress
was appropriating about $5,000 per year for the library,
and through purchases, gifts, and government publications
the book stock was growing steadily.  In 1832 part of the
legal collection in the library was removed to form a library for the Supreme Court, but this remained under the
jurisdiction of the Librarian of Congress for some time.
By 1850 the library had reached some fifty thousand volumes, second only to Harvard University's library in size.

Once again, a fire in the Capitol destroyed much of the library in 1851, including about two-thirds of the original Jefferson collection.

At mid-century, the Library of Congress was considered to be little more than a collection of books of use to members of Congress; its emergence as the "National Library" was to come under the persistent and enlightened leadership of Ainsworth Rand Spofford, who served as Librarian of Congress from 1864-1897. However, there was a library in Washington at mid-century that was billing itself as "national" in scope. That library, which constituted part of the newly formed Smithsonian Institution, was directed by America's most prominent librarian, the determined and controversial Charles Coffin Jewett.

When Jewett was appointed Librarian at the Smithsonian in 1847, he fully intended to make the Smithsonian Library the national library of the United States. However, he reckoned without the influence and eventual victory of the Secretary of the Smithsonian, the prominent scientist Joseph Henry, who was determined to allocate the Institution's limited resources to the support of scientific research and publication programs.

At first Jewett appeared to be making some headway. He was able to bring about the passage of a copyright deposit law which stipulated that one copy of each copyrighted work was to be deposited at both the Smithsonian and the Library of Congress. He worked diligently to make the Smithsonian the "centre of bibliographical knowledge" in the country, and pioneered a number of venturesome, but frustrating, cooperative cataloging programs. Finally, he published his famous Notice of Public Libraries in the United States of America (1851), which is now recognized as the pioneer attempt to survey and assess the Nation's library resources.

Before too many years had passed, the strong-willed Librarian and the determined Secretary of the Smithsonian clashed over policy, and Jewett was forced to resign, moving to Boston where he later became the first Superintendent of that city's new public library. Secretary Henry promptly proceeded to dismantle Jewett's national library plans, and in 1866 transferred the Smithsonian's 44,000-volume collection to the Library of Congress, making the LC collection the largest and most impressive in America.

In addition to the libraries of the federal government, most of the states also maintained one or more government libraries. Even before the Revolution, there were collections of legal works available in the provincial legislative halls for the use of officials and legislators. Virginia had a small library in the office of the provincial secretary as early as 1661, and at least fifty books have survived that belonged to the colonial government before 1776. In that year Thomas Jefferson suggested a bill for a state library for Virginia, but nothing came of it until 1828, just two years after Jefferson's death, when the state established a state library and gathered into one location all the books then belonging to the state's offices. In 1831 the Virginia State Library in Richmond had 5,500 volumes, and in 1856, 17,500.

Pennsylvania's state capital had a small library as early as 1777, and the other colonies probably had at least collections of law books for the use of their officials and legislators, but it was not until after 1800 that most of the states began to form official state libraries. South Carolina had one by 1814, Pennsylvania by 1816, New York and New Hampshire by 1818, and most of the Eastern states by 1840. Michigan's state library began in 1828, and Illinois' in 1839, with most of the other Midwestern states forming libraries by 1850. Territorial libraries often preceded state libraries in the more western states.

The early state libraries were usually made up mainly of legal works and official government publications, but from the beginning there were many historical or geographical works. These acquisitions came largely from gifts, via exchanges of state publications with other libraries, and through receipt of federal publications through acts of Congress. The use of the libraries was ordinarily restricted to state officials, and to borrow books even they sometimes had to leave deposits. Librarians were generally political appointees. Some of the state libraries, however, were from the beginning for general public use, as that of New York, which was established as a "public library for the use of the government and of the people of the state." Financial support for the early state libraries was usually erratic and most of them grew only slowly. Shortly after the Civil War there were forty-six state and territorial libraries, but only ten of them had over thirty thousand volumes and the largest was that of New York with ninety-five thousand.

Canadian Libraries

The history of Canadian libraries parallels to some
extent that of the United States, but there are also many differences.  First, there are the French origins of eastern
Canada and the continued domination of French language and
culture in Quebec.  Then, there is the long colonial status
of Canada and the close political and cultural ties with Great
Britain, even after the achievement of Dominion and Com-
monwealth status.  Finally, there are the vast distances, the
sparse population, the slow development of transportation,
and the long winters that accentuate the other difficulties in
socialization and communication.  Despite these difficulties,
the development of Canadian libraries has been steady, and
today they are in much the same position as those of Europe
and the United States.

There seems to be little doubt that books accompanied
some of the earliest French explorers to Canada.  Certainly
men such as Marc Lescarbot, Samuel de Champlain, and the
Sieur de Monts had small libraries even on their earliest
visits to Canada, and Lescarbot, at least, is reported to
have made some of his volumes available for use by others.
Also, the early missionary priests brought books with them,
and as early as 1635 there was a small library attached to
the earliest Jesuit "college" founded in Canada.  But for the
French fur trapper and trader in the wilderness, and even
for the Acadian farmers in Nova Scotia, books were virtually
unknown.  Small religious collections and the private libraries of priests and officials made up the sum total of
books in French Canada for a hundred fifty years, or until
after the British took over in 1763.

Even before the British flag flew over the St. Lawrence, the Hudson Bay Company had carried it into the fur
country of northern Canada, and a few boxes of books were
available to traders at the Company's outposts, and even the
early explorers into western Canada, whether overland or
via the Pacific, carried a few books with them.  Once the
English were firmly settled in Quebec, Governor Frederick
Haldemand promoted the establishment of the first subscription library in 1780, providing books in both French and English for subscribers who could afford to pay £5 down and
£2 per year.  A little later, in Upper Canada (Ontario),
Governor John Graves Simcoe gave his private library of legal and historical works to the Legislature of that Province
in 1791.  Stimulus for education, and secondarily for li-

braries, came from the Loyalists who had fled from the
United States during and after the American Revolution.
Most of these people represented what had formerly been the
upper class of New England and the Middle Atlantic colonies,
and although they were seldom able to bring their libraries
with them, most of them had been accustomed to owning
books, and as soon as they were able in their new homes
they began to establish private and social libraries. A social library was formed in Montreal by 1796 and another in
Niagara by 1800, with perhaps a dozen others before 1820 in
various Canadian towns and villages. The College of New
Brunswick was founded in 1795 and King's College in Nova
Scotia by 1802. Each of these institutions had small libraries, but like their neighbors in the United States, they
grew largely from gifts for their first few decades.

By the 1830s, the social libraries were joined by Mechanics' Institute libraries, semi-charitable agencies patterned after similar organizations in England. Providing lecture series and other educational encouragement for the working classes in addition to libraries, these Institutes received
not only approval but some financial aid from provincial governments. Among the earliest such libraries were those at
Montreal, York and Halifax, and by 1850 some forty others
had been established, although not all survived. In 1851 the
Canadian Parliament passed legislation regulating the establishment of mechanics' institutes and similar libraries, allowing a government grant of £50 each annually. When many
of the institutes failed to report properly on the use of the
funds, they were discontinued in 1860. Many of the institute
libraries survived, however, and after the Confederation of
Canada was formed in 1867, several of the provinces provided small grants to them. Some eventually became public
libraries, while others survived into the twentieth century as
"association libraries," a type of subscription library. The
services were at best minimal, but they provided an element
of library service for those interested, particularly in the
smaller towns.

After 1846 Ontario and eastern Canada tried the school
district library, similar to those then under way in New
York and New England. Operated by the schools but intended
for public use, these libraries were part of the program
for general public education planned by Egerton Ryerson.
By 1874 there were 1,334 such libraries in Ontario, containing some 266,000 volumes, or an average of about 200 vol-

umes each, according to the annual report of the Ontario Department of Education.  They were bought through the Department of Education from a selected list, and were generally more suitable for adults than for children.  Joseph
Howe, in Nova Scotia, was similarly involved in establishing
schools and libraries in the 1840s and 1850s.  In Quebec,
parish libraries were established in much the same manner.
On the whole, the success of the school district libraries in
Ontario was more apparent than elsewhere, but they were far
from providing anything like public library service.  They
did form a beginning by acquainting a few users with worthwhile reading material, and in their public support they set
the precedent for both public and school libraries of the future.

A few other developments in Canadian library history
prior to Confederation are worthy of mention.  The Library
of Parliament was founded in 1815 in Ottawa, and in 1841 it
was joined by a smaller collection from Lower Canada or
Quebec.  Unfortunately, a disastrous fire occurred in 1855
and destroyed most of the books, but they were quickly replaced and by 1882 the Parliamentary Library contained
nearly 100,000 volumes.  From the late eighteenth century,
provincial legislative libraries existed at least in name, but
they were usually small legal collections under the care of a
clerk until late in the nineteenth century.  Private libraries
of more than a few volumes were scarce in early Canada,
but records of several notable ones have survived.  Jonathan
Odell, Provincial Secretary of New Brunswick from 1784 to
1812, left a library of nearly a thousand volumes, probably
the largest private library in Eastern Canada at that time.
Robert Addison, a missionary sent out by the English Society for the Propagation of the Gospel, brought some 1,250
volumes with him to Niagara in 1792.  They were largely
theological, and were apparently made available to other Anglican ministers and to interested parishioners.  Even out on
the Pacific coast, early explorers and fur traders brought
along a few books.  Dr. John McLoughlin, agent for the Hudson Bay Company at the mouth of the Columbia River, maintained a large collection of reading matter in the early nineteenth century for his own use and for his frequent visitors.
When the Red River Library, the first to be founded in the
Province of Manitoba, was begun in 1847, its core was a
private collection donated by Peter Fidler, a trader and land
speculator.  Other government officials, professional men
and businessmen gathered sizable collections, many of which
later came to rest in public and college libraries.

Conclusion

The development of libraries in America, North and
South, projects an ever more complex mosaic upon the historical canvas.   However, certain similarities are evident.
First, it is obvious that a certain percentage of the residents of each new settlement in the New World possessed the
ability to read, and brought a few precious books with them
when they journeyed to their new homes.   Furthermore, they
set about importing reading material from their native lands,
and ultimately, producing newspapers, magazines, and books
locally.

Furthermore, as conditions stabilized, as the population grew, and as the amount of leisure time available to
many people increased, the small privately owned collections
began to prove inadequate to the information and recreational
needs of readers.   By the early nineteenth century nearly
all of the settled regions of America had experimented with
various forms of the "public" library--all designed to make
books and other reading material more readily available to
an ever-increasing number of readers.

At the same time, academic institutions were being
established throughout America, and, reflecting the practice
common to European civilization, they were nearly always
equipped with some semblance of a library.   While the collections were generally small, ill-housed, and little used,
they nevertheless represented the seeds of contemporary
American academic libraries.

But much was yet to be done.   In 1850, while the
need for a form of "public" library was viewed as essential
by many literate individuals, the idea of a "public library"
open to all, supported by tax-funds, and administered as a
public trust was only just gaining some attention.   Similarly,
while academic libraries were common ingredients in the
educational recipe, they were to gain a truly significant role
in American education only during the last few decades of
the century.   Other library types remained in a similar em-
bryonic stage.

And yet, much had been done, and the stage was set
for momentous library developments in America.   Before
these can be considered, however, we must turn our attention back across the Atlantic in order to survey the rise of
the modern European library.

Additional Readings

The literature on American library history is vo-
luminous. The following items are considered excellent treatments of the major aspects of early
American library history, but the list is highly selective. Those who care to pursue the literature
further should see Michael H. Harris, Guide to
Research in American Library History, 2nd ed.
(Metuchen, N. J.: Scarecrow Press, 1974). Chapter 3 of the Guide is devoted to a description of
bibliographies and other guides to the literature
of the field. Also of note are the annual reviews
of the "year's work in American library history"
which appear in the Journal of Library History.

Beard, J. R.  Canadian Provincial Libraries.  Ottawa, 1967.

Bell, W. J., Jr.  "The Old Library of the Pennsylvania
     Hospital," Bulletin of the Medical Library Association
     60 (1972): 543-50.

Boorstin, D.  The Americans: the Colonial Experience.
     New York, 1958.

Briggs, F. A.  "The Sunday School Library in the Nineteenth
     Century," Library Quarterly 31 (1961): 166-77.

Brough, K.  Scholar's Workshop: Evolving Conceptions of
     Library Service.  Urbana, 1953.

Cannon, C. L.  American Book Collectors and Collecting
     from Colonial Times to the Present.  New York, 1941.

Clayton, H.  "The American College Library: 1800-1860,"
     Journal of Library History 3 (1968): 120-37.

Clemons, H.  The University of Virginia Library.  Char-
     lottesville, 1954.

Constantine, R.  "The Vincennes Library Company: A Cul-
     tural Institution in Pioneer Indiana," Indiana Magazine
     of History 61 (1965): 305-89; 62 (1966): 121-54, 305-
     44; 63 (1967): 125-54.

Cushman, A. B.  "A Nineteenth Century Plan for Reading:
     The American Sunday School Movement," Horn Book
     33 (1957): 61-71, 159-66.

Ditzion, S.  "The District School Library, 1835-1855,"
Library Quarterly 10 (1940):  197-219.

_____.  "Mechanics' and Mercantile Libraries," Library
Quarterly 10 (1940): 197-219.

Donnelly, F. D.  The National Library of Canada. Ottawa,
1973.

Drolet, A.  Les Bibliothèques Canadiennes, 1604-1960.
Ottawa, 1965.

Granniss, R. S.  "American Book Collecting and the Growth
of Libraries," in Helmut Lehmann-Haupt and others,
The Book in America... New York, 1952.

Harding, T. S.  College Literary Societies. Brooklyn, 1971.

Harris, M. H. , ed.  The Age of Jewett; Charles Coffin Jewett and American Librarianship, 1841-1868.  Littleton,
Colo. , 1975.

Harwell, R.  "College Libraries," in Encyclopedia of Library and Information Science 5 (1971): 269-81.

Held, R.  Public Libraries in California, 1849-1878. Berkeley, 1963.

Jelin, V.  "The Instrumental Use of Libraries:  A Study of
the Intellectual Origins of the Modern Industrial Libraries in Nineteenth Century America," Libri 20
(1970):  15-28.

Jennings, J. M.  The Library of the College of William and
Mary in Virginia, 1693-1793.  Charlottesville, 1968.

Johnston, W. O.  History of the Library of Congress, 1800-
1864.  Washington, 1904.

Keep, A. B.  History of the New York Society Library.
New York, 1908.

Korty, M. B.  "Benjamin Franklin and Eighteenth Century
American Libraries," Transactions of the American
Philosophical Society, New Series, 55 (1965).

Kraus, J. W.  "The Book Collections of Early American
College Libraries," Library Quarterly 43 (1973): 142-59.

_____. "Libraries of the Young Men's Christian Associations in the Nineteenth Century," Journal of Library History 10 (1975): 3-21.

Kruzas, A. T. Business and Industrial Libraries in the United States, 1820-1940. New York, 1965.

Laugher, C. T. Thomas Bray's Grand Design. Chicago, 1973.

Leonard, I. A. Books of the Brave: Being an Account of Books and of Men in the Spanish Conquest and Settlement of the Sixteenth-Century New World. Cambridge, 1949.

Linglebach, W. E. "The Library of the American Philosophical Society," William and Mary Quarterly 3 (1946): 48-69.

Lockridge, K. Literacy in Colonial New England: An Inquiry into the Social Context of Literacy in the Early Modern West. New York, 1974.

McMullen, C. H. The Founding of Social and Public Libraries in Ohio, Indiana and Illinois through 1850. Urbana, Illinois, 1958.

_____. "The Founding of Social Libraries in Pennsylvania, 1731-1876," Pennsylvania History 32 (1965): 130-52.

_____. "The Prevalence of Libraries in the United States before 1876: Some Regional Differences," in Proceedings of the Fourth Library History Seminar. Tallahassee, 1972, pp. 115-39.

_____. "Social Libraries in Ante-bellum Kentucky," Register of Kentucky Historical Society 58 (1960): 97-128.

Mearns, D. C. The Story Up to Now: the Library of Congress, 1800-1946. Washington, 1947.

Metcalf, K. D. "The Undergraduate and the Harvard Library, 1765-1877," Harvard Library Bulletin 1 (1947): 29-51.

Predeek, A.  A History of Libraries in Great Britain and
    North America.  Chicago, 1947.

Ranz, James.  The Printed Book Catalogue in American Li-
    braries, 1723-1900.  Chicago, 1963.

Roseberry, C. R.  For the Government and People of This
    State; A History of the New York State Library.  Al-
    bany, 1970.

Rosenbach, A. S. W.  The Libraries of the Presidents of
    the United States.  Worchester, 1935.

Shera, J. H.  Foundations of the Public Library.  Chicago,
    1949.

Shores, L.  Origins of the American College Library, 1638-
    1800.  New York, 1935.

Skallerup, H. R.  Books Afloat and Ashore:  A History of
    Books, Libraries, and Reading Among Seamen during
    the Age of Sail.  Hamden, Conn. , 1974.

Sowerby, M.  "Thomas Jefferson and His Library," Papers
    of the Bibliographic Society of America 50 (1956):
    213-228.

Spain, F. L.  "Libraries of South Carolina:  Their Origins
    and Early History, 1700-1830," Library Quarterly 16
    (1947): 28-42.

Stone, E. W.  Historical Approach to American Library De-
    velopment.  Urbana, Illinois, 1967.

Thompson, C. S.  Evolution of the American Public Library,
    1638-1876.  Washington, 1952.

Thompson, L.  "The Libraries of Colonial Spanish Amer-
    ica," in his Essays on Hispanic Bibliography.  Ham-
    den, Conn. , 1970, pp. 3-18.

## Chapter 11

## MODERN EUROPEAN LIBRARIES

It is quite appropriate to end a discussion of early American library development with the middle of the nineteenth century. For it was the second half of that century which witnessed the rise of the library types and library services which characterize contemporary American libraries. Similarly, it would seem appropriate to begin our consideration of modern European libraries at the conclusion of World War I; a war that wreaked havoc across much of Europe, and had a major impact on library development.

On 28 June, 1914, the assassination of the nephew, and heir of the Austro-Hungarian emperor touched off a cataclysm that was to have profound implications for the world, and consequently for the development of libraries. Immediately obvious were the demands made on staffing and the financing of already established libraries, both aspects being severely proscribed as men were called to military service and money spent on peacetime activities was channeled increasingly into the war effort. Later developments included the destruction or capture of major library resources, such as the destruction of the Library of the University in Louvain on 27 August, 1914, and the gradual but increasingly mindless destruction of libraries as the fates of war sent first one victorious army and then another charging across the face of Europe. Finally, the war provided the Russian communists with the opportunity of reconstituting the now Soviet world in a hitherto unknown fashion; a fact that was to have an extremely influential effect on the development of libraries in that part of the world.

Given these justifications for picking up the history of European libraries at the conclusion of World War I, how is

this topic to be treated?  This question has proven exceeding-
ly difficult for library historians, for unlike the rather uniform nature of library development in the Americas--espe-
cially North America--the European library scene virtually
defies generalization.  This serious difficulty is further complicated by the fact of World War II, which had a devastating
influence on much of Europe, and led in effect to the emergence, in many countries, of a radically altered form of government, a development of great significance to libraries in
those countries.

In short, the history of European libraries from the
conclusion of World War I is not unlike a giant mosaic made
up of many pieces of varied sizes and irregular shapes--a
mosaic that, due to its size and complexity, clearly defies
ready interpretation.  And yet, the requirements of a book
of this type demand an attempt to discover the figure in the
carpet, the essential threads that dominate the pattern.  To
facilitate further investigation an extensive bibliography has
been appended to this chapter.

## The Continued Development of the National Library

In Chapter 9 it was noted that Europe's greatest libraries were her national libraries.  This fact is even more
apparent when we examine the history of these libraries in
the twentieth century.  France's Bibliothèque Nationale, Britain's British Museum (now part of the British Library), Russia's monolithic state library in Leningrad, and the new national library in Moscow, the Lenin Library, represent the
greatest libraries in their respective countries, in Europe
itself, and, indeed, rank among the finest in the whole
world.

Their growth has not been without trials and setbacks.
The two great wars, economic fluctuations, and changes in
governmental patterns have all contributed to the troubles to
be surmounted by those charged with the responsibility of
managing these ever more complex and important national
resources.  A brief examination of the history of some of
these libraries will help us to appreciate their development.

As noted earlier, the European national libraries were
well established, and generally thriving prior to World War
I.  In addition, their decidedly nationalistic emphasis and
their stature as the best financed and staffed libraries in

their respective countries allowed them to survive, and in
some cases, to benefit from the War. The Bibliothèque Nationale is a case in point. While it suffered seriously at
the hands of invaders during the two world wars, the library, due to its symbolic and real significance to the
French nation, enjoyed a rapid and substantial growth after
each of the conflicts. Book stocks were increased at a rapid rate, ever more people were employed by the library,
and financial support rose significantly. Today the Bibliothèque Nationale enjoys the reputation of being France's finest library, and ranks as a major library resource in all of
Europe. Like other European libraries, it has suffered of
late from the financial instability so prevalent in Europe,
but it remains the bibliographic and professional library center in France, and perhaps in all of Europe.

A similar consistent growth is evident in the history
of the British Museum Library in the twentieth century.
Recently, observers of the national library scene have been
impressed by the bold and imaginative creation of the British
Library in the short span of time from 1967 to 1972. This
new national library system consists of four main divisions:
the Lending Division (National Central Library and National
Lending Library of Science and Technology), located in Boston Spa; the Reference Division (the British Museum Library
and its various departments) in London; the Bibliographic
Services Division; and the Central Administration Division.
The objective of this unified and expanded service is:

> to provide the best possible library services for
> the United Kingdom ... preserving and making
> available for reference at least one copy of every
> book and periodical of domestic origin and of as
> many overseas publications as possible ... pro-
> viding an efficient central lending and photocopy-
> ing service in support of the other libraries and
> information systems of the country; and providing
> central cataloguing and other bibliographic services
> related not only to the needs of the central li-
> braries but to those of libraries and information
> centres throughout the country and in close coop-
> eration with central libraries overseas.

This new national library format promises to meet
the needs of the readers of the United Kingdom despite the
severe economic problems besetting the country, and to
greatly enhance the reference and lending library services
available throughout the nation.

In Russia, the Revolution of 1917, stimulated by the panic and political chaos engendered with the outset of World War I, resulted in the long run in the improvement of the national library. After a few months of disorganization and uncertainty the former imperial library was declared a national collection, and its holdings were enriched by the acquisition of many collections formerly owned privately by the Russian nobility. Under the new Soviet government this enormously enlarged library was designated the Russian Public Library, but it was later labeled the Saltykov-Shchedrin State Library. Its growth has continued unabated, and today its holdings number some 20 million volumes. Its importance has also grown in time, and its activities in every area of library, bibliographic and documentary services has increased in kind, although it serves now primarily as the national library for the Russian Federation.

While the State Library in Leningrad may be called the Russian National Library by virtue of its descent from the former imperial library, the Lenin State Library in Moscow has recently replaced it as the official national library and is even larger in size. Its predecessor was the collection of books housed in the Rumyantsev Museum, founded in 1862, which numbered nearly a million volumes prior to the Revolution. After 1917, it, too, was enlarged with books confiscated from private and other libraries, and a substantial amount of money was expended for new books. Today it contains over 25 million cataloged items, including books, pamphlets, and periodicals. Taken together, the two Russian "National Libraries" represent one of the largest and most progressive national library systems in the world, and their influence and control over library affairs in communist Europe is unrivaled.

Another example of national library development in Europe can be found in Germany. After World War I, the title of the Berlin library reverted to that of Prussian State Library, but its collection grew to more than 2,500,000 by 1930, with 55,000 manuscripts and over 400,000 maps. At that time it was receiving some 20,000 periodicals and cooperating closely with other major libraries, while continuing to be a bibliographic center for the entire nation. Among its many strong points were an almost unequalled collection on music and music history, and a collection on the history of World War I containing over 100,000 items. Under such librarians as Adolph von Harnack, Fritz Milkau, and Hugo Anders Kruess, the influence of the Berlin Library was felt throughout the library world.

During World War II the holdings of the Prussian
State Library were evacuated from Berlin, with some parts
going to various smaller towns where it was felt they would
be safer.  After the end of the war and the division of Germany into East Germany and West Germany, the holdings located in West Germany were brought together into the library of the University of Marburg.  Despite crowded conditions, this West German Library, as it was designated, had
grown to some 2,000,000 volumes by 1966.  The Deutsche
Bucherei at Leipzig, which had served Germany from 1912
to 1945 as a non-lending depository library and bibliographic
center, was located in East Germany after World War II.  A
West German counterpart was developed at Frankfurt when
the Deutsche Bibliothek was founded in 1946; it obtained a
new and modern building in 1959, by which time it had some
300,000 volumes.  Designed more for preservation than for
immediate use, this library serves West Germany as a national bibliographic center.

All of the other countries of modern Europe have national libraries, although some few go by another name.  In
nearly every case these libraries represent the finest libraries in their respective countries, and generally can boast
of the largest collections, the most impressive quarters, and
the best qualified and most influential staffs.  Their charge
is admittedly nationalistic, and as a result, use policies are
often characterized by restrictions that reflect the goals and
political philosophies of their respective governments.  Nearly all of these libraries are afflicted with serious space and
staff shortages, all incurred as a result of the consistent
and rapid growth of their collections.  Despite their problems
the national libraries of Europe represent a magnificent cultural heritage in graphic form, and they would appear to have
a bright future in the years to come.

## University Libraries in Contemporary Europe

Each of the countries of modern Europe can boast at
least one institution of higher learning, and these institutions
all possess some kind of library.  But, not unlike the situation with the national libraries described above, there is
more variety than standardization; more differences than similarities.  Nevertheless, the nature of academic library development in twentieth-century Europe can be illustrated by
a selective look at what appear to be representative countries.  Most of these libraries have struggled with the re-

current problem of the frequent destruction of their holdings and the disruption of services caused by the two world wars. Not infrequently, the history of a major academic library is characterized by a cycle of growth, destruction, rebuilding, destruction and a second major rebuilding.

Academic libraries in France were large and well housed prior to World War I. During that war a number of these libraries, such as the library at the University of Nancy, were destroyed. In World War II, the University of Caen, including its fine library, was destroyed by bombing, and a number of other libraries were destroyed or damaged in the invasions of northern France. After each war these libraries were rebuilt and French university libraries have enjoyed a steady growth since the end of World War II. Financial difficulties, and the consistent pressures to expand to handle the ever-increasing collections and meet new demands for services, remain the basic problems facing French academic libraries.

English higher education, once the monopoly of Oxford and Cambridge, has expanded with increasing rapidity in the twentieth century. These new libraries were generally spared any serious difficulty in World War I, but faced a severe test in the bombing of England that accompanied World War II. Today a number of major universities exist across England, and they are generally served by large and modern libraries. The University of London is typical, with its impressive library numbering over four million volumes. Oxford and Cambridge continue their leadership in academic library areas, although the libraries at both institutions are characterized by extreme decentralization. Both libraries contain in aggregate very substantial research collections, and are counted among the finest university libraries in the world.

The twentieth century has seen both great disasters and great progress for German libraries of all types. Although university libraries were not physically damaged during World War I, they suffered from a lack of staff, funds, and foreign publications. The needs of science and industry, emphasized by the war, encouraged the growth of technical institutes and colleges in the 1920s, but the uncertain political and economic conditions, with inflation followed by depression, prevented much progress. During the years after 1933, while Germany was under the dictatorship of Adolf Hitler, the university libraries were subjected to close gov-

ernmental control, although in general the scholarly libraries
did not suffer from book purges and book burnings as much
as the public libraries.  Funds were still short, however,
and staff members too few.  An indication of the low ebb of
library progress can be seen in the fact that not a single
new university library building was constructed in Germany
between 1914 and 1950.

World War II brought tremendous physical destruction
in the Allied air raids on Germany.  The university libraries at Bonn, Breslau, Frankfurt, Göttingen, Jena, Kiel,
Munich, Munster and Würzburg were either destroyed or
heavily damaged and many staff members were killed.  At
Jena, for example, sixteen staff members were killed in one
bombing raid.  At Hamburg over 700,000 volumes were de-
stroyed--almost the entire collection of the combined State
and University Library there--while at Frankfurt over 600,000
volumes were destroyed and at Würzburg over 350,000.  Other institutions suffered less seriously, but the combined
losses totaled millions of volumes.  Some valuable manuscripts and early printed books were saved by sending them
to areas less likely to be bombed.

After 1945 Germany was divided into eastern and western zones, with the former becoming a Communist state under the control of Soviet Russia.  Here the universities of
Jena, Leipzig and Rostock, for example, have been converted into centers of Communist learning and their libraries
have become part of a nationwide system dedicated to both
research and indoctrination.  At first the libraries were
purged of all pro-Nazi or anti-Communist literature; but
later, with the emphasis on books and learning that is an
earmark of Communist countries, the empty shelves were
filled with proper Communist literature and these universities have rapidly regained their position in the library world,
at least in number of volumes.  In the 1970s the six major
universities in East Germany together held over eight million volumes, with that at Leipzig being the largest.

In West Germany, the postwar period has seen remarkable recovery and advances in university libraries.  A
new university, the Free University of West Berlin, has already grown to nearly a million volumes, while the University of Frankfurt Library, after being almost destroyed, has
come back to nearly two million volumes.  Many new library
buildings and additions have been constructed, including
those at Bonn, completed in 1961; at the Free University in

Berlin, 1956; and at the University of Mainz in 1964. New
technical colleges have been formed in most of the major
cities, with their own specialized library systems. All told,
the eighteen major university libraries in West Germany and
West Berlin have bookstocks of nearly twenty million volumes. Major problems faced by these libraries, besides
rebuilding and recouping war losses, have been the acquisition of foreign publications missed during the Hitler years,
and the control of the myriad publications currently appearing. The training of new staff members for the tasks resulting from the large numbers of students and the new subjects being taught have also been major problems. Some
solutions have been found in cooperative purchasing, particularly of foreign materials, and liberal policies and practices
in interlibrary lending.

The central libraries of German universities have
traditionally been the workshops of scholars rather than
study halls or required reading rooms for undergraduates;
therefore, a new outlook or philosophy of librarianship was
needed for this new era. Moreover, German librarians
have generally been scholars rather than administrators or
specialists in public service, so that here, too, changes have
sometimes been in order. The problem of institute libraries connected with the universities still exists. These
libraries, usually specialized collections selected by profes-
sors, are often uncataloged or poorly cataloged, staffed by
untrained personnel, and outside the control of the central
library. They contain tens of thousands of useful volumes,
but the lack of a union catalog or of centralized selection
and acquisition results in much duplication and confusion on
most campuses. In East Germany, Communist state control
has forced centralization to some extent on the university libraries there, but in West Germany the institute and departmental libraries remain a problem. Despite these obstacles,
German university libraries continue to make progress and
are rapidly regaining their former position in the library
world.

In Russia, university libraries are quite a different
story. There, universities were late in beginning and grew
only slowly until the twentieth century. Since the Russian
Revolution, however, the university libraries have grown
tremendously, both in size and numbers, and they constitute
today an important part of the overall library program in
the Soviet Union. The oldest university in Russia proper
is the University of Moscow, founded by M. V. Lomonosov

in 1755. The Universities of Vilnius and Lvov, now in the
Soviet Union, but formerly in Lithuania and Poland, were
founded in 1570 and 1681 respectively, and in the nineteenth
century others were founded at St. Petersburg, Kazan, Kharkov, Kiev, Dorpat and Odessa. University libraries were
small in the early nineteenth century but the central collections were usually supplemented by both student and departmental collections. Moscow University grew most rapidly,
receiving over a hundred major gifts of private collections.
The University of Kazan Library was fortunate in having the
mathematician Nikolai Lobachevski as librarian from 1825 to
1835, and he made it the best-organized library in Russia,
complete with a full catalog and his own classification system. In 1834, it moved into a new building and shortly afterward began a card catalog, one of the earliest in Europe.

The development of Russian university libraries in the
late nineteenth century can be inferred from their bookstocks
in 1876 and 1910. During that period, Moscow grew from
some 150,000 to over 300,000 volumes, and other collections
grew as follows: St. Petersburg, 50,000 to 125,000; Dorpat
(now the University of Tartu), 125,000 to 400,000; Odessa,
40,000 to 250,000; and Kazan, 100,000 to 242,000. By the
beginning of World War I there were thirteen major universities in Russia with some 3,000,000 volumes in their libraries
for their 43,000 students. This does not generally count the
books available in libraries other than the central collections. The Russian Revolution of 1917 brought tremendous
changes to university libraries, and new universities were established even before the war was over. The Ural State University at Sverdlovsk was founded by Lenin himself, and others were established in 1918 in Tiflis and Tashkent. By
1925, when the higher education system was centralized under national control, there were universities in virtually
every part of the Soviet Union, and their libraries, often
aided by books taken from religious institutions and private
libraries, were seldom smaller than 100,000 volumes. Since
that time, the importance of the Soviet university libraries
can hardly be overestimated. The Communist effort to edu-
cate all the people to their highest capacity has brought an
emphasis on education and libraries unsurpassed anywhere
else in the world. Although the libraries have also served
a propaganda purpose and at times have been severely curtailed to keep out non-Communist ideas, they have undoubtedly helped bring the people of the Soviet Union from the Middle
Ages to the twentieth century in little more than a generation.

During World War II, many university libraries in the Ukraine, White Russia, and even in Moscow and Leningrad were severely damaged if not completely destroyed. The State University of Leningrad, for example, was almost completely razed in the fighting for that city, but most of its book contents had already been moved to Saratov, and after 1945 it was rebuilt even larger than before. All of the libraries at the University of Kiev were destroyed or heavily damaged, and damage was severe at Kharkov, Minsk, and other universities. Since 1945 these institutions have been rebuilt and new ones established, as for example at Daghestan and Yakutsk, along with scores of technical and scientific colleges and institutes. Holdings in the sciences, both Russian and foreign, are often excellent, but the humanities and social sciences sometimes suffer from neglect or regulated purchasing. The Marxist-Leninist philosophy, however, is represented by multiple titles and copies in all institutions, since it represents virtually a curriculum in itself in Russian colleges. The "Regulations for Libraries of Institutes of Higher Learning" issued in 1962 cover all phases of administration of college and university libraries, and include as part of the purpose of those libraries the "Communist training of student youth."

In the early 1970s the Moscow State University library had over six million volumes in its combined central and departmental collections, and it received over two thousand foreign periodicals as well as all major Russian publications. It has a total of forty-five separate reading rooms in its various facilities, with a seating capacity of over nineteen hundred. This is one of the largest of Russian university libraries, but there are many others with over a million volumes each, including the Academy of Science at Kiev with over five million. All university libraries are under the direction of the Ministry of Higher Education which controls the nearly 1,000 universities, colleges, institutes, academies, and conservatories. There are many subsidiary libraries on each university campus, but control is usually in the hands of the central library director and centralized acquisitions and cataloging are more effective than in the universities of western Europe. Library specialization, coupled with good bibliographic controls and easy interlibrary lending, give Soviet Russia a well-organized and efficient educational and research library system.

One further example of academic library development in Europe is the case of Poland. That country's university

libraries go back well into the fourteenth century, when the
University of Cracow was founded in 1364. Called the Jagellonian University since it was organized in 1400 by Ladislas
Jagellon, this university has played a prominent role in the
history of Poland. Copernicus studied there in the fifteenth
century. Although other early universities were established
in Lvov and Vilna, now in the Soviet Union, Cracow University remained the major institution of higher education in
Poland down to the nineteenth century. A university was established in Warsaw in 1808, and several others were added
when Poland was recreated as an independent state in 1918.
During World War II, the University of Warsaw was forced
to go "underground" when the Germans occupied Poland, and
its campus and libraries were virtually destroyed in the early
fighting in 1939, and again in the uprising of the Poles
against the Germans in 1944. However, these hardships only served to stir the students and faculty to higher efforts.
Today an entirely new university has been built, and its library of nearly 3,000,000 volumes is playing a major part
in the cultural development of the nation. In Cracow, the
Jagellonian University was closed by the Germans in 1939,
and then reopened with its library increased by books confiscated from the estates of executed Poles and Jews. In 1944
the loyal members of the library staff secretly collected Polish underground publications. When the German armies retreated near the end of the war, they carried away many of
the treasures from the University Library, but fortunately
most of these were later retrieved. Today, together with
hundreds of thousands of later acquisitions, these treasures
are housed in a completely new library building, one of the
most modern in Europe.

Since 1945, other universities have been established in
Poland, including the Marie Curie Sklodowska University in
Lublin, whose central library now totals over 500,000 volumes; the University of Lodz; and several other specialized
institutes and colleges for the various arts and sciences.
Two universities with old but excellent library collections are
located in areas reclaimed by the Poles from Germany in
1945. These are the universities of Wroclaw (Breslau), originally founded in 1505, and the Copernicus University at Tor-
un in Pomerania. University libraries in Poland, as in other
Communist-dominated countries, have a double role to play
as agencies of both education and indoctrination.

In organization and administration, the university libraries of Europe have many similarities and many differ-

ences.   Generally speaking, they differ most from American
universities in the large number of more or less autonomous
faculty and institute libraries.   These specialized collections
are valuable to their immediate clientele, but, though many
of them are large, they are often poorly cataloged, poorly
staffed, and virtually unknown and unavailable to students and
faculty of other departments on the same campus.   In classification, a variety of individual systems is used, but more
are turning in recent years to the Universal Decimal Classification system.   Catalogs are usually divided, with an alphabetical author catalog supplemented by a classed or topical
catalog.   Alphabetical subject indexes to the classed catalog
are sometimes found, but completely alphabetical subject
catalogs or combined author-subject-title catalogs are rare.
Closed stacks are more frequent than open ones, although
general reading collections on open shelves are becoming
more common.   Arrangement within the stacks is usually by
accession number or size, a system which aids in keeping
the stacks closed but also is useful in crowded conditions
and in storage collections.   Most libraries lend books for
outside use but usually have non-circulating collections which
vary considerably in size.   A major problem in most European libraries is the low salaries available for professional
librarians and the consequent scarcity of competent personnel.   By American standards most university libraries, particularly in western Europe, are understaffed, even at the
semi-professional and clerical levels.   However, the future
looks better; new buildings are under way or being planned
for many institutions, library training institutions are providing more trained personnel, and budgets are generally
higher.

    Since 1500 the university libraries of Europe have
borne more than their share of the task of preserving and
extending the cultural heritage of the western world.   National libraries have contributed to this task, and in the past
century the public libraries have joined in.   On the whole,
however, it has been the university libraries that have
served as the research centers in all fields--scientific, literary and historical.   In some instances and in some places
the university library has curtailed the search for knowledge,
limiting the acquisition and use of books according to some
preconceived religious belief or political philosophy.   But
fortunately this has not generally been the case, and the university library has served as a treasure house of old ideas
and a fountainhead of new ones.   Whether it was the university of 1500--with few books, few teachers and few students

--or the university of the 1970s, with millions of books, hundreds of teachers, and thousands of students, the basic story has been the same.  The university has been a combination of teachers, students, and books that have together preserved, passed on, and increased man's knowledge of himself and his world.


European Public Libraries

        Public libraries represent, in aggregate, one of the great cultural resources of modern Europe.  And while they vary significantly in size and function from one country to another, they do share one common feature:  they are invariably the most "popular" libraries in their respective countries, and as such, serve the people more extensively than any other type of library.  As we noted in our discussion of European public libraries in Chapter 9, by the beginning of World War I most European nations had arrived at the point where they agreed that some form of publicly supported library service was desirable.  This emerging support for the public library idea was based on a number of assumptions: the value of reading as a harmless form of recreation; the efficacy of the printed word in the control of social and political behavior; and the significance of the free access to information to the success of democratic forms of government.  Obviously, different governments placed varying emphasis on one or another of these justifications for public library support, but the fact remains that public libraries were a reality in most of Europe prior to the outset of World War I.  The years following this war were characterized by fifty years of strengthening and expansion as can be seen in the history of public library development in France, England, East and West Germany, and Russia.

        During World War I, there was considerable destruction of public libraries in northeastern France, including those at Rheims, Arras, Lille, and Verdun, and scores of smaller collections.  Many rare and valuable books were lost in the ruins of these libraries.  After the war, American aid helped in the establishment of model public libraries in Soissons and Paris.  Recognition of the public circulating library as distinct from the public research library became more common in France in the 1920s, and several cities made efforts toward reorganizing their libraries in this direction.  In 1929-30 a second nationwide library survey was made, with much the same outcome as a generation earlier.

This time, however, there were some results.  In the 1930s, despite the depression, experiments were made not only with public circulating collections but also with children's libraries, bookmobiles, branch libraries, factory libraries, and even a barge library for families living and working on the network of French rivers and canals.  Paris enlarged most of its popular libraries and placed them in larger quarters or separate buildings.  An Association for Public Libraries was formed to promote libraries and library services. In 1937 a special appropriation of two million francs was made by the French government for the purchase of public library books.  Some three hundred libraries throughout the nation shared in this distribution, all of them under the control and supervision of the Ministry of Public Instruction. They were divided into three types:  those with large or valuable collections, supervised directly by the national library office; those of smaller size or less-important collections, requiring at least one trained librarian to direct; and those smaller libraries without professional staff but visited regularly by supervisors from the national library office.  Despite this relative progress, the coming of World War II found France without a modern public library system and still generally under the impression that libraries should be for serious research only.

Because France fell to the German armies early in the conflict, war damage to French libraries was relatively light.  In 1944 and 1945, when the Allied invasion took place, there was some damage to libraries, but nothing to compare with that of World War I.  However, during the German occupation many libraries were closed, some valuable manuscripts were seized by the Germans, and a few libraries suffered confiscation of materials judged to be anti-Nazi or pro-Communist.  Some Jewish librarians and others active in the French underground were imprisoned or sent to concentration camps.  The librarian of the Bibliothèque Nationale, Julian Cain, was one of these.  After the war the new French government recognized the importance of public libraries by establishing a National Office of Public Libraries and Public Reading.  Today France has over five hundred municipal libraries and some cities have both central reference libraries and popular circulating library systems.  Facilities for children and young people's libraries, phonograph listening rooms, and rooms for public meetings are available in some of the more modern buildings.  Some of the French départements or regions have established department-wide lending libraries.  For example, the department of Haut-Rhin has a

central library at Colmar with over one hundred thousand
volumes for use through its five hundred lending   stations.
In Paris, each of the twenty <u>arrondissements</u> or divisions of
the city has its own central library with one or more branch
libraries.   Generally, however, public library service in
France is still poor compared with the best available in other parts of Europe and America.   Few trained librarians and
low salaries for those employed in libraries are two reasons
for relatively poor library service in France.   There is also a lack of appreciation of just what efficient public library
service is.   In the towns where local government has been
in the hands of left-wing parties, there is a greater realization of the value of reading matter and public libraries are
often strongly supported, possibly more for propaganda purposes than for education.   However, the promotion of library service in these towns stimulated other municipalities
to similar action and aroused the general public to the po-
tential value of public libraries.

Despite two world wars and a long period of economic depression in the twentieth century, England's public libraries have nevertheless grown and extended their usefulness
to all parts of the islands and to all walks of life.   In 1919,
the County Library Act removed the tax-rate limitations
previously imposed on local funds for libraries, and thus increased the financial support of library service considerably.
County libraries had been tried in a few places before this
date, but the great majority of the rural population had no
access to libraries.   With permissive legislation and aid
from the Carnegie United Kingdom Trust, more county libraries were established, and by 1926, county-wide library
service was available in all but five counties in England,
Scotland, Wales and Northern Ireland.   The depression years
saw increased demands on public libraries, but decreased
funds at the same time.   Nevertheless, the British public libraries have pioneered in branch libraries, bookmobiles, library service by mail, library service to hospitals and institutions, and in general library cooperation, so that they have
taken a lead in the library world and set examples of service
for all to follow.

One special element of British public library service
is that provided by the National Central Library in London.
Founded in 1916 as the Central Library for Students, to provide books for the city's adult education classes, it was enlarged in size and purpose in 1927 to provide a source of
books for students of all ages throughout the nation.   It also

serves as a clearing house for interlibrary loans and as a center for cooperative library and bibliographic projects. In 1933 it moved into a new building given by the Carnegie Trust, but this was largely destroyed by bombing raids in World War II. Since 1945 it has been reconstructed, and with its bibliographic tools and union catalogs it aids in making available to all British citizens any book in any British library. Connected with it is the British National Book Centre, which controls exchange and distribution of library duplicates. To supplement and expand the services of the National Central Library, a National Lending Library of Science and Technology was established in the 1960s. This institution, located in the north of England, not only provides the service that its name indicates but is also a national bibliographic and documentation center for the sciences.

The public libraries of London provide an interesting example of the growth of library service in a great metropolitan area. Under the Public Libraries Act each borough of London was entitled to establish its own library system but most of them were very slow in doing so. Not until the 1920s was a public library service general throughout the city and its suburbs, and the resulting system, or series of systems, included some 124 libraries with over 4,000,000 volumes by the 1950s. The London Government Act of 1963 reduced the governmental units in Greater London to a total of thirty-two, and each was to have its own library system. This entailed much reorganization and many administrative changes, but the results gave London a greatly improved library service. One interesting feature of the new service is the city-wide library borrower's card, which entitles the reader to use any unit of any public library in Greater London.

Many public libraries suffered great losses during the air raids of the war. The British Museum lost a wing that housed some 150,000 books and 30,000 volumes of bound newspapers, many of them unique. Public libraries in Manchester, Birmingham, Bristol, Liverpool, Sheffield, and Portsmouth were also hard hit by the enemy raids. Numerous smaller libraries and branches also suffered partial or complete destruction, and the total book loss of the war in Britain, including libraries, bookstores, and publishers' stocks, has been estimated at over 20,000,000 volumes. In the rebuilding, however, Britain has gained many modern library buildings, and library service has improved in proportion. In the 1970s, one hundred per cent of Britain's popu-

lation has available public library service.  There are some
500 public library administrative units with central libraries,
and over 2,000 branches and 20,000 part-time outlets.  The
public libraries of Manchester and Liverpool, and the county
libraries of Lancashire and Essex, each have over 1,000,000
volumes, and under the new British Library System public
libraries throughout Great Britain have access to enormous
library resources.  Nearly thirty per cent of the total population are registered library users, making Great Britain one
of the most library-conscious nations in the world.  No account of the library service of modern Britain should omit
the work done by the Library Association, founded in 1877
and now having over 15,000 members.  In promoting library
education and research, improved library legislation, and
the progress of library service in general, the Library Association has played an important part in greatly improving the
status of libraries and librarians, not only in Great Britain
but throughout the world.

        World War I did not seriously affect the physical con-
dition of German public libraries but it slowed down library
service in general.  After the war, the new Republic of Germany paid more attention to the need for popular library
service, and town libraries became more common, particularly in northern and eastern Germany.  By 1926 there were
356 Volksbibliotheken, but they were usually small, and since
the name implied that they were for the use of the lower
classes, they were neither well used nor adequately supported.  In the same year there were 273 public research libraries (including state universities and "national" libraries)
with holdings of more than 34,000,000 volumes.  The gulf
between research libraries and popular libraries remained as
wide as ever.  However, there was now a federal governmental agency to promote library service by assisting the
smaller libraries in selecting and acquiring books, and a Society for Library Service in the Frontier States helped provide popular libraries in the eastern area.  Among the larger
cities, Hamburg and Berlin took the lead in providing popular service, and a few of the smaller towns revised their libraries along western lines with circulating and juvenile collections.  Berlin's Municipal Library was given quarters in
the former royal stables, and in these quarters it contained
over 260,000 volumes by 1930.  A systematic buildup of all
Berlin's library services was begun, with the public, special,
and university libraries cooperating to provide the best possible library services, but this progress was slowed in the
depression years following 1929.

When the Nazis came into power in 1933, the development of libraries in Germany was seriously curtailed except
for a few favored institutions.  All public libraries were
placed under strict government control, and censorship over
their contents was rigidly enforced.  Books by Jewish or
Communist authors were removed from circulation and often
publicly burned.  Acquisition of books from other countries
was virtually stopped.  Libraries were made a part of the
propaganda system, and all efforts were directed toward the
development of a strong German nationalism.  In the Slavic
areas of eastern Germany, books and libraries were employed to make good German citizens out of the former Poles
and Czechs.  Not only was the freedom of the press curtailed but the Nazis tried to control the minds of the people
as well, and the public library was considered an essential
part of this plan.

During World War II, popular and research libraries
suffered from the Allied bombing raids.  State libraries in
Kassel, Stuttgart, Dresden and Würtemburg were completely
or largely destroyed.  Less damage was done at Darmstadt,
Kiel, Dortmund, and Düsseldorf.  In thirty-one major municipal libraries, with over fourteen million volumes between
them, more than fifty per cent of the book stock was destroyed.  Many smaller public libraries also suffered, and
it is estimated that in all of Germany more than one-third of
all public library books were destroyed or damaged.  Along
with popular reading matter, which could eventually be replaced, many irreplaceable manuscripts and unique copies of
printed works were lost.

Since 1945 the story of public libraries in West Germany has been one of reconstruction and rapid growth.  Particularly on the popular library level, there has been a tremendous increase in service and books available.  Some of
the larger Volksbibliotheken are now adding scholarly collections and reference services to take some of the research
load off of the reference libraries, while in other cities
Einheitsbibliotheken or unified reference and popular libraries
are being tried.  By the 1970s there were over ten thousand
popular libraries containing together over fifteen million
books and circulating over fifty million volumes per year.
However, at the same time there were over 600,000,000
books borrowed from commercial lending libraries, indicating that the public libraries are still far from meeting the
public demand for popular reading material.  Church libraries for congregational use are also popular in Germany,

and although they were small there are nearly eleven thousand of these including both Catholic and Protestant.    In each German state (Land) there are central library agencies to coordinate the work of the public circulating libraries, and in addition they are promoting publicly supported libraries in factories, mines, hospitals, prisons, and even in large department stores.    Munich provides a good illustration of the library situation in the larger cities.    There one finds a Stadtsbibliothek or public reference library of some 500,000 volumes, and a Stadtbücherei or public circulating library with 600,000 volumes and twenty-eight branches. Indicative of Bavaria's cultural interests, there is also a public music library with over 100,000 volumes.    In West Berlin, the American Memorial Library, opened in 1954, not only serves that isolated city, but is also an example of western-style library service for all of Germany.    Elsewhere in Germany, there is still a strong division between the public libraries and the research libraries, even to the extent of having separate library associations and separate programs for the training of librarians.

In East Germany, the library situation has developed somewhat differently.    As in all Soviet-dominated countries, the emphasis on library service has been high, and Leipzig continues to be a strong library and bibliographic center. However, books and libraries are strongly controlled.    All public libraries are under the control of the Ministry of Culture, and a Central Bureau for Scholarly Literature controls all access to non-Communist publications.    Under the pretense of removing pro-Nazi literature from the public libraries after 1945, a general housecleaning of all books unacceptable to the Communist commanders was made, and thousands of volumes were destroyed or confiscated.    Russian and pro-Communist works were substituted and their reading was made practically compulsory.    Throughout East Germany, the books and libraries are considered a definite part of the propaganda war.

Since the Russian Revolution, the printed word has become a much-used tool and weapon in Soviet Russia. Books by the million are poured through thousands of libraries to reach an eager public which apparently makes good use of them.    This library movement was off to a good start even by 1920.    Madame L. Haffkin-Hamburger, who had struggled long before the Revolution for library service for the Russian people, continued to work for libraries under the Soviets, and Madame Lenin (Nedezhda Krupskaya) also encouraged and sponsored libraries.   A pamphlet entitled "What Lenin Wrote and Said About Libraries" was printed and widely distributed.   By the time Soviet control was firmly established, libraries were growing rapidly, both in numbers and size.   State libraries were established in the capitals of the various Soviet Republics, and municipal libraries in the larger towns.   For example the state library of Turkmenistan in Ashkabad was organized in 1925, grew to over 150,000 volumes by 1934, and to nearly a half-million by 1960. Books in Russian public libraries increased from about 10,000,000 before the war to over 125,000,000 in 1934, while the number of readers in the same period jumped from 120,000 to 15,000,000.   To encourage and improve libraries --and to control them--library departments were established in each of the Soviet Republics, and library sections in the regional and provincial departments of education.   Besides the regular public libraries, there were libraries in factories and on collective farms, in construction camps where great projects were being built, and even on the trains of the Trans-Siberian railway.   Reading rooms were available in army camps and on naval vessels, in fact wherever large numbers of workers or citizens came together for any purpose.   Of libraries of all types--public, school and special --there were nearly 200,000 in 1934, with some 272,000,000 volumes in them, according to Russian official statistics. This averages out to one library for approximately every twelve hundred people in Russia, and that average library would have contained about fourteen hundred volumes.

World War II caused immense damage to libraries in the areas overrun by the Nazi armies and also in the major cities affected by air raids, not only in Moscow and Leningrad, but also in large provincial cities such as Minsk, Kiev, Orel and Kharkov.   Dozens of buildings were destroyed or seriously damaged, and losses in books ran into millions of volumes.   Since 1945, however, the public libraries of Russia have made a comeback, and new modern library buildings, some of them immense in size, have sprung up in the once-ravaged cities.   The post-war era has also brought new types of libraries especially designed to meet the needs of the millions of war veterans--including hospital libraries, veterans' society libraries, vocational libraries and libraries for the blind.   The war also brought a realization of the value of technical and scientific libraries, and the greatest growth since 1945 has been in the spread of scientific literature on the public, academic, and research levels.

As of the 1970s, all Russian libraries are organized into basic library networks controlled from Moscow. Three of the most important of these networks are the public, or "mass" libraries, the scientific and technical libraries, and the university libraries. The mass libraries are directed by the Ministry of Culture of the U.S.S.R., and at a lower level by the departments of culture in the various Soviet Republics. At the head of the mass libraries stands the Lenin State Library in Moscow. Besides the state or republic libraries, many of which have millions of volumes, there are also large regional libraries, city libraries, district libraries, and rural libraries. In addition to these are the trade union libraries, collective farm libraries, and public children's libraries, as well as others which are semi-public. For Russia's public libraries, the established aims are threefold: to propagate the Marxist-Leninist philosophy, to disseminate the government and Communist party news and propaganda, and to improve the material and cultural level of the people so that they can become better Soviet citizens. All public libraries are limited in accessions to books published in Russia or officially approved for Russian use. Some foreign literature, particularly scientific, is available in translation, but only a few of the larger research libraries are permitted to obtain actual books and magazines from foreign countries. Book collections must frequently be "weeded," not for worn-out books, but for books containing undesirable information. In 1950, for example, a government decree ordered the discarding of books including obsolete technical and agricultural titles; political, economic and Communist party literature published prior to 1938; and legal, war and defense literature published prior to 1941.

As of the late 1960s, there were reported to be about 400,000 libraries of all kinds in the Soviet Union. Of these, some 92,000 were larger municipal libraries with over 80,000,000 registered readers. There were 5,200 special public libraries for children, while the remainder were academic libraries, rural libraries, trade union libraries and others of special types. Altogether they held nearly two billion volumes, but such magnificent statistics require at least a small amount of interpretation. Many of the "libraries" are little more than a few shelves of books, open a few hours daily with a voluntary worker, in a village community hall or in a factory workers' lounge. Also, the large number of volumes results from multiple copies of the favorite Communist writings, and from the counting of all pamphlets and in-

dividual issues of periodicals.  Some of the larger public
libraries have hundreds of copies of the writings of Lenin
and Karl Marx.  However, even granting the duplication and
some exaggeration, the fact remains that the library picture
in Soviet Russia sets an example for serious consideration
by the rest of the world.

In other countries of Europe public libraries have also
experienced significant growth since World War II, following
the patterns already discussed.  To summarize, Europe's
publicly owned libraries have long contained treasures of literature and history that cannot be duplicated anywhere else
in the world, but these libraries have been poorly housed,
supported and used.  On the other hand, public circulating
libraries were largely developed by private groups, social,
religious, commercial or benevolent, and eventually taken
over in the late nineteenth or early twentieth centuries for
public support and control.  The concept that the only worthwhile libraries are research libraries, and the only users
of libraries scholars, has handicapped the development and
use of popular circulating collections.  Users of public libraries are often handicapped by fees, short hours of service, poorly cataloged collections, closed stacks and limited
staffs.  The result has been that even today the percentage
of library users in many parts of Europe is small.  Library
services available to the public vary considerably between
Western Europe and Eastern Europe, but despite this variety
the overall picture is one of enlarged interest and continued
progress.  Many European countries are experimenting with
new forms of organization and support, and serious attention
is being given to the education of library staffs and the utilization of the latest technologies.  Given these trends, public
libraries in Europe would appear to be in a position to expand significantly and improve services to their respective
clienteles, if the serious financial crises facing these countries, especially those in Western Europe, can be successfully met and overcome.


## Special Libraries in Modern Europe

So far, three types of libraries in modern Europe
have been considered--the national libraries, the university
libraries, and the public libraries.  Although each of these
is in a way a special library, its holdings are general in
subject content, and its reading public is broad if not universal.  There are other libraries, however, that are lim-

ited in subject content or in types of users, or both, and
these have come to be designated by the term "special libraries." Although the term is usually used in a more restricted sense, for the purpose of this chapter it will be
broadened to include religious and public school libraries.

One way to begin our examination of special library
history in Europe is to examine the development of one of
the world's most impressive special libraries--The Vatican
Library in Rome. After its re-creation in the fifteenth century, the Vatican Library experienced further growth in the
sixteenth century, and in 1588 moved into magnificent new
quarters provided by Pope Sixtus V. He also added to its
bookstock with various gifts, and in 1600 it was further enlarged with the library of Fulvio Orsini, a most valuable collection. Pope Paul V (1605-1621) divided the papal library
into archives, manuscript, and book collections, and added
two large halls to hold the increased number of books. The
Palatine Library, a gift of Maximilian I, Duke of Bavaria,
was added in 1622, and later came the large and valuable
manuscript collection formerly belonging to Queen Christina
of Sweden. Important gifts followed each other with regular-
ity in the seventeenth and eighteenth centuries, and the Vatican Library became one of the most important storehouses
of treasures in Europe. During the French Revolution, however, it was the Vatican Library's turn to suffer, and five
hundred of its choicest manuscripts were taken by the victorious French to the libraries of Paris. Fortunately, most
of these were restored in 1815. By the 1820s the Vatican
Library contained over 400,000 books and 50,000 manuscripts.
More gifts followed in the nineteenth century, the major one
being the library of Cardinal Angelo Mai, a collection of almost 40,000 volumes amassed over a lifetime and containing
histories and records of Christianity from all over the world.

In the late nineteenth century the Vatican Library experienced a rebirth and renovation, and its great masses of
books and manuscripts were arranged and organized; the
books at least were made more available to the public. Under Pope Leo XIII a reading room was opened in 1888, and
a public reference collection was made available. New collections continued to pour in, and the beautiful halls and
rooms soon became crowded. After 1920 another reorganization took place, and American librarians were invited to
act as consultants in modernizing the collection. In 1926,
the Carnegie Corporation sent Dr. William Warner Bishop
to survey the Vatican Library and make recommendations

for its future growth and development.  Pius XI was then
Pope and, as a former librarian both at the Ambrosian Library and at the Vatican, he was intensely interested in the
suggested reforms.  A new cataloging system was adopted,
modern book stacks were installed, new quarters were added,
and in general the whole purpose of the institution was directed toward making its collections available.  In 1931 a
tragedy occurred when a section of roof over a reference
room collapsed, destroying about a thousand volumes and damaging many others.  This, however, was only a temporary
setback, and rebuilding and enlarging continued.  During
World War II, library treasures from other Italian collections
were taken into the Vatican for safekeeping.  Since the War,
the Vatican Library has taken its place as one of the greatest libraries in the world.  Scholars from everywhere make
use of its treasures, and the services of the library and its
staff aid not only other Roman Catholic libraries but libraries
in general in virtually every country of the globe.  Many of
its rarest possessions have been made available in facsimile
or photograph, and bibliographies of its collections are available to scholars everywhere.  Its modern acquisitions tend to
relate more directly to the history and activities of the
Church, but its nearly one million volumes still make it one
of the world's great bibliographic centers.

Elsewhere in Italy, the special libraries are varied
and numerous.  Many of the great libraries of the Renaissance survive as either private or public collections, and other endowed libraries of considerable size were added in later
centuries.  Such libraries as the Ambrosian in Milan, the
Biblioteca Estense in Modena, the Casanatense in Rome, and
the Medicea-Laurenziana in Florence, with their valuable collections of manuscripts and incunabula, are unequalled anywhere in the world.  Many less famous but significant collections are located in other Italian towns and cities.  The monastery library at Monte Cassino, with about twenty thousand
printed books and thousands of manuscripts, some going back
to the seventh century, was declared a national monument in
1866.  Unfortunately, this famous landmark in western civilization was virtually destroyed in World War II.  Another
monastic collection to survive into the twentieth century is
that at La Cava near Salerno, with manuscripts dating from
the eleventh century.

As in most of Europe, the universities of Italy are
surrounded by institute and faculty libraries in many specialized fields.  A few of these reach 100,000 volumes in size,

but most of them are much smaller, and there may be fifty
or more of them around the larger universities.  Though
some are well organized and staffed, most of them are unavailable outside their respective departments.  In addition,
there are the libraries of the technical institutes not connected with the universities.  The library of the Polytechnic
Institute in Milan, for example, was founded in 1863 and now
has some 95,000 volumes.  In Rome there are over 300
special libraries, many of considerable size.  The Library
of the International Institute of Agriculture (now a part of
the United Nations Food and Agriculture Organization's library system) contains over 300,000 volumes, with files of
some 3,000 periodicals in agriculture and related fields.
Founded in 1905, it went into a new building in 1933.  It is
organized along the lines of American technical libraries and
serves not only its own organization but also agricultural
scientists throughout Italy.  Its bibliographies and interlibrary
loan service are available around the world.  A somewhat
smaller special library is the Biblioteca Romana, formed in
1930 to be the historical library for the city of Rome, specializing in political, social and economic history.  It also
maintains a union catalog of all such materials located anywhere in Italy.  Most of the departments of the Italian government have headquarter libraries in Rome, some of considerable size and importance.  The Library of the Ministry
of Agriculture and Forestry has over a half-million volumes,
while that of the Ministry of Industry and Commerce has
about 100,000 volumes.  Many other special libraries are
found in Rome, ranging from such small collections as the
Keats-Shelley Memorial House Library with 7,000 volumes
to the library of the Council of National Research with over
250,000 volumes.

Other major Italian cities also contain many special
libraries.  Florence, for example, has twenty-six major
special libraries, not counting those connected with educational institutions.  These include such libraries as the Che-
rubini music library with some 35,000 volumes, the Geor-
gofili agricultural economics library, the Colombaria library
of the Tuscan Academy of Science and Letters, and such
smaller ones as the Dante Society Library with 10,000 volumes.  The two large art collections are those of the Art
History Institute and the Academy of Fine Arts.  Many
church-related libraries are scattered throughout Italy, although in some cases their collections are relatively new,
where older libraries were confiscated in the late nineteenth
century.  Libraries of Catholic schools and colleges, mon-

asteries, cathedrals and religious societies are also significant.

School libraries in Italy are largely a twentieth-century development, but, although government financial support
is available, they still lag behind those of the United States
and England.   This is due in part to a lack of trained school
librarians, and in part to the continued emphasis on textbook teaching rather than individual study and reading.
Since World War II the new emphasis on public education
has brought an increased interest in school libraries, which
are currently improving.   Library service to schools through
the public libraries is being tried, particularly in the villages
and rural areas, and the larger towns and cities are experimenting with centralized school library services for the entire urban area.   One interesting phase of Italian library
service to children, although not restricted to them, is the
park library, available out in the open during the warmer
months of the year.

The special libraries of France are similar in many
respects to those in Italy, although more numerous.   Some
of the libraries of Paris, including several now associated
with the Bibliothèque Nationale or the University of Paris,
have histories going back into the Middle Ages, while others,
such as the Savoy Library of the Sciences, are products of
the 1960s.   The library of the National Civil Engineering
College (L'Ecole Nationale des Ponts de Chausées) was
founded in 1747 and now has over 160,000 volumes.   The
Bibliothèque de l'Arsenal, formed in the eighteenth century,
is, despite its name, a remarkable library of French literature, containing over 1,500,000 volumes with thousands of
rare literary manuscripts.   The Catholic Institute of Paris
has a theological library of nearly 500,000 volumes, dating
from 1875.   The various technical schools and institutes of
Paris also have their own libraries, ranging from the general to the very specialized, and from the National Institute
of Aeronautics to the National School of Veterinary Science.
Many documentation centers supplement the technical libraries of Paris, such as the Documentation Center for
Chemistry with its library of 50,000 volumes.   The French
governmental departments maintain central libraries in Paris, some of them large, important and semi-public, while
others are small working collections for departmental employees.   Besides these, there are other special libraries
such as those of the Musée et Bibliothèque de la Guerre,
which aims at collecting all available printed material on

the two World Wars.  At the other extreme, there is the
Bibliothèque de l'Heure Joyeuse, a children's library founded
in the 1930s as a non-circulating model juvenile collection.

In other parts of France, there are technical libraries in the various public institutes and in the technical
schools of the universities.  Some of the larger municipal
libraries are establishing business libraries or special collections, but lack of trained staff members often curtails
their value.  The larger business firms, particularly banks,
the chemical industries, and the metropolitan newspapers,
are establishing research and information libraries for their
employees.  Scattered throughout France are military libraries, both popular ones for the average soldier or sailor
and specialized ones for training purposes.  The French
army has maintained such libraries since the French Revolution, and virtually every military post or naval vessel has
its library.  The French public schools have had libraries
of a sort since the early nineteenth century, but for many
years they were small, out of date, and of little use to students.  In Paris, an improved school library system was
established in 1862, and by 1880 there were 440 school libraries in the city, but they averaged only about a hundred
volumes each.  In more recent years, the French schools,
particularly the secondary schools, are paying more attention to library service and are providing not only books and
periodicals but audio-visual instructional materials as well.
Shortages of school librarians or teachers trained in library
work continue to limit the number of school libraries that
can provide effective service.  Rural areas and small towns
are still lagging behind the larger urban areas in school libraries, and France, too, must await a change in public
school methods and educational philosophy before any great
progress can be made.

Some of the most important special libraries in the
world are found in England.  London alone contains libraries on virtually every possible specialization, and many
of them are quite large and filled with rare and valuable
works.  The British Museum itself is composed of many
special collections, such as the Harleian Collection of Manuscripts, or the Sloane or Cottonian libraries.  Its newspaper
library is probably the largest single collection of newspapers in the world.  The various Royal Societies all have
notable libraries in their specialties, such as the Royal Society of Medicine, the Royal Geographical Society, and the
Royal College of Surgeons, whose library was founded in

1518. There are many specialized libraries connected with
the University of London, such as that of the School of Economics, particularly strong in economics and political science relating to all parts of the world. The Public Record
Office is the official archives of Britain, and its treasures
include Parliamentary records going back for hundreds of
years. The Patent Office Library is an outstanding example
of the many government departmental libraries, ranging in
content from agriculture to foreign affairs. Among the oldest special libraries in London are those of the various law
schools known as Gray's Inn, The Inner Temple, and Lincoln's Inn. The latter, founded in 1497, is the largest law
library in London and one of the most famous in the world.
The Science Museum Library and the Victoria and Albert Art
Museum Library are among the best in their fields, and the
India Office Library has one of the greatest collections known
on the history and culture of India. The Royal College of
Music Library specializes in English music and has the original scores of many English and foreign composers. The National Library for the Blind takes a lead in providing talking
books and books in Braille for blind readers throughout the
British Isles. Not the least interesting of London's special
libraries is that of the Library Association with its 25,000
volumes relating to the field of librarianship.

One of the latest developments in special libraries in
England is the formation of the National Lending Library for
Science and Technology, now a part of the British Library.
This institution provides a national center for technical documentation, and is a clearinghouse for interlibrary loans for
all technical and scientific libraries throughout the nation.
These include public library technical departments, technical
college libraries, research libraries and industrial collections. The public libraries in particular have created and expanded library service to business and industry since World
War I. Leeds established a public technical and commercial
library in 1918, and since that time most of the larger municipal and even some of the county libraries have established
such collections. In the 1970s attention is being paid to the
problems of cooperation between such special libraries, and
in one particular area the Liverpool and District Scientific
and Industrial Research Libraries Advisory Council has taken
a lead in this direction. With union catalogs, teletype service, and liberal photocopying and lending policies, the special
libraries of regions or of the entire nation can pool their
services. Special research libraries maintained by private
firms are also being brought into these cooperative ventures.

Above all, the Association of Special Libraries and Information Bureaux (ASLIB), formed in 1924, serves as the professional association and general mentor for the field.

The cathedrals of England and Wales still maintain libraries, although they are largely theological and historical
materials for the use of the clergy.   Many of them are very
valuable, with books and manuscripts surviving from medieval collections.   The Cathedral at Durham was one of the
largest such libraries, numbering well over forty thousand
volumes.   There are several notable English Catholic libraries, such as those at the Oratory at South Kensington,
established in 1849, and at the Catholic Central Library in
London.   The libraries of the Cathedrals of York and Canterbury are among the richest in rare books and manuscripts,
but there are a number of parish churches scattered throughout England that have small but valuable collections in theology and history.   A few still keep books chained to desks as
they were kept down through the eighteenth century.

England has been fortunate in the creation of endowed
libraries, some specialized, some of rare books, and others
for the general public.   One of the largest is the John Rylands Library at Manchester, founded in 1899 by Mrs. John
Rylands in memory of her husband.   Its special holdings include medieval manuscripts, rare Bibles, and some 2,500
incunabula among its total collection of 500,000 volumes.   Its
scholarly staff issues a regular bulletin relating to the collection and the general field of bibliography.   A famous endowed theological library is the Dr. Williams Library,
founded by the will of a Presbyterian minister and opened in
1729 in London.   It was moved into a new building in 1873,
and its 118,000 volumes are strong in Presbyterian history
and theology, but also include material on other denomina-
tions and religions.   Many public libraries in English and
Scottish cities stem from endowed collections formed in the
nineteenth century and earlier, but later taken over with public support.

School library history in England is a comparatively
recent development, although many of the private schools
have had libraries since the seventeenth century.   English
public school libraries became a possibility after the passage
of the Public School Laws of the 1870s, but for the most
part implementation of the laws did not come until the twentieth century.   Books were sometimes placed in schools by
the public library systems, and county libraries used the

rural schools as distribution points.  Improvement in school
library service came in the 1920s, but a group of visiting
American librarians in the 1930s found poor library quarters
and unsatisfactory staffing in many localities.  They found
much to compliment, however, in the quality of the books
available, and in the interest shown by the children in their
school libraries.  The Education Act of 1944 recognized the
importance of school libraries, along with the modern adjuncts of audio-visual and teaching materials, but noted that
progress during the Depression and war years had been
slow.  Since then, much progress has been made in school
libraries, the concept of the library as a teaching materials
center is widespread, and standards of library service are
approaching the best in the world.  Cooperation between
school and public libraries remains high, and the use of
school libraries per pupil is greater than in most American
school libraries.

West Germany is another European country with many
special libraries.  Berlin alone had over two hundred special
libraries before 1939.  These included government office libraries, special libraries of universities and institutes and
libraries of scientific societies.  Governmental libraries
were strong, with the library of the Reichstag (Parliament)
having over 175,000 volumes; that of the Patent Office,
118,000 volumes; and the Census Office, nearly 200,000.
The German Army was supplied with technical libraries, the
major one being at the general headquarters in Berlin.  These
libraries, like the units they served, were disbanded after
World War I, but were reformed during the Hitler era.
Even in 1924, Germany had some 275 major research libraries with total holdings of over 34,000,000 volumes.
Eighty-four of them contained over 100,000 volumes each,
thus making Germany one of the most important sources of
research information in the western world.

Elsewhere in Germany, the former royal or ducal libraries of the various states that existed before the unification of Germany form a particular type of special library,
although they are generally classed as popular reference libraries.  Each of them is a special library on the history
and culture of its particular area, and most of them contain
unique manuscripts and rare books.  Each of the great German universities is surrounded by scores of institute and departmental libraries, and in addition there are many Hochs-
chule or colleges and technical institutes that have special
libraries.  Some of the larger cities have developed com-

mercial or business libraries, and some of them have public
music libraries as well.  Industrial firms are following their
western counterparts and developing research libraries with
the latest microcopying facilities and the most modern techniques in storing and retrieving information.  Hamburg's
commercial library was founded as early as 1735, or at
least it is based upon a collection that goes back that far.

Some special libraries that have emerged in Germany
since 1945 would include the American Library in Berlin,
the International Youth Library in Munich, and a new technical library at Hanover that contains a book collection, a
translation center, and a bureau of documentation to give a
complete research service.  The new national library at
Marburg is also a post-war development, and in the sense
that it is a bibliographic and reference center, it, too, is
a special library.  The German research libraries as a
group are well organized through their librarians' association
and through many public and private cooperative arrange-
ments.  There is cooperation not only in union catalogs, union lists of serials, and interlibrary loans, but also in the
selection and acquisition of specialized subjects and materials.  For example, some libraries concentrate on acquiring
material from specific geographic areas, so that there is
a complete coverage of literature from all parts of the world.
The ultimate aim is that in some German reference library
there will be found books or information on almost any subject and from almost any place on earth.

School libraries in West Germany, that is the libraries of the lower schools corresponding to American elementary and high schools, have been very slow in developing.
Emphasis on the textbook and lecture have prevented the
growth of usable school libraries down to the mid-twentieth
century, and where there have been libraries in the schools,
they have usually been small collections of old books rather
than living, working libraries.  The movement toward popular libraries has often been made with the idea of serving
the school children as well as adults, and some of the better
public libraries have excellent rooms or collections for children and young people.  Central education libraries in the
cities and states serve the teachers and school personnel
rather than the children.  However, since World War II, the
influence of American school libraries, particularly the libraries in the schools for children of American military personnel stationed in Germany, has led to an increased interest in the need for improved school libraries and to wide
experimentation in the field.

In Russia, the special library is a vital part of the complete library picture of that library-minded nation. Whereas in all of Russia before 1917 there were only 475 libraries that could be classed as special, there were over 6,000 by the 1920s, and over 50,000 by the 1970s. In addition to special collections in the national, public, and university libraries already discussed, Russia and its various federated republics share a widespread system of technical libraries. Many of these are concentrated in the library network of the Academy of Sciences of the U.S.S.R. The Academy library alone has over 7,500,000 cataloged items, and its activities are closely tied to those of the various institutes, academies, museums and other technical libraries in all parts of the Soviet Union. A series of agricultural libraries is centered in the Central Agricultural Research Library in Moscow, with its 2,500,000 volumes, and a medical library system is headed up by a State Central Research Medical Library in the same city. In most of the constituent republics, there are similar central technical libraries and each of them stocks books in the local languages as well as in Russian. Much foreign technical literature may be found in Russian libraries, but it is usually translated or digested into Russian and the major local languages.

The trade union library is a type of special library that is well developed in Russia, less so in other parts of Europe. This library serves as a technical or sociological library on trade union history and programs, but also on a lower level as a popular library for the workers. The system is headed up by the Gorki Reference Library of the All-Union Central Council of Trade Unions in Moscow. This unit serves labor specialists and advanced students rather than the general public. In addition, it assists in the work of trade union libraries all over the USSR by training library workers, providing bibliographies and booklists, and by publishing material in the trade union field.

In Moscow there are technical libraries embracing almost every conceivable field of interest. Some of these not already mentioned would include the Geographical Society Library, the Botanical Institute Library, and those of the Institutes of Physiology, Ethnography, Linguistics, History, and Russian Literature. The Fundamental Library of the Social Sciences has over 5,000,000 items, and the All-Union State Library of Foreign Literature contains 3,000,000 volumes in 126 different languages. In the capitals of the other Soviet states, there are similar professional and technical libraries,

although usually on a smaller scale. Some of the special libraries in other parts of the country are quite large, as for
example the Pushkin Science Library in Yakutsk, which has
over a million items. Throughout the Soviet Union access
to these technical and scientific libraries is free and readily
available to any serious student.

The Russian Army libraries form a network all their
own and the number of books involved is tremendous. Library service for the Red Army troops began during the
Revolution when package libraries by the hundreds were sent
to the Communist troops in training camps and even on the
front lines. The libraries for the troops became permanent
after the establishment of the Soviet Union, and they continued to grow in size and usefulness until the mid-thirties,
when there were over 16,000,000 volumes in the various
military libraries. The military headquarters library in
1941 was a seventeen-story building in Moscow, containing
over 1,000,000 volumes. These libraries proved their worth
during World War II, both for technical and morale purposes,
and since the war they have continued to expand.

Public school libraries in Russia are under the jurisdiction of the National Ministry of Education, which controls
libraries in elementary and secondary schools and in teacher-
training institutions. Russian school libraries and textbooks
are carefully controlled as to content; not only are the books
themselves carefully censored and written for full propaganda
effect, but the libraries are remarkably alike in all parts of
the country and in all schools of the same grade level.
Teachers are in charge of libraries in the smaller schools,
but the larger ones have one or more trained librarians. Instruction in the use of the library is mandatory, and in some
cases the reading of specific books is also required. Close
records are kept of each student's reading, both in the
school libraries and in the children's sections of the public
libraries that are also easily available. In the secondary
schools, the libraries are more practical, and the library
reading becomes a required part of the school curriculum.
At this stage, the student has reached a point where his concentration on mathematics, science, foreign languages and
Communist theory makes it almost impossible for him to have
time for leisure reading, so popular literature, available on
a small scale in the lower school libraries, tends to disap-
pear on the secondary school level. Whatever the library
contents, technical or popular, the library is part of an educational system that is designed to produce the same end

product--the well-trained and well-indoctrinated Soviet citizen. Certainly no country on earth makes as much use of the printed page in all its forms as the Soviet Union.

In other Soviet-dominated countries of eastern Europe, the pattern of special libraries follows the Russian system, although it is tempered by local customs and situations and modified to some extent by contacts with western libraries. Special libraries generally fall into four classes: governmental departmental libraries; scientific and technical libraries; libraries for special classes, such as soldiers or workers; and academic libraries. All these are public; private and theological libraries of all types have either been closed or considerably restricted in their activities. In Poland, for example, there were some 7,000,000 volumes in technical and scholarly libraries before 1939, but over half of these were lost during the war. By 1950 this figure had again been reached, and today the hundreds of specialized libraries in Poland contain over 15,000,000 volumes. Some of Poland's best known special libraries were founded in the nineteenth century or earlier; the library of the Medical Society in Warsaw dates from 1820; the Polish Society of Friends of Science was founded in 1802. School libraries in Poland have developed for the most part only since 1919. By 1939 there were some 26,000 school libraries, although most of them were small, and only 7,000 survived the war in usable condition. Again, it was 1950 before the pre-war levels were regained, but thanks to favorable library laws the progress has been tremendous since that date.

School libraries in southeastern Europe were slow in developing before World War II, and since that time have been patterned largely on those of the Soviet Union. The numbers of school libraries have increased, and also the size of the collections, but with strict state control they leave much to be desired by western standards. Larger schools are served by central libraries, but smaller ones receive rotating collections from a district or regional school library center. Librarians are usually scarce, so teachers fill in to the best of their abilities. Under these conditions, the amount of school library service is limited, but according to the library statistics in each country, the collections are well used, and this is confirmed by reports of visiting librarians from other countries.

Elsewhere in Europe special libraries are also prevalent. For instance, in Belgium and the Netherlands there

are a wide variety of special libraries.  As elsewhere, there
are special collections associated with universities and large
public libraries, and the governmental libraries are notable
for their history and size.  The Library of the Belgian Ministry of National Defense in Brussels has over 300,000 volumes, and that of the Ministry of Foreign Affairs is almost
as large.  The library of the Royal Conservatory of Music
was founded in Brussels in 1832, and now constitutes something of a national library of music and drama.  The Plan-
tin-Moretus Museum in Antwerp, founded in 1640, contains
a library of some 40,000 printed works and 15,000 manuscripts relating to the Plantin family and the development of
printing in the fifteenth and sixteenth centuries.  Another
special library on the history of books is that at the Musée
du Livre in Brussels.  In the Netherlands the Society for
the Literature of the Netherlands, founded in 1766 at Leiden,
has one of the most important national literature collections
in Europe.  Connected since 1877 with the library of the
University of Leiden, it contains over 100,000 volumes and
2,000 manuscripts relating to Dutch literature and literary
history.  The Hague contains an important library of international law in the Peace Palace.  In Rotterdam there is an
interesting private library, the Lesekabinet, which offers its
members the advantages of a club, a restaurant, and a library.  Its 115,000 volumes include popular, technical, and
even children's books.  Amsterdam has had a noted music
library since 1937, when the music division of the public library joined with the library of the Society for the Advance-
ment of Music to form the Amsterdam United Music Library.
There is much cooperation between the special and public libraries in Holland, and this cooperation has recently been
extended to include the research libraries of large business
and industrial firms.

Belgian and Dutch school libraries were not well developed according to American standards prior to World War
II, and in fact they were often non-existent in the smaller
schools.  Service to schools from the public libraries was
sometimes available, as for example in Deventer, Holland,
where collections of books were rotated among the schools
at the rate of 1.5 books per student.  Since 1945, a greater
effort has been made toward providing school library service.  In Belgium the public library system is charged with
supplying children with books, both in and out of school,
while in the Netherlands various methods of school library
service are being tried.  The Bureau of Books and Youth,
in the Central Association for Public Libraries, serves the

Netherlands as a center for information on children's books and libraries, with bibliographies, book reviews and traveling exhibits to stimulate library service to children, both in school and out.

Scandinavian countries are as well known for their special libraries as for their public and university collections. Moreover, library service to children is well developed, although it is done through public libraries rather than through school libraries in many cases. In Sweden, since 1919, schools have administered their own libraries by law, and some feel that library service has suffered through this arrangement, because many school libraries are of necessity small, and, being permanent collections, do not benefit from rotating deposits. Since 1955 each school may have its own library or share in a central district library in the case of smaller schools. Children in Sweden are taught to use the school library in special units during the upper elementary grades. Norway's public schools, except in the larger towns and cities, rely on deposits of books provided by public library systems. These deposits may be small, but since they are rotated they often introduce the children to a large number of books in a single year. Norway's Public and School Library Act of 1955 provides government funds for both services. In more densely populated Denmark, public library branches or stations are often in, or adjacent to, the public schools and serve them directly. Where public libraries are not easily available, basic collections of about four hundred volumes each are provided for the schools. Denmark also has a system of folk schools, or adult education centers, which often have large and well-used libraries. The library of the adult education school at Askov, for example, has over 30,000 volumes and dates back to the 1840s.

The Scandinavian countries have carried the idea of library cooperation farther than most countries. One example of this is seen in the Scandia plan, a voluntary means of cooperation between university, college and special libraries in Denmark, Finland, Norway, and Sweden. The cooperation is largely in the form of concentration in research collections, with specialization by country and individual libraries in subject, area, and language fields. Duplication in rare, little used and expensive research materials is thus avoided, and by means of interlibrary loan and photocopying, anything in any Scandinavian library is readily available to any other library in the four countries.

In Europe as a whole, the special libraries meet special needs and supplement the services of more general collections.  Their progress, size and effectiveness vary from
country to country, and from library to library, but in general, their development in the period since 1945 has been
tremendous.  In numbers, in size, in variety, and in techniques used, the European special library is a field in itself.
The demands of education, industry and scientific research
have led to the use of photographic and electronic means of
producing, duplicating, storing and retrieving information.
Documentation centers are appearing where public library
service is hardly known, and in some cases, particulary in
eastern Europe, it seems that the transition from manuscript
to computers was made almost overnight.  Progress is
uneven, however, and much remains to be done, particularly
in school libraries in central and southern Europe.


Conclusion

The impressive growth of European libraries since
World War I is clearly obvious to anyone familiar with the
history of these libraries.  And yet, in many parts of Europe
the gains made in the past sixty years appear to be threatened by the tenacious and widespread financial depression besetting the continent.  It remains to be seen whether library
development in countries like England, France, and Italy will
be permanently stunted by lack of nourishment, or whether
these nations will recover their economic vitality, and find
the resources necessary to continue the development of their
extensive library services.


### Additional Readings

The literature on modern European libraries is both
extensive and difficult to locate.  In the following
list we have included those items most useful for
the student who desires to pursue the topic in more
depth than could be offered here.  Items were
chosen on the basis of availability, recency, and
especially, for the fact that they contain useful
bibliographies and documentation.

Aitken, W. R.   A History of the Public Library Movement
in Scotland to 1955.  Glasgow, 1971.

Allred, J. R. "The Purpose of the Public Library: The Historical View," Library History 2 (1972): 185-204.

Assman, Kurt. Sachsische Landesbibliothek Dresden, 1556-1956. Leipzig, 1956.

Bednarski, Hanna J. "Warsaw University Library: A History of War Time Survival," Canadian Library Journal 32 (1975): 34-39.

Birkelund, Palle. "The Royal Library of Copenhagen: Historical Perspectives," Library History Review 1 (1974): 83-96.

Busse, G. and H. Ernestus. Libraries in the Federal Republic of Germany. Wiesbaden, 1972.

Buzas, L. Geschicte der Universitats-Bibliothek Munchen. Wiesbaden, 1972.

Campbell, H. C., ed. "Metropolitan Public Library Problems Around the World," Library Trends 14 (1965): 1-116.

Chandler, G. Libraries, Documentation and Bibliography in the USSR 1917-1971. London, 1972.

Chapman, M. "Public Librarianship in the Federal Republic of Germany Since 1945," Library Quarterly 36 (1966): 299-320.

Csapodi, C. "Geschichte der ungarischen Bibliotheken," Biblios 19 (1970): 276-85.

Danton, J. P. Book Selection and Collections: A Comparison of German and American University Libraries. New York, 1963.

_____. United States Influence on Norwegian Librarianship, 1890-1940. Berkeley, 1957.

Ellis, A. Library Services for Young People in England and Wales, 1830-1970. Oxford, 1971.

Ferguson, J. Libraries in France. London, 1971.

Fonotov, G. P. "Lenin and Libraries," UNESCO Bulletin

for Libraries 24 (1970): 118-25.

Francis, S.  Libraries in the USSR.  London, 1971.

Harrison, K. C.  Libraries in Scandinavia.  2nd ed.  London, 1969.

Hassenforder, J.  Development Comparé des Bibliothèques Publiques en France, en Grande-Bretagne et aux Etats-Unis dans la Seconde Moitié du XIXe Siècle (1850-1914).  Paris, 1967.

Hobson, A.  Great Libraries.  New York, 1970.

Horecky, P.  Libraries and Bibliographical Centers in the Soviet Union.  Bloomington, Indiana, 1959.

Houghton, B.  Out of Dinosaurs:  The Evolution of the National Lending Library for Science and Technology.  London, 1972.

Jackson, S.  Libraries and Librarianship in the West:  A Brief History.  New York, 1974.

Jones, G.  "Political and Social Factors in the Advocacy of 'Free' Libraries in the United Kingdom, 1801-1922,"  Doctoral dissertation, Strathelyde University, 1971.

Kelly, T.  History of Public Libraries in Great Britain, 1845-1965.  London, 1973.

Kildal, A.  "American Influence on European Librarianship,"  Library Quarterly 7 (1937): 196-210.

Kirkegaard, P.  The Public Libraries in Denmark.  Copenhagen, 1950.

Kunz, F.  "Bibliothekswesen in der DDR, 1949-1974:  Zwiftafel."  Bibliothekar 28 (1974): 622-39.

Leyh, G.  Die Deutschen Bibliotheken von der Aufklarung bis zur Gegenwart.  Leipzig, 1963.

Marcel, T.  "Les Bibliothèques de France,"  Tendances 24 (1963): 473-504.

Mearns, D., ed.  "Current Trends in National Libraries,"

Library Trends 4 (1955): 3-116.

Metie, A. "Libraries on the Left: Ideology in the Communist Library," PNLA Quarterly 33 (1969): 4-11.

Miller, E. That Noble Cabinet: A History of the British Museum. London, 1974.

Minto, J. A History of the Public Library Movement in Great Britain and Ireland. London, 1932.

Mohrhardt, F. and C. Penna. "National Planning for Library and Information Services," Advances in Librarianship 5 (1975): 62-123.

Munford, W. A. Penny Rate: Aspects of British Public Library History. London, 1951.

Murison, W. The Public Library: Its Origins, Purpose, and Significance as a Social Institution. 2nd ed. London, 1971.

Nelson, K. Nordiska Bibliotek, 1947-1964: En Oversikt. Goteborg, 1964.

Neylon, M. Public Libraries in Ireland. Dublin, 1966.

Pietsch, E. et al. "Germany, Libraries and Information Centers in," Encyclopedia of Library and Information Science 9: 395-545.

Rotzsch, H., ed. Deutsche Bucherei, 1912-1962: Festschrift der Deutschen Nationalbibliothek. Leipzig, 1962.

Salvan, P. "France, Libraries in," Encyclopedia of Library and Information Science 9: 37-66.

Serrurier, C. Bibliothèques de France. The Hague, 1946.

Simsova, S. Lenin, Krupskaya and Libraries. London, 1968.

_____, and M. Mackee. A Handbook of Comparative Librarianship. 2nd ed. London, 1975.

Sule, T. Bucherei und Ideologie; Politische Aspekte im Richtungsstreit Deutscher Volksbibliothekare, 1910-1930. Cologne, 1972.

Thornton, J.  Medical Books, Libraries and Collectors.  2nd
    ed.  London, 1966.

_____.  Selected Readings in the History of Librarianship.
    2nd ed.  London, 1966.

Vosper, R., ed.  "European University Libraries:  Current
    Status and Developments," Library Trends 12 (1964):
    475-623.

Whatley, H., ed.  British Librarianship and Information Sci-
    ence, 1966-1970.  London, 1972.

## Chapter 12

## MODERN AMERICAN LIBRARIES

Since about 1850, American libraries have grown significantly in number and scope. The rapid growth of American libraries was due to the happy mingling of a number of positive factors: 1) the enormous natural resources of the country, which offered a continuing stimulus to the economy, thus generating great wealth, part of which was available for the support of cultural institutions like libraries; 2) the rapidly increasing population, which supplied the voracious needs of American industry, and in turn provided an ever larger audience for libraries; 3) the amazing industrialization of the country which required ever more sophisticated information sources for its continued development, and demanded an increasingly sophisticated level of knowledge among its workers; and 4) the democratic caste of American life which encouraged the free flow of information and depended, at least in theory, upon the "informed citizen" as the very foundation of its existence.

Using economic terms, the "take off" in the development of American libraries can be said to have occurred between 1850 and 1900, and by the latter date most of the library forms known to modern librarians were firmly established, and their patterns of development clearly visible.

## The Rise of the American Public Library

While greatly stimulated by the positive factors influencing American life, the American public library developed as the natural outgrowth of a number of social and political changes sweeping the country in the late ante-bellum period. One of the most significant developments for public library growth was the slowly changing attitude towards the establishment and support of public services generally. As has already been pointed out, the social library form was flawed by its dependence on the "voluntary" support of its members and the beneficence of its supporters. In difficult financial times, or times of cultural indifference, the social library was threatened by a loss of financial support, and not infrequently with extinction. All of the publicly supported institutions so common to modern Americans had to await the time when the people, or at least those in control of the government, reached the conclusion that the principle of voluntarism was inadequate to the needs of the Republic, and that some form of government support must be instituted. This change of mind came during the late Jacksonian period, when many Americans became convinced that what was needed, in Lee Benson's words, was "a positive liberal state" where "the state had the responsibility to ... regulate society so as to promote the general welfare."

This change of mind was prompted by the serious, and, in many cases, disturbing changes taking place in antebellum America. To the establishment in America, the increasing industrialization of the country was viewed as a mixed blessing. On the one hand it promised prosperity and continued economic growth; on the other, it was giving rise to large cities with their manifold problems, and it was luring millions of poorly educated immigrants to the country-- immigrants, who in the eyes of the "Best men" of America, were ill-equipped to function effectively as citizens of a democracy.

The appearance of ever larger numbers of immigrants in the large urban centers, and the general feeling that older socializing and stabilizing voluntaristic institutions like the church and the family were disintegrating, led the country's leadership to cast about for ways of channeling the restive and potentially disruptive elements in American society into constructive channels. Increasingly, they came to view formal, carefully organized, and publicly funded educational institutions as the best means of securing the Republic against the winds of destructive change.

But while the "Best men" had inordinate power in relation to their numbers, they could never have established public schools and libraries without at least the tacit approval of the people. This support began to emerge in the late 1820s as the nascent Workingmen's movement in America

came to identify publicly supported education as an important
bulwark of democracy and an essential ingredient in the
Workingman's aggressive drive for political power and economic prosperity.  And while they soon came to view more
immediate concerns such as the ten-hour day, better working conditions, and child labor laws as their most pressing
issues, they nevertheless maintained a firm belief in education as the surest shield of the political authority of the people, and came to view universal public education in an ab-
stract sense, as the panacea that once achieved, "would
eradicate obstacles to democracy and maintain equality and
prosperity."

Thus, by 1850, the ground was prepared; the democratic dogma was generally accepted.  Few would quarrel
with its basic premise: that the success of the Republic was
inseparably tied to the enlightenment of its citizenry.  While
this faith in the democratic dogma was based on drastically
different conceptions of the purpose of education, the general
consensus was nevertheless complete.

It only remained for educators and civic leaders to
demonstrate the ways in which the public library might contribute to the enlightenment of the people.  Some scattered
attempts were made at this task before 1852, but in that
year the Trustees of the Boston Public Library issued their
now famous Report, which articulated, perhaps better than
any document before or since, the ideal conception of public
library service.

This Report, written jointly by Edward Everett, one
of the country's leading political figures, and George Ticknor,
the acknowledged social and intellectual arbiter of Boston,
traced the history of printing and libraries and then argued
forcefully for the establishment of a public library in Boston.
To Everett and Ticknor it was clear that:

> Reading ought to be furnished to all, as a matter of
> public policy and duty, on the same principle that
> we furnish free education, and in fact, as a part,
> and a most important part, of the education of all.
> For it has been rightly judged that--under political,
> social and religious institutions like ours--it is of
> paramount importance that the means of general in-
> formation should be so diffused that the largest pos-
> sible number of persons should be induced to read
> and understand questions going down to the very

foundations of social order, which are constantly
presenting themselves, and which we, as a people,
are constantly required to decide, and do decide,
either ignorantly or wisely.

To these men, steeped in enlightenment principles, there was
a direct connection between knowledge and virtue, and in
their report they stated the very heart of what was to become the public library creed: the future of a democratic
republic is directly dependent upon the education of its citizenry, and the library is an important element in the educational process. In 1854, as a result of the efforts of Everett and Ticknor and the city fathers, the Boston Public Library was opened.

Of course, the Boston Public Library was not the
first public library established in the country, not if we define a public library as one supported by local taxation and
open to all citizens of the community. Using this definition,
a few earlier examples of the public library form deserve
mention.

In Salisbury, Connecticut, in 1803 a collection of
books donated by Caleb Bingham was preserved and made
available by the town as the Bingham Library for Youth. It
survived to become a part of the modern Scoville Memorial
Library. In Lexington, Massachusetts, in 1827, the town
meeting voted to purchase a library for the youth of the town
and to employ a librarian to manage it. The collection was
deposited in the town church, but so small was the public
support that it went out of existence in 1839. In Castine,
Maine, a social library founded in 1801 became the property
of the town about 1827, and continued to operate as a free
public library. Other examples of small collections, more
or less publicly owned and supported, can be found elsewhere
in New England, but the town usually considered to be the
pioneer in permanent public library service was Peterborough,
New Hampshire. In 1833 it was decided by the town meeting
that a part of the State Literary Fund, usually applied to the
support of schools, should be used for the purchase of books
for a free public library. Other donations added to the size
of the book collection, and it was kept for public use in the
store that housed the local post office, with the postmaster
acting as librarian. By 1837 the collection numbered 465
titles, made up largely of religion, history, and biography.
The Peterborough Public Library was followed by several
similar ventures in New England towns in the next decade,

as for example in Orange, Massachusetts, where in 1846, $100 was voted to establish a free town library.

It was the passage of state laws enabling the local governmental units to levy taxes for the support of public libraries that really began the modern library movement. New Hampshire took the lead in 1849 with a law authorizing towns to appropriate money for the establishment and maintenance of public libraries. In 1851 Massachusetts passed a similar law, to be followed by Maine in 1854, and after the Civil War by several other New England and Middle West states.

Despite this early activity, it was the founding of the Boston Public Library which really gave impetus to the public library movement. Boston was the leading social and intellectual center in the country, and other cities watched jealously for new developments in Boston, and quickly followed its lead. The inordinate influence of the Boston Public Library, based partly on the impact of the widely read 1852 Report, partly on the leadership of its first two Superintendents: Charles Coffin Jewett (1858-68), and Justin Winsor (1868-77), and partly on the substantial resources available to develop the collection and innovate in matters of library service, continued unchallenged until the end of the nineteenth century.

At the outset, the administration of the Boston public library was focused on the collection and organization of books. Charles Coffin Jewett is remembered as one of the greatest bookmen in American library history, and his leadership in cataloging practice has led experts on this subject to label the third quarter of the 19th century the "Age of Jewett" in American cataloging history. His successor, the prominent historian and literary figure, Justin Winsor, focused his attention on "getting books used" in an attempt to implement Ticknor's concept of the library as a great civilizing and stabilizing force in America. His establishment of branches, utilization of selected reading lists, and provision of popular reading fare attest to his commitment to the popular nature of public library service.

Other municipalities throughout the country followed a pattern similar to that already seen in Boston and New York in their attempts to establish public library service in their respective communities. Tax support became the obvious key to library development and civic leaders quickly pushed for its adoption as the principal means of library

support.  In the beginning stimulus was frequently provided
by public-spirited benefactors who provided substantial sums
of money for the construction of buildings and the acquisition of library materials.  Also common was the process
whereby an existing social or endowed library would be donated or purchased by the city as the nucleus for a new public library.  By 1913 the U.S. Office of Education could report that the process had advanced to the stage where the
nation boasted some 3,000 public libraries containing over
1,000 volumes each.

In the last quarter of the nineteenth century three developments occurred which contributed mightily to the rise
of public libraries, and indeed, libraries generally.  First,
the American Library Association was organized in Philadelphia in 1876.  The ALA provided librarians with the long-
needed organizational structure and public forum required if
the library profession was to develop professional cohesive-
ness and philosophical consistency.

Second, the long-standing and frequently lamented
lack of a professional literature designed to provide guidance
and inspiration to librarians was met with the publication of
the now classic 1876 Report on Public Libraries in the
United States of America, and the establishment of the Library Journal in that same year.  The former, a massive
compendium of articles written by the nation's leading library
authorities, dealt with every conceivable aspect of library
development and management, and represented the standard
handbook of library practice for years to come.  The latter,
founded by the publishers R. R. Bowker and Frederick Ley-
poldt, and edited by the dynamic and controversial Melvil
Dewey, came to represent the library profession's most ar-
ticulate and influential medium of communication, a position
it still holds some 100 years after its founding.

The third, and perhaps most immediately obvious impetus to public library development was the wholesale philanthropy of history's greatest library benefactor, Andrew
Carnegie.  This immigrant from Scotland had made millions
in the steel industry and in his later years turned his interest toward the gifts of funds for the erection of libraries in
the United States and the United Kingdom.  As early as 1881
he began to encourage the construction of free public libraries with the gift of a library to the Pittsburgh area
where many of his steelworkers lived.  After this he began
to offer library buildings to any municipality that would

guarantee to maintain a public library, and by 1920 he had
provided some $50,000,000 for the construction of no fewer
than 2,500 buildings. In explaining his choice of libraries
as an outlet for his philanthropy, Carnegie was reported as
saying in 1900:

> I choose free libraries as the best agencies for
> improving the masses of the people, because they
> give nothing for nothing. They only help those who
> help themselves. They never pauperize. They
> reach the aspiring, and open to these the chief
> treasures of the world--those stored up in books.
> A taste for reading drives out lower tastes.

Despite his generous motives, some cities did not want Carnegie's "tainted" money. In 1901 Detroit was offered
$750,000 contingent on its raising another $500,000, but op-
position was so strong that the offer was not accepted until
1910. It is true that in some cases the libraries begun in
substantial buildings never fulfilled their promise, and were
poorly stocked and staffed, but in most cases the libraries
were continued and provided at least a moderate amount of
library service for millions of people. Besides Carnegie,
other philanthropists turned their attention to aid to public
libraries, and various buildings with "memorial" names still
dot the nation. The Enoch Pratt Free Library in Baltimore,
the Cossitt Library in Memphis, and the Pack Memorial Public Library in Asheville, N.C. are a few examples.

The establishment of the American Library Association, the development of a professional literature, and the
widespread philanthropy of Andrew Carnegie and other library
benefactors firmly rooted the public library in American life.
As public libraries spread across the nation, their staffs
worked diligently to expand and strengthen the services offered to users. In the late nineteenth and early twentieth
centuries branches were established, women and children
were recognized as legitimate clientele for the library, the
concept of open stacks was generally accepted, hours of
service were greatly increased, and the belief that the library should provide informational or reference service to
its patrons was widely endorsed. All of this was done despite the intrusion of financial crises like the great depression of 1929.

The development of public libraries in America was
at times a mindless and careless process; at others, it was

accompanied by a consistent attempt to systematize and ar-
ticulate both philosophy and practice.  Public library philosophy up through the nineteenth century was characterized by a
decidedly authoritarian and missionary caste.  Justin Winsor,
who served as President of the American Library Association
for the first ten years of its existence, clearly stated this
thrust when he noted that the public library could be wielded
as a "great engine" for "good or evil" among the "masses of
the people."  Using a similar analogy in one of his presidential addresses to his colleagues, he said that he thought of
the public library as "a derrick, lifting the inert masses and
swinging them round to the surer foundations upon which the
national character shall rise."  Following Winsor's lead, librarians were soon touting the public library as a panacea
for most of the country's social ills:  crime, disease, illiteracy, prostitution, intemperance, and the reckless and un-
American ways of the waves of new immigrants sweeping into the country.  In the latter case librarians viewed as one
of their most sacred trusts the "Americanization of the
immigrant," and led the way in developing programs to contribute to the success of this movement.  Similarly, during
the recurring financial depressions of the nineteenth and early
twentieth centuries, the library was hailed as a stabilizing
force in society.  As one librarian put it:  "if society cannot
provide work for all, the idle--chronic or temporary--are
much safer with a book in the library than elsewhere."

In the early decades of the twentieth century, librarians, faced with the rapid increase in the number and
size of libraries and their concomitant complexity as administrative organizations, seemed to turn inward and focus increasingly on internal matters of management, attempting to
make public librarianship what Melvil Dewey frequently re-
ferred to as a perfect "mechanical art."  However, by the
1930s librarians were again struggling with the purpose of
the public library, and in the light of the Nazi and Fascist
advances in Europe the public library's role was being rede-
fined as a "guardian of the people's right to know."  This
new view of the library's purpose represented an abandonment of the earlier authoritarian and elitist philosophy of
service, and emphasized the librarian's obligation to provide
a balanced and unbiased picture of issues so that the citizen
might decide for himself.  This philosophy, gaining increasing acceptance in the forties, is generally subscribed to by
all public librarians, at least in theory, and is embodied in
all basic policy statements, such as ALA's Library Bill of
Rights and Statement on Labeling, both currently in force.

More recently, public librarians, stung by criticisms
of the lack of use of the public library, have taken a more
aggressive stance in the area of service, and have initiated
numerous "outreach" programs designed to increase the
availability and use of library facilities by those, especially
the lower classes, who formerly made scant or no use of
public libraries.  This new thrust was greatly facilitated by
the widespread funding of library programs by federal and
state government in the late fifties and the sixties.  Access
to such large sums of money contributed to the exuberant
nature of American public librarianship, and soon led to the
development of a system of public libraries unrivaled in the
world.  It remains to be seen whether this renewed commitment to the aggressive delivery of public library services to
all classes of American society can survive the serious financial restraints evident today, or whether public librarians
will retreat to the more efficient and less expensive pattern
of serving only the intellectual minority in American society.


## College and University Libraries

As was noted in chapter 10, college libraries before
1850 were generally small and unimpressive collections of
books--poorly housed, little used, and strictly guarded.  After 1850 a number of developments conspired to alter radically the nature of American higher education and, concomit-
antly, to revolutionize the nature and role of the library in
the academic setting.  These developments can be discussed
under three basic headings:  financial, educational, and professional.

It is clear that the nation underwent an enormous and
momentous commercial and industrial development after 1850.
This rapid and unprecedented growth in financial resources
influenced American colleges and universities in a number of
ways prior to 1900.  First, the development of a surplus of
wealth, a proportion of which found its way into the coffers
of academic institutions, had a significant effect on the development of American higher education.  Increasingly,
large-scale philanthropy was being directed towards American higher education, and not a small proportion of this
money was being devoted to the construction and development
of library resources.  At the same time, American business,
industry, and government were becoming acutely aware of
the need to produce the specialized technical experts necessary to staff the burgeoning research and development wings

of American industry.  Consequently, all of these sectors
pushed actively for the establishment of institutions of higher
education explicitly charged with the responsibility of training
such personnel, and perhaps the most significant outgrowth
of this movement was the passage of the Morrill Land Grant
Act of 1862, which provided federal land grants for the establishment of technical and agricultural colleges.  This stimulus led to the establishment in many states of educational
institutions that were to become some of America's most
prestigious universities in the early twentieth century, and
as a result of their burgeoning financial support, their libraries soon became some of the finest in the land.

A number of developments in the nature of American
higher education also influenced the development of academic
libraries.  First, the introduction of a number of new
courses, especially in the biological and physical sciences,
contributed to an increased specialization.  Further, the
gradual acceptance of the "elective system," as opposed to
the prescribed curriculum so common to earlier higher education, provided for the development of a more sophisticated
curriculum and a degree of specialization among students
and faculty that had previously been unknown.  Finally, the
influence of the German educational system contributed greatly to the rise of American higher education and the development of academic libraries.  Perhaps most important was
the growing emphasis on the significance of research as a
major component of the academic institution's role in society.  This concept, combined with the German idea of the
seminar as a principal means of education, especially with
graduate students, made library resources a high priority.
All of these developments placed increased pressures on the
academic library and contributed to the emerging consensus
that the library constituted the very "heart" of any self-re-
specting academic institution.  This new awareness of the
importance of the library in the academic setting quickly
generated increased financial support for library programs,
and by 1900 the academic library was firmly established as
a central component in the educational process.

A last, but not unimportant, series of professional developments contributed to the rise of the academic library.
The establishment of the American Library Association, and
the emergence of a number of vigorous and respected library administrators, like Melvil Dewey of Columbia and
Justin Winsor of Harvard, heralded the rise of a new class
of professional librarians dedicated to the ideal that books

in libraries were an essential ingredient in any educational
recipe.  Librarians like Dewey and Winsor articulated the
growing consensus relating to the library's new significance
to the educational effort, and provided effective professional
leadership in the development of library services and collections.

Given these influences the academic library developed
with rapidity.  Book collections grew with such speed that it
was soon accepted as a fact of life that these libraries could
be expected to double in size every sixteen years.  This
growth was at first welcome, but it placed enormous strains
on the staffs charged with the responsibility of acquiring and
organizing the ever larger collections for use, and would
eventually create nightmarish strains on library building programs.

For example, in the East, Harvard's University Library, plus the other collections on its campus, totaled over
225,000 volumes by 1875 and over 560,000 by 1900.  By
1925 it had reached nearly 2,500,000, and by 1940 nearly
4,000,000 volumes were crowded into its varied facilities.
In 1900 Harvard's main library was still in Gore Hall, but
in 1915 it moved into the new Widener Library, a building
that was supposed to meet the university's needs for a half-
century at least.  By 1930, however, it was filled to overflowing, and the Widener Library has since been supplemented by the Houghton Library for rare books and the Lamont Library for undergraduates.  In addition, in the 1930s
there were some seventy departmental and associated libraries, many of them almost definitive in their subject coverage, plus hundreds of thousands of books in storage.

Among other university libraries, Yale had nearly
300,000 volumes in its library by 1900, and over 1,000,000
by 1925; Princeton University had moved its library into a
new building in 1873, and by 1900 this was crowded with
over 150,000 volumes; the University of Pennsylvania had
182,000 volumes at the turn of the century; Columbia had
reached 250,000 in all of its collections; Brown University's
library was about half as large.  In 1897 Columbia had
moved to a new campus at Morningside Heights in New York
City, and the next year Low Memorial Library, planned to
hold 750,000 volumes, was opened.  By 1934 the Nicholas
Murray Butler Library, with its fifteen-tier bookstack and
capacity for 3,000,000 volumes, was added to meet the expanding demand for space.  Cornell University Library at

Ithaca, New York, nonexistent before 1865, had about 40,000
volumes in 1875 and over 200,000 by 1900.  Its rapid growth
was aided by a generous endowment and the support of a
sympathetic administration.  It moved to its own building,
Sage Hall, in 1891.  By 1900 Dartmouth had only 90,000 volumes; Amherst, 72,000; Rutgers, 41,000; and in Washington,
D.C., Georgetown University Library had 88,000.  Among
the larger state university libraries in the South, Virginia
had about 50,000 volumes, North Carolina about 30,000 and
the University of Texas, 34,000.  Vanderbilt University in
Nashville, founded in 1872, had a library of 32,000 volumes
by 1900, but elsewhere in the South college libraries were
generally smaller than 20,000 volumes.

In the Middle West, the new University of Chicago,
founded in 1892, had taken a commanding lead in bookstock
by 1900, with nearly 300,000 volumes, making it one of the
leading libraries of the nation.  Backed by the philanthropy
of John D. Rockefeller, whole libraries were acquired in
both Europe and America to build up the University of Chicago Library, and even one entire bookstore, that of S. Cal-
vary & Company of Berlin, was purchased.  The University
of Michigan library bookstock had reached 145,000 by 1900,
but other neighboring collections were smaller, with 65,000
at the University of Minnesota, 42,000 at the University of
Illinois, and 34,000 at the University of Missouri.

Total numbers of volumes do not, of course, tell the
whole story of library development in the colleges and universities of this era.  The approach to library service on
the campuses was changing rapidly, with longer hours, better
catalogs, and more efficient library service to students and
faculty.  The development of the Indiana University Library
in the latter quarter of the nineteenth century may be typical
of many other university libraries.  In 1880 the library of
about ten thousand volumes was poorly cataloged and open only a few hours a week.  In that year the first full-time librarian was employed and, despite a disastrous fire in 1883,
a card catalog was prepared and new books purchased; by
1888 three additional library staff members were needed.  In
1891 the library moved into a new building, Maxwell Hall,
with a large reading and reference room.  In addition to a
law library, other departmental collections were started in
the 1890s.  Additional staff members, student assistants,
longer hours of service, and a reserve reading room gave
the library a twentieth century air by 1900, and the library
budget in that year was twenty times what it had been in 1875.

Throughout the country, the university libraries in the early part of the new century continued to grow more and more rapidly, with bookstocks expanding far beyond the capacity of old buildings, and new buildings quickly filled to capacity. New buildings appeared on many campuses, and for the first time they were being planned for library purposes rather than for architectural splendor. On larger campuses, departmental libraries and special collections grew both in size and numbers, although in a few cases there was a tendency to return all books to a centralized collection. Library staffs became more professionalized as library schools developed, although many a small college did not have a trained librarian until the 1920s, and the one-member staff was all too common. But gradually the college library ceased being a museum and became a more active part of the academic program. Newer teaching methods called for more student use of the library, more faculty interest in book selection, and larger expenditures for the library. The seminar method of teaching especially called for greater emphasis on the use and proximity of books. Growing graduate schools demanded rare and expensive books and periodicals for research. Moreover, the increased size of libraries meant that books and other materials had to be better organized and arranged, so that in many cases whole libraries had to be recataloged and new classification systems employed. Fortunately, this was also a period of library philanthropy, when most of the major universities and many of the colleges received substantial gifts in money, buildings and books. The Carnegie Corporation in particular gave money for buildings on literally hundreds of campuses. Later in the century, the same institution provided funds for library schools, surveys, recataloging projects, and publications. Public interest and support of the state institutions also increased and library budgets grew, although usually not in proportion to the need.

The 1920s saw a number of university libraries in the South and West beginning to compete in size and importance with the older ones in the Northeast. The Universities of Virginia, North Carolina, Florida, and Texas, along with the private universities of Duke, Tulane, Emory, and Vanderbilt, began to attract attention as major area research centers. Of these, the library of the University of Texas was largest, with some 400,000 volumes in 1929, while North Carolina was second and the others contained well over 100,000 volumes each. In the West, the University of California at Berkeley was in a class by itself with over 700,000 volumes, but the university libraries of Colorado, Washington, Oregon and

Nebraska each contained over 200,000 volumes by 1929. The libraries of liberal arts colleges, teachers' colleges, technical and agricultural institutions, although much smaller than those of the universities, increased in size and significance in their own fields. On many campuses, there was a conflict between those who wanted departmental libraries and those who wanted everything in a central collection, and as new buildings were constructed, the latter often won out. Each type of organization had its own good and bad points, but the departmental systems, by choice or necessity, remained in vogue in most of the larger institutions. As the donations of books and funds for library purposes became smaller in comparison to needs, many libraries turned to the formation of Friends of the Library groups, where many could give small gifts to take the place of the few large ones formerly received.

The economic depression in the 1920s hit hard at college and university libraries. Building programs were shelved, staffs and budgets were curtailed, yet needs and demands for services remained high. Fortunately, federal government assistance in the form of the Works Progress Administration and the National Youth Administration provided much needed assistance, and useful projects in binding, cataloging, indexing, and building repairs were carried out. In a few cases, library buildings were constructed with federal aid, and on almost all campuses federally-aided student assistants were plentiful. Moreover, the W.P.A. public records projects gave great aid to libraries in general through their indexing, abstracting, microfilming and publishing of research materials.

Probably the most important beneficial effect of the depression on college and university libraries was that it caused them to pause and reflect on their nature and purpose in the general educational scene. Library standards, codes of ethics, and education for librarians received serious study at both general and special library conferences. The need to extend services with strained budgets led to a search for new and more efficient means of providing library service. Various new methods of book charging and circulation control were introduced, some of them being widely adopted and others soon disappearing. As book acquisitions far exceeded stack space, ideas for reducing the size of book forms were investigated, and from these experiments came a wide variety of microforms as means of storing large quantities of graphic materials in a small space. Micro-

films and microcards in particular became widely used, and
newspapers, periodicals, and government publications were
soon reproduced in these forms.  Cooperative acquisition programs, especially for foreign publications, were tried and
some of them adopted.  Duke University, North Carolina and
Tulane, for example, cooperated in the acquisition of Latin
American materials, each specializing in one or more of the
countries south of the border.  On a larger scale, the Farm-
ington Plan, uniting many of the major research libraries of
the nation, assured complete coverage in the acquisition of
foreign newspapers and governmental publications.  Union
catalogs and interlibrary loans furthered this cooperation, and
photomechanical means of reproducing printed materials made
possible the acquisition of copies of rare materials at a reasonable cost.

Before the college and university libraries had recovered from the effects of the depression, World War II
caused new problems.  Colleges and universities were called
upon to supply the special training for soldiers and specialists needed in the war, and their libraries felt the strain.
Funds were usually plentiful but staff members were scarce,
and the demands for books and services for the new programs, the newly organized academic departments, and the
war information centers severely taxed the abilities of even
the largest libraries.  Under pressure, however, new methods were employed, new tools were developed, thousands of
new workers were introduced to the library field, and by the
end of the war the nation's college and university libraries
were stronger than ever.  Not only were their bookstocks
larger but their position on the campus was stronger.  The
trite expression that "the library is the heart of the college"
became nearer the truth than ever, and from one end of the
nation to the other, college and university administrators
pressed for more funds, bigger buildings and larger staffs
for their libraries.  The thousands of war veterans flooding
the campuses after 1945 made these library needs more ur-
gent, and library progress was rapid, if not spectacular.
Both graduate and undergraduate enrollments rose to new
heights, and the presence of the older veterans on the campus made all students more serious in their work.  Capacity
use was made of all library facilities, and once again the libraries faced a crisis with more demands for their services
than facilities to fill them.  By the 1950s most college and
university libraries had building programs, either in the
form of new buildings or annexes, often accompanied by reorganization of library procedures and reclassification of the

book collections.  The increasing use of non-book materials
in the teaching processes led the academic library to widen
its viewpoint and include in its programs a wide variety of
audio-visual materials including tapes, discs, films and filmstrips.  Once again departmental libraries flourished even on
small campuses, due to lack of space in the main libraries,
and storage facilities for little used materials became a necessity.  The new library buildings were constructed with the
new services in mind, and most of them adopted the modular
arrangement, with open shelving and divisional plans to make
books and other library materials as easily available as possible.

In 1975 Harvard University's library still led the nation in bookstock with some ten million volumes,  not counting manuscripts, maps, recordings and micro-materials.  In
addition to the Widener, Houghton, Lamont and Pusey libraries, over ninety other library units served the university,
some of them numbering into the hundreds of thousands of
volumes themselves.  Yale's library was probably second
largest, with some five million volumes, but Columbia University, the University of Illinois, and the University of California at Berkeley were close behind.  Tremendous new buildings were completed or under way on many major campuses
in the late sixties and early seventies, one of the most ambitious at the University of Chicago.  In 1968 alone, there were
at least sixty-eight major library building projects in process
on American college campuses.  Throughout the nation, university libraries of a million volumes, budgets of over
$1,000,000 and staffs in the hundreds became almost the
norm.  On the other end of the college scale, dozens of junior colleges became four-year colleges without sufficient re-
gard to adequate library facilities, and as many more four-
year colleges began offering graduate work without research
libraries.  Scores of new junior or "community" colleges
were formed throughout the nation, often without respectable
high school libraries.  Some states established entirely new
universities, planned from the start to serve thousands of
students, and here library facilities were usually adequately
planned, and often designed with all the newest facilities and
theories of library operation in mind.  Thanks to microforms
and widely reprinted source materials, it was possible to begin these institutions with collections that were reasonably
adequate on opening day.

However, there were still many college and smaller
university libraries that were far from adequate for the

needs of their faculties and students. Among these were some of the newer colleges, small church-supported institutions, Negro colleges, and institutions in the economically poorer areas. Colleges in the South were particularly noted for their inadequate library facilities, but meager collections and small staffs were not restricted to any particular area. Regional accrediting agencies, such as the Southern Association of Colleges and Secondary Schools, have done much to improve library conditions in colleges and universities through their library standards. As late as 1950, however, it was still true that almost two-thirds of the colleges in the Southeastern states failed to meet Southern Association standards on one or more points. Once again, federal aid to education has provided both funds and a new stimulus to college library growth. The Higher Education Act of 1965 provided funds for college library resources, for training librarians, and for research in the field of library science. Over eighteen hundred institutions received funds during the first year of operation of this act and its impact on book collections, library schools, and higher education in general has been tremendous.

While most institutions were having trouble getting enough books to meet demands and standards, many of the larger university libraries were having difficulties in finding space to house all of the books and other informational materials produced by the "information explosion." When microforms and compact shelving failed to provide the answers, these libraries turned to various forms of storage plans. Some found the necessary space on their own campuses, or in rented areas nearby, while others turned to interlibrary storage centers. The first of these was the New England Deposit Library in Boston, maintained by the major libraries of that area, including Harvard and the Massachusetts Institute of Technology. In it are deposited newspaper files, runs of older periodicals, sets of little-used works, state and foreign documents, and miscellaneous ephemeral material. In most cases, this material is not duplicated in any of the member libraries, but is available to any of them. Duplicates are not usually kept in the storage centers either, but are sold or exchanged. Another major storage library, the Midwest Inter-Library Center at Chicago, was the result of cooperation among a dozen or so Middle Western university libraries. It was formed in 1951, with a capacity of over two million volumes. This center functioned much the same as that in New England, but it also has the task of acquiring certain types of little-used materials itself, thus reliev-

ing its constituent libraries of that task.  Since 1965, this
Center has broadened its activities under the new title of
Center for Research Libraries, but its functions are essentially the same.  Cooperation between college libraries in
other fields also became more general in the 1960s.  Ohio's
College Library Center at Columbus was established to provide a computerized regional library facility to serve all academic libraries in Ohio in a cooperative cataloging and union
catalog service.  In the seventies the OCLC, aided by increasing pressure on library budgets, has vastly expanded
its program and influence, and has spawned a number of similar bibliographic networks throughout the nation.  Elsewhere
in the nation, other cooperative projects are in the planning
stage, and the advanced techniques of computers, teletypes,
and even closed circuit television have been employed to extend and strengthen library services.  Within the libraries
themselves, continued efforts have been made to improve library efficiency.  The rapid growth of library resources,
new educational methods, burgeoning student populations, and
the increasing sophistication of faculties have forced academic libraries to explore every new technical development in
their search for improved library service.

The recent past has witnessed a return of tight budgets
in the wake of the nearly uncontrolled growth of the sixties.
Academic libraries, large and small, are entering into a
multitude of cooperative agreements designed to stretch the
budget dollar.  At the same time, the cherished ideal of
"local self-sufficiency" is being abandoned by even the largest
and most respected academic libraries.  How well academic
libraries can meet the increased demands of users in the
face of stable or decreasing funding will dictate their success
in the years to come.


School Libraries

While some feeble beginnings in the area of school library services were made early in the nineteenth century,
it was not until after 1900 that school libraries in the modern
sense of the term became fairly general.  Before that, there
was a period of confusion and experimentation in the provision of library service to children.  The failure of the school
district library idea in many areas resulted in a setback for
school library development.  Often, school district books
were brought together in an attempt to form township libraries
but this, too, was unsuccessful.  As public libraries began to

be formed, taxpayers in many areas were reluctant to support two systems of public library service, and many attempts were made to serve the school children through public libraries. In some towns and villages, the public library or a branch would be located in the vicinity of the school, and opened for school use by groups during school hours and by individual children afterward. In others, public libraries simply provided books to the schools in deposits, either by classrooms or in central collections. In a few cases the public library was actually located in the school building, serving both school and public from one point. None of these plans was particularly successful, and by 1900 there was a controversy between those who favored public library service to schools and those who favored independent school libraries. In 1896 the National Education Association formed a Library Section that was interested in bringing library service to all children by the best means possible. In 1898, at its national conference, this group was divided, with strong voices raised in favor of both types of library service. After 1900, however, the majority seemed to favor independent school libraries, and particularly classroom libraries selected according to the reading level and interests of each grade. The discussion over the two methods of reaching school children was lively in both school and library circles for another decade, but by 1910 the concept of the independent school library had become widely adopted. Although in some cities and counties the link between public and school libraries has been successfully maintained, the main trend has been toward separate library systems.

Although public high schools had begun in New England even before the Civil War and were fairly widespread in much of the country before 1900, their libraries, if any, were usually small and little used. The books were often old, poorly selected, unavailable for much of the time, and under the care of teachers or other school personnel with little interest in their condition or use. By 1900 this situation was changing in a few states and in most of the larger cities. Whether the high school library was a unit in itself, a part of a school system library or of a public library, its content became up-dated, its financial support more regular, and, more important, it became available to the students. Full-time librarians were employed in the larger schools, teacher-librarians in the smaller ones, and the trained school librarian began to appear. Some colleges and normal schools had offered courses in library science as early as the 1870s, but it was not until the 1890s that Melvil Dewey's library

school at Albany and the Pratt Institute in Brooklyn began to
turn out professionally trained librarians.  Erasmus Hall
High School in Brooklyn had a trained librarian in 1900, and
Brooklyn Girls High in 1903.  Morris High School in New
York City obtained its first trained librarian in 1905, and in
the same year there were high school librarians in Albany
and Rochester, New York, New Jersey and Washington, D.C.
in the East; Michigan and Minnesota in the Middle West.
California and Oregon in the Far West took the lead in the
establishment of high school libraries and in the employment
of full-time librarians for them.  Elsewhere in the nation,
particularly in the South, the development of independent high
school libraries was spotty, but by 1915 most of the larger
high schools had some kind of central library, however inadequate.

One reason for the trend toward the independent school
library as distinct from the public library school deposit can
be found in the newer methods of teaching adopted after 1900.
The idea of learning to read for the pleasure of reading was
stressed, and the importance of having good books in addition to textbooks in the schools began to be realized.  The
newer theories of the child-centered school, where the pupil
was educated not for a profession but for a well-rounded,
meaningful life, called for the availability of books at all
times.  Such programs of learning as the platoon school,
which varied the school day into a work, play, study routine;
or the Winnetka plan, which emphasized the individual abilities of each pupil, called for free and frequent use of library
materials, and hence for a permanent school library and a
trained school librarian.  After this idea was adopted, there
was still the debate over the single, central library or multiple classroom libraries.  The elementary schools that had
libraries usually preferred the classroom collections, but
most secondary schools preferred the central library.  By
1913 the U.S. Office of Education could report that there were
approximately ten thousand public school libraries in the nation, but only about two hundred fifty of them contained over
three thousand volumes.  Most of the others were characterized as being out of date or too small, poorly housed, unclas-
sified and uncataloged, and sometimes completely unavailable
for use.  A few cities, including Washington, D.C., Spokane,
and Detroit, were commended for having excellent school library systems, but for the rest of the nation there was still
a long way to go in school library service.

The idea of the school library as a vital part of the

public school was becoming generally accepted by 1915, with
one writer calling it "the laboratory of the social sciences
and humanities and the laboratory annex for the sciences."
In that year, the number of school librarians had increased
so much that the American Library Association formed its
School Librarians Section, and "the new high school library"
was widely discussed. This more or less idealized library
was described as a large, airy, well-lighted room, cheery
and inviting, with books readily available for all grades and
all subjects taught in the school. There was to be a "librarian's office and work-room" next to the library room.
Something anticipating the audio-visual program of later years
was included with the listing of lantern slides, pictures, post
cards, and "Victrola records" as suitable adjuncts to the
book and magazine contents of the library, and a well-organized clipping file was heartily recommended. This type of
library and library service was described as "dynamic," in
contrast to the old "static" library that merely preserved
collections of unused books in out-of-the-way places. It was
admitted that libraries of this type were scarce, but they
were held up as goals for all schools to approach.

After 1920 this "ideal" school library became more
common, and new developments in the field of school library
service came rapidly. In 1920 the N.E.A. Committee on Library Organization and Equipment issued its Standards for Library Organization and Equipment for Secondary Schools, and
in 1925 this was followed by Elementary School Library Standards, prepared by a Joint Committee of the N.E.A. and the
A.L.A. These standards enabled schools throughout the nation to compare their libraries with adequate school library
conditions, and provided school administrators and local government officials with the definite goals needed for school library support. Other national organizations interested themselves in school library improvement, as when the National
Council of Teachers of English created a permanent committee on the use of school libraries. Regional accrediting associations conducted surveys of school libraries within their
areas and prepared standards of library service for accredi-
tation. Surveys of school library conditions by towns, cities,
and states brought out the strengths and weaknesses of existing libraries and pointed the way for future improvement.
These surveys culminated in a national secondary school library survey conducted in 1932 for the U.S. Office of Education by Dr. B. Lamar Johnson. This was a selective survey
of some 390 schools throughout the nation, and although it
did not make specific recommendations it provided the basis

from which school administrators could draw their own conclusions.  Probably the most important factor in school library progress, however, was the work done by state and
local governments in promoting school libraries.  Many
states, for example, created the office of school library su-
pervisor to encourage and supervise the development of
school libraries throughout the state.  Selected book lists,
school library handbooks and other valuable library aids were
prepared by these state offices.  Cities, towns and counties
followed this lead and employed library specialists who advised school librarians in the larger schools and the teachers
and teacher-librarians in the smaller ones.

In addition to progress in the general school library
scene, there were many changes in the school library itself.
In addition to more trained librarians and more cooperation
between librarians and teachers, there were also new and
better library quarters within the school buildings.  Instead
of occupying any available room, school libraries were being
planned for library services.  In 1922, when a large bond issue was passed for the construction of new schools in Los
Angeles, library quarters were planned in each building, and
a committee of librarians was invited to help plan those
quarters.  With the growth of school systems in the more
populated areas, the necessity for centralizing the purchasing
and processing of school library materials became obvious.
In 1927 Los Angeles began centralized purchasing and cataloging for its high schools, special schools and a junior college.  Centralized cataloging was also tried in Seattle, and
other larger cities had adopted the idea by the early 1930s.
The advantages were not only the obvious ones in economy;
librarians also were given more time to spend in working
with students and teachers rather than in processing duties.
Probably more important than physical changes was the
change in the approach toward school library service.  In
the better libraries throughout the nation, the emphasis was
being placed on service to students and teachers and on making the library an active part of the school program.  To
this end, the teaching of the use of the library was widely
recommended and units on the library were available for English and social science courses at almost all grade levels.

Charitable foundations continued to aid the development of libraries, and school libraries benefited directly in
several instances.  In 1929 the Julius Rosenwald Fund provided aid for eleven county library systems to demonstrate public library service to rural schools.  These demonstration

libraries were in the South, and library service was provided
on equal terms to both white and Negro schools. This same
organization also gave direct financial aid to Negro high and
elementary schools for the purchase of library books and materials in the early depression years. The Carnegie Corporation's aid to library schools also aided school libraries indirectly, as did the work of the General Education Board and
the Rockefeller Foundation. Publications to aid the school
librarian came from the American Library Association, the
National Educational Association, the U.S. Office of Education, and most of the state library and education departments.
In some states, state aid for the purchase of school library
materials was available, but in most this was left entirely
to the local school system.

Unfortunately, the school library progress begun in
the 1920s was to be seriously hampered by the depression
era after 1929. School budgets were hard hit and the library
was often the first to suffer. Funds for new books, or even
to pay for current periodicals, were often unavailable when
even teachers were going unpaid for months. For example,
the state of Tennessee reported, as late as 1936, that eighty
per cent of its high schools had no funds at all for books.
But there was still some progress in the 1930s in spite of,
and partly because of, the depression. After 1933, federal
aid came in the form of W.P.A. - and N.Y.A. -paid workers
in the school library, and W.P.A. and P.W.A. built schools.
With federal aid, the trend in consolidating small schools into larger, more modern and more efficient ones progressed,
and these new buildings provided quarters for school libraries. State aid for school libraries became more general, particularly in the states with large rural populations.
In 1938-40, in the South alone, Tennessee, Georgia, Louisi-
ana and Virginia were providing direct state aid to their
school libraries.

The depression also brought about a reappraisal of
the relationship between public and school libraries, and cooperation between the two took several forms. In some
cases, there was a single library system, with a public library in the county seat providing rotating book deposits for
the schools. This had many advantages in lower operating
costs, and in having to supply only one set of books for both
school and public library use. In other systems the school
libraries were permanent collections but they were bought
and processed by the central public library. Either way
brought obvious benefits but also some disadvantages, such

as the slowness of obtaining new books, lack of participation
by the teachers in book selection, and lack of trained librarians to give the necessary library service along with the
books.   Often, centralized purchasing and processing meant
that all the available professional staff would be employed at
the central library and the schools would be left with good
books but no librarians.   Where professional libraries for
teachers were incorporated into the public library-school library cooperative system, the advantages were even greater,
and this feature often proved very popular.

        The effect of World War II on school libraries was
similar to that on libraries in general.   Population shifts
brought the building of new schools and the abandonment of
old ones.   Emphasis on training for special skills, and on
the rapid flow of information, was as important to school libraries as it was to college and public libraries.   Hence,
the school library scene during the war years was hectic,
with rapid developments and often increased funds, but with
librarians almost impossible to obtain.   Out of this period
of change, however, came a new appreciation of the value of
school libraries and a thorough rethinking of their nature and
function in the educational system as a whole.   Plans for future library services were made even before the war ended,
and their implementation was to come, slowly but surely, in
the post-war years.

        In 1945 the American Library Association published
School Libraries for Today and Tomorrow, which outlined
programs and established guidelines for the future development of the nation's school library services, including a
statement of objectives, necessary services, and required
facilities for that development.   Implementation of these standards, however, was slow, although much progress was
made in many individual instances.   In 1953 it could be
pointed out that more than half of the nation's schools still
lacked adequate libraries.   The combined efforts of state and
local governmental units were not enough to assure good libraries in all schools.   Fortunately, the mood of the country was changing, and the necessity of federal aid for the
improvement of educational facilities was recognized.   The
National Defense Education Act of 1958 led the way, and although its action was not directly aimed at library service,
its funds for the improvement of training in mathematics,
science and foreign languages often led to the purchase of
additional books and teaching materials for the school libraries.   Similarly, the Vocational Education Act of 1963

provided funds for school libraries in some cases.  The
most important federal legislation for school libraries, however, came with the Elementary and Secondary Education
Act of 1965.  Title II of ESEA, in particular, provided millions of dollars for the purchase of books, periodicals, tapes,
records and other instructional materials for school libraries,
and other parts of the act also had promising implications.
Under Title III, for example, demonstration libraries have
been established with new facilities and services hitherto un-
tried and unavailable.  Finally, the Higher Education Acts of
1965 and 1966 have aided school libraries in their provisions
of aid in the training of school librarians.

      To supplement the various federal acts and to help put
them into effect, several significant special library projects
were inaugurated.  The Knapp School Libraries Project, financed by a grant from the Knapp Foundation, provided demonstration libraries in eight schools from 1963 to 1968.  In
five elementary schools and three high schools, ranging from
New York to Oregon, libraries were provided with the best
book collections, equipment and staffs that could be obtained
to demonstrate what ideal school library service could be.
Thousands of librarians and educators visited these demon-
strations and profited from their experiences.  The American
Library Association, with funds from the Council of Library
Resources, carried out a School Library Development Project to show how its 1960 Standards for School Library Programs could be achieved.  Many states and school districts
used ESEA Title III funds to carry out their own demonstration library projects.  By the late 1960s, there was no longer
a question of how good school libraries could be achieved,
but where the librarians could be found and when the local
school systems would take advantage of the many aids available.

      With aid and stimulation from many directions, the
decade after 1965 will probably be one of the greatest in the
history of American school libraries.  In fact, it may well
be remembered as the era when the school library disappeared and the teaching materials center took its place.
Changes in this direction had begun as early as 1947, when
California established central teaching materials centers in
each county.  The idea spread to other states in the 1950s,
and such centers were established within libraries, or outside of libraries in separate systems, and on both district
and school levels.  The cost of the equipment and materials
needed usually resulted in centralized district collections un-

til federal funds made it possible for the larger schools to
establish their own teaching materials centers. Today, the
expanded school library, or teaching materials center, is a
far cry from that of the 1930s. It is equipped to supply all
kinds of instructional aids, including books, periodicals,
pamphlets, pictures, charts, maps, films, filmstrips, micro-
films, tape recordings and disc recordings, and even three-
dimensional models. It includes a suite of several rooms,
with open-shelf reading rooms, offices, conference rooms,
a class room, work rooms, and individual study carrels. It
may have special audio-visual aids rooms where projection
equipment, record players, tape players, television, radio,
filmstrip and film-loop viewers, and even teletype equipment
are available.

One other bright aspect of the school library scene in
the 1950s and 1960s was the increasing number of elementary
school libraries. Long the stepchild of the school library
world, depending on small classroom collections or deposits
from public libraries, the elementary school library was finally coming to be realized as an important part of elementary education. Increased emphasis on individual effort by
the pupil and on learning by doing rather than memorizing
textbooks meant that a wider variety of materials entered into the daily elementary school teaching and learning experience. The classroom library, long favored by elementary
school teachers, became inadequate and was being replaced
by the centralized elementary school library, while the
trained elementary school librarian took her place as a part
of the teaching team. Both elementary and high school librarians have begun to place more emphasis on teaching the
students to use books and libraries. This wider concept of
the use of library materials as a subject in itself has greatly
enhanced the value of both the school library and the school
librarian.

Statistically, the school library scene at the close of
the 1960s was both gratifying and disturbing. Of the 88,000
schools in the United States, two-thirds had centralized libraries, but only about forty per cent had full-time librarians
and teaching materials collections. Moreover, of the elementary schools, only one-third had centralized libraries.
A.L.A.'s 1965 National Inventory of Library Needs found that
even those 56,000 schools with centralized libraries had less
than half (collectively) of the volumes to meet the 1960 standards. To fill this "volume gap," an expenditure of nearly
$1,000,000,000 would be necessary. Not only was there a

great shortage of volumes, but the "staff gap" was even greater. Instead of the 32,000 "professional" librarians employed in schools in 1964, the standards called for 112,000, and an additional $500,000,000 would be needed to provide these staff members. Still, the school library picture was a great improvement over 1960, and the rate of improvement was increasing. The school library and the instructional materials center had won their places in the educational scene.

## Libraries Serving Government

Since 1850, libraries serving federal and state government in the United States, like other types of libraries, have undergone rapid and revolutionary growth. By far the most significant of government libraries is the Library of Congress, a library which in terms of size of collection and extent and nature of services may well be the most impressive such institution in the world. The Library of Congress began its remarkable development when Ainsworth Rand Spofford was appointed Librarian of Congress by President Lincoln in 1864, and under his leadership the library soon became one of the most important in the world. It was still housed in the Capitol building, but it was rapidly overflowing its quarters.

As early as 1871, Dr. Spofford suggested the library needed a building specifically designed for the collection, and in 1874, Congress appointed a committee to look into the possibilities of building a national library structure. But the wheels of government grind slowly and it was not until 1887 that construction finally began. The resulting building, not completed until 1897, forms the present main part of the library, capable of holding nearly three million volumes and covering nearly four acres. It had all the latest in library equipment for its day, with everything from well-lighted reading rooms and steel stacks to book conveyors and inter-office speaking tubes. Though Librarian Spofford's staff of 1864 had only five members, the new building required one hundred eighty-five workers in 1900, with an additional crew of forty-five in the copyright office. The old system of classification, an adaptation of Jefferson's original private library scheme, was outmoded by the multitudes of new books of the late nineteenth century. To meet this need, a number of classification schemes were considered, but in the end a system particularly adapted to the needs of the Library of Congress was developed, and the entire library was reclassified

and cataloged.  As the books were reprocessed, printed catalog cards were produced and made available for purchase to
libraries all over the nation.  Thus the Library of Congress
card distribution program was begun, one of its most valued
and appreciated services to the library world.

    Although the Library of Congress was still essentially
a collection of books designed to aid the Congress and other
government officials in the performance of their duties, by
1900 it had come a long way toward being the national library.  After that date it soon became the nation's largest
single library, and under the capable leadership of Dr. Her-
bert Putnam it extended its influence far beyond the needs of
Congress or the confines of Washington.  Its services soon
went beyond the printed catalog cards to published bibliographies and other library tools, to the maintenance of a national union catalog, the sponsorship of national and international
book exchanges, and many other library innovations.  The national library for the blind is centered in the Library of Congress and reaches the blind readers throughout the nation
with deposit libraries in each state.  In 1937, the completion
of the new National Archives removed many of the public
records and manuscript materials from the Library of Congress, and in 1938 the completion of a new annex relieved
the crowded conditions in the forty-year old main building.
This new addition more than doubled the available space, but
there was still hardly enough room to meet the needs for
book preservation and library service that the growing nation
demanded.  A third major addition, named after President
James Madison, has recently been completed, but it also
promises to be filled to overflowing in a few years.

    Something of the enormous work done by the Library
of Congress can be seen from the statistics related to the
Library's holdings.  It now contains some 60,000,000 items.
A staff of nearly 2,000 serves these collections and adds to
them nearly a half million items each year.  The National
Union Catalog, with its records of the location of some
14,000,000 volumes in North American libraries, is a most
valuable part of the Library, and the Legislative Reference
Service for the Congress and other government officials provides a most valuable service.  Like the British Museum,
the Library of Congress is many libraries in one, with, for
example, a collection of over 350,000 volumes in Chinese,
and an equal number in Russian or about Russia.  Its files
of newspapers, music scores, motion pictures and maps are
unsurpassed.  Its additional services in publications, catalog

cards, books and recordings for the blind, cultural programs
and exhibitions, and photoduplication make it indeed the cultural center of the nation.

Besides the Library of Congress, the city of Washington and its immediate vicinity contain more than a hundred
other government libraries, many of which are notable collections.   Two in particular bear the well-deserved titles of
"national libraries."   The National Library of Medicine, at
suburban Bethesda, Maryland, is probably the largest single
medical library in the world.   Its interesting history began
in 1836, with the creation by Congress of the Army Medical
Library, but its growth was slow until after the Civil War,
when Dr. John Shaw Billings became its librarian.   From
a miscellaneous group of some eighteen hundred books in
1865, he developed it into a well-organized library of fifty
thousand books and sixty thousand pamphlets by 1880.   He
made it one of the major medical libraries of the world, developed a subject card catalog for it, began indexing medical
journals, and published a comprehensive bibliography of medical literature.   By 1910 the Army Medical Library had over
100,000 volumes, and after moving into its new building in
1962, its cataloged items now number over 1,300,000, and
its staff over 300.   Serving the nation's physicians and scientists, it has pioneered in the computerized storage and retrieval of medical information as evidenced in MEDLARS,
the Medical Literature Analysis and Retrieval System.   From
this, it produces the current index of medical literature,
Index Medicus, and is able to provide almost instantaneous
information on any medical question.   The National Agricultural Library has developed out of the Department of Agriculture Library, founded in 1862.   It, too, grew slowly at
first and had only 7,000 volumes in 1875, but by 1929 this
figure had passed the 200,000 volume mark.   In the early
1970s it had some 1,300,000 volumes and a staff of about
200.   Its contents are virtually definitive in subjects relating
to agriculture, including botany, chemistry, forestry and
zoology.   One of its strongest points is its holdings in agricultural periodicals and the publications of societies, institutes, and government agencies in the field of agriculture
from all over the world.   It, too, has pioneered in the ap-
plication of electronics to the storage and dissemination of
information and produces indexes and bibliographies of tremendous value to its field.

The rapidly increasing number of government agencies that have come into being in the twentieth century have

multiplied the number of government libraries in Washington, and they vary widely in subject and size. New departments, such as Commerce and Labor, have libraries in the neighborhood of 500,000 volumes, and even the Department of Housing and Urban Development, created in 1965, has combined earlier housing agency collections with new purchases to build up a 300,000-volume library. Such agencies as the Federal Reserve System, the Federal Aviation Administration, and the Civil Service Commission have libraries of around 100,000 volumes each, while those of the National Archives and the Patent Office are even larger. By contrast, there are dozens of smaller, more specialized agency libraries in the 10,000- to 50,000-volume class, such as those of the Selective Service System, the Naval Intelligence School, and Walter Reed Army Hospital, to mention only a few examples. Possibly one of the most unusual libraries in Washington is that of the Government Printing Office whose nearly 2,000,000 items consist largely of U.S. government publications. These libraries, considered along with older collections like those serving the Department of State and the Treasury Department, constitute a significant resource for the federal government.

Not all United States government libraries are in Washington. In fact, there are more libraries, and probably more volumes belonging to the government, outside the capital than in it. Some of them are completely independent libraries, others are branches of libraries that have their main collections in Washington. The military services, in particular, have libraries in large numbers, scattered almost around the world. The Military Academy at West Point, New York, has a library that was founded in 1812, with about 20,000 volumes in 1850 and 25,000 in 1875. In the 1970s it had over 250,000 volumes, with some 40,000 more in departmental reference libraries. The Naval Academy Library at Annapolis was organized in 1845, and by 1875 it had some 16,000 volumes. Today its bookstock totals over 200,000 volumes and it is rapidly catching up with the older service academy. The Coast Guard Academy has a library of some 75,000 volumes at New London, Connecticut, and the new Air Force Academy has a library at Colorado Springs that was approaching the 250,000 mark in the early 1970s.

From the Civil War onward, the United States military services have attempted to provide libraries for all service men, whether in war or peace. In 1861 the U.S.

Military Post Library Association was founded to provided
reading matter for the soldiers in the field, and although
largely voluntary, has been successful.   By 1875 nearly every military post and garrison with a permanent staff was
supplied with a small library from about 50 to about 2,500
volumes, depending upon the number of troops.   For example,
the first library in the newly acquired territory of Alaska
was a garrison collection at Sitka.   With benevolent funds,
post petty cash, soldiers' reading clubs, and a little official
support, these post libraries survived down to the period of
World War I.   During this war, with the aid of the American
Red Cross, the American Library Association, and the
YMCA, a renewed effort was made to provide the best library service possible for the men in uniform, and from it
developed a system of permanent government-supported libraries for all the military and naval services.   After 1920
there were libraries with full-time librarians in all posts,
camps, and stations of over 2,500 men, and smaller collections under special service officers at smaller posts.   During World War II a wide network of military libraries was
developed.   Wherever servicemen were stationed--in training
camps, at permanent bases, on naval vessels, overseas or
in hospitals--there were books available.   At the larger
posts, well-stocked and well-staffed libraries of several thousand volumes were maintained, while even the smallest units
had package libraries of fifty or a hundred paperbacks, considered expendable and passed from man to man until they were
worn out.   In 1943 there were over two thousand post and
hospital libraries in the United States alone, requiring more
than six hundred trained librarians and hundreds of service
personnel to staff them.   About the same time, the U.S.
Navy had over sixteen thousand library stations serving its
various ship and shore units.   To meet the need for inexpensive editions of desirable books, the book publishers produced the Armed Services Editions of popular and serious
works that were printed and distributed by the hundreds of
thousands.   Since the war the military library services have
continued their important role, providing technical and professional as well as recreational books for all phases of the
defense program.   The Bureau of Naval Personnel, Library
Services Branch, serves over thirteen hundred libraries for
naval units around the world, while hundreds of other base
and unit libraries are provided by the Army and Air Force.

        Other federal government libraries outside of Wash-
ington are operated by many agencies.   The Veterans' Administration provides libraries in each of the many Veterans'

Hospitals throughout the country.  The Department of Agriculture has technical and professional libraries in many
places in connection with its experimental stations and research posts.  The Atomic Energy Commission has libraries at its research bases, such as Oak Ridge, Tennessee, and the Savannah River Authority in South Carolina.
One of the newest research agencies, the National Aeronautics and Space Administration, is rapidly providing library
service at its bases in Houston, Cape Canaveral and Hamp-
ton, Virginia.  The scope and variety of federal agency libraries outside the nation's capital can be exemplified by the
state of Washington on the west coast.  In this one state, in
the 1960s, there were five Veterans' Hospital Libraries,
three U. S. Air Force Base Libraries, five Army installation
libraries, five Navy installation libraries, one Fish and Wild-
life Service Library, one Department of Commerce Library,
and a library at the U. S. Penitentiary on McNeil Island.
These were the ones large enough to have professional librarians in charge; they do not include smaller government
libraries without full-time librarians.

A new type of government library, or at least one
that is under the control of a government agency, the National Archives, is the presidential library, usually located at
the birthplace of a former president, and containing books,
documents, manuscripts and momentoes relating to his life
and administration.  The first of these, possibly the largest
and best known, is the Franklin Delano Roosevelt Library at
Hyde Park, N. Y. , established in 1939.  In 1955 the Presidential Libraries Act provided for the government administration of this and other collections honoring former presidents,
although most of the funds for the construction of such libraries would have to come from private donations.  The
Harry S Truman Library at Independence, Missouri, the
Dwight D. Eisenhower Library at Abilene, Kansas, and the
Lyndon Baines Johnson Library in Austin, Texas are examples.

All in all, in its hundreds of libraries the United
States government operates the greatest system of organized
information in the world today.  In fact, its very size and
diversity present immense problems, and there was much
discussion and study in the 1960s concerning the future of
government library services.  Various groups, committees
and associations concerned themselves with the problems of
space, staff and availability that trouble all libraries, but
also with automation, bibliographic control, cooperation,

duplication, photo-reproduction, and the many questions brought on by the astronomical growth of recorded information. Several new agencies were organized to help solve some of these problems. The Clearinghouse for Federal Science and Technical Information was established in 1965, and the Educational Resources Information Center (ERIC) in 1966. The former attempts to coordinate and disseminate technical bibliographic information, while the latter does the same service for educational research. ERIC operates clearinghouses throughout the United States, each specializing in a particular phase of educational information. The Library of Congress has developed a system of Machine-Readable Cataloging (MARC) by which complete catalog cards can be transmitted on electronic tapes and printed out by a receiving library. To coordinate information concerning the use of automation in libraries, LC has set up the Library of Congress Automation Techniques Exchange (LOCATE). In these and many other instances, the government libraries are in the vanguard of library progress in the United States and in the world.

A second major type of library serving government in the United States is the state library. While many state libraries can trace their origins to the early nineteenth century, they began their most rapid development after 1900. By this date and later, many of the state libraries were taking on other functions designed to serve the state as a whole rather than merely the state officials. In Ohio, a state law of 1882 opened the state library for reference use to all citizens, and in 1896 it began to offer circulation service to the entire state with a few special restrictions. By that time, the services of a typical state library might include a legislative reference division, a library organizing division, and a traveling library service. The latter two functions were added to state library duties in some states, while others created special library commissions for these purposes. The promotion of public library service, with or without financial aid from the state, and the distribution of reading material by mail service or package libraries to citizens without local libraries became accepted state library functions. The allocation of library extension services varied considerably from state to state, since they could be found under the state library, a library commission, the state department of education, or even a state university.

Development of state library agencies has continued to vary greatly since the 1920s. Some state libraries have grown into major research libraries, such as those of Massachusetts, New York, Illinois and California. Others have concentrated on public library development and library extension services, and serve as headquarters or coordinating agencies for statewide library networks. The Pennsylvania State Library at Harrisburg heads up a statewide system of four research centers and thirty district library centers. Indiana's State Library at Indianapolis is an example of a central research center connected by teletype with county libraries throughout the state. Hawaii's public libraries are all in one statewide library system, headed up by a central library and processing center in Honolulu. Maryland, on the other hand, has a library extension division under the State Department of Education, which in turn contracts with the Enoch Pratt Free Library of Baltimore to serve as a state library center. The Library Services Act of 1956, and later acts of the Federal Government designed to aid library development, have had tremendous impact on the states' official libraries. The federal funds for library aid have generally been made available through a central state agency, and this has usually been the state library. These federal funds have been wonderful assets, of course, but they have also brought problems. Their allocation and use called for more staff members, often difficult to obtain. Some funds had to be used for surveys, to determine the greatest areas of need and how the federal funds could best be employed. Other funds went for equipment and supplies necessary to handle the great influx of books, particularly where they came into centralized processing centers. Some funds went for demonstration libraries and bookmobiles. Most, however, went for books and materials that went directly into use in the state's public libraries. Increased federal funds often brought increased, matching state funds, and thus library finances expanded rapidly in a few years. By 1962 the states were spending three times as much as the federal government for library service, not including county and municipal library appropriations.

In addition to the central state libraries, the twentieth century has seen the growth of many specialized libraries at the state level, generally designed to aid the services of a state governmental agency. A few of these had been established before 1900, such as Massachusetts' Department of Labor and Industries Library in 1869. Most state departmental libraries, however, began in the 1920s and later, but as of the 1970s there were a wide variety of state agency libraries serving public welfare departments, departments of education, or public health, state museums, highway commissions, insurance commissions, mineral boards, and even geological surveys. Most of these are small, but a few are in the twenty to thirty thousand-volume class. Even on the local level some government collections such as county law libraries and county medical libraries are found. In the larger cities, metropolitan departments of health, police and welfare sometimes have official libraries for the use of public employees in those fields. Thus, at all levels of government, the necessity of organized collections of information is felt, and specialized libraries are the answer. Whether centralized or decentralized, statewide library systems or local library units, the development of government libraries proceeds at a rapid pace, and as in almost all other fields of library service, demand often exceeds supply. All possibilities of cooperation, automation and bibliographic control are being studied and considered by the nation's government librarians in their attempts to provide ever better service.

One other type of governmental library found in the United States is the international library, serving the United Nations or other multi-nation organizations. The United Nations headquarters library in New York City is the Dag Hammarskjold Library, founded in 1947 and already containing over 300,000 volumes in the 1970s. Its contents, in all of the five official languages of the United Nations, plus many others, are strongly related to international law and relations, plus history and the social sciences. One of its strongest holdings is in the history and publications of the League of Nations. It also contains the Woodrow Wilson Memorial Library, particularly devoted to the history of peace efforts in the modern world.

## Special Libraries in the United States

Although all libraries are specialized to a certain extent, the special library in the United States is in a category of its own and deserves separate attention. Two types of special libraries, schools and government agencies, have already been considered, but there are a large number and a wide variety of libraries which contain some of the most valuable single collections in the country. Where the general collection stops and the specialized collection begins is difficult to delineate exactly, but for the purposes of this chapter the term "special library" can be defined as that library which is restricted in content and, usually, also in clientele served.

On the whole, special libraries tend to be smaller
than general ones, and the average special library is usually
in the 10,000-volume range rather than the 100,000. Furthermore, the special library usually differs considerably in size
and training of staff, in hours of service, general organization, and materials handled. It can often experiment with
new ideas, new methods, new machines and new services
more easily than the older, larger, and more standardized
libraries. Thus, it is fortunate for the library profession
that special libraries exist, not only for the services that
they render but also for their leadership in the library world
generally.

Special libraries may be divided into two types: those
that are independent in themselves, and those that are part
of, or related to, general public or university libraries.
Also, they may be classified into three other groups: professional, business, and government. The more general governmental libraries have already been discussed, but there
are many smaller technical libraries in governmental agencies that are special libraries in the fullest meaning of the
term. Professional libraries are those that serve professional schools and organizations. Business libraries include
a wide variety of libraries, while early medical societies with
libraries included the Worcester, Massachusetts Medical Society, and the Boston Society for Medical Improvement.
Each of these had collections of five thousand volumes or
more by 1875, as did also the Rhode Island Hospital of Providence, the Cincinnati Hospital, and the Massachusetts General Hospital in Boston. There were also the medical libraries that were part of general collections, such as the
eleven thousand volumes in the Boston Public Library, or the
five thousand volumes on medicine in the Boston Athenaeum.
It should be noted that the preponderence of medical libraries
was in the Northeast.

By 1875 there were also a few libraries in public institutions such as prisons, reformatories, and insane asy-
lums. For the most part, they were the result of gifts from
charitable individuals and groups, and were cared for by interested inmates. A library in the State Penitentiary at
Philadelphia was begun in 1829 with a gift of books, and that
at Sing Sing in New York started with a donation from Governor William H. Seward in 1840. One prison library, at
Alton, Illinois, began with books donated by the inmates of
another prison at Charlestown, Massachusetts, in 1846. By
1867 thirteen prisons reported libraries with an average of

about fifteen hundred volumes each.  Sing Sing had the largest at that time with some four thousand volumes, but thirteen states reported the appropriations of small funds for
books in their prison libraries.  Ten years later the number
had risen to forty, and most of them reported their contents
as well used.  Most of the titles included were classed as
"entertaining," although a fair proportion were "instructive"
or "religious."  The reformatory movement for young crimi-
nals began in New York in 1825, although most of the similar institutions in other states came after 1850.  In 1875, of
fifty-six reformatories in the United States, forty-nine reported libraries ranging from one hundred fifty volumes to
four thousand, for an average of about one thousand.  Again,
the largest was in New York, this time in the New York
City House of Refuge.  Both prisons and reformatories reported heavy use of their books by all the inmates who could
read.  Besides the small funds received in a few states, the
institutional libraries depended almost entirely on gifts for
their acquisitions and on inmates for their staffs.  There
were a few libraries reported in 1875 in hospitals for the
insane, but they were apparently for the use of the staffs
rather than for the inmates.

    One other nineteenth-century special library worthy
of mention is the newspaper library.  This institution tended
to take two forms:  the "morgue," a specialized file of clippings of past newspaper issues, topically arranged and forming something of an index to the paper as well as an information file, and the regular research library for the use of
staff reporters and editors.  The New York Tribune had a
research library before 1850, and by 1874 it contained over
five thousand volumes.  Its morgue, which was begun in
1860, was largely biographical and designed to provide quick
information on the lives and careers of all important and
newsworthy people in New York and the nation.  The New
York Herald had a well-established reference library of some
eight thousand volumes in 1870, but its morgue was not begun until later.  Two other newspaper libraries, established
shortly after the Civil War, were those of the Boston Herald
and the New York Times.  Most newspapers in larger cities
followed suit in the late nineteenth and early twentieth centuries, and the morgue in particular became standard equipment for the average newspaper office.  The research library, on the other hand, was confined to the very largest
papers, and for smaller ones a few standard reference works
usually sufficed.

The period after 1875 and before World War I was
one of slow growth in the special library field, but one in
which the special library came into its own and was recognized as an institution in itself. Although in types of
libraries and fields of service it varied more than those
in any other library group, it was recognized that the
special libraries, whether large or small, part of a
larger system or not, had something in common, and so
in 1909 the Special Libraries Association was founded.
The formation of such a group was first proposed at the
Bretton Woods Conference of the American Library Association, when some forty-five special library representatives
followed the suggestion of John Cotton Dana in joining together.   After its formation, the Special Libraries Association
took a prominent part in promoting the interests of special
libraries and in giving leadership and direction to the profession.

Although there had been a few small "company libraries" in existence before 1910, it was not until after that
date that the special library field was enlarged to any great
extent by business and industrial libraries.   At first, their
libraries were largely collections of company records and
studies made by the firm's specialists, but soon they began
to include specialized reference materials, technical journals
and general scientific works of value to the particular industry.   In the East, some of the early industrial libraries
were those of the American Brass Company, the United Gas
Improvement Company, and the New York Merchants Association.   The National City Bank of New York and Harvey Fisk
and Sons were among the earliest banks and financial houses
to provide research libraries for their employees and customers.   In smaller cities, Chambers of Commerce and other businessmen's associations sometimes provided business
libraries for their members, and public libraries also began
to provide "business and technical" branches in some instances.

Among all special libraries, one of the most valuable
is the endowed reference library, of which the nation is most
fortunate in having a reasonably large number.   The trend
was already beginning in the nineteenth century, but even
more have been added in the twentieth.   Although these libraries may not be limited in subject content, they are not
public in either support or general use, and are usually limited to a restricted clientele of scholars and special students.
Two of these, the Lenox and Astor Libraries, have already
been mentioned in connection with the formation of the New

York Public Library, but another most valuable one is the
Folger Shakespeare Library in Washington, D.C.   Henry
Clay Folger began collecting Shakespeare material as a youth
at Amherst College in the late nineteenth century, and by
1909 his collection was noted as the largest in the United
States.   A few years later it was called the largest Shakes-
pearean collection in the world, and before his death he arranged to have it housed in an appropriate building and eventually opened to research by serious scholars.   This library
was opened in 1933, containing besides books and pamphlets,
many manuscripts, documents, relics, curios, drawings,
paintings, prints, medals, coins, tapestries, playbills,
prompt-books, and even furniture and costumes relating to
Shakespeare and the time in which he lived.   Today, the
Folger Library contains over 260,000 volumes, not counting
its other thousands of prized possessions.

Chicago is fortunate in having two major research libraries, the Crerar and Newberry libraries.   The Newberry
Reference Library was founded in 1887, by Walter L. Newberry, as a public reference library in the humanities and
social sciences.   The John Crerar Library was begun by its
namesake in 1895, as a scientific library to balance and complete the work begun by the Newberry collection.   In the late
1960s, the Newberry Library had some 930,000 volumes.
The Crerar Library, now housed in a new building on the
grounds of the Illinois Institute of Technology, makes its
more than 1,100,000 cataloged items available to the students and also continues to serve as a public reference library.   In New York City, the Pierpont Morgan Library is
particularly strong in the history of the book, incunabula and
Americana.   On the West Coast, the Henry E. Huntington
Library in San Marino, California, is one of the finest rare
book collections in the world.   Its 425,000 volumes and over
1,000,000 manuscripts make it a scholar's paradise, and
much of the research completed in its resources is published in the Huntington Library Quarterly.   Also in California, on the campus of Stanford University, is the Hoover
Library on War, Revolution and Peace, with its hundreds of
thousands of books, pamphlets, government documents, newspapers and periodicals dealing largely with the history of the
twentieth century.   Elsewhere in the nation are such endowed collections as the Linda Hall Library of Science and
Technology in Kansas City, and the Lloyd Library and Museum in Cincinnati.   The former has some 350,000 volumes
while the latter collection contains about 275,000 books and
pamphlets.   The Robert Browning Collection on the Baylor

University campus in Waco, Texas is an example of a very
specialized collection, while the William L. Clements Library
of American History at the University of Michigan in Ann
Arbor is much broader in its content.  Its 40,000 volumes
and 200,000 manuscripts, together with an appropriate building, were given to the University in 1923.  Among more recent libraries of this type is the Marshall Research Library,
opened in Lexington, Virginia, in 1964.  In memory of General George C. Marshall, this collection focuses on its subject in particular and the diplomatic and military history of
the United States in the twentieth century in general.

By 1920 or shortly after, most of the university libraries had become so large and unwieldy that they had begun to break up into many departmental or special college
libraries.  This trend was noticeable in a few cases in the
nineteenth century with the formation of law, theology and
medical libraries on a few campuses, but in the twentieth
century it extended to other subject fields.  A reverse trend
can be noticed after World War II, with some universities
returning their departmental collections to a new central library, or at least attempting to do so.  The special library
on the campus, however, seems to be well established, and
with the proliferation of literature in the special fields, there
seems to be no end to them.  The University of Michigan,
for example, has some twenty-eight special or departmental
collections on its campus, and it is only about average in
this respect among the larger universities.  Its special libraries range in subject from architecture to transportation,
and from a few thousand in the smaller collections to more
than 100,000 in the medical library and over 300,000 in the
law library.  Besides these special libraries, moreover,
there are also many special collections inside the main university library, some of them running into thousands of volumes.  This situation is duplicated on a hundred other campuses, and it is obvious that the special library is a definite
part of the university library program.

The few industrial research libraries established before World War I have been followed in more recent years
by thousands of similar establishments.  The technical and
scientific revolution that accompanied and followed World War
II has particularly emphasized the value of research to the
industrial firm, and the company library has become a necessity.  The E. I. du Pont de Nemours Company not only
has seven technical libraries in its headquarters city of Wilmington, Delaware, but also has branch libraries in Du Pont

plants in fifteen other cities.   The libraries in Wilmington
range in size from a few thousand volumes to over 57,000
in the Central Research Library.   Among the specialties in
the Du Pont libraries are not only such subjects as chemistry, physics, engineering, business, and manufacturing, but
also biology, bacteriology, biochemistry, and even a legal
research library.   Westinghouse Electric Corporation has
four libraries in Pittsburgh, with another in East Pittsburgh.
General Electric Company has five libraries in Schenectady,
with forty others scattered among its plants elsewhere.
These are representative of the larger industrial library systems, and there are hundreds of examples of companies with
a single research library.   For example, the Corning Glass
Works of Corning, New York has a library of some twenty
thousand volumes; General Tire and Rubber Company of Ak-
ron, Ohio has eight thousand; and the Allied Chemical Corporation of Morristown, New Jersey has some eleven thousand.   Although the preponderance of special libraries remains in the East and Middle West, there are also others in
all parts of the country.   The Texas Instruments Company
of Dallas has four libraries containing some twenty thousand
volumes between them, and the Humble Oil and Refining Company of Houston not only has a main library of some twenty-
five thousand volumes, but five others including a law library,
a geological library, a medical library, and an employee relations library.   In central North Carolina, a Research Tri-
angle grew up in the 1960s and there are today almost a
score of research agencies, complete with technical library
facilities, where only piney woods existed a few years ago.
The growth of industry on the West Coast, from San Diego
to Seattle, has been accompanied by the development of industrial libraries, and there are at least twenty-five major
ones in the Los Angeles area alone.

      If industry has come to appreciate the research li-
brary, the fields of banking and insurance are not less re-
sponsive to the value of books in the conduct of their business.   Banking and insurance companies were among the
first to develop special libraries, but again their widespread
use has come only since the 1940s.   New York City is a center of such libraries, and those of Chase Manhattan Bank
(forty thousand volumes); Dun and Bradstreet (seventeen
thousand); Bankers' Trust Company (twelve thousand); and the
American Bankers' Association (twenty thousand) all bear this
out.   Among the insurance firms, Equitable Life Assurance
Society has a library of nearly forty thousand items and
New York Life Insurance Company has over twenty-five thou-

sand.  However, this type of library is not limited to the
Northeast, and such firms as the Prudential Insurance Company of Chicago, the National Bank of Detroit, the Bank of
America in San Francisco, and the Southwestern Life Insurance Company of Dallas all have research libraries for their
employees and clients.  In some cases, insurance firms and
agents join together to support libraries, as in the case of
the Insurance Society of Boston with its sixty thousand-volume
library and the Insurance Library Association of Atlanta with
thirty-five hundred.

Newspaper libraries have come far since the early beginnings in the nineteenth century, and today there are scores
of them ranging in size up to many thousands of volumes.
The New York Times has a reference library of some 38,000
volumes, plus some 10,000 maps, 3,000,000 prints, and a
morgue of over 1,500,000 clippings.  In Boston, the Globe
has a library of 15,000 volumes, 350,000 pictures, and
3,000,000 clippings, while in Chicago the Tribune has a library of 22,000 volumes besides its morgue of clippings.
Elsewhere, the book collections in the newspaper libraries
may be smaller but the collections of clippings and pictures
are constantly growing.  In recent years, the newspaper library has been joined by the magazine headquarters library.
For example, Time, Incorporated, has a headquarters library
of some 85,000 volumes; Newsweek has some 20,000 volumes
with nearly 200,000 other additional items of information on
file; McGraw-Hill Publishing Company has a library of some
30,000 volumes for its several publications; and the Curtis
Publishing Company has libraries in both Philadelphia and
New York.  Other popular magazines, such as McCall's,
Popular Science and Reader's Digest, to name only a few,
have libraries at their headquarters offices.  This system of
research and reference libraries to provide quick and accurate information on persons, places and events is considered
most important in the operation of magazines, particularly for
the news weeklies.

Not the least important of modern special libraries
are those of national and international organizations.  Professional societies, educational associations, labor organizations, and many other types of associations have developed
headquarters libraries for the use of their professional staffs,
visiting members, and even for the public.  Some of these,
as for example the Engineering Societies Library of New
York with its 190,000 volumes, not only provide a magnificent library, but carry on publishing activities as well.  The

Engineering Societies Library began the Engineering Index, now compiled and published by its own firm.  A few others, among many such libraries in New York City alone, are the Explorers' Club with its twenty thousand books and pamphlets; the Family Service Association with three thousand volumes; the International Ladies' Garment Workers' Union Library with seventeen thousand volumes; and the National Association of Manufacturers Library with about twenty thousand.  Chicago has the National Association of Real Estate Boards Library, the American Library Association headquarters library, and the National Livestock and Meat Board Library, among others.  Washington, D.C. has its share of associational and institute libraries, and still others are to be found in almost all of the states in the union.

Hospital libraries and prison libraries have also come into their own in recent years.  Particularly in the hospital field, the number and size of libraries have increased considerably since 1945.  Both technical libraries for the use of doctors and nurses and popular libraries for the patients have become standard items in the larger hospitals.  Chicago, for example, has at least forty-four medically related libraries, including those in hospitals, medical and nursing schools, and others in various association headquarters. The Children's Memorial Hospital there not only has a doctors' library and a nurses' library but a children's library as well.  Prison libraries, led by those of the Federal prison system, have grown in importance and size, with many professional librarians employed.  The larger libraries in correctional institutions range from twenty to thirty thousand volumes.  In addition to its value as a recreational and educational aid in the reform program, the library is now being studied for its inspirational and psycho-therapeutic value. Both the American Correctional Association and the Association of Hospital and Institution Libraries are concerned about the quality of prison and reformatory libraries, and the two together have drawn up standards for such institutional libraries.  However, a survey conducted in 1965 indicated that in number of volumes, size of staff, and adequacy of budgets, the nation's correctional institution libraries still have far to go.

Special libraries in general, and more particularly those in the technical and scientific fields, were faced in the 1960s with the tremendous task of controlling the vast amounts of information pouring from the presses and processing machines all over the world.  Even in the relatively re-

stricted field of an individual industry, the information has
increased in geometric proportions in recent years, and the
special librarian and information specialist have the task of
organizing this material for quick and orderly use by scientists and researchers. Time is money for the industrial
concern, and the quicker the information can be retrieved
from the books and files, the more valuable it is to the
company. Add to the quantity of material available the fact
that it comes in many varieties of format, and it is easy to
see what a task special librarianship can be. Information in
a technical library can be in the usual form of books, periodicals, and films, but it can also be in the form of maps,
oilwell logs, meter readings, punched cards, perforated
tapes, sound-recorded tapes, and other electronically recorded materials, as well as manuscript, typed, processed, or
filmed reports. The tasks of organizing all of this information call for new techniques, and the special librarian has
risen to the challenge with a variety of devices for information storage and retrieval. Automated processes in library
routines and services were first employed, in most cases,
by special libraries, and special libraries in general have
taken the lead in exploring new ideas and services.

Closely allied to, or perhaps encompassing, the field
of special librarianship is the field of documentation or information science. Documentation has been defined as "the
complex of activities required in the communication of specialized information including the preparation, reproduction,
collection, analysis, organization and dissemination...." It
is generally accepted to mean the storage and retrieval of
technical information, but it can also be applied to all recorded or preserved knowledge, in which case it would include all of library service itself. The term "documentation" seems to have been replaced in the late 1960s by "information science" as best describing the multiple connota-
tions to be included. The American Documentation Institute
was organized in 1937, and concerned itself largely with
micro-reproduction in its early years, but broadened its interests considerably during World War II with the flood of
technical and intelligence reports that failed to fit neatly into
the librarian's usual processes. Through the journal American Documentation, the Institute provided the library world
with research and interpretation during documentation's in-
fancy and adolescence. Now with the Institute's new name of
American Society for Information Science, the same services
are continued and enlarged, and it is joined by the A.L.A.'s
new Information Science and Automation Division and the

Journal of Library Automation to provide the extended coverage which the subject deserves.

The Special Libraries Association continues to be one of the most effective and productive groups of its kind, and it has in recent years been joined by several other groups in even more restricted library areas. These include the Music Library Association, the Theater Library Association, the American Association of Law Libraries, the Medical Library Association, the American Theological Library Association, the Association of Jewish Libraries, and the Catholic Library Association, among others.

## Canadian Libraries

Significant progress in the development of Canadian libraries came only in the last quarter of the nineteenth century. New colleges and universities were established, particularly in the western provinces; more attention was paid to school libraries; and legislation by the provinces provided for the formation of municipally supported free public libraries. The Ontario Free Libraries Act of 1882 authorized towns to levy taxes for free libraries, and by 1900 there were some 390 public libraries listed in the province. However, most of these were small holdovers from the mechanics' institutes and association libraries. In 1895 the partially subsidized mechanics' institutes were given the choice of either becoming free public libraries, with support, or joining the subscription-type association libraries. This resulted in more free public libraries, and by 1900 interest in libraries had reached the point where the Ontario Library Association was formed. Portland, New Brunswick, formed a free public library in 1882, and St. John, in the same province, followed the next year. The St. John Free Public Library started in two rooms in the City Market Building, where it remained until a Carnegie building was erected in 1904. In Halifax, Nova Scotia, the Mechanics' Library, formed in 1831, was given to the city in 1864 and combined with an earlier circulating library to form the Halifax Citizens' Library, housed in the City Hall. In the western provinces, British Columbia enacted a public library law in 1891, and libraries were begun in Vancouver and Victoria. Elsewhere, from Ontario to the Pacific, subscription libraries remained the general rule before 1900, and several of them were quite large and successful. Among new colleges founded during this period were Dalhousie University in Halifax, begun in 1867; Acadia Uni-

versity in Wolfville, Nova Scotia in 1877; Ontario Agricultural College in 1874; and McMaster University in Toronto in
1887.   Each of them had libraries of only a few thousand volumes at the turn of the century.   McGill University in Montreal, founded in 1855, with about 100,000 volumes, and Laval University in Quebec with about the same, were Canada's
largest university collections at this time.

Public library development was faster in the early
twentieth century, thanks to Andrew Carnegie's philanthropy,
improved transportation, and heightened interest in education.
Between 1901 and 1917, 125 Carnegie library buildings were
constructed in Canada, the great majority of them public libraries and the remainder on college campuses.   A survey
of public library facilities in 1909 found Ontario fairly active,
with 131 free public libraries and 234 association libraries.
Together they made over 1,000,000 volumes available to the
people of the province, the Public Library of Toronto being the largest with its 150,000 volumes.   In Quebec, a public library was founded in Montreal in 1903, but it was initi-
ally limited to technical and scientific works.   Quebec City
had the Fraser-Hickson Institute, an endowed public library
with some 38,000 volumes, of which 13,000 were in French.
Elsewhere in the province, there were library associations,
usually small, serving the English population, and religiously-
oriented parish libraries available in French.   In the Mari-
time Provinces, there were public libraries in Halifax, Nova
Scotia and Saint John, New Brunswick.   The western provinces were beginning or enlarging public libraries, particularly in Winnipeg, Edmonton, Victoria and Vancouver.   An
interesting development after 1900 was the formation of the
McLennan Traveling Libraries, privately endowed but serv-
iced by McGill University.   This service, beginning in 1901,
loaned collections of thirty to forty books for a fee of $4 for
three months, including transportation costs.   It was available anywhere in the Dominion, to almost any responsible
group or individual, from small colleges to mining camps,
even including some theological collections for ministers and
churches.   Some of the western provinces began similar
traveling libraries as a free public service, such as the Saskatchewan Traveling Library Service, begun in 1914.

By the 1920s another mild spurt of progress took
place in Canadian public libraries.   Trained librarians began
to appear in the larger libraries, and branches were established.   Broader public library acts were passed, with provincial aid and encouragement to a small degree.   Toronto

still had the largest public library in Canada; it moved into
a new central building in 1930, and served some 500,000
people with its 16 branches, including the first branch exclusively for children in the British Empire.  Other large
public libraries in Ontario were those at Ottawa, Hamilton
and London, but despite the fact that this one province contained over half the public libraries in Canada, there was
still some forty per cent of its population not reached by
them.  Quebec still lagged in public libraries in the 1920s
and 1930s, although the Montreal Public Library opened
branches, and in the English-speaking suburb of Westmount
a public library flourished and opened a children's room in
1922.  Also in Montreal, the Bibliothèque Saint Sulpice, an
old and valuable library formed in 1845, was given to the
city in 1931 and opened as a public reference library.  In
Nova Scotia, the Halifax Public Library had 89,000 volumes
in 1927, while in New Brunswick the St. John Free Public
Library had some 45,000 volumes.  Two experiments in regional library service came with Carnegie funds in the early
1930s.  One of these, on Prince Edward Island, resulted in
the formation of a province-wide library service, centered in
the town libraries of Charlottetown and Summerside.  The
other, in the Fraser River Valley of British Columbia, was
also successful, demonstrating the feasibility of regional libraries by serving forty thousand people over several hundred
square miles with seven branches and a book-truck.  In British Columbia's major city, the Vancouver Public Library had
its first public libraries in 1921 and opened its first branch
in 1922.  Its collection numbered some forty thousand volumes by 1927, and the provincial capital city of Victoria had
a library that was slightly larger.  The inland provinces of
Manitoba, Alberta and Saskatchewan had good public library
services in their major cities of Winnipeg, Calgary, Edmonton, and Regina, but the smaller towns continued to be served
by subscription libraries or by traveling libraries from the
provincial capitals.  In 1930 a survey of Canadian public library services, conducted by John Ridington, librarian of the
University of British Columbia, reported a general lack of
interest in promoting public libraries except in the provinces
of Ontario and British Columbia.  The report also noted public apathy on the subject of libraries, but that where services
were available, as in the Fraser Valley demonstration, libraries were well used and appreciated.  The recommendations of the survey were unfortunately slow in being imple-
mented due to the depression and World War II.

Since 1945, however, the public library scene in Can-

ada has shown remarkable progress.  One of the suggestions
of the Ridington Survey had called for the creation of regional libraries for more efficient service to small town and rural areas.  This form of library has proven particularly
adaptable to the Canadian provinces and has been widely used
in almost all of them.  Ontario continues to be the most library-minded province, but it was being challenged in the
1960s by several others.  New library laws have provided
for multiple unit services, and cooperation between large and
small libraries have extended public library service to over
seventy-five per cent of all Canadians.  Local taxes continue
to provide most of the support for public libraries, and this
became more generous in the 1960s in most cases.  There
is some provincial support, but virtually none from the Dominion government.

Toronto Public Library, with its more than one million
volumes, its widespread branch library system and its many
specialized services, remains Canada's largest public library,
but it cooperates closely with suburban and other nearby collections under the Metro Public Library Board.  Ontario's
many small public libraries, in the 1960s were joined into
fourteen regional systems, each coordinated into a single
service unit with centralized purchasing and processing and
region-wide availability of all library materials.  Ontario's
provincial grant to public libraries reached nearly $5,000,000
in 1966, but still it claimed to reach only about eighty-five
per cent of its widespread population.  In Quebec, a modern
public library system seemed to be nearly achieved in the
1960s, also thanks to the use or planned use of regional libraries.  The Quebec Services des Bibliothèques, created in
1960, planned to serve the province with twenty-three regional libraries.  One of the first of these, the West Island Regional Library at Pointe Claire, serves about a dozen small
towns and suburban areas west of Montreal.  In Montreal,
the Public Library now has some 1,000,000 volumes and 25
branches, including four especially for children.  In the Montreal area, the Westmount Public Library now has some
75,000 volumes; the Verdun Municipal Library has over
100,000, and the Jewish Public Library has some 75,000.

In the eastern provinces, the regional library has also proved to be a satisfactory solution to the problem of
many relatively small, isolated towns.  Newfoundland serves
a bare majority of its population with a single system, reaching 54 small libraries, including three in Labrador, and some
400 library stations, with about 350,000 volumes.  Prince

Edward Island also has a single, island-wide library service
with 24 branches.  Nova Scotia has seven regional libraries,
with ten bookmobiles to serve over seventy per cent of its
population.  Major single public libraries are those at Halifax, Annapolis and Sydney.  New Brunswick's major public
library is the St. John Free Public Library, with some
100,000 volumes in the 1960s.  Over sixty per cent of the
province's population is reached by public library service.

In the West, regional libraries alternate with large
municipal systems to provide services ranging from Manitoba's sixty per cent coverage to British Columbia's eighty-
five per cent.  In the latter province, Vancouver's Public
Library now has over 600,000 volumes and nine branches,
while Victoria has over 225,000.  Three regional systems
and a number of smaller public libraries cover the remainder
of the province.  The Okanagan Regional Library, for example, serves a headquarters library at Kelowna, three
branches and 20 smaller units, with 128,000 volumes for
102,000 people.  In Manitoba, Winnipeg Public Library has
over 375,000 volumes and seven branches, while Alberta has
libraries of 350,000 volumes and 580,000 volumes at Calgary
and Edmonton respectively.  Regional libraries have joined
smaller collections in these two provinces.  Saskatchewan
has large libraries at Saskatoon and Regina, three regional
libraries, and a traveling library service for remote villages
and lumber camps.  Even the Yukon Territory has a new and
modern public library at Whitehorse, constructed in 1961, to
serve the sparse population in that far northern area.

In the early years of the twentieth century, Canada's
university and college libraries were, like their counterparts
in the United States, usually small, poorly organized and
staffed, and of doubtful value to their students and faculties.
A few of the older institutions had book rarities, often the
results of the gifts of private libraries, but these too were
hardly usable.  In Ontario, Queen's University at Kingston
had about 40,000 volumes in 1909, and the University of
Toronto Library was slightly larger.  McGill University in
Montreal and Laval University in Quebec had collections of
more than 100,000 volumes, but Dalhousie University in Halifax had only about 20,000 volumes.  One of Canada's oldest
colleges, King's College at Windsor, Nova Scotia, was destroyed by fire in 1920, and when it was reestablished in
1924 it moved to Halifax and joined with Dalhousie.  Their
combined libraries came to only about 30,000 volumes.
Even in the late 1920s university libraries were still rela-

tively small, numbering their books in the tens of thousands,
with the exception of the University of Toronto with some
210,000 in 1927, and Queen's University with 175,000 volumes.  Several new colleges were added during this era, including the University of Western Ontario and most of the provincial universities in the West, but in addition to inadequate
collections on the individual campuses, there was too little
cooperation between libraries, and many of them actually depended more on their neighbors in the United States than on
each other.

The great growth in university libraries has come
since World War II, and this growth has been not only in
size, but in numbers of institutions, new buildings, and new
approaches to library service.  Among the new institutions,
Ontario alone has four, all founded since 1945:  Guelph,
Trent, Brock and Carleton.  Each has constructed its library
along the latest lines and taken advantage of the best techniques introduced in both British and American universities.
Quebec has, among others, the University of Sherbrooke,
founded in 1954, with a library of 220,000 volumes in 1968;
and Sir George Williams University at Montreal, founded in
1948, had a library of some 100,000 volumes two decades
later.  A recent study of Canadian university libraries indicates that only one, the University of Toronto with its nearly
2,000,000 volumes, approaches a true research collection,
but there are several others that are rapidly developing.
Laval University and the University of Montreal each have
about 500,000 volumes in their libraries, and the University
of Ottawa has about 350,000.  In the western provinces, the
libraries of the Universities of British Columbia and Alberta
have about 500,000 volumes each, while those of Saskatchewan and Manitoba are somewhat smaller.  A number of new
university libraries were constructed in the 1960s, including
Acadia, Dalhousie, University of New Brunswick, Toronto,
McGill and Laval.  In addition to the universities, there are
also regional and specialized colleges, plus those with religious affiliations, especially in Quebec.  Junior and community colleges are not as numerous as in the United States,
but there are a few.  Cooperation among university libraries
has taken the form of interlibrary loans, teletype, and in the
metropolitan areas particularly, a few tentative moves have
been taken toward selective purchasing to avoid duplication
of rare and expensive materials.  The Canadian Association
of College and University Libraries takes a lead in enabling
its member libraries to work together and solve mutual
problems.  Since one of the most important problems is

staff, the work of Canada's two library schools at McGill
and Toronto was supplemented by a new one at the University of British Columbia in 1962 and one at Dalhousie University in 1969.  By 1975 there were seven accredited Canadian
Library schools.

Canada's school libraries in general have also lagged
until recent years.  Ontario's schools have had small libraries throughout the twentieth century, but only since 1945
have there been serious efforts to staff and use them properly.  In 1916 the western province of Alberta reported that
ninety per cent of its 2,300 schools had libraries, but the
average size was only about 50 volumes.  In 1927 Manitoba's
1,800 public schools had libraries ranging from 50 to 400
volumes each.  Even in 1965, Quebec's 1,043 school libraries
averaged less than 500 volumes.  On the other hand, many
schools have been at least partially served by public libraries,
either by deposits in the schools or by direct service after
school hours.  In fact, in several of the provinces the public libraries are administered from the provincial departments of education.  In British Columbia, for example, the
Public Library Commission is directly under the provincial
Minister of Education.  Thus, cooperation between public and
school libraries is excellent, as it should be.  Recent developments in school library service in Canada are similar to
those in the United States, with concern for centralized libraries in the elementary schools, multi-media centers in
the high schools, and with making school and public library
resources interchangeably useful.

Government libraries in Canada consist of those of the
Dominion and those of the Provinces.  In the early years of
the twentieth century the nearest thing to a national library
was the Library of Parliament, which had some 250,000 volumes.  However, this was largely a legal and legislative reference library and served only the Parliament members and
their employees, together with a few other government officials.  In 1953 the National Library of Canada was created
and in 1967 it moved into an entirely new and modern building.  It serves as the legal depository for all copyrighted
materials appearing in Canada, and as the bibliographic center for the nation.  It also coordinates interlibrary activities
among Canada's research libraries and maintains a union catalog of the holdings of some two hundred major libraries.  In
1968 its bookstock had already passed the 1,000,000 mark.
There is also a National Science Library of some 700,000
volumes in Ottawa, the outgrowth of a national science re-

search center established after World War II, and the Canadian Supreme Court Library serves as a national law library.   There is still a large and active Parliamentary Library of nearly 350,000 volumes as well as many specialized
libraries of the various government departments.   There are
at least fifty-seven government libraries in Ottawa, and about
the same number situated elsewhere in the Dominion, mostly
small research collections.   The Department of Agriculture
in particular has research station libraries all over Canada.

Each of the provinces also has one or more provincial libraries.   There is usually one major collection known
as the Provincial Library, and/or the Legislative Reference
Library, a Supreme Court Library, and several departmental collections.   The Provincial Libraries range in size from
Prince Edward Island's 10,000 volumes to British Columbia's
380,000.   Alberta, for example, has a Provincial Library of
some 75,000 volumes, an Attorney General's Library, a Department of Mines and Minerals Library, and a Department
of Education Library, among others.   Provincial Libraries,
especially in the western provinces, often provide mail library service, or rotating book collections for citizens outside the reach of public libraries.   Reference service by
mail or telephone is another valuable Provincial Library
service.

After academic libraries, special libraries are probably the most rapidly growing book collections in both size
and numbers since World War II.   Earlier years had seen
a moderate development in theological libraries, historical
collections, and governmental research units, but in recent
years there have been added many industrial, banking and
private research libraries.   Law and medical society libraries are among the oldest and most active special libraries, with many of them dating well back into the nineteenth century.   The Advocates Library in Montreal, for example, was founded in 1849, and contained some 70,000 volumes in 1970.   In British Columbia, the Law Society has
major libraries in Victoria, Vancouver and New Westminster,
with smaller courthouse libraries at fourteen other points in
the province.   Victoria's Medical Society Library was founded
in 1922, and its counterpart in Vancouver dates from 1906.
Throughout Canada, hospital libraries have been formed, particularly since 1945, and they often provide separate book
collections for doctors, nurses and patients.   Vancouver, to
use one major western city as an example, has two major
hospital libraries, two nursing libraries, the British Colum-

bia Medical Centre Library, the Department of Health and Welfare Library, and the University of British Columbia Medical Faculty Library among its medical research facilities. Another type of special library is the headquarters collection of a national association. There are several of these in Canada's eastern cities. Montreal contains those of the Canadian Jewish Congress, the Canadian Red Cross Society, and the National Film Board, and Toronto has libraries of the Royal Astronomical Society of Canada, the Canadian Manufacturers' Association, and the Canadian Association for Adult Education, among others.

Among industrial libraries, those of insurance, mining and chemical firms are the largest. Sun Insurance Company of Montreal has a library of some eighty thousand volumes, while the Aluminum Company of Canada has a library of seventy thousand items at Kingston, Ontario. Atomic Energy of Canada, Ltd., in Toronto, has a research collection of over sixty thousand volumes, while out in the new petroleum fields of the West, British American Oil Company has a fifteen thousand-volume library at Calgary, Alberta. One of the largest Canadian newspaper libraries is that of the Toronto Star. Not the least important of Canada's special libraries are those connected with the universities, either as departmental or institute libraries, or as special collections in main libraries. For example, one of the largest collections in Braille is the Charles A. Crane Memorial Library at the University of British Columbia.

Thus, one can see in the history of Canadian libraries a long era of slow growth followed by a few decades of rapid change. There are still millions of Canadians without good public libraries, and hundreds of schools with inadequate supplies of books and teaching materials. College libraries are small, and most university collections have far to go before meeting the needs of modern research. But on the positive side there is the new National Library, the mounting financial support for libraries, the active library associations, and the willingness to break with tradition and try new methods as illustrated in the Toronto materials center. Canada is in the fortunate position of being able to benefit from the library developments of both Europe and the United States; her bilingual status can be a major asset instead of a handicap. Her resources, both economic and human, are relatively limitless, and the future of libraries there can be just as hopeful. Canada will be an interesting nation to watch in the future development of libraries and information control.

Latin American Libraries

   Library development in Latin America over the last
century is extremely difficult to characterize in a concise
manner.  For, unlike the history of libraries in Canada and
the United States, where development has been rapid and
fairly even, the history of Latin American library development
is widely varied from country to country; indeed, it is so uneven as to defy generalization.  Some countries of Latin
America--Brazil for instance--appear to have made the transition from underdeveloped countries to industrialized nations
with burgeoning economies and flourishing libraries.  The
majority of Latin American countries, however, remain in
the pre-industrial stage and little money has been available
for the development of social institutions like libraries.
Then too, the unstable and varied nature of government in
the various countries dictates wide variations in the nature
and extent of library service available to the people.  Given
these conditions, the following discussion can only be suggestive of the complex and rapidly changing nature of Latin
American libraries.

   The greatest library development has taken place in
the ABC countries--Argentina, Brazil, and Chile.  Argentina
in particular has made excellent progress in the twentieth
century.  There were only 49 public libraries in all of Argentina in 1915, while in the 1970s there were some 115 major public libraries, with over 1,700 public library outlets,
including the smaller "bibliotecas populares."  Altogether
these public collections contain some 10,000,000 volumes.
Similarly, book collections in 24,000 Argentine public schools
place another 7,000,000 volumes at public disposal.  Buenos
Aires has over 70 major libraries, ranging from the Biblioteca Nacional with its 700,000 volumes, and the National Congressional Library with 300,000, down to many small academic and special collections.  Public libraries are under the
direction of the Commission for the Protection of Public Libraries, formed in 1870.  One interesting feature of Latin
American libraries is that banks and newspapers often have
libraries open for public use.  In Buenos Aires, the Central
Bank has a library of 42,000 volumes, and the newspaper
La Prensa has a collection of 75,000 volumes, also open to
the public.  Other interesting and important libraries of
Buenos Aires include the Biblioteca Nacional de Maestros,
an education and reference library of some 100,000 volumes,
and a public art library.  Government libraries include the
Department of Agriculture Library of some 75,000 volumes;

the Ministry of Foreign Affairs Library, almost as large, and such smaller ones as those of the Department of Treasury, and of the Bureau of Geology and Mines.

Outside the capital city, there are major libraries at the larger universities, such as those of Cordoba, Santa Fe, and Tucuman, and also some significant public libraries. The university libraries, like those in Europe, have separate departmental and institute libraries outside the main collection, and these constitute both an asset and an administrative problem. The largest of the university libraries is at Santa Fe, with over 1,500,000 volumes in all its collections. The Juan Alvarez Public Library in Rosario is one of the largest provincial public libraries, with some 120,000 volumes, but there are other public libraries in each of the provinces and in most of the larger towns. In 1964 the Argentine National Commission on Education recommended the extension of school libraries to the elementary level, and much progress has been made in this direction. Leadership in the Argentine library world stems from the School of Library Science at the University of Buenos Aires. A center for research in bibliography, information science and library science has been established there with the aid of UNESCO. Today, Argentine libraries are making progress on all levels and the other nations of Latin America are looking to them for leadership.

Brazil's libraries are also progressive, but vast areas to be served and millions of uneducated people make the task much more difficult. Much of Brazil's hinterland in the Amazon valley is still unexplored and inhabited by primitive Indian peoples. Since the early nineteenth century, however, Brazil has had major libraries in her larger cities, and Rio de Janeiro in particular has been the home of several internationally known collections. Today the capital city has such libraries as the National Library of over 1,000,000 volumes, the municipal library of over 100,000 volumes and ten major branches, and the Library of the Chamber of Deputies with over 100,000 volumes. Rio de Janeiro has two old and respected special libraries in the Biblioteca Britannica, founded in 1826, and the Royal Portuguese Reading Room, founded in 1837. The former, relatively small, is a library of English language works of interest to Brazilians; the latter, with over 200,000 items today, serves as a cultural link between the Portuguese and Brazilian peoples and concentrates on the history and literature of those two nations. Government libraries include those of the Ministry of Finance, with

50,000 volumes; the Ministry of Mines and Power, with
75,000; the Ministry of Labor, Industry and Commerce, with
over 250,000. The latter has a valuable cartographical collection of over 30,000 items in its "mapateca." An interesting endowed library was founded by the author, lawyer and
philologist, Rui Barbarosa, and is now housed in his former
home, open to the public with some 45,000 volumes.

Sao Paulo, Brazil's largest city, also has an interesting variety of libraries. Its municipal library, the finest in
Latin America, has over 400,000 volumes, housed in a modern twenty-story building, with branches throughout the city.
Sao Paulo has many specialized libraries, ranging from state
government libraries, such as the Department of Agriculture
Library with over fifty thousand volumes, to private industrial libraries, academic libraries and religious collections.
One interesting feature is the separate library for children,
a fortunate development found in a few other Latin American
cities.

Although there are other state, college and religious
libraries outside the major cities, the most significant recent development in Brazilian library history has been in
the new capital established at Brasilia, several hundred miles
in the interior. Here there are not only the libraries of the
Brazilian Congress (other government agencies may or may
not move their major collections to the new capital) but also
exciting new library developments at the University of Brasilia. The new library building, begun in 1968, houses
about two million volumes, and seats about four thousand students. It has open shelves, an innovation for Latin American libraries, and serves as a public library also for Brasilia and the surrounding area. The university will have
a school of library and information science, and the library
will house a union catalog of all major research holdings in
the nation. Together with the services stemming from the
National Library in Rio de Janeiro, which include a catalog
card service, national bibliographical publications, and a national legal depository, the university at Brasilia will provide the nation with the planning and leadership necessary
for library progress. A National Federation of Library Associations also promotes library development at all levels in
Brazil.

Chile's national library in Santiago has long been considered one of the major collections in Latin America. With
nearly a million volumes, it heads up a system of over one

hundred public libraries throughout the nation.  It has several specialized reading rooms, including the Medina Collection of Historical Manuscripts which is one of the most valuable in the Western hemisphere.  Other significant libraries in Santiago include the forty or more special libraries at the University of Chile, academic libraries at the School of Fine Arts, the Catholic University and the national military and teacher training institutions.  The central library of the University of Chile contains over 200,000 volumes, as does also the Chilean Congressional Library.

Three other nations of the northern and western part of South America present a varied library picture, in general unfavorable.  These are Venezuela, Ecuador and Bolivia. Venezuela has several modern cities, and with its new-found wealth from oil it is rapidly becoming industrialized.  But it still has large rural areas that are quite primitive, and its libraries are scattered and generally poor in size and content.  Its national library in Caracas has some 400,000 volumes, and there are several other government libraries including those of the National Congress, the Supreme Court, and various ministerial departments.  The National Academy of History Library, founded in 1888, serves as something of a second national library, specializing in the history of Latin America.  Major Venezuelan university libraries include those at the Central University of Venezuela, Caracas, and Los Andes University at Merida, but there are also thirty-eight other institutions of higher learning in the nation.  Special industrial collections are maintained by several international firms in Caracas, but these are not publicly available. Public and school libraries are small where they exist, and often there are none.

In Ecuador public libraries are largely confined to reference services, and of the twenty-four listed in the nation in 1955, only one had more than fifty thousand volumes. University libraries include those at Central University in Quito, and at the Catholic University in the same city.  In the 1960s, the latter received considerable aid in books and advice from St. Louis University in the United States.  The university library at Cuenca has a modern collection of some sixty thousand volumes.  Only four per cent of Ecuador's secondary schools had working libraries in 1964, and this represented less than one book per student for the nation as a whole.  Bolivia was even less adequately supplied with libraries than the other Latin American countries.  Only one of its secondary schools reported a workable collection of

library materials in 1960, and this one had only about five
hundred books.  Elsewhere in Bolivia, the National Library
and Archives at Sucre has only about thirty thousand volumes, while the national Congressional Library at La Paz is
only half as large.  The Ministry of Foreign Affairs has a
modern library of ten thousand volumes, and the Municipal
Library of La Paz has about thirty thousand.  The seven institutions of higher education in Bolivia have libraries that
average fewer than twenty-five thousand volumes each, while
the twelve publicly available libraries including the National
Library, average fewer than twenty thousand volumes each.
Bolivia is undoubtedly one of the poorest nations of the western world in library facilities.

Among the Central American countries, Mexico has
the best system of libraries, but even here there is much to
be desired in library service.  There were private and religious libraries from the sixteenth century onward in Mexico
City and a few scattered points throughout the nation.  Before
Mexico obtained its independence in 1823, there were no public libraries in the nation, but in 1833 the national library
was formed from sequestered religious collections.  It had
little support, however, and was not publicly available until
1869, receiving only small funds from the government until
after 1882.  By 1910 it had over 150,000 volumes, and by
1926 over 250,000, but it was still housed in a former church
building and poorly organized.  By the 1970s, with over
800,000 volumes and housed in a beautiful building on the
campus of the national university, it was a modern library
in every sense of the word.  Some other large libraries in
Mexico City include those of the National Anthropological and
Historical Society with 250,000 volumes; the National Academy of Science Library with 120,000; and the National Teachers College Library with about 100,000.  Various government
departments have effective libraries, including the Congressional Library of 50,000 volumes; the library of the Ministry
of Economics, 65,000; and a national library of periodicals
with over 100,000.

Public libraries in general made little progress before
the 1920s.  As late as 1915 there were only ninety-two libraries of all kinds except private in all of Mexico.  In 1923
Jose Vasoncelos, Minister of Public Education, began establishing public libraries and secured the formation of a Bureau of Libraries in his Ministry.  By 1926 there were some
sixteen hundred small libraries and reading centers throughout Mexico.  The first Congress of Mexican Librarians met

in 1925, and a training school for librarians was established in the National Library. By 1965 Mexico reported 263 major public libraries, averaging around 5,000 volumes each. School libraries are being established, but still hardly one in ten of Mexico's secondary schools has a library. Elementary library services are even less satisfactory, but public collections often emphasize books for children. Outside Mexico City the major libraries are those of colleges and universities, although there are a few special libraries in the major cities, such as that of the Technical Institute at Monterrey with its 100,000 volumes.

In Central America, the library pattern is much the same as in the smaller countries of South America. This means a national library and one or more university libraries, with few or no public libraries and only a smattering of library service for schools. The national libraries of Costa Rica, Guatemala and Nicaragua are nearing the 100,000-volume size, and a few of the larger university libraries, with all their departmental collections, approach this number. Panama is an exception because an effort has been made to supply public library service and most of the towns have small public libraries. The Bank of Guatemala provides a public reference library in Managua. In British Honduras, there is a National Library Service which supplies seven branches, and some forty stations throughout that small dependency. In each country, the national library provides a moderate amount of leadership to the profession, and often serves as a bibliographic center as well.

In Latin America as a whole, library service has made only slow progress. This is partly due to social and cultural conditions in general, to economic and political problems that must be solved first, and to a lack of appreciation of the value of books and libraries. Unstable governments and lack of economic security have prevented the financial support necessary to library development. But lack of respect for learning, added to a lack of respect for the profession of librarianship, has handicapped the growth of libraries even when economic support might have been available. Fortunately, the scene is gradually changing. Organizations of professional librarians, many trained in other countries, and the growing number of library schools are combining to upgrade the profession in Latin America and provide many new librarians to fill the growing number of positions. Support and encouragement from the outside, such as that from the United Nations, the Pan-American

Union, and the various United States agencies, have done
much to encourage library development "south of the border." Finally, cooperation between libraries, between nations, and between interested groups is beginning to solve
some of the numerous problems involved. The provision of
adequate library service for all Latin Americans is not likely in the immediate future, but in the long run, the pros-
pects are bright.


## Additional Readings

The literature on American library history is volumi-
nous. The following items are considered excellent treatments of the major aspects of early
American library history, but the list is highly
selective. Those who care to pursue the literature further should see Michael H. Harris, Guide
to Research in American Library History, 2nd ed.
(Metuchen, N. J.: Scarecrow Press, 1974). Chapter 3 of the Guide is devoted to a description of
bibliographies and other guides to the literature
of the field. Also of note are the annual reviews
of the "year's work in American library history"
which appear in the Journal of Library History.

Adams, F. B., Jr. An Introduction to the Pierpont Morgan
Library: an Account of the Origin and Growth...
New York, 1964.

Aldrich, F. D. The School Library in Ohio. New York,
1959.

Bay, J. C. The John Crerar Library, 1895-1944: an Historical Report. Chicago, 1945.

Beard, J. R. Canadian Provincial Libraries. Ottawa, 1974.

Berthold, A. B. "The Library of the Department of State,"
Library Quarterly (1958): 27-37.

Bixler, P. The Mexican Library. Metuchen, N. J., 1969.

Bobinski, G. S. Carnegie Libraries: Their History and Impact on American Public Library Development. Chicago, 1969.

Brough, K. J.  Scholars' Workshop:  Evolving Conceptions
of Library Service.  Urbana, 1953.

Brown, E. F.  Bookmobiles and Bookmobile Service.  Metuchen, N. J. , 1967.

Campbell, H. C.  Canadian Libraries.  2nd ed.  Hamden,
Conn. , 1971.

Carrier, E. J.  Fiction in Public Libraries, 1876-1900.
New York, 1965.

Carroll, C. E.  The Professionalization of Education for Librarianship, with Special Reference to the Years 1940-
1960.  Metuchen, N. J. , 1970.

Cecil, H. L. and W. A. Heaps.  School Library Service in
the United States.  New York, 1940.

Churchwell, C. D.  The Shaping of American Library Education.  Chicago, 1975.

Cole, J. C.  Ainsworth Rand Spofford:  Bookman and Librarian.  Littleton, Colorado, 1975.

Commons, E.  "The Libraries of the Departments of Health,
Education and Welfare,"  Library Quarterly 27 (1957):
173-86.

Coughlin, V. L.  Larger Units of Public Library Service in
Canada.  Metuchen, N. J. , 1968.

Cramer, C. H.  Open Shelves and Open Minds:  A History
of the Cleveland Public Library.  Cleveland, 1972.

Dain, P.  The New York Public Library:  A History of its
Founding and Early Years.  New York, 1972.

Dale, D. C.  The United Nations Library; Its Origins and
Development.  Chicago, 1970.

Danton, J. P.  Book Selection and Collections:  A Comparison of German and American University Libraries.
New York, 1963.

Ditzion, S.  Arsenals of a Democratic Culture:  A Social
History of the American Public Library Movement in

New England and the Middle States from 1850 to 1900.
Chicago, 1947.

Donnelly, F. D.   The National Library of Canada.   Ottawa,
1973.

Gambee, B. L.   "An 'Alien Body': Relationships Between the
Public Library and the Public Schools, 1876-1920, "
Ball State University Library Science Lectures.   Mun-
cie, Indiana, 1973.

Garrison, D.   "The Tender Technicians:   The Feminization
of Public Librarianship, 1876-1905, " Journal of Social
History 6 (1973): 131-59.

Gleason, E. A.   The Southern Negro and the Public Library.
Chicago, 1941.

Harris, M. H.   The Role of the Public Library in American
Life:   a Speculative Essay.   Urbana, 1975.

_____, ed.   Reader in American Library History.   Wash-
ington, 1971.

_____, and G. Spiegler.   "Everett, Ticknor and the Com-
mon Man; The Fear of Societal Instability as the Moti-
vation for the Founding of the Boston Public Library, "
Libri 24 (1974): 249-75.

Harwell, R.   "College Libraries, " Encyclopedia of Library
and Information Science 5 (1971): 269-81.

Held, R. E.   The Rise of the Public Library in California.
Chicago, 1973.

Holley, E. G.   Raking the Historic Coals:   The A. L. A.
Scrapbook of 1876.   Urbana, 1967.

Jackson, S. L.   Libraries and Librarianship in the West:
A Brief History.   New York, 1974.

Jamieson, J.   Books for the Army; the Army Library Service in the Second World War.   New York, 1950.

Johns, A. W.   Special Libraries:   Development of the Concept, Their Organization, and Their Services.   Metuch-
en, N. J. , 1968.

Jones, H. G.   The Records of a Nation.   New York, 1969.

Kalisch, P. A.   The Enoch Pratt Free Library: A Social History.   Metuchen, N. J., 1969.

Kruzas, A. T.   Business and Industrial Libraries in the United States, 1820-1940.   New York, 1965.

Lee, R. E.   Continuing Education for Adults through the American Public Library, 1833-1964.   Chicago, 1967.

Long, H. G.   Public Library Service to Children; Foundation and Development.   Metuchen, N. J., 1969.

McCarthy, C.   Developing Libraries in Brazil: with a Chapter on Paraguay.   Metuchen, N. J., 1975.

Mearns, D. C.   The Story up to Now: The Library of Congress, 1800-1946.   Washington, 1947.

Mohrhardt, F. E.   "The Library of the U. S. Department of Agriculture," Library Quarterly 27 (1957): 61-82.

Peterson, K. G.   The University of California Library at Berkeley, 1900-1945.   Berkeley, 1970.

Pomfret, J. E.   The Henry E. Huntington Library and Art Gallery: from Its Beginnings to 1969.   San Marino, 1969.

Rider, F.   The Scholar and the Future of the Research Library.   New York, 1944.

Roseberry, C. R.   A History of the New York State Library.   Albany, 1970.

Rothstein, S.   The Development of Reference Services through Academic Traditions, Public Library Practice and Special Librarianship.   Chicago, 1955.

Schullian, D. M. and F. B. Rogers.   "The National Library of Medicine," Library Quarterly 28 (1958): 1-17, 95-121.

Thomison, D. V.   "The History and Development of the American Library Association, 1876-1957."   Ph. D. Dissertation, University of Southern California, 1973.

Thompson, L. S. "Historical Background of Departmental and Collegiate Libraries," Library Quarterly 12 (1942): 49-74.

Towner, L. An Uncommon Collection of Uncommon Collections: The Newberry Library. Chicago, 1970.

Utley, G. B. The Librarians' Conference of 1853: A Chapter in American Library History. Chicago, 1951.

Vann, S. K. Training for Librarianship before 1923. Chicago, 1961.

Waserman, M. J. "Historical Chronology and Selected Bibliography Relating to the National Library of Medicine," Bulletin of the Medical Library Association 60 (1972): 551-558.

Whitehill, W. M. Boston Public Library; a Centennial History. Cambridge, Mass., 1956.

Williamson, W. L. William Frederick Poole and the Modern Library Movement. New York, 1963.

Woodford, F. B. Parnassus on Main Street: A History of the Detroit Public Library. Detroit, 1965.

Wright, L. B. The Folger Library, Two Decades of Growth: An Informal Account. Charlottesville, Va., 1968.

PART IV

THE LIBRARY IN HISTORY

## Chapter 13

## THE LIBRARY IN HISTORY

If we define "history" as that period of man's existence since he began to keep records, then libraries are almost as old as history. Indeed, if our knowledge of when man began to keep records is based entirely upon surviving records, and if we define a library as any orderly collection of preserved records, then the library is exactly as old as history. We know that soon after man learned to write and to put down in graphic form some evidence of his experiences and observations, if not of his thoughts, he began to save those graphic records for religious, legal, economic, or purely sentimental reasons. Whatever the reasons, these collections formed an archive or proto-library. As we have seen, these libraries have been in existence in the western world for close to five thousand years. As man's civilization has progressed, so have his libraries. Regardless of the format of his records or books, whether clay tablet, papyrus roll, parchment codex, printed book, or microfilm reel, man has devised a means of arranging, preserving and using them. Once arranged, preserved, and used, they become libraries, and as such they parallel the cultural state of western man from the Nile to the Hudson, from the Euphrates to the Amazon.

This relationship of culture to libraries raises an interesting question. Does man's cultural advance come as a product of the knowledge preserved in the form of libraries, or does this cultural advance merely produce libraries as a by-product? Great works of art, music and literature tend to be produced only in advanced, relatively highly cultured societies. Are libraries in the same category? A secondary query along the same lines might well be: Are libraries the products of a communal desire for preserving knowledge, or

are they formed largely by individual efforts, either selfish-
ly or for the benefit of the community?  Have any people as
a majority of a community ever risen up and demanded libraries, public libraries, free libraries, or library service
in the same way that they have opposed tyranny or taxation,
or espoused liberty or a new religion?  The second query
can be answered more easily than the first, and the answer
is simple:  No.  But the answer to the second query throws
some light on the first, and with this in view we might quickly review the development of libraries in the western world
in the light of our first query:  Which comes first, the library or cultural progress?

        Going back to the ancient Egyptians, it can be argued
that the beginning of the library was purely functional.  It
came about only after a written language had been developed,
a social structure with a complicated government and religious system had emerged, and at least a small portion of
the population had become literate.  The library was functional because it was kept largely to know what had trans-
pired in the past.  It was necessary to keep the laws and
decrees of former kings, the land ownership records of former generations, and the formal rituals of the church.  As
the number of these laws, records, and rituals grew beyond
a few score, it became necessary to organize them for easy
use, to preserve them in a permanent location, and to desig-
nate one or more persons to be responsible for their arrangement, preservation, and availability.  But once they had
been so arranged and preserved, they became a durable part
of the cultural heritage, a stepping stone to further progress.
With records of the past available, it was no longer necessary for each generation to make the same mistakes, redis-
cover experimental approaches to progress, arrive at the
same solutions for problems.

        As an individual grows from infancy to adulthood
through a learning process, so a society develops from sav-
agery to civilization through the same experiential movement.
But just as the individual, without adult guidance, learns only what he experiences himself, so the society without records of past experiences must relearn any progressive developments with each generation.  Oral accounts of previous
group and societal experiences are a part of social growth,
but the fantasies of legends and myths indicate the unsound
basis of oral tradition for substantial growth.  In Egypt, the
cumulative graphic recordings of social and cultural progress
preserved a single culture for nearly three thousand years

and brought gradual progress despite political and military
upheavals.  If no more rapid progress was made it is possible that a reason can be found in the restricted use of the
cultural records because of the low literacy rate during
much of Egypt's history.  Generally, the records of past
history were available only to a few literate scribes, and the
masses of people during most Egyptian eras remained in a
cultural rut, living for the most part just as their ancestors
had lived, no better or worse.  Records of past experience,
no matter how well kept, have no effect upon the progress
of society unless they are used.

    In the storehouses of clay tablets of the Babylonians
and Assyrians, another element enters the story of cultural
progress and library development.  Some of the rulers of
the Mesopotamian kingdoms, particularly the Assyrians, collected libraries with the idea of preserving all that was
known to man, not only the records of his experiences and
observations but also the products of his reasoning and imag-
ination--his philosophies, theologies, and literature.  Records of land ownership or legal acts may be kept of necessity, but philosophy and literature are kept for the love of
learning.  Although much of the "literature" kept on the clay
tablets was functional and utilitarian, there is evidence of
an effort to preserve all that had been or could reasonably
be committed to graphic form, whether business record or
epic poem.  If the "book-keepers" of Egypt were largely ar-
chivists, those of Assyria came close to being bibliophiles.
Certainly the Assyrians reaped from their libraries the benefits, economic and cultural, of two thousand years of Sumerian, Chaldean, and Babylonian civilization.  Yet even here
the great libraries came at the height of a cultural epoch,
after a relatively prosperous and semi-urban society had
produced wealthy rulers and a prosperous priesthood with
great palaces and temples to house and protect their records.
And again we note that only a small minority of the people
could read and benefit directly from the knowledge preserved
in their libraries.

    With the Greeks the purely utilitarian record becomes
supplemented by the literary work, and the library begins to
preserve graphic materials for their literary value alone.
The idea of starting a public library so that the correct texts
of dramas can be both preserved and readily available is a
far cry from the preservation of tax records or genealogies,
yet it still serves a utilitarian purpose.  In this sense, the
early Athenian public library served as a copyright office

with the right of legal deposit.  And when the Greek master
teachers compiled libraries of texts to read to their students,
or to allow their students to copy, they added the educational
motive to the functions of the library, and the knowledge contained in books was put to use by larger groups of people.
Of course, the temple libraries of Egypt and Babylonia were
also used to teach, but here the function was more the teaching of language or the training of scribes rather than the
teaching of literature or philosophy.  With the building of the
great Alexandrian libraries, still another function for the library appears.  Not only were records preserved and literatures collected with the idea of saving everything ever committed to writing, but now there was the task of editing,
criticizing, translating, and correcting texts to preserve literary purity and accuracy.  Whether the Septuagint was prepared in the library or not, it could easily have come
from such a scholarly institution.  With the zeal of the Hellenic scholars and the wealth of the Ptolemies, the libraries
of Alexandria approached a completeness never before known,
and probably never since.  But the libraries and the museums were not all of Alexandria, and Alexandria was not all
of the Hellenic world.  The thousands of rolls were only a
microcosm of learning in a world of ignorance, and this
great center of learning was more the result of Alexandrian
Greece than the cultural forefather of Rome.  Or was it?

For finally, with the Romans we begin to see how
cumulative cultural resources of societies distant in time or
space bring forth the flowering of a new civilization.  Certainly the Romans borrowed culturally--books and teachers
and ideas--from the Greeks and others, whether from Alexandria or Pergamum, Carthage or Syracuse, or directly
from Greece itself.  When books became spoils of war, and
educated slaves came with them, a new Rome emerged.  A
literature was begun, a language was formalized, a wealthy,
cultured nobility arose, and a republic became an empire.
The cultural debt of Rome to Greece was great, and much of
that debt was incurred when the rolls of papyrus and parchment passed from the eastern Mediterranean to the Italian
peninsula.  The early libraries of Rome were mainly the
toys of the wealthy nobility, but this nobility was relatively
numerous, and probably a larger percentage of the citizenry
was literate and used those libraries more during the height
of Roman culture than ever before in the history of man.
Rome had achieved a stable society, strong armies, and
wealthy leaders before it acquired large libraries, but from
those libraries it developed a strengthened, reinforced and

enlarged culture that was in many respects the sum total of
all that had gone before.  Moreover, under the Roman Empire the great libraries were open to the public, supported
by the government, and free at least for reference use:
they were truly public libraries.

Books can preserve ideas, and they can spread them.
This is nowhere better demonstrated than in the history of
the early Christians.  The lessons taught by an itinerant Hebrew known as Jesus--lessons at once both simple and pro-
found--caused a social revolution from one end of the Mediterranean to the other in a little more than a hundred years.
Much of the teaching of Christ and his followers was spread
by word of mouth, by teachers and preachers speaking to
their followers; but with the writing down of the Gospel of
Mark and the Epistles of Paul, Christianity adopted the graphic word, and a new dimension was added.  The parchment
codex carried the story of Christ and the teachings of his
followers wherever the Roman legion ruled.  From Ethiopia
to Ireland, from the Black Sea to the Baltic, a new era was
born.  Certainly Christianity spread with the book--The
Book--and though Christians were persecuted by Rome for
nearly three hundred years, the Empire nevertheless provided them with a relatively peaceful and stable society in which
to grow, and in the end Christianity won out.  No one can
doubt that the heart and strength of Christianity for nearly
two thousand years has been in the written word; and the library, whether of priest or Pope, monastery or cathedral,
has been an essential organ of the church from the days of
Paul to the present.  Did Christianity grow out of the graphically preserved culture of an earlier era?  Certainly the
culture in which Christianity arose had available the Hebrew
literature of a thousand years, and the Hebrews in turn may
well have borrowed from other Near Eastern peoples of even
earlier ages.  The Dead Sea Scrolls tend to confirm this,
even if one ignores the evidence in the Bible itself.  Also,
the early Christians had the Greek and Roman cultures to
draw upon, and used their languages if nothing else.  Thus,
the rise, spread and durability of Christianity easily demonstrates the value of the written word and its preservation in
libraries.  Similarly, the perseverance and stamina that have
enabled the Jewish religion to survive in the face of almost
continuous persecution for over two thousand years stem directly from the written word that is the Jewish scripture.
Surely the Torah and the Talmud have played just as great a
part in the survival of Judaism as the Bible has played in
the spread of Christianity.

But it was in the Middle Ages that the true value of
the book and the library was proven.  When barbarians
swept over much of the civilized world, and when the sword
and flame almost destroyed the Roman world, it was in the
rolls and codices collected into a few isolated monasteries,
or brought together at Constantinople by a zealous Christian
emperor, that the heritage of both the Christian church and
classical civilization was preserved.  In the Byzantine civilization centered in Constantinople for a thousand years after
the decline of Rome, the works of the early Christians
joined the classics of Greece and Rome.  Here they were
copied, abridged and edited, but too often they were little
understood or appreciated.  In the Moslem world, the classics of the Greeks at least were borrowed, and here they
were studied in translation and enlarged and fused into a
Moslem learning that was to far surpass anything that western Europe possessed in the Middle Ages.  Meanwhile, in
western Europe, from 500 to 1500 A.D., thousands of monks
bent over their desks in secluded monasteries, copying and
recopying old parchments that they barely understood, em-
bellishing them with ornaments, but seldom adding to them,
or extracting from them, any ideas.  There were, of course,
bright flashes of light in the Dark Ages, light that spread
from an Isidore or an Alcuin, a Carolingian renaissance or
a brilliant thirteenth century; but on the whole, the western
world retreated rather than advanced.  During the Middle
Ages, the library--in monastery and cathedral, in the occasional noble's study, in the scholar's room--truly fulfilled
one of its functions, that of preservation, but its greater
function of communicating ideas was little realized.  Many
works of the classic era were lost, but some survived and,
like seed waiting for a favorable season, lay dormant await-
ing the inquiring mind of the Renaissance, the mind that
would understand them, translate them into action, and put
them to use.

What brought on the Renaissance?  Why should a Europe, long bound in a feudal system which thrived on ignorance, gradually awaken and emerge into a "modern era" in
which ideas flourished--ideas like humanism, neo-classicism,
nationalism, Protestantism, capitalism and Communism?
Was it the Crusades that brought to western Europe new
ideas, new tastes, new methods--and a new look at the classics?  Or was it the economic prosperity, brought on by
the revived trade, stimulated by the Crusades and promoted
by rising nationalism that led Europe into a new age?  The
answer is, probably both, not wholly either, plus other fac-

tors less tangible and provable.  One fact stands out, however, and that is the connection between the Renaissance and
the rediscovery of the classics.  Another is that the Renaissance began in Italy, an area that had never been completely
separated from the Byzantine, Jewish and Moslem cultures
of the eastern Mediterranean.  It was usually from Italy that
the Crusaders took ship for the Holy Land, and it was usually through Italy that their remnants returned.  It was the
Italian cities of Venice and Genoa and Florence that first became merchant metropolises as a result of ferrying Crusaders and carrying the trade that resulted from western
Europe's discovery of Eastern luxuries.  It was the princely
and merchant families of Italy that encouraged and financed
the recovering, translating, copying, and disseminating of
the Greek and Latin classics.  To their libraries came the
manuscripts rediscovered in declining European monasteries,
or purchased from Greece, Asia Minor or Constantinople.
And it was in these Italian private collections that the classics were studied and preserved until the development of the
printing press could make them available to the world.

     The coming of printing is probably the most important
event in the history of libraries between writing and electronics.  If history began with writing, modern history begins
with printing.  The printing press made hundreds, or even
thousands, of copies of a book available where only one had
been before.  This meant that literature and learning could
be made available to the majority, rather than to a select
few.  From one press alone, that of Aldus Manutius in Venice, came more copies of Aristotle's works in twenty-five
years than the world had known in the previous two thousand.
More copies of more books meant more libraries, larger libraries, more ideas and information available, and more
people capable of making use of them.  The library was finally on the verge of achieving its fullest purpose--that of
making the heritage of the past fully available to all the people all the time.  But it was still to take nearly four hundred years before this goal could be reached, even approximately.

     In modern Europe--since 1500--the library in its role
of preserver has almost reached its ultimate goal as far as
the printed word is concerned.  The great libraries of Italy,
France, Germany and England have gathered and preserved
virtually every important item in manuscript or print that
survived the Dark Ages or came after them.  But on the
whole, these libraries have still been available to only a

few of the people--the collectors, librarians, teachers, a few
students and scholars--and the concept of popular libraries,
of mass culture, has been realized only in the twentieth century, if at all.  Has modern Europe's culture stemmed from
its libraries, or have they resulted from it?  Shakespeare
found the sources for his plays in many ways, from history,
folklore, and other writers' works; in almost every case he
found them in print.  Karl Marx's ideas came out of the
British Museum, possibly warped to fit preconceived opinions; nevertheless, his long studies undoubtedly gave form
to his theories.  Could well-used popular libraries have prevented the rise of a Hitler?  Possibly.  Certainly he made
use of his brand of librarianship to sell his racist and Nazi
theories.  Would an educated Russia have adopted communism?  Possibly.  Certainly no country on earth has so
adopted the book and the library as a means of controlling
the minds of the people as the U.S.S.R. since 1918.  But
where did libraries come from before the days of the popular revolutions?  Largely from the efforts of princely collectors, bibliophilic philanthropists, ecclesiastical scholars, and
a few ordinary book lovers.  Only a society that is relatively stable, with at least a small class that is economically
prosperous, can provide the setting in which libraries can
grow.  For hundreds of years Europe has seen the founding
and preservation of libraries by the few and for the few.
There was little popular education until the late nineteenth
century, and until the people could read there was little popular demand for books and libraries.  Nevertheless, there
was a gradual increase in the number of books and libraries
and in the numbers of their users.  More important, the
leaders of the people--academic, religious, economic, political, scientific--had access to libraries and made good use
of them.  Thus, directly or indirectly, modern European culture is a product of its preserved heritage in graphic form--
in other words, of its libraries.

If Europe demonstrates the interdependence of libraries and cultural growth in a continuing society, then the
European colonies in America well illustrate the value of the
written word in the transformation of a culture from one
background to another.  It was the written word that brought
many, if not all, of the first settlers to America--the explorers' glorified accounts of the New World, the joint stock
companies' charters, and the land promoters' pleadings and
promises.  Once in the new land, the settler was more often
occupied with the plow and the gun than with the pen; but
even if he had only two books, the Bible and the almanac,

he relied on them and on his leaders who, political or clerical, were never far from the printed word.  When the
American Revolution came, it was made inevitable by the
tyranny of printed laws; inspired by the printed philosophies
of a bygone age; promoted by letter, newspaper and broad-
side; and fanned into flame by the publication of a single
pamphlet: Thomas Paine's Common Sense.  The Declaration
of Independence drew from many sources, including the com-
posite heritage of the western world from the Greek democracy, through the Roman republic, the English freedoms,
the French philosophies, and the American colonial experiences of a century and a half.  Behind every significant
event in American history there has been a book, a pamphlet, a printed law or treaty, or a written contract.  Everywhere one turns in American history, the idea or fact preserved in graphic form has shaped events for better or
worse.  If colonial America did not develop great libraries,
it nevertheless made good use of books and, probably more
than any society ever developed before, it owed its nature
and very existence to the printed word.

In the nineteenth century, however, the United States
did develop great libraries.  Slowly but surely over a hundred years, it developed from a frontier nation of a few
books to the single most library-minded nation in the world.
By 1900 the United States had the most libraries, the largest
libraries--with a few exceptions--and certainly the most-
used libraries in the world.  For a nation founded on books
revered the printed word, and as political independence and
economic security made it possible, libraries of all types
and sizes were formed.  Governments formed libraries; societies formed libraries; schools and colleges formed libraries; individuals formed libraries; companies formed libraries; and last but not least, libraries were opened freely
to the public.  With a few exceptions, these libraries were
formed for use, not merely for preservation.  Books and libraries in the United States came to be meant for the reader
--for educational, recreational, inspirational, and informational use--and the printed word came to be used in its ultimate form as a means of communication of ideas and facts
from one mind to another.  The value of the graphic word
came to be appreciated more than ever before in any time
or place.  The role of the library as an adjunct to education, as a device for information, as a partner to recreation, as a boon for business, or as an assistant to science,
has been widely acclaimed and to a large extent realized.
As western civilization has reached what we like to think is

its highest point, the library has come into its own as a key
part of that civilization.  We still do not have all the libraries and all the books that are needed, but we realize
that our culture would not and could not have reached its
present level without those libraries that we consider still
inadequate.

All this indicates the part that libraries have played
in the development of the western world to date, but does it
answer our main question?  The answer at which we have
arrived seems to indicate that neither cultural progress nor
the library necessarily comes first.  Each is at one and the
same time to a large extent the cause and result of the other.  Cultural progress comes from accumulated experience
and knowledge; records of that experience have been best
kept in graphic form--in the form of books and libraries.
But the preservation of graphically recorded knowledge is
not automatic or self-generated.  Recorded knowledge does
not become a usable library or archive without the conscious
effort of some person or persons.  The accumulation of large
collections of graphic materials, and the organization of that
material into libraries, seems to depend upon the activities
of relatively few people in a society that has reached a high
degree of culture, an advanced civilization that is relatively
peaceful and prosperous.  War, poverty, famine and ignorance are as much the enemies of books as they are of people.  Despite the value of their contents, books and libraries are not indestructible and history shows by many examples that in times of great crises, books are among the
first items to be destroyed, whether intentionally or accidentally.  Thus it would seem that libraries and cultural
progress have an interdependent relationship rather than one
of cause and effect.

Yet, despite the value of libraries to cultural progress, there has never been a great popular demand for them.
Most of the great libraries of the world have a history of
long neglect, of constant struggles for funds, for quarters,
and for staff.  Throughout history, their very existence has
been the result of the efforts of a few, and they have been
used intelligently by only a few more.  Only in the last century or so have they been generally supported, used, and
appreciated.  Perhaps in the twentieth century we can see
popular demands for services that can be considered within
the realm of libraries.  The cheap, paperback book, for example, seems to meet a demand for popular reading that
perhaps the public library has failed to supply.  The demand

of the businessman and the scientist for readily available,
specialized information may result in an information science
that could develop inside the library field, outside it, or in-
clusive of it.   Certainly, as the library of today seems to
be on the verge of fulfilling its destiny as a medium of communication, new challenges are arising from many directions.

What of the future of libraries in the western world?
How will the libraries, archives, information and documentation centers be able to cope with the tremendous outpouring
of graphic and other recorded materials of the near future--
and the distant future?   It has been estimated that more than
half of the graphic materials ever produced have appeared
since 1900; that more than half of the scientific research
completed in the history of man has been done since 1939.
With recorded information increasing in geometric proportions,
the tasks involved in collecting, organizing, and making
readily available this mountain of materials on paper, film,
disk, and tape seem insurmountable.   Apparently the answer
to the problem of controlling this informational "wave of the
future" lies in electronics and automation.   Certainly good
minds are at work on this problem.   Steps in the right direction have been made with microfilm and its related forms,
with the computer and its electronic allies.   We may even
be headed for a micro-microfilm that can reduce the printed
page to little more than pinpoint size.   One such extra-re-
ducing camera can reportedly produce a film in which a million pages could be stored in one cubic foot, or approximately three million average volumes in one ten-foot cube.   Add
to this reduction in volume an electronic system capable of
locating in a few seconds any page wanted in those millions
of volumes and reproducing it anywhere on a television
screen, and you have what might be termed the ultimate in
library service presently in view.   Another such system
would reduce a twenty thousand-volume library to an eight
by ten-inch sheet of nickel aluminum foil.

But somewhate in the midst of this super-mechaniza-
tion, this Jules Verne world of information storage and retrieval, let us hope that there will always be a place for the
ordinary book, and for the librarian who knows books and
enjoys the supreme satisfaction of bringing a book and a
reader together.   The human element has always been upper-
most in the history of books and libraries; let us hope that
it always remains that way.

Aside from the physical problems in the future, the

library and its related institutions have a tremendous task to
perform in human relations, whether on the local, national,
or international level. Modern means of transportation and
communication have brought the peoples of the world closer
together than ever before in the history of mankind. Close
contact of peoples of different cultures has, in the past, usually resulted in tragedy--in wars, in conquest of one people
by another, or, at best, in colonialism. Today we are
faced with a conflict of cultures on all levels, from the Cold
War on the international level to the "generation gap" at
home. Mutual understanding is one way, perhaps the only
way, that these conflicts can be resolved, and the library is
one of the best means of reaching this understanding. Instantaneous communication, via electronic means, has
reached the point where it is conceivable that one man's
voice could be heard at one time by all the people on earth.
This is good, but it also presents dangers. By accident or
intention, these electronic means of communication could
plunge the world into chaos in seconds. Graphic communication, on the other hand, is a somewhat slower process.
It can and must be a more considered process. Through
the books, magazines, newspapers, recordings, pictures--
the tools of the library--graphic communication must be employed to bring the element of thoughtful contemplation into
the consideration of world, national, and local problems.
They must be used to bring people together, to teach them
to understand each other, to arbitrate and mediate differences, rather than to hurl insults and diatribes. A push-
button war can be started in split-seconds; a permanent
peace can be achieved only through years of patient effort,
of growing appreciation of mutual interests, of education toward an understanding tolerance of other people, their cultures, and their problems. Books and libraries can play a
most important role in this effort toward world peace and
toward arousing the people of the world to fight ignorance,
intolerance, disease, and poverty instead of each other.
Books and libraries have clearly contributed significantly to
the rise of what we call western civilization. What remains
unclear is the direction and nature of library development in
the future, but certainly the availability of the cumulative
record of man's fears and hopes, failures and achievements,
frailties and strengths, as preserved, organized, and disseminated through libraries will continue to figure significantly in the process of cultural evolution.

## Additional Readings

Few works dealing directly with the role of the library in society are available, but the following are suggestive of the thinking that has been done on the subject.

Benge, R. C. Libraries and Cultural Change. Hamden, Conn., 1970.

Butler, P. An Introduction to Library Science. Chicago, 1933.

Jackson, S. L. Libraries and Librarianship in the West: A Brief History. New York, 1974.

Landheer, B. Social Functions of Libraries. New York, 1957.

Licklider, J. C. R. Libraries of the Future. Cambridge, Mass., 1965.

McCrimmon, B., ed. American Library Philosophy: An Anthology. Hamden, Conn., 1975.

Reynolds, M. and E. H. Daniel, eds. Reader in Library Information Services. Washington, 1974.

Shera, J. H. The Foundations of Education for Librarianship. New York, 1972.

Thompson, J. Library Power: A New Philosophy of Librarianship. New York, 1974.

Wasserman, P. The New Librarianship: A Challenge for Change. New York, 1972.

# INDEX

Alcuin, Bishop of Tours, 101
Alexander the Great, 46, 53
Alexandrian Libraries, Egypt, 19, 44, 46-50, 334
Allan, John, 188
American Antiquarian Society Library, 188
American Documentation Institute  see  American Society for Information Science
American Library Association, 270, 272, 274, 288, 290, 295, 308
American Philosophical Society, 209, 211
American Society for Information Science, 308
Amherst College, Amherst, Mass., Library, 194
Andover Theological Seminary, Andover, Mass., Library, 209
Aristotle, 42-43, 44, 59, 88
Armaria (bookcases), 68-69, 106, 109, 121
Association of Public Libraries, Paris, 237
Assurbanipal, 19-21
Atticus, Titus Pomponius, 62, 69
Austria. National Library, Vienna, 148-149
Automation, 308-309

Bale, John, 154
Bavaria. State Library, Munich, 148
Belcher, Jonathan, 191
Benedict, Saint, 98-99
Benedictine Order, 98-99, 102, 104, 105
Benson, Lee, 266
Bentley, Richard, 144
Berkeley, George, 190
Berlin Library, 227
Berlin Municipal Library, 168, 240
Bessarion, Cardinal, 131
Biblioteca Romana, 248
Bibliothèque Nationale, Paris, 142-144, 147, 163, 225, 226, 237